First Edition

Facing Our Future: Hurricane Floyd and Recovery in the Coastal Plain

Edited by

John R. Maiolo

John C. Whitehead

Monica McGee

Lauriston King

Jeffrey Johnson

Harold Stone

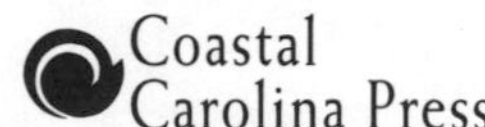

Facing Our Future: Hurricane Floyd and Recovery in the Coastal Plain
Edited by: John R. Maiolo, John C. Whitehead, Monica McGee, Lauriston King, Jeffrey Johnson, and Harold Stone

Coastal
Carolina Press
Coastal Carolina Press
www.coastalcarolinapress.org

First Edition August 2001

Book design by Maximum Design & Advertising, Inc.

Printed in the United States of America
Applied for Library of Congress Cataloging - in - Publication Data

ISBN 1-928556-30-2

Cover: An infrared satellite image of Hurricane Floyd shortly after making landfall along the North Carolina coast on September 16, 1999. On an infrared image, the gray color is relatively warm, blues are cooler, and red indicates clouds that are the coldest, tallest, and most likely to produce rain.

Dedication

Reflecting upon the meaning of a distant funeral bell, John Donne wrote:

No man is an Island, intire of it selfe...
Any man's death diminishes
me, because I am involved in
Mankinde; and therefore
never send to know for whom
The bell tolls; it tolls for thee.

— *Devotions upon Emergent Occasions, 1624*

But Donne would not give death the last victory, and in his Holy Sonnet 10, his religious beliefs on life after death were expressed in the poem *Death, Be Not Proud* (n.d.).

Death, be not proud, though some have called thee
Mighty and Dreadful, for thou are not so;
For those whom thou think'st thou dost overthrow
Die not, poor Death, nor yet canst thou kill me...
One short sleep past, we wake eternally,
And death shall be no more; Death thou shalt die.

We dedicate this book to the fifty-two people who died directly because of Hurricane Floyd and its aftermath, to the other individuals who later died because of problems caused by the event, and to the countless thousands of North Carolinians who continue to suffer.

Contents

A Community Perspective

III. Dynamics of Hurricanes and Floods: Achieving New Insights

Historical Reflections

Improving Our Understanding of Natural Systems

IV. An "Extreme Event"—Hurricane Floyd, September 1999

Impacts on Groups and Individuals

Impacts on the Natural Environment

V. A Better Blueprint for the Future

VI. Recommendations

Acknowledgments

The conference on which this book is based was made possible only because many people and organizations were willing to devote their time and money to make it happen.

Sponsors

American Red Cross, North Carolina Chapter
Aramark Catering
Branch Bank and Trust (BB&T)
Carolina Power and Light
Carteret News Times
Catalytica Pharmaceuticals, Inc.
Center for Transportation and the Environment
Centura Bank
Coastal Carolina Press
Coastal Resources Management Program, ECU
Division of Research and Graduate Studies, ECU
Eastern North Carolina Poverty Committee
Federal Emergency Management Agency (FEMA)
First South Bank
Flood of the Century Archive, Joyner Library, ECU
Grady White Boats
John J. Kirlin, Inc.
N.C. Division of Emergency Management
N.C. Sea Grant Program
PCS Phosphate
Pitt County Memorial Hospital
The News and Observer, Raleigh, N.C.
Trade Oil Company
University Book Exchange
Weyerhaeuser Corporation
WCZI Radio
WNCT-TV

Other Contributors

Coastal and Marine Resources Program, ECU
Department of Economics, ECU
Department of Sociology, ECU
Overton's Sportscenter
U.S. Army Corps of Engineers

We are especially grateful to the extraordinary efforts made by the following individuals for assistance in organizing and implementing the conference: Katie McDermott, James Martin, and Pam Cloer, the Center for Transportation and the Environment; Laura Edwards, Coastal Resources Management, ECU; Margaret Pio and Andrea Harrell, Research and Graduate Studies, ECU; John Whitehead for his wonderful work in establishing and maintaining the conference web site; Ron Mitchelson and Stephen Culver who put together a moving and informative multimedia room at the conference; Gene and Sandra Grigg who took the fear out of using audio/visual aids; Ruth Maiolo and Terry Harne who were willing to do whatever detail work was needed to keep the conference on track; and Kristen Kochekian for her assistance in publicizing the event. Kristen was one of ten undergraduate students in Professor Maiolo's political sociology class in the fall of 1999 who dropped everything to assist him in coming to grips with the human impacts of Floyd and the flood. The others were Rachael Coston, Chris Fowler, Johnny Holden, LaWanda Jones, Don Leffew, Steven Matea, Jason McHone, and Jamara Wallace. Some of these students were victims as well; thus, the class work they did on behalf of the recovery served the dual purpose of information gathering and therapy. Their hard work and the many sacrifices they made contributed greatly to the conceptualization of the conference.

Within a very short time frame, the Conference Planning Committee put in many hours forming and organizing the program. The committee met two or three times a month, from November 1999 through May 2000, planning, reviewing, and revising. Additionally, committee members spent countless hours outside of the meetings seeing that details were given proper attention, including creating and obtaining visual aids, establishing conference content, contacting people whose participation was needed, and assisting in notification of potential registrants.

The Committee

Dr. John R. Maiolo
Committee Chair, Professor Emeritus, Department of Sociology, ECU
Mr. Chris Coudriet
Planning and Support Branch Manager, N.C. Division of Emergency Management
Dr. Stephen Culver
Chair, Department of Geology, ECU
Ms. Kelly Dickens
Director, Disaster Recovery Program, Eastern Area Health Education Center
Mr. Gary Faltinowski
Natural Hazards Program Manager, N.C. Division of Emergency Management

Dr. Thomas Feldbush
Vice Chancellor for Research and Graduate Studies and Committee Organizer, ECU

Dr. John Fisher, P.E.
Professor of Civil Engineering, N.C. State University; Director, Center for Transportation and the Environment, Raleigh

Dr. Susan Gustke
Executive Director, Eastern Area Health Education Center; Associate Dean for Continuing Medical Education, ECU

Dr. Jeffrey Johnson
Professor of Sociology and Senior Scientist at the Institute for Coastal and Marine Resources, ECU

Dr. Lauriston King
Director, Coastal Resources Management Ph.D. Program, ECU

Dr. Christopher Mansfield
Adjunct Associate Professor of Sociology and Director of the Center for Health Services and Development, ECU

Dr. Ronald Mitchelson
Chair, Department of Geography, ECU

Dr. William Queen
Director of the Institute for Coastal and Marine Resources, ECU

Dr. Harold Stone
Assistant Professor of Planning, ECU

Dr. John Whitehead
Professor of Economics and Chair, Coastal and Marine Studies Program, ECU

Mr. Glenn Woodard
Director (Retired), Response and Recovery Division, Federal Emergency Management Agency, Region IV, Atlanta

Message from the Chancellor of East Carolina University

Richard Eakin

Seldom does a university have the opportunity to put its accumulated knowledge to such good use as East Carolina University (ECU) has in the aftermath of Hurricane Floyd. Even before the Tar River crested in September 1999, ECU faculty, staff, and students were lending their hearts and their hands to the rescue and relief efforts throughout eastern North Carolina. At the same time, we began planning how we could effectively make our faculty expertise available to assist the ongoing recovery effort. Almost as soon as the highways became passable, we put a busload of our experts on the road to ask government officials, business owners, school officials, church leaders, and others what they needed and how we could help them get it. We've done our best to provide that assistance. In a more scholarly fashion, many researchers from departments throughout this university have been carefully studying and recording the physical, economic, and emotional impacts of the storm and its associated flooding. Many of their findings were reported in fact for the first time at the conference, which formed the basis for this book. Only through a complete and careful examination of disasters such as Hurricane Floyd can we hope to make eastern North Carolina more resilient in coping with extreme weather events in the future.

Preface

Thomas Feldbush

Vice Chancellor, Division of Research and Graduate Studies, East Carolina University

Several days after Hurricane Floyd drenched eastern North Carolina, a number of faculty and staff came together to discuss how the university could use its faculty, staff, and students to help with the region's short-term and long-term recovery needs. It seemed to us that East Carolina University (ECU), together with the other fifteen campuses of the University of North Carolina system, had a wealth of technical, intellectual, and human resources that could help in the recovery of our region. We quickly realized that it would be necessary to first find out just what type of help our communities needed. The best way to do this was to go to the communities and to talk to the people most affected by the flood. During the week of 13 October 1999, ECU faculty and administrators boarded a university bus and participated in town meetings throughout the stricken area.

During our visits several things became abundantly clear to me. First, it was obvious we had learned a great deal about how to respond to such a natural disaster. We also realized that we could have, and should have, been better prepared to prevent some of the devastation that occurred and to provide appropriate, immediate relief. Second, while it was apparent to us and to all the world that the area suffered a great deal of physical damage, perhaps the more profound and long-lasting effects would be the emotional and economic impacts, especially to the least advantaged members of our region. Third, we realized that we needed to record what we had learned from the ordeal and use the experience as a basis for research, discussion, and planning. If we did a good job at this, we would all be far better prepared to mitigate and respond to the next natural disaster that strikes our region.

These were the ideas that provided the rationale for our conference, *In the Aftermath of Hurricane Floyd: Recovery in the Coastal Plain.* At every stop on our bus tour, I promised people that I would make sure that ECU would bring together the experts and citizens who could explain and evaluate why the flood occurred, how we responded to it, how we can respond more effectively and compassionately to such crises, and how we can better handle the economic and emotional impacts on all our citizens. Our goal was not to cast blame nor to find a scapegoat for our troubles, but to identify what we did right and what we should have done better.

I believe our conference made a very good start at dealing with these issues, as is suggested by the contributions in this book. However, it was only a start. Now we need to vigorously pursue the recommendations that emerged from our discussions and continue to anticipate and identify problems and opportunities to mitigate the worst effects of future hazards.

To this end, the Conference Planning Committee and I have begun discussions on how to continue this dialogue between scientists, elected officials, city and county administrators, and citizens. The next step will be a second conference to be held in late 2001, again on the ECU campus.

Part I / Introduction and Overview

An Overview of the Perfect Flood

John R. Maiolo

Dr. Maiolo is currently Professor Emeritus in the Department of Sociology at East Carolina University. He served as the chair of the planning committee of the conference In the Aftermath of Hurricane Floyd. *He is also a member of the East Carolina University team that is involved in researching the socioeconomic aspects of hurricane evacuation behavior and disaster impacts. For twenty-five years he taught, trained graduate students, and shared his knowledge and experience with the students and faculty of ECU. He served as chair of the Department of Sociology and Anthropology for sixteen years (1975–1991), which was renamed the Department of Sociology, Anthropology and Economics in 1982. In 1986, he helped found what is now the Department of Economics. His research projects include studies of coastal zone and fisheries management issues, and he is co-editor of the book* Modernization and Marine Fisheries Policy. *He has presented numerous papers at professional meetings. He has published many articles in social scientific journals and has published twelve sociology textbook ancillaries. He also served as a consultant to the National Academy of Sciences and as president of the North Carolina Sociological Association.*

Introduction

Over a seventeen day period in 1999 two hurricanes jolted eastern North Carolina. In the last days of summer, the strong winds of hurricanes Dennis and Floyd downed trees and electrical lines and damaged property. But it wasn't the winds that shook North Carolina. The combined downpour from the two hurricanes flooded nearly half of North Carolina's 100 counties, all in the eastern region of the state. The deluge of September 1999 created flooding that resulted in the worst natural disaster in North Carolina's storied history.

The aftermath of Floyd might be appropriately labeled the "Perfect Flood" because of its similarity to the "Perfect Storm," which hit the northeast coast of the United States in late October and early November 1991. Hurricane Grace combined with a high-pressure system moving from the west, a low-pressure system east of Nova Scotia, and three storms to create a gargantuan weather event that ravaged coastlines from Jamaica to Nova Scotia and caused $100 million in damages to Massachusetts alone. The series of hurricanes that ravaged eastern North Carolina in 1999 piled up water to the west, while the winds from Hurricane Dennis pushed coastal water into Pamlico Sound, essentially making the sound a dam that restricted the drainage of three large river systems and caused the whole system to enter into what Dr. Len Pietrafesa labeled a "storage mode."

A family home is destroyed. This house in Princeville, N.C., apparently rose with the Hurricane Floyd floodwaters and eventually settled atop the family truck. (Photo by Dave Gatley, courtesy of FEMA News Photo)

For seven days, from 30 August to 6 September, Hurricane Dennis wobbled back and forth along the coast of northeastern North Carolina, hitting the region twice before moving inland, penetrating the central part of the state, and then heading north. During its long visit, Dennis saturated the land. A rainfall total of 19.13 inches was recorded in the Outer Banks village of Ocracoke, and from three to ten inches of rain were reported elsewhere across the state's eastern region. Ten days later, on 16 September, Hurricane Floyd had weakened to a category two storm when it made landfall at Cape Fear, near Wilmington, North Carolina. It quickly moved to the north, toward the New England states, but the rains that fell as it passed were extreme. Rainfall totals as high as fifteen to twenty inches were recorded in portions of eastern North Carolina. In Wilmington, a storm total of 19.06 inches was recorded, including a twenty-four-hour record of 15.06 inches. But Dennis and Floyd were not the end of the hurricane season. Nearly one month after Hurricane Floyd, Hurricane Irene swept along the East Coast. This wet October storm caused severe flooding in southeast Florida. It strengthened to a category two storm as it headed toward the Carolinas. Irene's ninety-five mile per hour winds brushed the Outer Banks of North Carolina on 16 October.

Without question, the floods that followed Hurricane Floyd were devastating, and this disaster will surely take its place among the most costly storms in U.S. history. Although the human death toll was low compared with other hurricanes, the hurricanes and floods of September 1999 damaged or destroyed tens of thousands of homes, flooded nearly half the counties in the state, caused fifty-two human deaths, millions of livestock deaths, ruined much of the state's 1999 summer crop, eliminated 30,000 jobs, and caused countless hours of human misery for people of all ages, ethnic groups, and social classes (Table 1).

This book documents a journey to uncover reasons for the magnitude of this disaster, to propose solutions to problems, and to work toward preventing a disaster of this severity from happening again. Readers will find some parts of the book depressing, but there are stories here that will tug at your heartstrings, while others will provide hope for the future.

The Conference

Table 1. A factual overview of the 1999 hurricane and flooding disaster.

Landfall in North Carolina (Floyd)	16 September 1999; c. 2:30 A.M.
Rainfall from Dennis	10+ inches
Rainfall from Floyd	20+ inches
Number of Counties Impacted	44
Number of North Carolina Deaths	52
Homes Impacted	50,000 to 55,000
Homes Made Uninhabitable	15,000+
Homes Destroyed	8,000+
Economic Impact (Agriculture)	$800 million
Crop Losses	$543+ million
Livestock Losses	$13+ million
Employment Impacts	Loss of 30,000 jobs
Estimated Total Cost	**$6 Billion**

The conference on which this book is based was conceived and designed as a forum to identify many of the problems that contributed to and resulted from the disaster. But more importantly, the goal of the conference was to provide solutions and to make specific recommendations for how to rebuild eastern North Carolina's communities in a way that will make them more resilient to extreme weather events in the future. Immediately following the hurricane and the inception of the flood, East Carolina University (ECU) administrators thought it was crucial to understand what went right and what went wrong with regard to the preparation for and response to the disaster. Chancellor Eakin and Vice Chancellor Feldbush quickly convened a committee to design and implement the conference. Nearly 300 people attended, including a few elected officials, federal and state agency employees, social scientists, environmental scientists, students, educators, farmers, volunteers of religious-based groups, representatives of charitable organizations, and ordinary citizens.

While representatives of disadvantaged minorities and lower socioeconomic groups were present, several other groups were either absent or underrepresented. For example, no developers, crop farmers, or small business owners were in attendance (although one hog grower and one representative from a hog grower's association were present). This is unfortunate, particularly since *all* of the stakeholders in North Carolina's future need to be involved in the rebuilding process. We cannot develop sensible policies with regard to the many issues that surround hog farming without a thorough discussion among the people whose lives depend upon this activity and the consumers whose budgets are tied to proposed solutions. We cannot continue to develop housing for students, retirees, vacationers, and people relocating for newly developed industries without involving developers in the planning process. Other than emergency and health planning personnel, only a few officials from counties and municipalities attended the conference. Yet, the policies needed to rebuild in a sensible manner require courage from the elected officials who are entrusted to lead their communities.

Several types of presentations were made at the conference and are represented in this volume. We were fortunate to have as our keynote speaker Dr. Robert Sheets, the well-known expert on hurricanes and former director of the National Hurricane Center. His vast forecasting experience and his years of witnessing the impact of hurricanes can teach us a great deal about preparing for this type of disaster. Leaders in the fields of city and regional planning, public policy, disaster studies, and natural sciences gave plenary presentations. Their papers provide a broad, often historical, insight into identifying large-scale problems and offering solutions. The results of original research give us detailed, quantitative data of the immediate impacts of the hurricane and floods on the environment and on people. Many of the results in these papers support issues that are outlined in the plenary papers.

Five roundtable discussions provided an opportunity for people with diverse backgrounds to identify problems and recommend solutions for issues that specifically arose from the hurricanes and flooding. The "Dialogue" papers in the book are a summary of these valuable discussions. Finally, Dr. Lauriston King moderated firsthand commentaries on the impact of the disaster on seven groups whose voices are not always heard. These commentaries, titled "Looking into the Face of the Storm," appear at pertinent places throughout the book.

The final section uses recommendations that were gathered throughout the conference to summarize the lessons learned from this disaster experience and to list specific recommendations for changing our approach to disaster preparation, recovery, and prevention.

Why Didn't We Know This Could Happen? Or, Did We?

We should have taken a clue during the hurricane season in the late summer of 1996. Tandem hurricanes, Bertha and Fran, took direct aim at the Tar Heel state within a matter of weeks. Dr. Sheets presents data in his paper showing that since 1995 there have been a total of forty-one hurricanes—an all time record. In 1998, Hurricane Bonnie paid our state a visit. This storm was similar to Hurricane Floyd, as it mostly battered the coastline and waterfront communities along our major rivers (i.e., Pamlico, Pungo, Neuse, Roanoke, and Chowan rivers). Nineteen ninety-six should have been the beginning of a collective transformation of our perceptions of risk from hurricane-related disasters. In the aftermath of Bertha and Fran, we should have recognized our vulnerability to extreme weather events, many of which are hurricane driven (e.g., heavy winds, tornadoes, and rain).

Robert Sheets, former director of the National Hurricane Center, joins in a discussion at the *In the Aftermath of Hurricane Floyd* conference. (Courtesy of the ECU News Bureau)

Even less severe weather events now can pose a threat to public safety. This is due to the explosive and increasing population density in the coastal zone, much of it in the floodplains east of Interstate 95. In his plenary paper, Mr. Delia discusses eastern North Carolina's gradual transformation from a sparsely populated area to a region with more urban-like densities (although the region is still mostly considered rural). With two exceptions, North Carolina's coastal counties have experienced anywhere from a near doubling to a quadrupling in population size since the 1970s (Maiolo et al. 1998). We have also seen increasing property values. According to a report completed with my hurricane research colleagues at ECU:

> Eastern North Carolina now supports a combination of industries, including corporate agriculture and fishing, retirement, recreation, higher education, ecotourism, manufacturing, and a repository for the transshipment of goods and people through the Global Transpark system. As a beautiful and comfortable place to live, work, and play, the region attracts people from all over the nation, indeed, the world (Maiolo et al. 1998).

One of my colleagues, Bob Edwards, commented as we were writing the 1998 report for the Division of Emergency Management that "hurricanes only become disasters when you build out in front of them." And that is exactly what appears to have happened. Geologist Dr. Stanley Riggs discusses the incompatibility between the natural, normal functioning of rivers and humankind's propensity to alter and build in river floodplains. He has argued for years that human development in North Carolina's coastal zone is dangerous because draining swamps, filling wetlands, rechanneling streams, and creating large areas of impervious surfaces in regions adjacent to rivers change the natural character of land surfaces. These kinds of alterations to our natural systems tremendously exacerbate the effects from a rainfall event like Floyd.

This is what Dr. Dennis Mileti means by "Disasters by Design." Costs from natural disasters continue to rise and show no signs of abating. In his recently published book on the topic, Dr. Mileti, a renowned disaster researcher, reports that current research reveals most people are unaware of the risks they face. They do not associate their spatial location with degrees of danger from extreme events, such as hurricanes and floods. Furthermore, most people do not properly plan or estimate what is needed to cope with disasters, and there is too much reliance on emergency relief from government agencies.

Who Was Impacted?

Many people were impacted by the storms. But as the presenters and audience participants came to conclude, an event like Floyd is "not an equal opportunity disaster." Dennis Mileti states that minority populations and people in lower socioeconomic groups are at greater risk than other segments of the population. These groups live in lower quality homes that are often located in disaster-risk areas (e.g., floodplains).

The driver of a supply truck slowly makes his way down a flooded section of the Highway 264 bypass in Greenville, N.C., while behind him boaters quickly cross the road. (Courtesy of the city of Greenville, N.C.)

Mr. Billy Ray Hall touched on this same theme. While he presents an informed *respect* for North Carolina's strengths, he presents an informed *disdain* for her persistent and enduring problems. He notes that businesses, as well as homes, often are built on cheap floodplain land in order to save costs, but this places them at high risk to flooding. He also notes that Floyd tended to exacerbate sociological issues, such as poverty, racism, and access to quality education. As evidence of his concern, information received from the North Carolina Division of Emergency Management indicates that fewer than 50% of the homes impacted by Floyd even had homeowner's insurance. Furthermore, the issues outlined by Mr. Hall have endured throughout North Carolina's history, especially in rural counties. He makes a compelling argument that recovery from Floyd must occur in the context of these "enduring issues."

Measuring the Impact: The Human Experience

The "Looking into the Face of the Storm" accounts, which occur throughout the book, provide a firsthand account of the flood experience of several groups. These are important commentaries on how communities responded to the different problems people encountered during and after the storms.

Researchers took an empirical look at some of these problems and other issues. In many cases, the results from the studies presented here are preliminary and many projects are ongoing. But the quick response of these researchers to study the impacts of the flooding is a tribute to their commitment to understand underlying problems and to initiate change. Often, research findings can have a tremendous positive impact on public policies and programs.

Karen Becker examined hospital records to characterize the immediate hurricane-related injuries and illnesses, and the illness and injury pattern one month after the storm. The author provides very important cautionary steps that can be used to minimize death and injury during hurricanes and floods.

The work of several researchers reinforced the disproportionate distribution of disaster impacts among different types of people. In their study of ECU staff, East Carolina University geographer Holly Hapke and her colleagues underscore the differential impact of Hurricane Floyd on African American inland residents. Their data support the research results of a study conducted after Hurricane Bonnie by

ECU faculty members Bob Edwards, John R. Maiolo, John C. Whitehead, Kenneth Wilson, and Marieke Van Willigen, where African American and low-income residents in coastal counties incurred greater costs *in proportion* to their household income when compared to other socioeconomic groups.

Sadly, many residents in Princeville, N.C., discovered that flood impacts included the disturbance of loved ones' final resting place.

The experience among the elderly in several coastal counties did not mirror that of younger segments of the population. The paper by Eleanor Krassen Covan, Marlene M. Rosenkoetter, Beth Richards, and Anita Lane underscores the need to identify the pre-disaster and post-disaster assistance needs of older adults. Floyd impacted ECU students in terms of damages, but Marieke Van Willigen and her colleagues found that the most disruptive and stressful aspect of the experience for students was trying to keep up with their schoolwork. There are several universities and colleges along North Carolina's coast. These institutions will need to determine how they should respond after students experience a stressful event. The response should be humane and yet not neglect the integrity of the educational experience.

Given the results of these studies, it's imperative that we determine how to design recovery programs that address the realities of differential impacts. Several roundtable dialogues discussed this issue, agreeing that a key to resolving this problem is including representatives from vulnerable groups in disaster planning and preparation programs. (See "A Dialogue—Communities at Risk and Access to Disaster Recovery Assistance" and "A Dialogue—Responding to the Long-Term Recovery Needs of Disaster Victims.")

Other research actually points to some positive affects from the disaster. Ken Wilson and his colleagues examined differences in people's perceptions of economic development and technology before and after the Hurricane Floyd events. Although the results indicate that the storm did not affect perceptions of economic opportunity, it did appear to motivate people to install Internet access for use as an information source for disaster preparation and recovery. Households were more likely to have a personal computer and Internet access after Floyd than before. Three papers (Hapke et al.; Van Willigan et. al.; and Covan et al.) showed high levels of volunteer participation after the storm, especially among ECU staff but also including students and the elderly. However, there is an indication that recovery work was largely dominated by those who engaged in volunteer work before the storm, and although a significant body of research suggests that volunteer work has a positive impact on individuals' well being, the validity of this research has been questioned.

In the Van Willigan study, ECU students indicated many positive changes in their life priorities as a result of their experiences with Floyd. The hurricane and flooding disaster caused stress and anxiety, but perhaps we should not assume that these kinds of experiences necessarily have only negative effects. Some ECU students may have learned valuable skills and a sense of self-reliance that will benefit them in the future.

The Pattillo A+ Elementary School disaster relief project gave some ECU students the opportunity to help children recover from the effects of the disaster. It is noteworthy that some of these students had lost their homes and/or belongings to the flood. This project represents the gallant work of Carmen Russoniello and other faculty and students in the School of Health and Human Performance at ECU, and focused on the psychological recovery needs of the schoolchildren in the hard-hit Tarboro area. The project is the first of its kind. It demonstrates the effectiveness of a planned bio-psychosocial intervention and provides a point of reference for future disaster relief efforts.

Measuring the Impact: The Natural Environment

In his "Anatomy of a Flood" paper, Stanley Riggs describes the link between the earth's natural systems, the particular characteristics of North Carolina's river systems, and the floods of September 1999. People choosing to intimately live with dynamic natural systems must understand these systems. As Dr. Riggs asserts, if we come to understand and appreciate the earth's natural processes, perhaps we will stop believing that we can manipulate and manage our river systems and instead weave their normal cyclic patterns into our lives.

Several papers looked at the natural dynamics of flooding and hurricanes. As noted previously, Dr. Len Pietrafesa and his team of researchers concluded that a series of unusual events, involving wind and rain that began with Hurricane Dennis, created a previously unseen set of circumstances in Pamlico Sound that substantially contributed to the severe inland flooding. The group also concluded that these types of conditions, as unusual as they were, can be predicted in the future. Professor Wang and his colleagues address the problem of accurately determining the total extent of flooding for an area. They propose a useful method that could aid government officials in identifying hard-hit areas, thus facilitating response, recovery, and disaster-planning strategies.

Scott Lecce and his collaborators looked at how sediments are deposited in a river floodplain after a large flood. Based on preliminary data for the Tar River drainage basin, they found that the floods of 1999 deposited little sediment in the Tar River floodplain. This research may have implications for how flood zone lines (e.g., the 100-year flood line) are drawn. Additionally, as these researchers continue this study and begin focusing on tracking where heavy-metal contaminants were deposited in the Tar River and in the

Pamlico Sound, they may be able to provide a perspective on the long-term impacts from the floods.

There was much local and national media attention on the biological impacts of the floods on the Pamlico and Cape Fear rivers. Images of floating animal carcasses and the flow of sewage, industrial, and agriculture waste into these major rivers led many scientists to predict that large fish kills would soon result. Conditions that were stressful to many organisms did occur immediately after the storm. But as Hans Paerl and his collaborators state in their study of the Pamlico Sound, the winds of Hurricane Irene helped stir up the water, increasing dissolved oxygen levels (i.e., the concentration of oxygen in the water), and thus preventing the predicted fish kill. However, there may be severe long-term impacts of the floods on the Pamlico River Estuary system. Since the storms, there has been a higher incidence of lesions on certain fish species, particularly Atlantic menhaden (see Luczkovich et al. this volume). Also, because Pamlico Sound has a very restricted exchange with the open ocean, the higher than normal levels of organic material in the estuary, as well as lower salinity levels, may have a significant long-term impact on the sound's food chain.

The water quality study of the Cape Fear River by Lawrence Cahoon and fellow researchers at the University of North Carolina at Wilmington shows that all rivers and estuaries are not alike. Unlike the Pamlico Sound, the Cape Fear River has a broad connection to the coastal ocean. The high volume of floodwater that resulted due to Hurricane Floyd was able to quickly flow to the open ocean, and dissolved oxygen did not fall low enough to cause fish kills. However, the paper by these researchers, as well as the study by ECU professor Joe Luczkovich and his colleagues at the North Carolina Department of Environment and Natural Resources, point toward a need for long-term monitoring of North Carolina's rivers and estuaries. Determination of the impacts from severe natural events will only be educated guesses unless they can be compared with comprehensive, detailed baseline data. Researchers cannot tell us anything about the "after" if they don't know have enough information about the "before." Drs. Joseph Ramus and Hans Paerl describe a project that will begin to address this research need.

In July 2000, information was received from the North Carolina Division of Marine Fisheries indicating that the 1999 hurricane season did have a devastating impact on commercial fishing, but not on recreational fishing. In 1999, the total weight of commercial seafood landings was 153.4 million pounds, with a value of $98.9 million. Although record landings of crabs and shrimp were reported, the overall harvest (all marine species) was the smallest in twenty-six years. The menhaden catch was the lowest on record. Recreational anglers, on the other hand, hauled in an estimated 18 million pounds, the second largest catch since 1990 (the year estimates first became available).

The difference between the two fishing groups is accounted for by *where* the fish are caught and the *type* of species harvested. For example, in terms of *pounds*, most of the recreational catch comes from the ocean, where the hurricanes had less of an environmental impact. (A bumper harvest year for offshore tuna in 1999 inflated recreational statistics.) Most commercial landings come from inshore and nearshore, where the hurricanes and flooding significantly impacted the water quality. After Floyd, individual catch statistics from commercial fishers qualified a large number of them for hurricane relief funds. An examination of comparable data from inshore and nearshore fisherman along the coast verifies that where the hurricanes of 1999 hit the hardest, the fishing statistics were the poorest. Data examined in the fall of 2000 indicated that finfish landings seemed to approximate normalcy, shrimp landings were normal or above, but crab landings were suffering, especially in the Neuse River and to a similar extent in the Pamlico River.

Research on this topic continues as the specific effects of Floyd on types of fisheries are examined. Detailed information about catches by time period, type of fishing activity, and geographical area can be obtained from the North Carolina Division of Marine Fisheries at <www.ncdmf.net>.

The Institutional Context of Disaster Recovery and Regulation

Emergency response planning

Evacuation warnings, orders, and the actual process of evacuating an area are common experiences for those living in a disaster-prone area. Evacuation was certainly a large part of the Hurricane Floyd experience. The mandatory evacuation orders for communities from Florida to Virginia resulted in the largest peacetime evacuation in U.S. history. Several researchers evaluated people's evacuation behavior and their trust in official sources of disaster information after the Floyd experience. For several years, David Sattler has researched the effect of multiple exposures to natural disasters on people's evacuation behavior in the hurricane-prone city of Charleston, South Carolina. He presents results from several studies that looked at how past experience affects people's willingness to evacuate for future hurricane threats. This is a particularly important issue in coastal South Carolina because a snarl of traffic resulted from the evacuation order issued before Floyd, causing stress and anger. ECU researchers (Marieke Van Willigen, Stephanie Lormand, Bob Edwards, Jayme Curry, John R. Maiolo, and Kenneth Wilson) found that university students, as a result of experiences during Floyd, reported a lack of trust in official sources of disaster warnings. Is this a cause for concern in terms of whether individuals will evacuate in the future when an evacuation is recommended or even when it is ordered? According to the research of John Whitehead and his colleagues, households generally make decisions about evacuation that are consistent from one hurricane to another and from one hurricane season to another. Therefore, how concerned do we need to be about reports stating that people are less trusting of experts and that they may not evacuate next time? It is clear, however, that understanding the motivation for people's evacuation decisions provides insights into the economic impacts of their behavior during disasters and is essential information for emergency managers.

Government disaster policy and assistance programs

While deaths related to natural disasters have declined, the economic impacts continue to rise. The cost of disasters is increasing for disaster victims, the insurance industry, and governments. This was a theme repeated many times at the conference and is addressed in several papers included in this volume (see Mileti; Hall; Platt). Both Dr. Mileti and Dr. Rutherford Platt state in their papers that the estimates of disaster costs are often not accurate—actual total costs are probably higher than reported costs. Many costs are not figured into the total, including the out-of-pocket expenses to property owners, business losses not covered by insurance, and costs to nongovernmental relief providers. Both authors call for the creation of a central data processing center that would collect and organize all disaster-related costs. It will be difficult to accurately evaluate the effectiveness of recovery and relief programs if we cannot identify where assistance was needed in previous disasters.

Professor Platt shares his unique perspective on the causes for the increased cost of disasters. He gives an overview of our national disaster policies, identifies many problems, and proposes possible solutions so that we can better plan for the extreme weather events in our future.

For instance, Congress has initiated a variety of strategies in response to natural disasters during the past half century. But how effective is our current national disaster policy? Dr. Platt emphasizes the need to coordinate disaster response and recovery efforts, particularly during the rebuilding process after a disaster. As Professor Platt explains, one reason federal efforts to reduce the impact of natural disasters have fallen short is because the federal government is expected to play the major role in disaster response but state governments *limit* the federal government's ability to initiate disaster mitigation programs. Redevelopment and new construction is often allowed in disaster-prone areas. The future social costs of natural disasters cannot decrease until the rights of private property owners are reconciled with larger public interests.

Contributing to the increase in disaster costs is the number of federally declared disasters, which nearly doubled in the 1990s compared with the previous decade. This is not due entirely to an increase in the number of disasters, but may reflect a tendency for the president to issue multiple declarations for a single disaster across many states. But often the need for assistance is not equal across states. A region that is impacted by a serious disaster, which causes widespread damage and threatens human life, should receive federal assistance. But too often states receive federal money for less than severe disaster impacts, such as those resulting from heavy rain or snowfall or simply "bad weather."

For a federally declared disaster, the Stafford Act specifies a 75 to 25 ratio of federal to nonfederal cost sharing. According to Professor Platt, too often "the nonfederal (state and local) share is interpreted liberally to include staff salaries and repair costs that would be incurred even without a disaster. . ." In some cases, the president has reduced the nonfederal share (e.g., Hurricane Fran) or waived it entirely (e.g., Hurricane Andrew). This encourages local governments to request federal money to rebuild damaged infrastructure in the same location because there is no cost to local taxpayers. The combination of an increase in federally declared disasters and the discretionary approach to the application of the Stafford Act has discouraged self-reliance at the regional and local levels. States, local communities, businesses, and households will not decrease their probability of being impacted by a future disaster as long as there is federal money available to make everything the way it was before the disaster.

There are also several problems with how disaster assistance benefits are distributed. Lower income communities and families are at a distinct disadvantage in the assistance/recovery process. This problem was echoed throughout the three-day conference. Billy Ray Hall, who for many months oversaw the North Carolina Hurricane Floyd Redevelopment Center, believes that our ability to identify and reach vulnerable communities is crucial to the recovery process after Floyd.

The role of the insurance and real estate industries

Many presenters emphasized an imbalance between the choices people make before a disaster, such as where they choose to live and build, the risks they are willing to take, and the amount they pay for insurance policies and for needed recovery activities after a disaster. A consensus emerged that preparation and recovery costs should directly correspond to the choices people make and the conscious risks they are willing to endure. Much of the burden in dealing with this issue falls on the insurance and real estate industries. Both industries should integrate disaster risk information and education into their business practices. The insurance industry also needs to create rates based on better data. Rates should reflect the property owner's actual risk. Often homeowners in high-risk areas, such as coastal regions, do not pay rates that reflect their true risk. And the insured in other parts of a state may pay higher rates to compensate the industry for losses suffered in high-risk areas.

The real estate industry needs to be more upfront with consumers about the risks associated with the specific location of a business or home. According to Mr. William Wall, Executive Vice President of First South Bank, lending institutions, in order to gain a competitive market advantage, often ignore important information about property location that would force consumers to purchase appropriate protective insurance policies. Real estate agencies contribute to this problem by improperly designating a property as not being in the flood zone when it is actually in the flood zone.

UNCW economists examined the monetary costs associated with choices that homeowners make to decrease their risk to flooding disasters. Specifically, they looked at whether a homeowner should purchase flood insurance or spend money on defensive measures that would protect the home in the event of a flood. They note from a purely "rational" economic perspective that, at present, there is no financial incentive for a typical North Carolina coastal resident to spend money on defensive measures or on flood insurance. Although their choice of a "typical" resident is questionable, given other arguments about differential impacts as well as demographics of the region, the research brings up two important issues. First, flood insurance and defensive measures have been promoted by the groups that financially benefit from marketing them (including the federal government); there is probably a need for information about what measures really "work." Also, given the experiences in eastern North Carolina, we are now painfully aware of how inaccurate floodplain maps are. Some people paid for flood insurance that they did not need, while many others did not qualify for flood insurance, although they were flooded. Second, what is the utility of using a purely economic rationale for understanding human behavior? The model presented by the UNCW economists does not take into account the sentimental value of objects. Can we afford to underestimate the importance of these kinds of factors in human choices?

How Can We Make Individuals and Communities More Resistant to Events Like Floyd?

Eastern North Carolina communities have faced rapid growth since the 1950s. This is also a region that is vulnerable to hurricanes and tropical storms. The consensus among the forecasting experts is that extreme weather will continue to hit this region, and the frequency of these events will likely increase in the future (see Sheets, this volume). So, now more people are living in a disaster-prone region. As Dr. David Godschalk informs us, if communities want to improve or maintain their quality of life, they must be able to quickly rebound after disasters like Hurricane Floyd. Old ideas and behaviors of how a community grows and develops must change. There must be a balance between our desired quality of life, the economy, and the environment.

Dr. Godschalk argues for a strategy that combines hazard mitigation and smart growth. *Hazard mitigation* "protects people and property from the destructive impacts of natural hazards . . .," while *smart growth* "connects development and the quality of life, and leverages new growth" to improve community resources, even as it protects environmental resources. This approach creates a sustainable community. That is, a community, according to Professor Goldschalk, "whose buildings, facilities, organizations, and activities are strong and supple in the face of natural hazards." He sees the resilient community in the future as one that can weather any flood or hurricane, "while sustaining its economy, environment, and quality of life." On a positive note, he provides several examples of communities in the Tar Heel state that have learned how to be more resilient after experiencing weather impacts.

But as Drs. Platt, Godschalk, and Mileti suggest, this process must begin with the accurate measurement of each community's disaster risk and vulnerability. And all these experts agree that this will not be easy. It will take compromise, coordination, sacrifice, and strong leadership. For example, municipalities located near rivers cannot allow homes to be built in the floodplains. Unfortunately, as Dr. Godscahlk notes, "Most of the seventy towns and counties affected by Floyd are choosing not to curb floodplain development. . . ."

Now What Do We Do?

Concern for pets was a source of stress for many people as they evacuated from their homes. Here, search and rescue team members bring in stranded dogs from the flooded town of Princeville, N.C. (Photo by Dave Saville, courtesy of FEMA News Photo)

Hurricane Floyd taught eastern North Carolina many lessons. There were disaster response strategies that worked, others that failed, and many that were never anticipated. For instance, the city manager of Elizabeth City, in the far northeastern coastal county of Pasquotank, indicated that had they received the brunt of the storm, about forty curious people who rushed to the downtown waterfront to see the rising water would have been killed. The next time a severe storm threatens this region, the downtown area will be blocked off, according to the manager.

Several schools in Johnston County that were used as shelters had not been wired to run electrical generators. The city of Tarboro was without an operating radio system. This was an unforeseen problem that confounded their ability to alert the community about the storm and floods. Greenville, on the other hand, was fortunate to have WNCT-TV communicate with the citizenry around the clock, alerting the community as a third of the city was inundated with floodwaters that cut off access on three sides. But city officials found that the National Guard was not prepared to respond adequately during several crucial situations. In general, the emergency management plans at ECU worked well; lives and expensive equipment were saved. But the scope of the disaster revealed a weakness in the university's ability to deal with evacuation. These and other stories indicate the good, the bad, and the ugly of our ability to respond to a large disaster (also see Shaw [2000] for additional examples).

At the end of this book, we present a list of specific recommendations on what should be done to prepare eastern North Carolina for future storms. As you read the many excellent papers that lead to this final chapter, you will see the following recurring and interrelated themes:

- More extreme weather is coming; don't be lulled into thinking anything else.
- Many of our communities not only remain vulnerable to hurricanes and flooding, but some are repeating pre-Floyd mistakes.
- Illnesses and death related to disasters like Floyd continue months after the event occurs.
- There are lessons to be learned, not only from Floyd, but also from communities who have become proactive.

- We must adopt ways to make a dangerous future less catastrophic than the tragedy that resulted from Hurricane Floyd and its flooding aftermath.
- In the process of making our communities more resistant and resilient, other social issues haunting eastern North Carolina need to be recognized and addressed.
- Reassessments of warning systems and evacuation plans are in order. There were near chaotic situations in some of the potentially impacted areas during the Hurricane Floyd episode. Evacuations are costly, so care must be taken to provide the appropriate mix of moving people out of harm's way and keeping unnecessary expenditures to a minimum, for both businesses and households.
- Household evacuation decisions are not just economic in nature, nor do they rest solely upon the safety of the residents. They involve a number of other issues, including health, whether people have pets, types of dwelling, etc. Policies that intend to improve the evacuation processes need to take these kinds of measures into account.
- The combination of hurricanes Dennis, Floyd, and Irene created extremely unusual conditions in the floodplains, rivers, and for the Pamlico Sound. New floodplain maps and risk assessments are in order, as are new predictive models and measurements.
- As severe as the impacts were, it could have been worse. Hurricane Dennis cooled coastal waters, which decreased the wind velocity of Hurricane Floyd. The impacts on the marine environment would have been far worse had the winds of Hurricane Irene not stirred the waters to improve the levels of dissolved oxygen in Pamlico Sound.

Hurricane Floyd was an awful disaster, but it also provides a unique opportunity for those of us who live in the region, all of us, from every walk of life, to create and rebuild a smarter future. It will cost just as much, or more, to rebuild "stupid" as it will to build "smart." So why not build smart? If anything came out of the conference with a resounding unanimity, it was just that message. We should all take a moment to see how this natural disaster can create the basis for a new way of looking at and living in the "east" as we undertake the journey into the new millennium.

References

Junger, S. 1997. The perfect storm: A true story of men against the sea. Thorndike, Me.: Thorndike Press.

Maiolo, J. R., A. Delia, J. C. Whitehead, B. Edwards, K. Wilson, M. Van Willigen, C. Williams, and M. Meekins. 1998. A socioeconomic hurricane evacuation impact analysis and a hurricane evacuation impact assessment tool (methodology) for coastal North Carolina: A case study of Hurricane Bonnie. Greenville, N.C.: East Carolina University, Regional Development Services (RDS), Department of Sociology, Department of Economics.

Shaw, M. 2000. Floyd was a disaster we never planned for. CountyLines (a publication of the North Carolina Association of Country Commissioners). February.

Living with Future Extreme Weather Events

Robert Sheets

Dr. Sheets is familiar to anyone who has watched hurricanes weave their way along our nation's East Coast. He has spent most of his life studying severe weather events. While at the National Hurricane Research Laboratory, he studied hurricanes, directed field operations, and made more than 200 high-risk flights through the "eye" of hurricanes. In 1980 he became a hurricane specialist at the National Hurricane Center (NHC), where he was also deputy director and finally the director from 1987 to 1995. Since leaving the NHC, he has been a meteorological consultant, providing on-camera services for the Florida News Network, its affiliates, and the ABC network. His other activities include lectures and workshops on hurricane threats and preparedness and serving on numerous committees and boards. He is the author of many scientific and popular articles on weather events and has received numerous honors and awards. Dr. Sheets gave the keynote presentation at the conference and was introduced by Philip Williams, chief meteorologist at WNCT-TV, Greenville, North Carolina.

Introduction

We have learned many lessons from past hurricanes and other severe weather events. I've learned many lessons, having been through Hurricane Andrew and a few other significant hurricanes, about preparing and planning for severe weather. I want to share these lessons so that perhaps education can be a substitute for direct experience. In the future, it would be preferable if we didn't need to have conferences that identify how to lessen the impacts of future storms. It would be best if we could recognize and apply the lessons that are evident in the damage we see each time a hurricane or severe storm beats a path along the East Coast.

Historically, North Carolina has been very susceptible to hurricanes, and according to recent forecasts it will be in the future. The accuracy of forecasting and predicting the path of hurricanes has improved tremendously in recent years. We have made far less progress in changing how we prepare and plan for hurricanes. This paper will describe the forecasting process, including details of the progression of Hurricane Floyd, but more importantly it will outline how the impacts from future severe weather can be reduced. This includes practical construction techniques and issues relating to insurance and coastal development. We cannot divert the path of a hurricane away from the North Carolina coast, but North Carolina and other states in this region of the country can live more harmoniously with future severe storms.

Forecasting Hurricanes

The origin of forecasting began with a benchmark hurricane in 1900, the Galveston hurricane. This hurricane severely impacted the booming town of Galveston, Texas, and was essentially the same strength as Hurricane Hugo—a category four storm that devastated the West Indies and the southeastern United States in September 1989. In fact, when I superimposed the satellite image of Hurricane Hugo on the track of the 1900 Galveston hurricane, they were very similar. The hurricane that hit Galveston was one of the deadliest in the nation's history, yet today most people, even those living near the town, have not heard of the Galveston hurricane. The 1900 hurricane came ashore in what was then the second wealthiest city in the United States. Approximately 6,000 to 8,000 people drowned as a result of the storm—one-third of the population of the town. Another couple of thousand people from nearby communities also drowned.

The deaths in the Galveston disaster were due to the storm surge. In 1900, they really didn't know a whole lot about the surge of tidal water that can occur as the result of a hurricane or other intense storms. The normal, average sea level can be significantly increased by strong winds blowing water shoreward. In 1893, a famous meteorologist, Isaac Cline, was telling the chamber of commerce that Galveston didn't have a storm surge problem because of all of the shallow water buttressing the island. In fact, it was just the opposite.

Isaac Cline, although a smart man, didn't understand storm surges. When the water is shallow, the wind blows the water up to the coast, and then ashore; if the water is deep, the wind blows it up to the coast, where it sinks and recirculates. The long and relatively shallow shelf in the Gulf of Mexico creates ideal conditions for a storm surge like the one experienced in Galveston. If that same hurricane struck near the Hawaiian Islands, where the water is deeper close to shore, than the storm surge would add only three or four feet to the normal sea level.

There were other large and devastating hurricanes in the early part of this century. In 1926, a hurricane a little bit stronger and larger than Hugo and not very different than Hurricane Floyd crashed into South Florida. Miami Beach was beaten up badly as a result and the death toll exceeded 1,800. In 1938, 600 lives were lost when a hurricane hit the northeast.

As a result of losses of life associated with storms occurring over the past century and because scientists did not really understand storm surge dynamics, we started modeling storms. The first models were used with Hurricane Camille in 1969. This was the first storm for which surge estimates were available. Bob Simpson, the director of the National Hurricane Center at the time, said that the crude model predicted storm surge heights of about 25 feet. The highest measured surge of 24.2 feet was measured within the city limits of Pass Christian, Mississippi, close to site of the hurricane's landfall. By the time of Hurricane Hugo's arrival the model had been refined. The height of the surge from Hugo that produced the devastation on Folly Beach, South Carolina, was well predicted. Currently, predictions are believed.

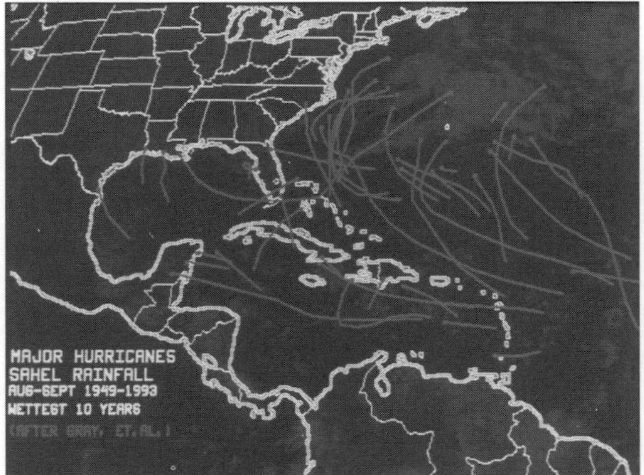

Figure 1. The relationship between HIGH rainfall totals in the Sahel region of western Africa and hurricane activity. The track of major hurricanes that impacted the East Coast and the Gulf of Mexico in the *wettest* ten years in Sahel, between 1949-1993.

Figure 2. The relationship between LOW rainfall totals in the Sahel region of western Africa and hurricane activity. The track of major hurricanes that impacted the East Coast and the Gulf of Mexico in the *driest* ten years in Sahel, between 1949-1993.

There are cycles of hurricane activity. Periods of great hurricane activity alternate with periods of relatively little activity. For instance, there was a very active period of hurricane activity that began in the 1950s and lasted until the mid-1960s, which was followed by a twenty-year lull in activity. Professor Bill Gray of Colorado State University has studied the reason for these cycles. He first discovered that the amount of rainfall in the Sahel area of western Africa seemed to be associated with hurricane activity (Figure 1 and 2). During the 1940s and 1950s, rainfall in this region of Africa was above normal, and there were a lot of major hurricanes. From the mid-1960s through the early 1990s, rainfall was below normal and hurricane activity was less. There was an exception to this pattern. In 1988 and 1989 the rainfall was above normal in the Sahel, and there was a lot of hurricane activity in both years. The dramatic variations in rainfall in Africa and the hurricane activity in the Atlantic Basin may be related to water temperature and salinity levels in the North Atlantic. Presently, the rainfall is near or above normal, and it is predicted to stay that way for the next couple of decades. Data from recent seasons show a tremendous increase in hurricane activity, starting in 1995 when there were almost a record number of storms, nearly duplicating the record year of 1933. In 1997, we had an El Niño event that accounted for decreased hurricane activity. But in 1998 and in 1999 there were a flurry of storms. Looking at the five year total, beginning in 1995, there have been forty-one hurricanes—a record. Clearly we have entered an active hurricane cycle, perhaps similar to what was experienced in the 1940s and 1950s.

The Path of Hurricane Floyd

Hurricane Floyd was one of the more memorable hurricanes of recent years, in part due to its strength, but also because the combined effect of hurricanes Dennis and Floyd caused severe flooding, primarily in North Carolina (Figure 3). It also caused the largest evacuation in U.S. history.

Figure 3. Extensive flooding of an eastern North Carolina neighborhood just days after Hurricane Floyd.

Floyd's start was unimpressive. It initiated as a tropical wave that emerged from western Africa on 2 September. By 13 September, Floyd was at the upper limit of the category four intensity on the Saffir/Simpson Hurricane Scale. It started to weaken a little as it passed through the Abaco Islands in the Bahamas on the 14th, but it was still a borderline category three/four hurricane. Floyd continued to turn gradually to the right, and subsequently the center of the hurricane paralleled the central Florida coast. The size of the storm surge from a paralleling storm is much less than for a storm that directly strikes a coastline. Therefore, it appeared that Florida was not going to get the big storm surge that was originally depicted on the generalized maps. Yet, the human response to the hurricane was as if it were going to move directly at the Florida coast. I think we overreacted to Floyd, particularly with regard to the storm surge threat. The end result was an evacuation of over two million people all the way up the coast, from Florida to Virginia. Chaos and congestion occurred along most evacuation routes in South Carolina (Interstate 26) and Savannah, Georgia, as well as Interstate 95 up and down the East Coast (Figure 4).

If the call for an evacuation in the Miami area of Dade County had been delayed by about three hours, there probably would have not been a hurricane warning for Floyd. But it takes anywhere from thirty-six, forty-eight, or more hours to prepare for a severe hurricane, and if Floyd did continue to move on a straight line, there would not have been time to respond. Imagine if Hurricane Floyd had come ashore where all those people were sitting in their cars. A situation like the one that resulted from the massive evacuations is where we'd expect a big loss of life. It's clear that a reexamination of the whole evacuation planning process is essential.

By the afternoon of the 15th, Floyd was proceeding to the north, headed for the Carolinas (Figure 5). It was still a powerful hurricane, but not as powerful as it had been when approaching and striking the northwest Bahamas. It continued to weaken slowly as it moved near the North Carolina

Figure 4. After a state-issued mandatory evacuation, gridlock traffic resulted on the stretch of Interstate 26 leading out of Charleston, S.C.

Figure 5. Satellite image of Hurricane Floyd as it heads towards North Carolina.

coast. Floyd also cooled the waters as it moved north. Because the storm had weakened, there was a lot of beach damage and coastal erosion, but there was not a large storm surge. Had the hurricane been as strong as it was when it first struck the northwest Bahamas, the coastal destruction would have been massive and wind damage would have been catastrophic over much of eastern North Carolina. This destruction would be in addition to the damage caused by the floods. In someways, despite the massive flood damage, the impact easily could have been much worse.

In the Bahamas, where Floyd passed through with significantly stronger wind speeds, there was damage and a strong storm surge. But again, the problem for communities in the Carolinas was not strong winds and a storm surge. Instead, for many communities, one of the biggest problems was what had happened two weeks earlier. Hurricane Dennis came up the coast and soaked many areas, including eastern North Carolina, and then made a loop and came back and soaked the area again. A tremendous amount of water was already present prior to Floyd's visit. But Dennis also did something good. Dennis cooled the waters just north of the Bahamas, so when Floyd came over that area, it did not strengthen, it weakened.

Most of the loss of life from Hurricane Floyd occurred in North Carolina. In fact, the fatalities from Floyd are the most lives lost from a hurricane in the continental United States in many, many years. Most of the deaths occurred inland, with a great majority resulting from drowning as people became trapped in their cars after driving on roadway systems that were washed out.

North Carolina's Future Hurricanes

When an image of an Atlantic tropical system first appears on the satellite radar, residents along eastern North Carolina get nervous, with very good reason. In the last five years the eye of three hurricanes (Fran, Bonnie, and Floyd) have made landfall in North Carolina. Why North Carolina? First, there is a large high-pressure area in Bermuda that is centered in the ocean slightly south and east of North Carolina. Hurricanes are frequently steered by the circulation around this high-pressure area. Next, many tropical storms come off the coast of Africa, moving westward along a trade wind belt and on the south side of the clockwise circulation of the Bermuda high-pressure area. The storm may then turn toward the north on the western end of this high-pressure region. If the high-pressure ridge is built westward, this turn will not occur until the storm strikes Florida or moves into the Gulf of Mexico. However, frequently the western edge erodes away and the storms turn northward just off the east coast of Florida. The northeastern end of North Carolina juts right out into the ocean, so a storm that has turned north along the western side of the high pressure area has a good likelihood of affecting the Outer Banks and then proceeding right on through the state, entering near the south to central portion of the coastline.

North Carolina is a member of a community of states that by the luck of geology and geography will continue to experience hurricanes. But the probability of North Carolina experiencing a hurricane is not equal throughout the hurricane season. In June, most of the hurricanes form in the western Caribbean and the Gulf of Mexico. If a hurricane moved up the coast to North Carolina in June, it would probably be a very weak hurricane and would move mostly parallel to the coast. Maybe once every fifty years North Carolina might get a direct hit in June.

In July, hurricanes are continuing to form in the Gulf of Mexico and the western Caribbean, but a few are starting to form in the Atlantic, east of the Caribbean islands. North Carolina can get hurricanes in July, but they are very infrequent events, occurring maybe every thirty to forty years. By August, there is a great increase in hurricane activity in the Atlantic, with many storms forming near Africa. There is a well-established subtropical ridge, or a Bermuda high, at this time. August and September are the months in the hurricane season when North Carolina is typically threatened with storm activity. In October the pattern will start to shift again, with the great majority of storms originating in the Caribbean Sea and the Gulf of Mexico. North Carolina can still get hurricanes in from the south or east, but a good portion of these will move parallel to the coast rather than into the coast. The hurricane season is basically over by November. Once in a while a storm might occur, but it would be a very rare event, and it would normally be moving parallel to the coastline.

Hurricane Preparation

During the course of my work with the hurricane preparedness programs at the National Hurricane Center, I've documented a lot of hurricane-caused destruction. I took "before" pictures and matched them with the "after" pictures, and sometimes the destruction is unbelievable. Hurricane Camille made landfall in Mississippi with sustained winds of about 175 miles per hour—the last category five hurricane to strike the continental United States. The twenty-five foot storm surge breached an eight-foot seawall and leveled a three-story apartment complex. That is the power of wave action. One home on the Mississippi coast, built in the mid-1800s, was extremely well built, but it was destroyed by Camille.

The power of a storm often exceeds the strength of man-made storm barriers. For instance, rip-rap (large, organized piles of rock) are often placed as a barrier between the beach and an adjacent road or a housing area. The Phillips Petroleum Company made a well-advertised filter cloth on which rip-rap was piled. This cloth was used along oceanfront property in South Carolina. It failed to work as advertised during Hurricane Camille; the rip-rap wound up in the living room of a home that was in the second row back from the ocean. Those living in disaster-prone areas often have a false sense of security, which is based on perceptions of construction quality and a belief that protective structures will work.

Hurricanes are rare events. But they do come, and they destroy a great deal of what lie in their paths, often at great surprise to many people. There was a gentleman I met after Hurricane Hugo who lived up on a bluff, and he said, " [the] water's never been in my yard, I don't evacuate, I've been here since 1928." During Hugo, he almost died. He, his son, and his grandson survived by hanging onto a tree, but everything was gone. This is an example of people's perception of their risk. Their perception is based on what has been personally experienced, or maybe what their fathers experienced, or their grandfathers. Once that reference point is exceeded, disaster preparation ends.

Evacuation Planning

The technology that allowed us to develop models for hurricane and storm surge predictions also allowed us to better understand problems associated with establishing evacuation routes. In Lee County, Florida, the phonebook shows the areas that will be under water with a category one, two, three, four, and five storm. Also shown are the evacuation routes for the designated areas. Because we cannot predict precisely where a hurricane will strike, many other communities have done the same thing. But in many instances the number of people typically evacuating as a hurricane approaches has been excessive, resulting in massive traffic congestion. One source of the problem is that most communities take much longer to begin evacuating than the standard twelve to twenty-four hours of warning time that is given for an evacuation. Evacuation routes are clogged with evacuees that received evacuation notices at different times.

A forecast thirty-six hours before the expected landfall of a hurricane is uncertain. Many different scenarios can potentially occur. In the face of forecasting uncertainty, huge areas would have to be evacuated to remove everybody that might be impacted by the hurricane and storm surge. The problem results from the idea that everyone, from the people that might only get their feet wet to the people who are at risk of losing everything, is given the same evacuation orders. This is exactly what happened with Hurricane Floyd.

First the people in the most danger must be evacuated before road systems are cut off—those people who are truly in areas of life-threatening winds and flooding. We cannot afford to have people who would suffer only minor impact from a storm, or others who live inland, or those who live in substantial homes clogging up a limited roadway system.

This is particularly crucial in the Florida Keys. Hurricane Floyd scared everyone along the coast of Florida, and rightly so. But people in some areas were evacuated from areas where there was little danger. On the one hand, it's important to motivate people to take the right action. Satellite imagery is a very powerful tool for this because it gets people's attention. But only the communities that will suffer the direct power of the storm should be alerted to evacuate. As Floyd approached the south Florida coast, comparisons were made to Hurricane Andrew. There was a great deal of fear about where Floyd would strike. The people in south Florida, in particular those who had experienced Andrew, were scared to death. Those along the whole eastern coast of Florida were also getting pretty frightened. The models that were being used by the Hurricane Center were predicting that the storm would curve fairly close to the coast, perhaps heading slightly inland or remaining offshore, but definitely moving nearly parallel to the coast. But as was previously noted, the hurricane ultimately took an unexpected turn away from the Florida coast.

When I was the director of the National Hurricane Center, a member of the news media would frequently ask me where a hurricane was going to strike. If the storm was three or five days out, of course, we didn't know the answer. It was too early to make that kind of precise prediction. But the reporter would persist, asking where the storm would strike if it continued to move in a straight line. Well, I'd respond, "In about three weeks, it'll be in Tokyo." But that's not very practical. There is a real problem when people try to project a storm path along a straight line, without regard to the intricacies of forecasting, such as a change in direction or movement. Of course, even the experts using guidance models cannot guarantee that a predicated turn will take place. There is perhaps a 5% to 10% chance that it won't. The question for government and other officials is how much risk they are willing to take.

The number of people evacuating can also be reduced if safe shelters are provided. When Andrew came ashore there was about a 20-mile wide swath of destruction of many mobile and manufactured homes. Mobile and other manufactured homes are a quality, low-cost way of life, but they are not a place to be when a hurricane comes ashore. During Hurricane Andrew, several hundred homes were destroyed in a mobile home community in south Dade County, but not one life was lost, nor was anyone killed in other mobile home parks in the region. Each of these mobile home parks had a safe place for people to go during the event. We ought to require that every mobile home park or manufactured home community have a building that can withstand a hurricane or tornado.

Construction Standards

In August 1992, Hurricane Andrew ripped across Dade County. The Air Force Hurricane Hunter plane measured winds at about 186 miles per hour. One of the lessons learned from this hurricane was the type of houses most at risk. The houses in one planned community were built in a New England style; in fact, it was a style restriction stipulated in the building deed for every house in the community. They should have stayed in New England. The construction style and standards for these homes were not suited for a hurricane environment. The damage to this community was severe.

Many homes built in Dade County during the twenty years when there was a lull in hurricane activity were wood frame, perhaps with gabled ends, double entrance doors, overhangs, porches, or unreinforced garage doors. The construction of many homes was shoddy, some having walls attached with just two nails. Therefore, a portion of the damage resulting from Hurricane Andrew was due to poor design and construction.

But this problem is not restricted to Florida. In Charleston, South Carolina, one official stated, "If Dade County's buildings were built to our standards, they'd still be standing," and he continued, "After Hugo we didn't see the need to change our code much." The fact is that several counties in South Carolina do not even have applicable building codes! There were no codes to change. More importantly, false perceptions of construction quality are dangerous. When Hugo came ashore in South Carolina, Charleston was on the *weak side of the storm.* It really was only a category one or two hurricane in Charleston. The strong part was to the north in the Francis Marion National Forest, where Hurricane Hugo caused the greatest timber loss in U.S. history. Charleston, even with relatively weak winds by hurricane standards, experienced substantial damage, but it wasn't massive. Had that beautiful city experienced the full brunt of the hurricane, it would have been a totally different story.

Buildings can be constructed to resist the effect of wind. But quality construction must be accompanied by an appropriate building style. In hurricane-prone areas, special clips or straps are often used to tie the roof systems. But this will not prevent damage from occurring when a house is designed to trap wind. Three years before Hurricane Andrew, a house was built using many techniques that were considered the best strategy to reduce the potential damage from a hurricane (Figure 6). From the foundation to the roof trusses, the house was tied, bolted, nailed, and wrapped. But when Hurricane Andrew blew through, the house was demolished (Figure 7). The key was the style of the building. The architect seemed to have designed the house to catch every bit of wind. The old standard Florida-style home, and the modern version of it, did quite well during Andrew. And with plywood covers, the insides of most houses were fine. Current homes that are built with steel reinforced, poured tie beams with the tie column set every 4 feet, and straps tying the roof and trusses, should also do well during high winds.

Recently, the Florida Windstorm Insurance Underwriters decided to charge higher rates for

Figure 6. This house in south Florida was built using several structural techniques that were meant to protect it from the damaging effects of heavy winds

Figure 7. The house pictured in Figure 6, after Hurricane Andrew. Although measures were taken to protect the home from wind damage, its design actually helped to trap wind.

houses that are built with gabled ends, double entrance doors, overhangs, porches, or unreinforced garage doors. Also, the state of Florida passed, and the governor just signed, a statewide building code that requires all new construction that is built in the high-wind zone after the year 2001, except in the Florida panhandle, to have protection for the windows and doors. Dade County implemented this requirement right after Andrew, because even houses still standing after the hurricane were considered uninhabitable due to interior damage resulting from unprotected doors and windows. I estimate that at least $5 billion would have been saved if windows and doors had been protected before Hurricane Andrew's arrival.

Coastal Development and Insurance Rates

Quality construction and proper design have major implications for a building's risk of hurricane-caused damage, but neither will mean a thing if a home is built in a vulnerable location. The homes along North Carolina's coastline are not that different from many coastal regions in this country. Homes in these communities are not low-income houses, and very few are wind-resistant structures. Although the National Flood Insurance Program is self-supporting, which means that operating expenses and flood in-

Figure 8. Hurricane Hugo cut through Pawleys Island in South Carolina (below), but this didn't stop people from rebuilding larger homes in this exact location (above).

surance claims are not paid for by the taxpayer but through premiums collected for flood insurance policies, those in the high-risk areas are being subsidized by those in the low-risk areas. The *St. Petersburg Times* recently completed a study of the structures in the Tampa Bay area and found that 50% to 70% are subsidized. People who live in a low-risk area and pay flood insurance are paying a higher rate in order to subsidize the insurance costs for those living in a high-risk area. Former FEMA Director James Lee Witt stated that this practice will not continue. He advocated that *actuarially* sound rates be applied in high-risk areas, such as coastal regions. This is something that many people have been trying to get done for a long time. This policy should result in changes in the way we build and where we build.

I served on a state of Florida insurance commission task force after Hurricane Andrew that attempted to deal with the resultant insurance crisis. That crisis was created when State Farm, Allstate, and other insurance companies refused to insure homes on the coast due to the large losses they suffered after Andrew. But the state responded by stipulating that each insurance company operating in the state must take a portion of the risk on the coast, and furthermore they could not charge actuarially sound rates for coastal homes. This same regulation is in effect in North Carolina. Faced with this condition, the insurance companies, instead of losing money from insuring high-risk structures, increased the rates for people living inland. In essence, the entire insurance paying public is subsidizing construction along the coast.

As result of the type of damage that has resulted from hurricanes in the last two decades, the logical question is: Will we allow the use of subsidized insurance dollars to build again? Examination of the coastal areas affected by Hugo, Fran, or Andrew shows that the answer is yes. For example, as a result of Hurricane Hugo, the southern end of Pawleys Island, South Carolina, was devastated. The wind and water from the storm cut through a narrow spit of sand on which a single row of houses was built. After the storm, the sand was bulldozed back into the cut. It took three times before the sand was stable; each time it washed out and they'd fill it in. Later a house was built where the cut had been (Figure 8). Next door to it, a one-story home was replaced by a three-story building. I have no objection if somebody spends his or her money to build a grand house on the coast. That's fine. But they should do it at their own expense. Federal flood insurance that is subsidized by those in low-risk areas should not be available to residents in high-risk areas. They should be charged actuarially sound rates. When that happens, we will see better quality structures and fewer structures built in extremely high-risk areas.

Summary

Perhaps the best advice for any community dealing with the reality of severe storms was a message I read on a church marquee in Harlingen, Texas, in 1992: "I can not direct the wind, but I can surely adjust my sails." Anyone concerned with the aftermath of hurricanes and our response to these disasters must be willing to adjust their sails. It is up to all of us to participate in our future. We must implement policy changes to direct how we build and develop our land, how we plan for evacuations, and how we apply insurance rates. We can't continue to stumble over past mistakes.

Hurricane Information Resources

National Flood Insurance Program <http://www.fema.gov/nfip/ FEMA>.

National Hurricane Center, with links to National Oceanic and Atmospheric Administration (NOAA), the National Centers for Environmental Prediction, and the National Weather Service <http://www.nhc.noaa.gov/>.

Project Impact, FEMA's nationwide initiative that develops partnerships with communities, using a common-sense damage-reduction approach to reducing the impact of disasters. This web site has many helpful links <http://www.fema.gov/impact/>.

Anatomy of a Flood

Stanley R. Riggs

Dr. Riggs, Distinguished Professor of the College of Arts and Sciences, Department of Geology at East Carolina University, is a popular teacher and speaker, as well as a renowned researcher. As a coastal and marine geologist he studies sediments and sedimentary rocks that are formed in the sea—their form, arrangement, chronological succession, geographic distribution, classification, and the relationship between rock layers. His area of research extends from inland rivers and lakes, to estuaries and barrier island systems, and seaward across the continental shelf. He primarily examines geologically recent rocks (i.e., those that were deposited in the Quaternary and Tertiary periods) to determine the interrelationship between coastal and mineral resources and human civilization. Dr. Riggs has been actively involved in numerous technical coastal and mineral resource issues at the federal, state, and local levels, which has included appointments to many commissions, task forces, panels, and committees. These appointments, as well as many of his publications (more than 100 articles), focus on integrating scientific understanding and utilization with management of various coastal systems. Dr. Riggs brings a unique perspective to the issues surrounding development in eastern North Carolina and provides insight into how to reduce the impact of severe storms. He gave a plenary presentation at the conference and was introduced by Dr. Stephen Culver, chair of the Department of Geology at East Carolina University.

Introduction

Water, an essential resource for life as we know it on earth, is also the most powerful agent shaping the earth's surface. It does this through the timeless processes of weathering and mass movement of the surface layers of soil and sediments and the perpetual flow of rivers to the sea. The Urubamba River flows thousands of feet below the ancient mountain village of Machu Pichu as it boldly sculpts the Peruvian Andes, and the Colorado River incises its Grand Canyon deep into the belly of the Arizona desert. Erosion of the earth's surface by flowing river water occurs primarily during major storms and the resulting floods.

Evidence suggests that primitive societies ditched and drained wetlands and built irrigation canals into dry lands for millennia. However, the study of flowing water, or hydrology, was born in the Nile River valley 5,000 years ago. Egypt is a desolate country sustained by a narrow ribbon of water that slices northward through the absoluteness of the North African desert. The ancient Egyptian civilization was so intertwined with the flow of water that its fortunes rose and fell intimately with changing pulses of the river. The fellaheen worked the enriched soils of the lush valley floor and lived in desert villages above the floodplain. The great temples and tombs of the Pharaohs were built above the villages and often in adjacent uplands, far from influences of the flooding river valley. Nileometers were built along the banks to monitor the river and record floods, which were the basis for determining annual taxation rates. During years of active flooding, agricultural yield was good, the economy was healthy, taxation was up, and Pharaohs built great temples. However, during droughts, food was scarce, people were hungry, the economy was in shambles, taxation was down, and temples were destroyed by warring factions.

The scale of human modification of drainage systems was small until modern engines were developed to power draglines and bulldozers. With increasing population pressure, these symbols of the industrial age helped modern society redesign and re-engineer the earth's surface to fit its needs. The evolution from the industrial age to the high-tech age is removing us even further from direct interaction with basic earth processes. However, with each natural hazard event, we are rudely and temporarily shaken back into the reality of our intimate interdependence on our earth. The September floods of 1999 in eastern North Carolina have done that for us.

North Carolina's "Flood of the Century"

On 4 and 5 September, Hurricane Dennis made landfall in the Cape Lookout area after spending many days of indecision wandering off the Dare County coast (Figure 1). Dennis dropped enough rain on the coastal plain to saturate the ground and fill the major rivers to well above normal flood stage (Figure 2). When the first rain bands from Hurricane Floyd began to impact the region, the Tar River in Greenville was at about 17 feet and was still rising on 14 September (flood stage for the Tar River is 13 feet above mean sea level). The Floyd rains continued through 16 September, as the storm slowly moved from the Cape Fear area through eastern North Carolina along a north-northeast track (Figure 3). On 21 September an unnamed tropical depression delivered a small amount of rain that added slightly to the river height, which crested in Greenville on 22 September at about 30 feet (Figure 2). Then the rivers began their very slow retreat. But this was interrupted on 27 September when yet one more major rainfall inundated the area. This rain put enough water into the drainage basins to hold river levels above flood stage through the first week of October. Finally, by 10 October the rivers settled back into almost normal modes, only to be sent back above flood stage by the rains from Hurricane Irene on 16 October, causing the flooding to persist until almost the end of October (Figure 2).

Thus, the "flood of the century" was first and foremost the product of two months of severe rainfall in the North Carolina coastal plain. Five different rain events (three hurricanes, one tropical depression, and one frontal system) produced highly variable rainfall, ranging from twenty to forty inches depending on the specific location within the flooded region (Figure 2).

These five events produced different kinds of flooding and damage depending on where you were within the drainage basin. For example, there were three different flash floods that sent the tributary streams quickly out of their banks and severely impacted the upland areas adjacent to the upper tributary streams. These floods dissipated just as quickly, but with a severe price tag. As the flash floodwaters were discharged into streams, the main rivers began to rise, and water filled the primary and secondary floodplains, as well as downstream tributaries. With each new rain, the tributaries discharged more water into the rivers. The longevity of the flood was in part due to multiple rain events, as well as high sea levels that restricted the floodwaters from flowing out of estuaries and into the ocean and restrictions to flow that occur within the floodplains themselves (i.e., natural geometry, road dams, etc.).

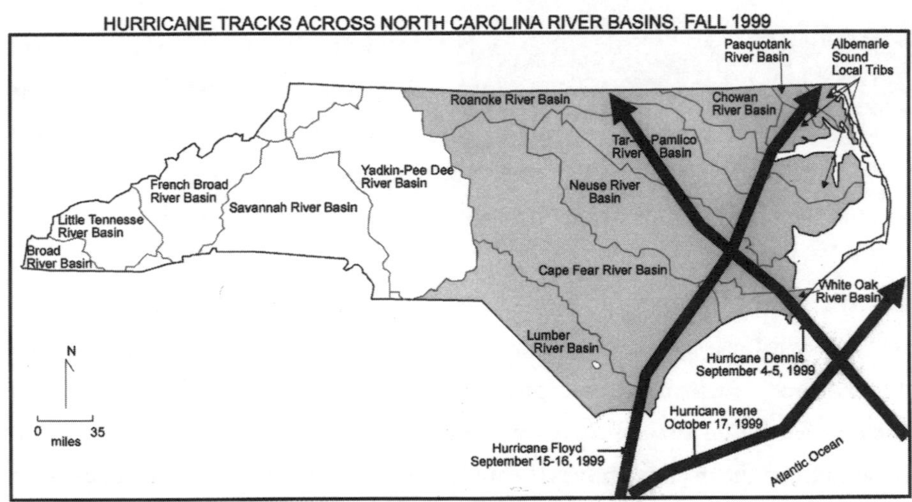

Figure 1. Map of North Carolina showing the river basins and the tracks of three hurricanes that resulted in the coastal plain flooding in September and October 1999.

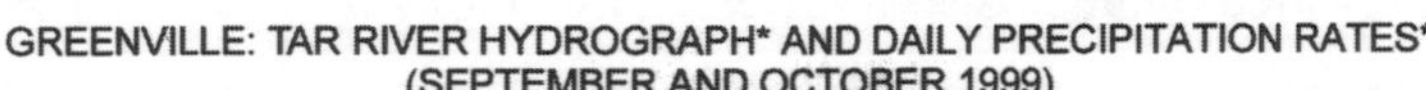

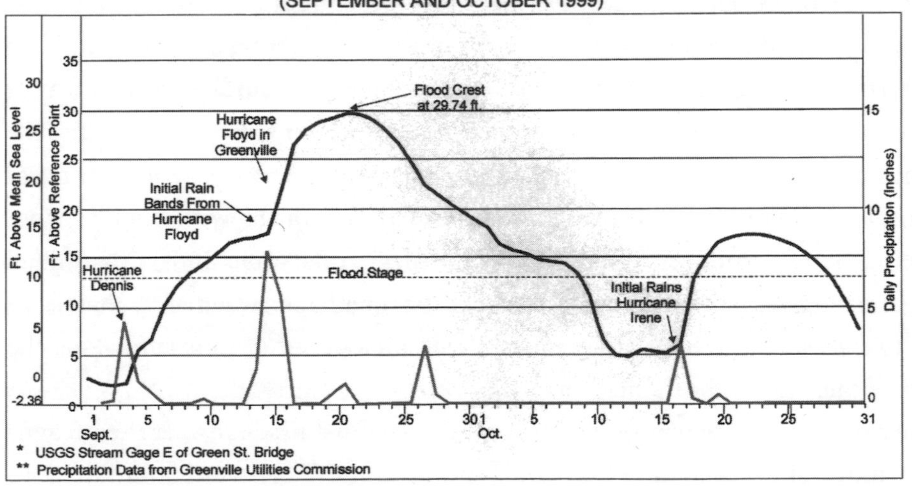

Figure 2. The hydrograph (in feet above mean sea level) for the Tar River is plotted against the rainfall data (in inches) for Greenville, North Carolina. Notice the relationship between each of the three major rainfall events and the changing pattern of river level elevation. It was the cumulative impact of a series of storms that created the severe flooding of 1999—timing was everything. The rains from Hurricane Floyd came a few days after the river rose above flood stage from Hurricane Dennis. If Hurricane Irene had come one or more weeks sooner, the rivers would have quickly risen back to record flood levels.

Figure 3. Satellite image of Hurricane Floyd as it makes landfall in southeastern North Carolina on 16 September 1999. The lighter shaded pattern represents areas of lower moisture content and the darker patterns represent areas of high moisture content. (Courtesy of the National Oceanographic and Atmospheric Administration (NOAA), National Climatic Data Center, Public Data Images web page.)

Understanding Water, Rivers, and Floods

The earth's hydrologic cycle

A fundamental concept in geology is the hydrologic cycle. The flow of water through the earth's plumbing system follows a basic set of complex rules. It is imperative that we completely understand and respect these rules if we hope to minimize future conflicts and flood hazards, which are increasing at alarming rates due to the ongoing population explosion.

About 98% of the earth's water supply resides in the ocean basins as salt water. This is the basic source and sink for all of the earth's fresh water, the other 2%. Today about 1.6% of the earth's fresh water is locked up in glacial ice in Antarctica and Greenland. The remaining 0.4% forms all the water that occurs within the biosphere, atmosphere, and the groundwater and surface water systems of the earth. The latter two resources are generally what drive modern civilization.

Fresh water is evaporated from the oceans, moves through the atmosphere to form the backbone of our climatic system, and is ultimately precipitated back to the earth's surface within weather systems, some of which are catastrophic storms. Solar energy drives this cycle, which represents the most fundamental component of heat distribution on the earth and is responsible for creating and maintaining a habitable planet. When storms discharge their energy load back to the earth's surface in the form of precipitation, the water is either taken into the biosphere, or through the force of gravity, it soaks into the ground to form our groundwater system or flows downhill to form our surface water system. All three of these pathways are intimately interconnected and are critical for human survival. However, in this paper I will only focus on the surface water portion, or about 0.04% of the earth's total water budget. This small segment of the water budget is the riverine system. This system consists of all open water areas that occur within a defined channel of a stream, as well as along intermittent stretches of streams and along the floodplains that develop on either side of the defined channel.

To understand the hydrologic cycle within North Carolina, we must first consider the oceanographic setup that supplies much of the rainfall to the region. A map of the U.S. Atlantic coast demonstrates how the North Carolina coast and its famous capes jut seaward into the Atlantic Ocean, well beyond the adjacent states. This results in a narrow continental shelf bounded by one of the strongest warm-water currents in the world's oceans—the Gulf Stream.

The Gulf Stream is a major component of the North Atlantic circulation system, or oceanic gyre. It is a critical link in the earth's heat machine that redistributes equatorial heat into higher latitudes. This warm-water current is also the feeding trough for cyclones. The storms utilize the current's heat energy to evaporate water off the warm ocean surface and then release this energy through precipitation either over cold ocean water or land. Because of North Carolina's geographic location relative to the Gulf Stream, it is situated to receive the direct and indirect effects of many cyclonic storms. Consequently, a major portion of the annual rainfall, as well as basic processes that build and maintain the barrier island system, are dependent on these seasonal low-pressure systems, which range from tropical depressions to hurricanes.

North Carolina's riverine system

Water falling on the earth's surface flows downhill in response to gravity. As it begins to flow, it has energy capable of eroding a rivulet into the underlying substrate and transporting the resulting sediments downhill. The rivulet is miniature, but it grows as it travels downhill, forming a gully and ultimately becoming a larger stream as it joins water flowing in other rivulets, which together form a network of streams. With time the entire system evolves through stages that carve the land's surface and creates the incredibly variable topography that is unique for each region of the country.

Together the rivulets, gullies, and streams form a drainage basin, which is characterized by a valley floor that is separated from the next basin by the upland, or interstream, divide. But each rivulet, gully, and stream has its own characteristic basin shape. Therefore, the drainage basin is really composed of many smaller sub-basins. In the downstream direction, as each stream discharges into larger streams, the gradient decreases, becoming flatter, and these sub-basins coalesce into the ever-expanding drainage basin. Each larger stream systematically collects all surface water falling within the upstream sub-basins, ultimately forming a trunk river. The trunk river is the largest or principal stream of a given drainage basin. It has a low gradient and discharges great volumes of water back into the ocean (Figure 4). Each tributary component within this complex network has its own set of characteristics, processes, and rules of operation that are different from the trunk river. Consequently, one simple set of management rules does not work equally throughout large drainage basins.

In North Carolina, the major rivers drain off the high eastern slope of the Blue Ridge in the Appalachian Mountains and flow through the rolling hills of crystalline rocks and red-clay soils of the Piedmont Province (Figure 4). All major drainage systems flowing across North Carolina's Piedmont Province and into the Coastal Plain Province form northwest-southeast elongate basins and from north to south include the Chowan, Roanoke, Tar, Neuse, Cape Fear, and Lumber rivers. Each drainage system crosses into the Coastal Plain Province along the rocky rapids of the "fall line" (Figure 4). Due to low stream gradients and gentle topography, the coastal plain rivers have broad valley floors characterized by vast wetlands or floodplains. As each river system approaches sea level, the river valleys are flooded by and mixed with ocean waters to form the vast drowned river estuarine system of coastal North Carolina.

Coastal plain rivers have several basic morphological components that are critical to their function. The main channel carries the normal day-to-day water flow. Adjacent to the channel is a series of floodplains that carry the additional volumes of water that occur during periods of greater water flow. Floodplains are morphological features recognizable as a series of river terraces eroded into the valley walls and containing distinctive vegetation (Figure 5). The primary floodplain carries the increased water volume resulting from small storms that produce the annual wet season. The primary floodplain consists of obvious wetlands that filter water and hold it like a sponge for slow release, helping maintain a more uniform river flow throughout the year (Figure 6A). The secondary floodplain carries high water volumes resulting from less frequent, large to extreme storm events. This floodplain is generally a transitional zone between riverine and upland areas and is characterized by less obvious wetland plant species (Figure 6A). The upper floodplain is less frequently used by rivers and is habitually modified for other land uses (Figure 6B). However, when the river system needs the secondary floodplain, it must be available. Many rivers have a tertiary floodplain, marked by distinctive river terraces eroded into the valley walls by rare extreme flood events that occurred in the past.

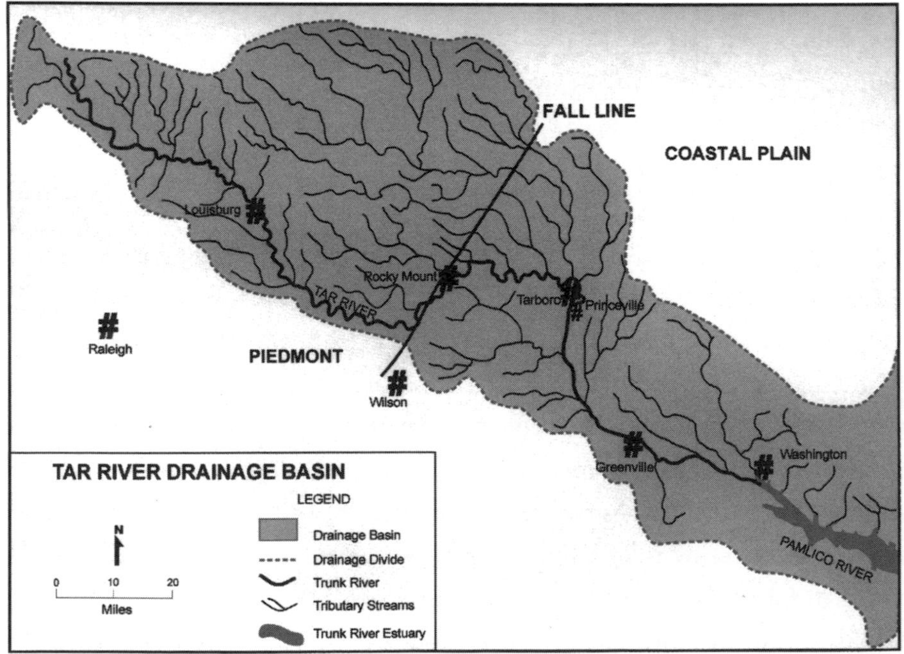

Figure 4. This schematic map of the Tar River drainage basin shows the river's generally asymmetrical pattern, with the trunk river flowing along the southern margin of the basin. This results in the highest land, which is associated with the drainage divides, generally occurring along the southern banks of the trunk river along with short, steep tributary drainages. In contrast, the northern side of the trunk stream is characterized by broad, low terraces that rise slowly northward to the next drainage divide and by long, low-sloping tributary streams. This asymmetrical pattern characterizes all North Carolina coastal plain drainage basins.

Above the river valley is the upland portion of each drainage basin. This can be the rise dividing adjacent streams in a drainage basin (the interstream divide) or the highest land that separates two adjacent drainage basins (Figure 5). This upland region will only contain the small headwater portions of tributary streams, which usually have steep gradients and are eroded into the underlying substrate with no or poorly developed floodplains. These streams rarely receive the backwater flooding from the trunk river, but they are subject to flash flooding in direct response to intense rain events. Minor modifications to these small drainages can have major responses that can be either good or bad depending on upstream land uses.

An extremely important characteristic of coastal plain drainage basins is the prominent basin asymmetry (Figure 4). In general, the trunk river flows along the southwestern side of the basin. This results in high riverbanks. The highest land forms in a narrow zone parallel to the river along the southwest side. Typically short, steep, and deeply incised tributary creeks flow north and northeast into the trunk river. The northeast side of the trunk rivers is characterized by a very wide, low series of primary and secondary floodplains that stair-step upward away from the river over distances of miles to tens of

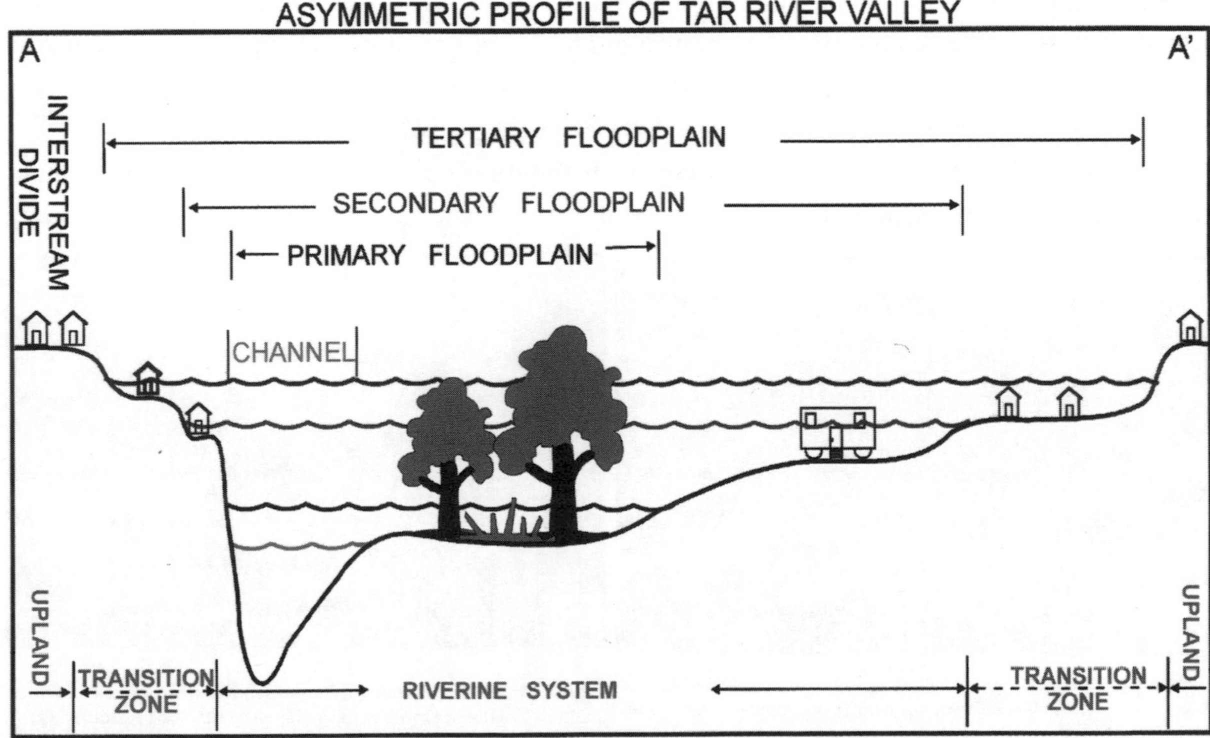

Figure 5. Schematic profile showing the topography across the Tar River and its various floodplains. This profile demonstrates the classic asymmetrical profile that characterizes all North Carolina coastal plain drainage basins. The channel carries the normal day-to-day water flow, while the primary floodplain is occupied and carries the additional water flow for several months during the wet season of each year. The secondary and tertiary floodplains are occupied. They carry the water flow during major flood events. An example of this type of asymmetry occurs in Greenville and is indicated as profile A-A' in Figure 11.

miles (Figure 5). The north side of the basin rises gently upland to the interstream divide and in close proximity to the next major trunk river to the northeast. This asymmetrical geometry results in south and southeast flowing tributaries that are very long, broad, low-gradient streams that drain extensive wetlands occupying the secondary and tertiary floodplains (Figure 4).

The asymmetric geometry of the drainage basins explains why towns were built and most development generally took place along the southwest side of the rivers. However, through time major land-use changes have greatly modified the low and poorly drained areas on the northeastern side of the drainage basins. Subsequent human encroachment into these marginal wetland areas will be primary factors in any riverine flood in coastal North Carolina.

Flooding rivers

A river basin is like a bathtub. Bathtubs flood when water is added faster than it can run out the drain. Rivers flood when rainfall exceeds the channel capacity to carry it downhill. The U.S. Geological Survey estimates that about 10,000 floods occur annually in the world. Most of these floods are local and occur in response to single thunderstorms over a drainage basin. However, some floods occur over multiple drainage basins in response to major weather fronts and cyclonic storm activity. These floods are the most costly type of natural hazard, accounting for major portions of both the annual economic cost ($150 billion per year) and number of deaths (150,000 people per year).

You can't pick up a major daily newspaper without seeing an article concerning one or more floods occurring somewhere in the world. Since North Carolina's "flood of the century," which barely

Figure 6 A: A 1976, oblique aerial photograph of a segment of the Tar River east of Greenville, showing the heavily vegetated primary floodplain, cleared agricultural land of the secondary floodplain, and the adjacent high upland. The secondary floodplain has been utilized for agriculture for centuries with the knowledge that occasionally a crop will be lost to flooding. However, during the 1990s, urban sprawl lead to extensive development of low-cost housing in this area—all of which were severely flooded during September 1999.

Figure 6 B: A 1973 photograph shows a landfill in the secondary floodplain of North Greenville with the Tar River in the background. Converting wetlands into good land for sale and low-cost urban and industrial development has been a common practice in eastern North Carolina. All subsequent development on this site was totally destroyed by the September 1999 flood.

made notice in *Time* magazine, there have been many larger storms and floods around the globe. For example, in February 2000, multiple cyclones hit the Limpopo and Save rivers in Mozambique, creating massive destruction and displacing hundreds of thousands of people. Over 20,000 people died in flooding in northern Venezuela in December 1999. In November 1999, cyclonic flooding along the east coast of India killed over 10,000 people. The Yangtze River in China flooded for months during the summer of 1999, killing over 800 people, while over 3,000 died in a similar flood during the summer of 1998.

Creating the "Flood of the Century"

Why was the September 1999 event considered to be the "flood of the century"? Several factors led to the extreme damage resulting from this flood event. First and foremost, a tremendous volume of water fell in five specific rain events that included two back-to-back hurricanes. Second, and of equal importance, portions of eastern North Carolina have recently experienced tremendous growth and development. During the period from the mid-1960s to the mid-1990s, the central coastal plain region experienced incredibly high levels of development and very few, minor hurricanes. This rapid growth and development led to modifications of coastal plain drainage systems, including channelization and wetland destruction, floodplain dams, and urbanization.

Channelization and wetland destruction

Coastal plain morphology, drainage systems, surface sediments, and soils are products of the past two million years of geologic time known as the Quaternary period. During this period, the Atlantic Ocean regressed and transgressed many times across the Coastal Plain Province in response to major climate changes and episodes of polar glaciation and deglaciation. The consequences are flat coastal plain surfaces with vast areas of clay soils and poorly developed drainage systems (Figure 7). This results in vast wetlands or "pocosins," an Indian word meaning "swamp on a hill." Early settlers drained these pocosins to use the land for agricultural purposes.

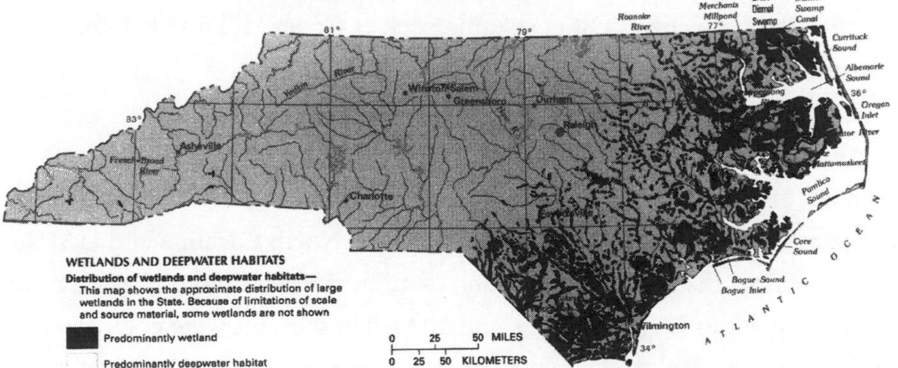

Figure 7. Map showing the distribution of wetlands in North Carolina. Notice that the wetlands are dominated by riverine swamp forests and upland pocosin swamp forests (or swamps on a hill) and are concentrated almost totally within the Coastal Plain Province. (Map from Dahl, T. E. 1996. Wetlands and deepwater habitats map of North Carolina. In: North Carolina wetland resources, edited by J. D. Bales, and D. J. Newcomb, U.S. Geological Survey, Water-Supply Paper 2425.)

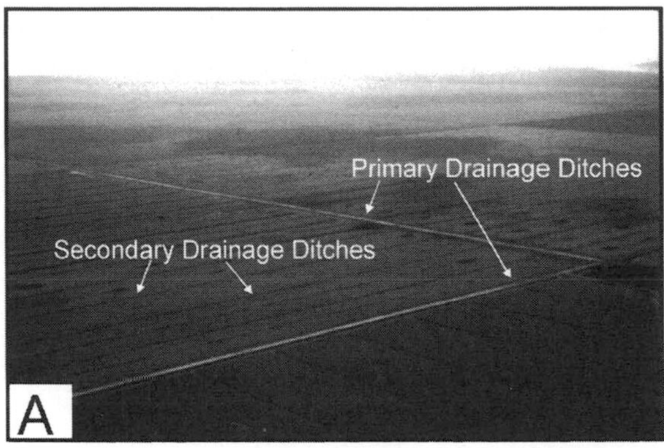

Figure 8 A: An oblique aerial photograph of a agricultural drainage system built within a pocosin wetland, which characterizes the secondary and tertiary floodplains of the North Carolina coastal plain drainage basins. These wetlands are cleared, a network of drainage ditches is dug, and then the land is planted for agricultural production.

Figure 8 B: Downstream from the drainage network in A, the tributary stream is channelized to carry the increased water flow off the land. Notice how the dredged channel sediments are piled into a berm adjacent to the straightened ditch, which essentially cuts off natural primary floodplain. This extreme modification allows for major land-use changes and increased encroachment, which in turn results in greater losses during abnormal conditions.

But severe drainage system modification really began in response to the late-twentieth century growth boom. Tens of thousands of miles of ditches drained vast acres of the marginal wetlands into adjacent tributaries (Figure 7 and 8A). To carry this increased water flow, thousands of miles of tributary streams were channelized by the U.S. Soil Conservation Service and U.S. Army Corps of Engineers, the former to improve marginal agricultural lands and latter for flood control (Figure 8B).

Channelization changed the tributary streams into pipe-like ditches for the sole purpose of getting more water off the land faster. The channels were straightened and deepened, and in some urban areas encased in concrete. Vegetation was cleared from the floodplains. The spoil removed from channels was piled in the floodplain, creating great dikes along one and sometimes both sides of the channel. However, this construction design severely limited both the hydrologic and biologic function of the adjacent floodplain. Natural, rural streams, such as Chicod, Grindle, Conetoe, Deep, Contentnea, and Ahoskie creeks to name a few, were extensively channelized. Other streams, such as Green Mill Run in Greenville, were straight-jacketed by urbanization.

Floodplain dams

While several government arms were working to increase rates of water delivery downstream, other arms were busy building partial dams across drainage systems. The North Carolina and U.S. Departments of Transportation were filling the floodplain for construction of new raised highways, using minimal-sized culvert and bridge openings (Figure 9A, 9B, and 10A). These roads were engineered to balance the flow of a specific size rain event against the minimization of economic costs. Upstream ditch-ing and draining increased the discharge through time, resulting in major land-use changes and encroachment by agribusiness, forestry, industry, and urban housing into the marginal riverine wetlands (Figure 9 and 10).

During the September 1999 storms, three flash floods severely impacted upland areas, including agricultural crops and animals, development on the pocosins, and roads that criss-cross the vast network of small tributary streams. Water flowed off ditched fields and developments, rapidly filled the narrowed and deepened stream valleys, and then was held back by road dams that couldn't discharge the water fast enough. Water levels exceeded the design of existing bridges and culverts. They were too small to handle the higher volume of water that was caused by upstream drainage modifications, harshly shocking those who initially benefited from encroachment into the marginal wetlands.

Temporary lakes formed behind the culverts then overtopped the road dam (Figure 9C). As the overflow undercut the road bed on the downstream side, many weakened roads finally blew out like the cork in a champagne bottle (Figure 9D). As the road bed blew out, so did any sewer, water, and power lines associated with it. The first flash flood resulting from Hurricane Floyd's rain bands took out many hundreds of road dams in a few hours. In addition, about 75% of the fifty-two known deaths attributed to the flooding occurred as people either got caught in a blowout or subsequently drove into a blown-out road segment. These flash-flooding events devastated the region's road infrastructure and basically shut down movement for the next month.

Increased discharge into the trunk river from the many overloaded tributary streams forced the water level to rise higher and faster than would have happened in an unmodified drainage system. In theory, the modified system should drain faster, causing the flood to dissipate more rapidly. However, in the lower portions of tributary streams and within the trunk rivers, the September 1999 flood event persisted for over a month. Part of this duration was due to the cumulative impact of the five different rainfall events. However, the slow discharge of floodwaters from the trunk rivers was also due to two other factors.

First, there is an extensive network of road dams across the trunk river floodplains. Extensive dikes, on which the roads are built, fill the entire secondary floodplain and most of the primary floodplain except for one or two small bridges to carry storm flow (Figure 10A and 10B). The main river channel is always bridged, but the bridge rarely extends much beyond the channel banks. Such construction is adequate for normal flow and small storm events when water backs up behind the upstream side of the partial dam and the stronger current flows into the bridge constriction. However, as the size of the discharge event increases and spreads into the secondary floodplain, greater proportions of flow are held back behind each road dam, increasing both flood levels and durations. The Tar River has about fifty such road dams between its headwaters and the town of Washington, most of which are 75% or more dam with about 25% or less bridge span.

Figure 9. These photographs show the sequential effect of a road dam on high-flow, flash flood conditions in a small tributary stream. **A:** A road dams the channel and floodplain of a small tributary stream with a small culvert that is more than adequate to carry the normal day-to-day low flow. **B:** A small storm fills the culvert through the road dam. **C:** During the flash flooding due to Hurricane Floyd rainfall, the water flow far exceeds the culvert capacity and forms a lake behind the road dam. The rising water level overflows the road dam and the water begins to undercut the road on the downstream side. **D:** With increased overflow, the road dam weakens and finally blows out, revealing this disaster after the water level begins to decrease to more normal levels. The remnants of the road can be seen in the upper right and the culvert in the upper left corner of the photograph. Between 300 and 500 roads in eastern North Carolina totally blew out and probably a thousand or more were partially damaged in response to flash flooding on tributary streams.

Second, the gradient, or river slope, decreases to zero as the lower stretches of the river approach sea level. On the Tar River this occurs between Greenville and Washington. At Washington, the Tar River opens into the Pamlico River, a drowned-river estuary. Because the Pamlico River is a large water body at sea level, its water level is controlled by wind driven tides produced by regional wind patterns. Northeast, east, or southeast winds create water levels that are above sea level in western Pamlico River, whereas northwest, west, or southwest winds blow water out of the Pamlico River, producing water levels below sea level. The storm events of September and October 1999 caused the Pamlico River water level to fluctuate dramatically, including an eight-foot storm surge at Washington with the arrival of Hurricane Floyd. Fluctuations in the Pamlico River water level affect the Tar River gradient and the resulting river discharge, which in turn affect the rise and fall of upstream flood levels (Figure 2).

Urbanization and the tale of two cities

Greenville, North Carolina. The oldest portions of most urban areas in the coastal plain in North Carolina are situated on the highest and best land along the southwest side of major trunk rivers. In general, these areas received no flooding during the 1999 event. However, urban growth during the latter part of the twentieth century has led to development in increasingly lower and poorer land. With the best land unavailable within the city core, adjacent lowlands along the trunk rivers and lower portions of tributary streams are increasingly modified and utilized in response to escalating development pressures. These lowlands are the primary and secondary floodplains that in the past were often used as landfills. There is a direct correlation between contour elevation and date of development. This relationship can be thought of as "contoured urban sprawl" (Figures 6B, 10B, and 11).

Urban sprawl also radiates outward into the surrounding countryside, converting forest and agricultural uplands to expansive subdivisions. This "radial urban sprawl" also increases the amount of impervious surfaces, such as the roads, footprint of buildings, and parking lots. The result is a significant increase in discharge of storm-water runoff that is piped directly into adjacent tributary streams. Rarely do urban comprehensive storm-water management plans incorporate the cumulative impacts resulting from ever-increasing runoff.

Greenville and surrounding Pitt County are an excellent example of both contoured and radial urban sprawl, showing a lack of long-term planning and storm-water management. Greenville is a growing city with a population of 58,951. Green Mill Run, a tributary to the Tar River, runs through a section of the town. In Greenville, the Tar River has a very asymmetrical valley (Figures 5 and 11). Immediately north of the river is a broad primary floodplain, which was severely modified and filled over the years, and a low, very wide, and marginally wet secondary floodplain. Together the primary and secondary floodplains are several miles wide and occur within the 100-year flood designation (Figure 11). Consequently, land in north Greenville is relatively cheap and over the past thirty years has filled with trailer courts, low-cost government housing, and industrial complexes.

A 1930 map shows the city limits at Green Mill Run, and the streets end outside the floodplain. East Carolina University, the largest single development component of Greenville, was located between Fifth and Tenth street at the edge of Greenville and outside the Green Mill Run floodplain. Over the years, Greenville extended its limits, channelized Green Mill Run to the south side of Tenth Street, filled the floodplain for the extension and expansion of Tenth Street, and built at least six road dams across the lower reaches of the stream (Figure 10 and 11). During this period the university significantly expanded its footprint, adding many new buildings and parking lots as well as locating portions of two recent buildings in the former floodplain. As the university grew, pressure for student housing caused Greenville to permit many new apartments. These developments seriously encroached on the remaining open lands, in both the Green Mill Run and Tar River floodplains. In addition, the city and county built office buildings and new infrastructure facilities, including water and sewage plants and power substations, on large tracts of the cheap floodplain land in north Greenville. Also, in 1973, a bypass highway was constructed around Greenville that resulted in a new road dam on the downstream side of the city (Figure 10). Unfortunately, it was built just downstream from north Greenville and the Green Mill Run discharge. It is situated on a dike that crosses the primary and secondary floodplains with three small bridges (Figure 10B).

Figure 10 A: A 1973 photograph of the construction of the Highway 264A/33 road dam across the primary floodplain of the Tar River on the east side of Greenville (see Figure 5 for the location of both A and B). This photograph looks north across the primary floodplain during normal winter flood conditions, with a small floodplain bridge in the foreground and the main channel bridge over the Tar River, where the cranes are located. The road becomes more effective as a dam and holds back increased volumes of water as river level rises and flood discharge increases.

Figure 10 B: A 1978 oblique aerial photograph of the Highway 264A/33 road dam across the primary and secondary floodplains of the Tar River on the east side of Greenville. Notice that most of the highway was built on an extensive berm that filled the primary and secondary floodplains with only one bridge immediately over the channel and two small bridges over small portions of the primary floodplain. This photograph looks south across the river system to the uplands of Greenville and shows the Green Mill Run tributary stream discharging into the Tar River just above this major road dam. Notice the amount of primary floodplain filled over the years, during which Greenville utilized this low wetland as their major landfill; this landfill also acts as a partial dam that significantly decreases the cross-sectional area of the floodplain.

These expansion projects increased storm-water runoff into Green Mill Run during the flash-flooding events of September 1999. All of the new student apartments were located in the 100-year flood zone, and all were severely flooded during the September 1999 event. Road dams inhibited discharge into the Tar River and increased the back flooding (Figure 9). The two university buildings that received extensive flood damage were those that encroached into the Green Mill Run floodplain. The city and county water, sewage, and power stations located in the floodplains were severely flooded, which led to major breakdowns at crucial times in the crisis. Water backed up in the floodplains behind the three small bridges built for the highway. This caused floodwater to back up further upstream and increased flood heights in both the Tar River and Green Mill Run.

The university is presently building its largest building even further into the floodplain. Officials claim they that are building it above recent flood levels and have increased the size of drainage pipes to discharge water faster into Green Mill Run. An important question is how the combined effects of this new encroachment and increased storm-water runoff will impact flooding in upstream portions of Green Mill Run. During the postflooding economic boom, building within these same flooded areas along the Tar River continues at full steam ahead.

Princeville, North Carolina. Princeville is a community of African Americans founded in 1865 by freed slaves and incorporated in 1885. It is a small town situated on the lowland side of the Tar River, opposite the colonial town of Tarboro (Figure 4). The northwest side (Tarboro) has a high and steep bank while the southeast side (Princeville) has a low and broad floodplain system that extends eastward for many miles. The land Princeville is located on is characterized by the paleo-topography of an ancient meandering river and point bar system that produced a series of alternating sand ridges and swampy swales. The original roads and houses in Princeville were built along the sandy ridges. The next river bend north of Princeville has the low floodplain occurring on the Tarboro side of the river, and has not been developed.

These towns are situated within a unique geometric feature of the Tar River. The underlying geology produces a series of right angle river bends (Figure 4) that cause the river channel and its primary floodplain to become greatly restricted, creating a bottleneck effect. To make matters worse, the largest tributary sub-basin in the Tar River drainage system discharges into the Tar River immediately upstream from Tarboro and Princeville (Figure 4). Fishing Creek represents 16% of the total drainage basin and drains vast areas of pocosins. Consequently, much of the upland area has been extensively ditched and drained for agricultural production, and many tributary branches flowing into Fishing Creek have been channelized.

Due to six previous floods in Princeville since incorporation, the U.S. Army Corps of Engineers in 1965 built a two-mile long, twenty-two foot high flood-protection dike along the north and west banks of the Tar River. A new four-lane highway (Highway 64) was built on a major dike across the floodplain along the downstream side of Princeville, creating a potential road dam.

The floods of September 1999 were initially kept out of the town by the flood dike and the highway road dam that enclosed the town. When flooding finally occurred, it flooded fast and the town was totally inundated. By peak flood, no one was left in Princeville to observe the flooding process. However, the pattern of flooding can be extrapolated from flow dynamics preserved in sediments and debris left behind when floodwaters receded. The town did not flood due to the failure of the dike. Rather, it flooded first through the low spot in the dike occupied by the railroad tracks and then around the north end of the dike, creating "Lake Princeville" behind the dike. Finally, the rising river spilled over the top of the dike in a broad zone that included the Riverside Trailer Court. When the river overtopped the dike, the water level in "Lake Princeville" was already to the top of the trailers, as evidenced by the pattern of dike scour and associated sand deltas deposited into the "lake." The trailers in front of the overtopped zone floated off their cinder blocks and were stacked like dominoes in a broad arcuate band at the back of the trailer court.

Once Princeville was flooded, the dike and road dam appear to have held the floodwaters within the town after river levels receded. Floodwaters could neither flow along the floodplain due to the road dam or back into the main channel due to the dike. The new four-lane Highway 64 road dam was probably responsible for significantly aggravating the flooding. Based on aerial photographs taken during peak flood, it appeared that floodwaters could only escape from Princeville through two locations in this impressive road dam: one discharge point occurred during the highest flood stage, when floodwaters overtopped the road, and the other was the Highway 33 underpass. Also, the Fishing Creek subbasin received among the greatest amounts of rainfall. Thus, very large volumes of water were discharged rapidly into the Tarboro-Princeville bottleneck.

Figure 11. Map showing the trunk Tar River and Green Mill Run, a tributary stream, flowing through Greenville, N.C. Note the designation of the approximate location of the 100-year flood line designated by the U.S. Federal Emergency Management Agency (FEMA). The old and major portion of Greenville occurs on the highest land south of the river, while to the north of the river is the low-sloping land of the primary and secondary floodplains and the location of more recent, low-cost development. Notice also that Green Mill Run discharges into the Tar River just above the Highway 264A and 33 road dam across the primary and secondary floodplains of the river. All land within the 100-year flood line was severely impacted by the September floods. Also notice the location of the old Greenville landfill directly in the floodplain. Line A-A' is the location of Figure 5, a schematic profile across the Tar River and its various floodplains. (This map is from the U.S. Geological Survey 1:24,000 topographic map (Greenville Quad) with a 2 meter contour interval.)

On November 23, 1999, headlines in local newspapers announced that "Princeville board opts to fix dike—instead of accepting a government buyout." Less than two months after floodwaters destroyed 850 homes , the Town Board of Commissioners decided to totally rebuild the town within the floodplain because "this is our heritage." The federal government agreed to either fix the dike to its original condition or move the town out of the flood-prone land. It would not sponsor a rebuilding effort that would end in another flood. Now the 2,100 residents, most of whom had no flood insurance, are left to their own resources to rebuild their homes and lives, and pray that future hurricane seasons are gentle ones.

Summary

For millennia, the ancient Egyptians understood the river and intricately interwove its cyclic patterns into the fabric of their lives. However, this interaction between a civilization and its environment is disappearing today as increasing portions of the population move off the land and into the confines of four walls. We are forgetting some basic "rules of the earth" as we encroach into the conflict zone. Our engineering mentality has led us to believe that we can manipulate and manage major earth processes. We're shocked and devastated by each new disaster and declare we will do better. How soon we forget the pain and suffering and focus on the money flow, jobs, and the economic stimulation that is created with each natural catastrophe. The result is an ever-increasing "hazard-based economy." To begin to turn this around, society must fully acknowledge the crucial role of water and protect water as it cycles through the earth system. By living with and protecting our water resources, we will also protect humans from the devastation of the natural processes of river flooding.

When we look back at the events in the fall of 1999, we can draw many important conclusions about how our current relationship with the natural processes in North Carolina's coastal plain created this disaster:

1. The "flood of the century" was not a natural disaster. The rivers were doing exactly what they were supposed to do—carrying the surface water off the land. This was a human catastrophe.
2. Society contributed significantly to the 1999 flood crisis through modification of drainage systems that resulted in major land-use changes and subsequent encroachment into marginal wetlands by agribusiness, forestry, industry, and urbanization. Modification of the drainage system and encroachment into marginal land has major impacts on both the flow dynamics and flooding response.
3. Each portion of a drainage system responds differently to specific rain events and must be utilized and managed in sympathy with these specific dynamics.
4. Since we are locked into an expanding growth mode, it is more important than ever for society to understand how the most basic resource (water) works on our finite planet.
5. Rivers operate within a set of natural rules. We must learn to live with our rivers and rebuild within constraints of the river's rules. If North Carolina rebuilds as it was before the flood, a similar disaster *will* happen again, and it *will be* sooner rather than later.

Part II / Evaluating Disaster Response Strategies—An Institutional Perspective

Congress and Natural Disasters: A Symbiotic Relationship?

Rutherford H. Platt

Rutherford H. Platt is a professor of geography and planning law in the Department of Geosciences at the University of Massachusetts at Amherst. He received both his Ph.D. and law degree from the University of Chicago and is licensed to practice law in the state of Illinois. His research focuses on federal, state, and regional management of land and water resources, especially in coastal regions, river basins, floodplains, and wetlands. He is also interested in problems related to urban growth, particularly the protection and management of urban and regional open spaces for diverse purposes. Dr. Platt has directed research on these topics under a variety of grants from the National Science Foundation and other government agencies. He has served on eight panels of the National Academy of Sciences/National Research Council and has participated in many international meetings. He has served as a consultant to many organizations, including the Environmental Protection Agency, the Federal Emergency Management Agency, the Lincoln Institute of Land Policy, and the Heinz Center. In 1998, he received the Merit Award from the Boston Society of Landscape Architects. Dr. Platt gave a plenary presentation at the conference and was introduced by Dr. Ron Mitchelson, chair of the Department of Geography at East Carolina University.

Introduction

This chapter first summarizes the nature and general effects of natural disasters in the United States. While deaths have declined, the economic impacts of disasters to victims, to governments, and to the insurance industry continue to rise. Over the past fifty years, Congress has embarked on a variety of strategies in response to natural disasters. I briefly describe these strategies and their current problems, limitations, and successes. The final section of this paper discusses a series of issues that are hampering the effectiveness of disaster relief programs. These issues are integral to reducing the impacts of disasters and should be addressed by both Congress and the Federal Emergency Management Agency (FEMA).

Overview of the Natural Disaster Experience in the United States

Geography of U.S. natural hazards

The United States, including Alaska, Hawaii, Puerto Rico, and its various territories, is vulnerable to a wide spectrum of natural hazards (National Geographic Society 1998). The principal hazards and geographic areas of vulnerability include:

- Earthquakes (California, Alaska, central Mississippi Valley, South Carolina).
- Hurricanes (Atlantic and Gulf of Mexico coasts and adjacent inland areas).
- Floods (riverine and coastal floodplains, urban areas with constricted drainage).
- Coastal erosion (most sandy or erodible cliff coastlines).
- Wildfire (urban-wildland areas in western states).
- Volcanoes (western states, including Alaska).
- Winter storms (Northeast and upper Middle West, western mountain areas).
- Tornadoes (south central and midwestern states).
- Tsunamis (Hawaii, West Coast).
- Drought (the entire country except Pacific Northwest coast).

While most hazards are geographically selective, few areas of the United States can be considered hazard-free. Between 1988 and 1995, only two states (Wyoming and Idaho) received no federal disaster assistance. Property owners in every state have received payments under the National Flood Insurance Program (NFIP), albeit of vastly different amounts.

The economic and social costs of disasters

It is an axiom of natural disaster managers in the United States that loss of life due to disasters has fallen dramatically while economic and social costs of disasters continue to rise (National Research Council 1994). Particularly in the case of hurricanes, improved warning and evacuation procedures have helped to save lives. While different disasters are difficult to compare, the following were the total of lives lost in five historic U.S. hurricanes: Galveston, Texas (1900)—over 6,000 deaths; Camille (1969)—256 deaths; Agnes (1972)—122; Hugo (1989)—86; Andrew (1992)—61. The last statistic is particularly notable considering that Hurricane Andrew left 250,000 people homeless in south Florida and Louisiana, with an estimated economic cost of about $30 billion. However, a slight northward shift in its point of landfall towards the Miami metropolitan area would have further magnified its impacts, including potentially increasing the death toll (National Academy of Sciences 1994; Ayscue 1996). Also, improved warnings appear to have reduced deaths due to tornadoes, which killed some 1,400 people between 1950 and 1960 compared with 521 between 1982 and 1992 (National Academy of Sciences 1994). Earthquakes generally occur without warning, but mortality has diminished due to improved seismic building standards, particularly in California. The 1906 San Francisco Earthquake and fire killed "some 3,000 people" (National Geographic Society 1998), while the Northridge Earthquake in January 1994, which cost an estimated $43 billion and damaged over 97,000 structures in Los Angeles County (Eguchi et al. 1996), killed "only" sixty-one people. However, worst-case scenarios of a potential catastrophic earthquake in California predict a much higher toll. Confirming this forecast, the Kobe, Japan, earthquake of 17 January 1995 caused 6,308 deaths, 43,000 injuries, left 300,000 people homeless, and cost $100 billion ($U.S.) in total damages (Burby 1998).

Estimation of the economic and social costs of natural disasters is extremely difficult to determine (National Research Council 1999; Heinz Center 1999). The costs of disasters are of many types: direct versus indirect, monetary versus nonmonetary, overt versus "hidden." Conventional assessments of disaster costs are largely confined to direct, monetary costs to insurers, to government, and to the economy of the community or region affected. Even these "overt" costs are difficult to identify and enumerate. Estimates of insurance losses due to the 1994 Northridge Earthquake were revised eight times, from $2.5 billion just after the event to $12.5 billion two years later (Institute for Business and Home Safety 1998). Furthermore, loss estimates for that disaster differed by an order of magnitude, as compiled by building inspectors and insurance adjusters respectively (Eguchi et al. 1996).

Not only are insurance costs and undocumented property owner costs difficult to estimate but so are the costs of governmental response and recovery. The federal government provides a wide array of different benefits and subsidies to communities, businesses, and individuals stricken by disasters. Yet the government has no comprehensive database on costs of government assistance across all participating programs and agencies. One cannot, for instance, easily ascertain all of the federal costs pertaining to the Northridge Earthquake or Hurricane Andrew. Nor can one readily ascertain the federal costs for a given disaster within a particular state, county, or local jurisdiction. After the 1993 Midwest Flood, a special study commissioned by the White House attempted to assess all of the federal costs pertaining to that disaster. The study yielded an estimated total of $4.2 billion in direct federal expenditures, $1.3 billion in payments from federal insurance programs, and more than $621 million in federal loans to individuals, businesses, and communities (Interagency Floodplain Management Review Committee 1994). This was probably the most complete inventory of federal outlays for a particular disaster ever conducted, but it did not break out the administrative or "overhead" costs to the federal government (including salaries, travel, consultants, etc.) that were required to administer those outlays. Nor did it reflect insurance and other costs of that flood, such as those of nongovernmental (NGO) relief providers, including the American Red Cross and the Salvation Army.

Such "overhead" costs are part of a vast penumbra of indirect and "hidden" costs that are seldom identified. Eguchi et al. (1996) raised the estimated costs of the Northridge Earthquake from $24 billion in documented costs to about $44 billion. The $20 billion increase resulted from the "hidden costs" of deductibles absorbed by property owners and damage to uninsured structures. Business losses not covered by insurance are another form of hidden disaster cost. The Heinz Center (1999) conducted a recent study of the "true costs" of coastal disasters in an attempt to identify (without quantifying) the full range of overt and hidden costs for Hurricane Hugo in 1989 such as business disruption, social costs to individuals and families, and environmental costs to natural resources, including fisheries, forests, and agriculture.

U.S. Federal Response Strategies to Natural Disasters

Like Australia, Canada, Germany, Japan, and many other nations, the United States has a federal system of government consisting of three tiers: federal, state, and local. Under the laws of the U.S. Constitution and acts of Congress, the federal government is theoretically limited to powers and functions conferred by states. But in practice, the federal government is clearly the dominant player in the American system of governance, particularly where spending is involved. States and local governments happily defer to the federal government and the national taxpayers for a vast array of spending programs, including national defense, water resource development, highways, economic development, and, most emphatically, financial assistance in times of disaster.

On the other hand, states and local governments resist federal intervention in the area of land-use planning and regulation. Oversight of private land-use practices is largely a local government function, under legal authority delegated by the state. Private property owners dislike any government-imposed limits on their desired use and development of their land; they prefer local or state regulations (which may be more supportive of tax-producing development) to federal restrictions. Thus, owners, local governments, and states present a united front in opposing federal land-use regulation, even when it is intended to curtail unwise development in areas subject to natural hazards.

The relationship between the federal and nonfederal sectors in the United States is a constitutional double standard and a paradox. On the one hand, since the 1950s the federal government has been increasingly expected to absorb the economic costs of disasters through a variety of programs (listed below). But on the other hand, the federal government remains relatively powerless to mandate hazard mitigation measures such as land-use restrictions that limit development and redevelopment in areas of recurrent natural hazards. This double standard poses a challenge to American society: reduce vulnerability to natural hazards through sustainable development or simply restore the *status quo ante* at national expense.

Today, subject to the foregoing limitations, the U.S. government is actively (and expensively) involved in disaster response and recovery. The dominant federal role in providing disaster assistance has emerged over the past half-century. Before 1950, the federal government remained aloof from disasters, except where flood-control projects were constructed along certain rivers and coastal shorelines. The costs of disasters were largely borne by states, local governments, insurers, charitable relief agencies, and the victims themselves. A series of hurricanes and winter storms that struck the Atlantic Coast during the 1950s and 1960s prompted states and local governments to demand increased federal economic as well as physical protection from the effects of disasters. At that time, Congress passed a series of laws that laid the foundation for the present multibillion dollar a year federal involvement in disaster response and recovery. There is still no comprehensive federal disaster policy or program, but one may identify several "strategies" that collectively define the major approaches now employed to alleviate or avoid the effects of natural disasters (Platt 1999).

Strategy 1—Structural flood protection

Structural flood control projects—including dams, storage reservoirs, levees, and coastal works—dominated federal response to flood disasters between the 1930s and the 1960s. Most federal flood control projects were constructed by the Army Corps of Engineers, the Tennessee Valley Authority, the Bureau of Reclamation, or the U.S. Department of Agriculture. Since the advent of the environmental movement in the early 1970s, few federal flood control or other water development projects have been built, although several are proposed.

Strategy 2—Warning and emergency response

The federal government has greatly improved its warning and response capabilities for weather-related hazards such as hurricanes, blizzards, and tornadoes. Today, the National Hurricane Center in Florida provides detailed, real-time forecasts of hurricane tracks to the affected public via broadcast media, the Internet, and other means of communication. This has reduced the potential loss of life on exposed shorelines as well as stimulating the boarding up of windows and removal of many boats, cars, etc. from areas of immediate threat. The National Weather Service also provides emergency warnings of tornadoes, thunderstorms, and other hazardous weather phenomena.

Strategy 3—Financial assistance

Billions of dollars are disbursed annually as financial disaster assistance under authority of the 1988 Robert T. Stafford Relief and Emergency Assistance Act (the "Stafford Act" P.L. 100-707). This act provides federal assistance to state and local governments so they can alleviate suffering and damage from disasters. The act expanded existing relief programs by encouraging disaster preparedness plans and programs, coordination and responsiveness, insurance coverage, and hazard mitigation measures. Federal disaster benefits are provided under the Stafford Act pursuant to a "disaster declaration" by the president of the United States. Presidential declarations specify the state and counties that are eligible for disaster benefits. Declarations have been more numerous in recent years (Table 1). According to FEMA's web site, a total of 460 major disaster declarations were issued by Presidents Bush and Clinton during the 1990s, nearly double the number issued for the previous decade. Since each declaration applies to a single state, this does not necessarily reflect an increasing number of disasters but, at some level, a tendency to issue multiple declarations for a disaster across more states than was done in the past. Thirteen states, from Florida to Maine, received a presidential disaster declaration after Hurricane Floyd.

Stafford Act benefits fall under two major headings: public assistance (PA) to states and local governments and individual assistance (IA) to eligible families and individuals, both administered by FEMA. About two-thirds of federal outlays ($14.8 billion during fiscal years 1990–1999) under the Stafford Act are for public assistance, which includes the rebuilding of public infrastructure and reimbursement of certain disaster-related expenses for eligible state and local governments. This assistance is *not* needs based; communities in declared counties may qualify for public assistance regardless of their tax base or ability to raise revenue locally. The other one-third of Stafford Act assistance ($6.3 billion during the 1990s) is spent on individual assistance, which *is* needs based and is largely in the form of grants to low-income households and temporary housing for people displaced by a disaster. The Stafford Act specifies a federal share of eligible costs at 75%, with the other 25% to be supplied by states and local governments. In certain very large disasters, however, the president has waived all or part of the nonfederal share, thus the federal government assumes up to 100% of the eligible costs. In theory, the federal assistance under the Stafford Act and its predecessors is intended only to "supplement" state and local resources, but currently in the U.S., the federal government bears the major cost of disaster response and recovery (Platt 1999). On 18 October 1999, Congress (PL 106-74) signed an appropriation of $2.48 billion for disaster relief, much of which was earmarked for the federal costs of recovery from Hurricane Floyd.

Table 1. The number of requested presidential disaster designations and the number of actual presidential disaster declarations for the fiscal years 1984–1997.

Fiscal Year	Number Requested	Number Declared	Percent Declared
1984	48	35	72%
1985	32	19	59%
1986	38	30	79%
1987	32	24	75%
1988	25	17	68%
1989	43	29	67%
1990	43	35	81%
1991	52	39	75%
1992	56	46	82%
1993	51	39	76%
1994	51	36	71%
1995	45	29	64%
1996	85	72	85%
1997	66	49	74%
1998	n.a.	65	n.a.
1999	n.a.	50	n.a.
Average			
1984–1987	35	25	71%
1988–1992	44	33	75%
1993–1997	60	45	75%

n.a. = not available
Sources: General Accounting Office 1995; Rhinesmith 1997.

FEMA has recently proposed, as a eligibility condition for public assistance under the Stafford Act, that public and certain nongovernmental entities be required to carry private insurance coverage to defray part of the cost of disaster losses to their buildings and infrastructure (Federal Register 2000). This proposal, if adopted, would diminish the tendency of the disaster assistance program, as now structured, to act as a disincentive for local governments to purchase insurance. Under this proposal, they could no longer assume that at least three-quarters of their losses would be supported by federal dollars in the event of a presidentially declared disaster.

Strategy 4—Government insurance programs

In the mid-1960s, Congress became alarmed by the apparent rapid rise in the cost of flood-related federal disaster assistance. To fill a void in private insurance coverage (which normally excludes flood-related losses), the National Flood Insurance Program (NFIP) was established in 1968. Besides shifting some of the costs of flood losses to an insurance-based scheme, the NFIP also incorporated hazard mitigation. Since the federal government cannot directly regulate land use in flood hazard areas, the program sought to encourage local floodplain management through a "carrot and stick" approach. Affordable flood insurance coverage under the NFIP (the "carrot") could be purchased only for property within communities that agreed to regulate future development in flood hazard areas (the "stick"). Such areas were identified in flood hazard maps prepared and distributed by the federal government. In 1973, amendments to the program compelled anyone that borrowed money from a federally supported financial institution for the purchase or improvement of property in a mapped floodplain to acquire a flood insurance policy. As Table 2 shows, the program has grown rapidly in recent years. Today, there are approximately 19,000 communities enrolled in the NFIP, representing over four million policies, with total coverage of flood-prone structures and their contents amounting to more than $482 billion. Approximately two-thirds of this coverage is in coastal communities. But contrary to Congress' intent, the NFIP has not noticeably reduced the scale of flood-related disaster assistance because both public assistance and individual assistance help with losses not usually covered by flood insurance.

Congress has also established a federal crop insurance program to supplement its agricultural disaster grant programs. After the Midwest Flood of 1993, the U.S. Department of Agriculture paid out more than $1 billion in crop insurance payments, along with over $1.4 billion in farm disaster payments (Interagency Floodplain Management Review Committee 1994). By contrast, payments under the NFIP totaled only $297 million.

Strategy 5—Disaster loans

Congress initiated the Small Business Administration (SBA) Disaster Loan Program in 1953. Unlike other SBA activities, authorized disaster loans are issued not only to small businesses but also to homeowners, tenants, and nonprofit organizations. Loans are made to entities that are victims of disasters (as declared by either the president or by the administrator of the SBA) to help cover uninsured losses. Most long-term disaster loans (up to thirty years) are made at below-market interest rates (currently about 4%); thus, they reflect a federal subsidy when compared with market loans. The SBA expects to be repaid and refers applicants who lack the ability to repay a loan to FEMA for a possible "Individual and Family Grant," which are available to low-income households after a presidentially declared disaster. The SBA secures its loans, when possible, with liens on the relevant real property and may foreclose in the event of nonpayment. However, its claim would be subordinate to those of prior mortgage lenders (Bipartisan Senate Task Force on Funding Disaster Relief 1994).

Since 1953, the SBA has approved slightly over 1.4 million disaster loans for a total of $25.5 billion. Loans to homeowners and tenants account for 77% of the number of loans and 41% of the dollar value, with the remainder largely extended to small businesses. The largest disaster event in the history of the program, not surprisingly, was the Northridge Earthquake in 1994, which contributed to a total for that fiscal year of 125,861 loans amounting to $4.1 billion, about four times the recent annual average of about $1 billion. The actual loss rate on SBA disaster loans over the life of the program is 8.27%.

Strategy 6—Hazard mitigation

The relentless rise of the costs of federal disaster assistance has long provoked demands for measures that anticipate and lessen the effects of extreme natural events. This has been especially the case with coastal and riverine floods, which are relatively place-specific and in the average year account for the bulk of national disaster costs (barring the occasional Northridge Earthquake). Flood hazard reduction has therefore served as the testing ground of methods for building safer and more sustainable communities through the concept of "hazard mitigation" (Platt 1998). The term, as currently used, embraces various actions to reduce vulnerability. David Godschalk provides greater details on hazard miti-

Table 2. The number of policies issued by the National Flood Insurance Program (NFIP) and the total monetary coverage and the net income or loss from these policies for the fiscal years 1974–1997

Fiscal Year	Number of Policies (1,000s)	Coverage in Billion Dollars ($)	Net Income or (Loss) ($)
1974	385	8.4	n.a.
1979	1,650	62.5	n.a.
1984	1,831	115	(61 million)
1984	1,955	133	273 million
1984	2.075	133	29.7 million
1984	2,079	158	171 million
1984	2,101	169	183 million
1984	2,200	179	(146 million)
1984	2,378	203	73 million
1984	2,506	219	169 million
1984	2,561	229	(20.4 million)
1993	2,725	254	(602 million)
1994	2,804	274	269 million
1995	3,264	325	(576 million)
1996	3,546	369	(536 million)
1997	3,811	422	(117 million)
1986-1997 Cumulative Total			**(1.1 billion)**

n.a.= not available
Source: Federal Emergency Management Agency/Federal Insurance Administration data.

gation elsewhere in this volume. In essence, hazard mitigation includes structural protection projects, warning and evacuation planning, creating and enforcing appropriate building regulations, developing sustainable land-use plans and regulations, property acquisition in hazard-risk areas, public education programs, and protection and restoration of wetlands and other natural habitats.

Mitigation has had a checkered history over the past three decades. While universally supported in principle, it has often proven to be the unwelcome guest at the post-disaster banquet. Rebuilding more safely may cost more, take longer, and sometimes conflict with private property interests, the public tax base, and economic priorities. And despite recent expansion of funding for mitigation, the lion's share of federal disaster assistance is still devoted to rebuilding the *status quo ante* as quickly as possible.

Needed Improvements for Increasing the Effectiveness of Disaster Assistance Programs

Coordinate programs

Over the past fifty years, the United States Congress has created a legal edifice of Byzantine complexity to cope with natural disasters. The federal disaster apparatus includes laws, agencies, programs, policies, and strategies, many of them intended to operate in "partnership" with state and local governments, nongovernmental organizations, and the private sector. Federal assistance is provided under approximately fifty different laws and executive orders to households, businesses, farms, states, municipalities, special districts, and nongovernmental organizations (May and Deyle 1998).

The number and variety of federal agencies involved in disaster-related activities are breathtaking. For example, agencies interested in coastal hazards include FEMA, the National Oceanographic and Atmospheric Administration (NOAA), the Army Corps of Engineers, the National Park Service, the Fish and Wildlife Service, and the U. S. Geological Survey (USGS), among others. Issues of overlap, competition, and cross-purposes arise among different federal entities, adding to the cost and delays of accomplishing pre-disaster and post-disaster actions. Comparable issues arise when disasters strike less-developed countries, where international aid agencies, national and local government authorities, churches, and other helping organizations may pursue uncoordinated efforts and agendas, resulting in confusion and a waste of time and resources.

Promote local and individual self-reliance

A number of recent U.S. disaster policy reviews have charged that the federal government discourages state, local, and individual self-reliance and prudence by offering federal disaster assistance too readily (Congressional Research Service 1992; National Performance Review 1993; U.S. Senate Bipartisan Task Force on Funding Disaster Relief 1995; Sylves and Waugh 1996; Platt 1999). One indicator of the increasing availability of federal assistance is the rising yearly average of presidential disaster declarations, which are increasing applied toward smaller disasters (see Table 1). In 1996 and 1998—both election years—President Clinton issued an average of more than one disaster declaration per week. Does the federal government try to do too much? Does the likelihood and generosity of federal assistance serve as a disincentive to states and local governments to provide for their own needs in routine, foreseeable natural disasters?

In fact, there are no objective criteria for presidential disaster declarations (Sylves and Waugh 1996). Few would quibble about the need for federal assistance in true catastrophes involving tens of billions of dollars in losses, such as Hurricane Andrew, the Midwest Flood of 1993, and the Northridge Earthquake. Certainly the next tier of disasters, those causing widespread or intense property losses and threat to human life such as Hurricane Fran in 1996, would be generally accepted as requiring federal response. But heavy rain and snow storms, flash floods, and simply "bad weather" now seem to be declared as well. Despite the urging of several recent policy reports, Congress and the president prefer the present discretionary approach to more objective standards for federal disaster assistance. (It should be noted that many federal benefits, such as flood insurance and SBA disaster loans, do not depend on a presidential declaration.) Some observers have charged that disaster assistance has become a new form of political "pork barrel," transferring federal resources to localities beyond the strict requirements of compassion and clear need. For instance, former Tennessee Valley Authority floodplain management administrator, James Wright (1996) writes:

> The historical record demonstrates that disaster relief policies and programs are fluid, being subject to public sentiment for the disaster "victims," often strong political pressure "to do something," and resultant legislative changes—often more liberalized assistance through federal grants. The flood control construction program of the 1930–1950 era now seems to have been replaced by an equally massive federal relief and recovery assistance program for flood disasters in the present era.

Comparable issues arise in the international context. When does national or international aid overwhelm local and individual self-reliance? To what extent should localities, regional governments, and nations be expected to plan and prepare for foreseeable natural disasters? Loss of life is more prevalent in disasters occurring in less-developed nations than elsewhere (Watson 1999). The international community must, of course, do its utmost to assist in rescue and medical care efforts. Local and national authorities, however, should be expected to play leading roles in planning and funding post-disaster reconstruction to the extent of their economic capabilities. International programs, like those in the

United States, should strive to train local emergency management personnel ("first responders") and to promote disaster resistance through building and land-use controls ("sustainable development").

Adhere to cost-sharing agreements

The Stafford Act specifies a 75 to 25 ratio of federal to nonfederal cost sharing of disaster assistance costs under a presidential declaration. The nonfederal (state and local) share is interpreted liberally to include staff salaries and repair costs that would be incurred even without a disaster (referred to as a soft match). In at least fifteen disasters during the 1990s, the president has reduced the nonfederal share to 10% (e.g., Hurricane Fran), or waived it entirely (e.g., Hurricane Andrew). This encourages local governments to request federal assistance for rebuilding damaged infrastructure at little or no cost to the local taxpayer. Since no federal aid would normally be available for such repairs in the absence of a disaster, some communities, when included in a disaster declaration, seek to upgrade their public facilities, even if they are only remotely affected by a disaster.

Federal cost sharing has declined or vanished for other sectors of public spending (e.g., wastewater treatment plants, parks and open space, and low-income housing). The silver lining of being struck by a disaster is that states and local governments included in a presidential declaration become eligible for federal benefits at a ratio ranging from 75 to 100. Furthermore, Congress has repeatedly approved emergency "supplementary appropriations" of billions of dollars to cover the federal costs of disaster assistance.

Create clear, well-defined hazard mitigation strategies

The Clinton administration has made commendable efforts to promote hazard mitigation both before and after natural disasters. Since 1994, FEMA has established a mitigation directorate, has issued a national mitigation strategy, and has launched several initiatives to stimulate community-level mitigation efforts (e.g., "Project Impact" in 1997). These are the latest in a long series of mandates, policies, and approaches to reducing vulnerability to natural disasters (Platt 1999). After three decades of the NFIP, two decades since the formation of FEMA, and over one decade since the Stafford Act, there has been no systematic effort to evaluate the effectiveness of various approaches to flood hazard mitigation, let alone mitigation of other natural risks. The federal government, and particularly FEMA, is still struggling to define, achieve, evaluate, and improve their efforts in hazard mitigation. Despite abundant rhetoric, it remains unclear what mitigation really means, and who should pay for it.

A critical issue of hazard mitigation is the problem of *repetitive losses*, particularly with reference to multiple payments on losses to the same property under the NFIP. In a major study of this problem, the National Wildlife Federation (1998) found that between 1978 and 1995 the NFIP paid repetitive losses on only 2% of the programs' policy base (74,000 out 3.3 million policies), but these amounted to 40% of total NFIP payments ($1.5 billion out of $6.3 billion).

Assess risks and vulnerabilities

Risk and vulnerability assessments are needed to guide state, local, and private development decisions and to inform hazard mitigation in general. Hazard identification, assessment, and mapping has been a longstanding activity of several federal agencies, for instance the USGS, NOAA, the Army Corps of Engineers, the Tennessee Valley Authority, the Soil Conservation Service, and FEMA. Hazard maps and supporting scientific reports of many types are available in published form, and many are now available on the Internet. Furthermore, the federal government supports studies of hazards by state and local governments, as under the federal Coastal Zone Management Program.

More sophisticated computer models are now being developed to estimate levels and distributions of economic and social costs from hypothetical disasters in specific locations. For instance, FEMA is developing a model named HAZUS to evaluate potential losses due to earthquakes and floods. The insurance industry, in collaboration with the federal government, is also developing models of potential loss exposures from hypothetical disasters (Heinz Center 1999).

The high-force winds and the high water of Hurricane Floyd damaged this Oak Island, N.C., home. Beach erosion has placed many coastal properties in danger, but many coastal property owners don't want erosion rate data included on national flood hazard maps because they may decrease property values, yet they seek federal assistance for disaster recovery. (Photo By Dave Saville, courtesy of FEMA News Photo).

Resolve the battle between property rights and public interest

As the ability to simulate and quantify vulnerability to natural hazards improves, it is essential that the results of such research be applied to reduce risk wherever possible. However, there is a countervailing resistance to the restriction of land development decisions that are based on scientific studies and modeling of disasters. Coastal property owners, for instance, have challenged the inclusion of erosion rate data on NFIP flood hazard maps because they threaten coastal property values. This issue is not limited to the United States; the government of New South Wales in the 1980s actually withdrew flood maps from circulation due to similar objections from affected property owners (Smith 1996).

During the 1990s, the United States has experienced an aroused property rights movement.

Private property owners enjoy a certain measure of freedom from governmental control under the U.S. Constitution provision that " . . . no private property shall be taken for public use without just compensation." Court decisions have interpreted this provision as applying not only to literal taking of property but also to regulation of land use that is deemed excessive or arbitrary. On the other hand, the protection of the public health, safety, and welfare requires that government restrain unreasonable use of private property through land-use and building controls without paying compensation to the owner. These two competing interests—private economic gain versus public interest—have struggled with each other throughout the twentieth century. While courts have tended to support governmental regulation most of the time, a more conservative Supreme Court in the 1990s has upheld property owners in a few highly publicized cases. These decisions have empowered property owners to threaten to sue governmental officials who limit their claimed freedom to use their property as they wish. Clearly, this has important implications for natural hazard mitigation. While local officials and property owners demand federal protection from the effects of natural disasters, they resist restrictions on land use in hazardous areas. In other words, the federal government is expected to remedy the effects of the bad decisions of disaster victims, without the power to prevent such decisions from being made in the first place.

Implement smart redevelopment plans

Disasters are often viewed as windows of opportunity to rebuild more safely than before. As stated earlier, FEMA emphasizes hazard mitigation as an objective in all of its programs. Congress has allowed up to 15% of public assistance funds to be used for hazard mitigation, which in large disasters may amount to hundreds of millions of dollars. The United States, however, usually tends to rebuild after disasters as quickly as possible, often recreating or worsening the level of vulnerability that allowed the disaster to happen. In Oakland, California, for instance, after the destruction of 3,300 homes in a 1991 wildfire, the burned area was substantially rebuilt with even larger homes (albeit with more fire resistant roofs and landscaping), even though a major earthquake has been forecast for the Hayward Fault that lies just downslope from the reconstructed area (Platt 1999). Similarly, coastal homes are rapidly replaced after hurricane damage, as in North Carolina after Hurricane Fran.

A major challenge for the U.S. and other countries is application of disaster recovery resources for the reduction of future vulnerability. FEMA currently promotes building more strongly, as in earthquake retrofitting and elevation of coastal structures. But the will to prevent any rebuilding in areas of clear and continuing risk is required. While politics drives the disaster assistance program, it should not be allowed to deter necessary adjustments to settlement patterns and infrastructure location that reduce vulnerability. And, as mentioned earlier, the costs of such intervention should not be entirely federal. Potential victims—communities and property owners—should be required to contribute to their own protection by refraining from repeating past mistakes.

Create a needs-based disaster assistance option

Federal disaster benefits that are available to victims of U.S. disasters are directed towards individuals with economic assets at risk. Insurance and government benefits likely cushion the financial impacts of disasters on affluent victims. But uninsured victims—particularly the destitute, minorities, the homeless, and the elderly—must bear their own losses, except for short-term charitable and governmental emergency relief.

The NFIP covers flood-related losses to insured structures and their contents. While tenants may purchase contents insurance, most coverage under the NFIP protects real estate owned by the policyholder. Similarly, the SBA low-interest disaster loans are extended to individuals and businesses that qualify in terms of their ability to repay. Public assistance administered by FEMA is provided to states and communities covered by a disaster declaration to reimburse their emergency-response infrastructure repair costs, subject normally to a 25% nonfederal cost-share. There is no needs-based test or sliding scale. While little research has been directed to this issue, it appears that public assistance is substantially allocated to communities that are capable of dealing with the federal bureaucracy and are able to contribute towards the nonfederal cost-share. Low-income communities, particularly unincorporated areas with urban or rural poverty, are likely to receive less public assistance per capita than more affluent areas. (An exception would be Hurricane Andrew, which predominantly devastated the lower income community of Homestead, Florida, and its vicinity.)

The only federal disaster program that is specifically needs based is individual assistance administered by FEMA under the Stafford Act. Individual assistance includes small grants for eligible individuals and families, temporary housing assistance, unemployment payments, and certain other benefits. Grants to families and individuals are intended to help them "meet those disaster-related necessary expenses or serious needs for which assistance from other means is either unavailable or inadequate" (44 Code of Federal Regulations Sec. 206.131). Any insurance coverage available to the victim is deducted from the grant. Furthermore, grants may not be used for the "purchase of items or services that may generally be characterized as nonessential, luxury, or decorative." In other words, federal assistance to low-income disaster victims is intended only to meet their minimal needs, not improve their condition in life. No such qualifications are attached to any other form of federal disaster benefits. A parallel may be drawn with the U.S. federal housing policy, where generous tax subsidies are provided for middle-class and upper-class homeowners, but the poor are placed on waiting lists for access to subsistence-level housing in depressing surroundings.

Both U.S. and international disaster policy makers have the commendable goal of "making people whole" after a disaster. But the moral that both must realize is that very different sets of benefits are being offered in relation to the recipient's socioeconomic status: The more you have at risk, the more you are eligible to receive government assistance after a disaster. This policy ignores the reality that the less you have, the more you may suffer from disaster in terms of personal, emotional, social, and economic impacts (Peacock et al. 1997). In other words, those with the least resources are the most vulnerable to natural disasters.

Summary

This paper has reviewed a number of strategies and issues pertaining to natural disaster policy in the United States. The issues I've outlined are obstructing the intended purpose of disaster assistance programs. Those who oversee disaster recovery and response programs must actively seek resolution of the need for program coordination, encouraging self-reliance, cost sharing, hazard mitigation, assessing risk and vulnerability, reconciling the rights of private property owners with public interest, and promoting equity in the distribution of assistance.

FEMA, in particular, has a leading role among disaster assistance programs. FEMA, of course, is a creature of the political system and is subject to the political oversight and direction of Congress and the White House. FEMA must administer the disaster programs entrusted to it in accordance with the legislation passed by Congress and pursuant to disaster declarations issued by the president. But FEMA also has certain discretion within these constraints. It can fine tune disaster assistance policies through the regulatory process. Its proposal to require local governments to carry casualty insurance as a condition to receiving public assistance under the Stafford Act reflects a creative use of the regulatory process (if this policy is adopted). Furthermore, under the National Flood Insurance Program FEMA has discretion in the degree of vigor it applies toward requiring effective local land management in floodplains. The tendency during the 1990s to relax enforcement of land-use regulatory standards in the face of an aroused property rights movement should be reversed. Mitigation of foreseeable natural hazards is not strictly a federal responsibility—local governments and property owners must share in the costs of avoiding future losses by accepting reasonable restraint of building and rebuilding in harm's way.

References

Ayscue, J. K. 1996. Hurricane damage to residential structures: Risk and mitigation. Natural Hazards Working Paper No. 94. Boulder, Colo.: University of Colorado Natural Hazards Research and Applications Information Center.

Burby, R. J. 1998. Natural hazards and land use: An introduction. In: Cooperating with nature: Confronting natural hazards with land-use planning for sustainable communities, edited by R. J. Burby. Washington, D.C.: Joseph Henry Press.

Congressional Research Service (CRS). 1992. FEMA and the disaster relief fund. Washington, D.C.: CRS.

Eguchi, R. T. et al. 1996. Analyzing economic impacts and recovery from urban earthquakes: The Northridge earthquake as an economic event: direct capital losses. (commissioned paper presented at the EERI Conference: Analyzing economic impacts and recovery from urban earthquakes: Issues for policy makers, Pasadena, Calif., October 1996).

Federal Register. 2000. Federal Emergency Management Agency advance notice of proposed rulemaking: Disaster assistance—insurance requirements for the Public Assistance Program. 65(36) (23 February): 8927–8931.

General Accounting Office (GAO). 1995. Disaster assistance: Information on expenditures and proposals to improve effectiveness and reduce future costs. GAO/T-RCED-95-140. Washington, D.C.: GAO.

Heinz Center (The H. John Heinz III Center for Science, Economics and the Environment). 1999. The hidden costs of coastal hazards: Implications for risk assessment and mitigation. Washington, D.C.: Island Press.

Institute for Business and Home Safety (IBHS). 1998. The insured cost of natural disasters: A report on the IBHS paid loss database. Boston, Mass.: IBHS.

Interagency Floodplain Management Review Committee. 1994. Sharing the challenge: Floodplain management into the 21st century. Washington, D.C.: U.S. Government Printing Office.

May, P. J., and R. E. Deyle. 1998. Governing land use in hazardous areas with a patchwork system. In: Cooperating with nature: Confronting natural hazards with land-use planning for sustainable communities, edited by R. J. Burby. Washington, D.C.: Joseph Henry Press.

Mileti, D. R. 1999. Disasters by design: A reassessment of natural hazards in the United States. Washington, D.C.: Joseph Henry Press.

National Geographic Society. 1998. Map: Natural hazards of North America. Washington, D.C.: National Geographic Society.

National Performance Review. 1993. Creating a government that works better and costs less: FEMA. Washington, D.C.: Office of the Vice President of the United States.

Natural Research Council (NRC). 1994. Facing the challenge: The U.S. national report to the IDNDR. Washington, D.C.: National Academy Press.

Natural Research Council (NRC). 1999. The impacts of natural disasters: A framework for loss estimation. Washington, D.C.: National Academy Press.

National Wildlife Federation (NWF). 1998. Higher ground: A report on voluntary property buyouts in the nation's floodplains. Washington, D.C.: NWF.

Peacock, W. G., B. H. Morrow, and H. Gladwin. 1997. Hurricane Andrew: Ethnicity, gender, and the sociology of disasters. London, England: Routledge.

Platt, R. H. 1998. Planning and land use adjustments in historical perspective. In: Cooperating with nature: Confronting natural hazards with land-use planning for sustainable communities, edited by R. J. Burby. Washington, D.C.: Joseph Henry Press.

Platt, R. H. 1999. Disasters and democracy: The politics of extreme natural events. Washington, D.C.: Island Press.

Rhinesmith, A. Data provided from Mr. Rhinesmith, Office of Management and Budget, to the National Research Council Committee on "Assessing the Costs of Natural Disasters," 15 December 1997.

Smith, D. I. 1996. Toward cooperative policies: Flood management in New South Wales. In: Environmental management and governance: Intergovernmental approaches to hazards and sustainability, edited by P. J. May et al. London, England: Routledge.

Sylves, R. T., and W. L. Waugh, Jr. 1998. Disaster management in the U.S. and Canada. Springfield, Mass.: Charles C. Thomas, Publisher, Ltd.

U.S. Senate Bipartisan Task Force on Funding Disaster Relief. 1995. Federal disaster assistance. Washington, D.C.: U.S. Government Printing Office.

Watson, R. 1998. Remarks to PPP 2000 Forum, World Bank Headquarters, 27 January 1999, Washington, D.C.

Wright, J. M. 1996. Effects of the flood on national policy: Some achievements, major challenges remain. In: The great flood of 1993: Causes, impacts, and responses, edited by S. A. Changnon. Boulder, Colo.: Westview Press.

A Dialogue: Communities at Risk and Accessing Disaster Recovery Assistance

William V. D'Antonio

Starting the Dialogue

The Question: *After Hurricane Floyd, were the recovery resources provided by public and private agencies distributed fairly and without discrimination to the diverse communities of eastern North Carolina?*

The discussion was guided by **Bob Edwards**, Professor, Department of Sociology, East Carolina University and **Don Ensley**, Professor and Chair, Department of Community Health, East Carolina University. About thirty people were present for this important discussion. Some represented local, state, and federal offices or agencies but the majority represented volunteer associations such as the Salvation Army and the Red Cross.

Introduction

When confronted by a disaster like Hurricane Floyd, impacted populations have many problems. As a society we have established a system, both formal and informal, to help those in need. But assistance is not always distributed randomly; some receive more help than others. The participants in this discussion were asked to reflect on how the benefits provided by public and private agencies were distributed after Hurricane Floyd, and how the pattern of distribution affected the short-term and long-term recovery of different groups.

The following summary attempts to capture the spirit of the discussion that ensued. The themes discussed were similar to those heard throughout the conference: a lack of coordination between government agencies and volunteer groups, a lack of coordination within and between government agencies, and a strong sense among disaster victims of being disconnected, ignored, and left out. The feeling of not being acknowledged during the disaster recovery process was especially evident for those segments of the population that were least able to cope with the formal structure of the recovery assistance process.

Confusion in the Recovery Process

As the dialogue between faith-based volunteer associations and representatives of public agencies developed, a significant amount of suppressed class, racial, and ethnic emotion surfaced. Some participants had very specific questions. And the agency officials did their best to provide answers. But it was clear that even people who would be expected to know the answers to the questions posed were uncertain about many crucial matters. For instance, there was some debate over the maximum size of the recovery assistance loans that are available or that would be available in the coming months. There was also a lack of understanding regarding loan eligibility and what specific groups the loans were designed to assist. Certain government officials in the audience did know the details and may have subsequently made the information available to volunteer associations and other government agencies. The serious point that emerged from the loan discussion was that communication about money matters is always problematic, even under the best circumstances. In a disaster such as Floyd, it can threaten to become its own disaster.

Government officials attempted to avoid appearing defensive as they tried to explain why it had been impossible, immediately following the aftermath of the storm, to provide the amount of substantial help that would have enabled people to get on with their lives. But it has been eight months since the flooding and people are still unclear about the process of accessing important recovery resources, such as housing funds. This discussion exposed a serious problem that is clearly impeding the progress of long-term recovery from the Hurricane Floyd disaster—communication, both among different government agencies and between government agencies and nongoverment organizations.

Identifying People at Risk

When a disaster like Hurricane Floyd hits, it is a great equalizer—everyone has an equal probability of being impacted. Regardless of economic or social status, the immediate risk to life and property is more or less equal. But after the storm abates, the people who are quick to recover are those who have knowledge of bureaucracies, a certain amount of personal wealth, or other resources, such as relatives and friends living outside the affected areas. At the same time, there was a general perception among discussion participants that people in lower income brackets were more likely than those in a middle socioeconomic class to get government loans to help them get back on their feet. Some participants asserted that the people most at risk of not receiving recovery assistance were those just above the poverty level.

Government officials must recognize that some people have a limited knowledge or ability to communicate when they are confronted with bureaucratic organizations. This was a major concern among the representatives of volunteer associations. One leader put it very bluntly when he said, "People with limited education don't know how to deal with bureaucratic organizations like FEMA." To which a leader in the African American community added, "The elderly and the less educated are so accustomed to being told 'No' that they are easily defeated by a single 'No' from any office. And they don't follow up. They don't know how to follow up. These are the people who are most disadvantaged by these disasters."

The poorest and most needy victims want simply to return to life as it was before the disaster. But the reality is that they have been displaced. They have lost their sense of community and have become forced to live in temporary quarters next to strangers. Although government agencies generally have good intentions, they may actually assist in excluding vulnerable people from the recovery process. These people quickly disappeared from view and were left alone as the larger effort to recover from the flood proceeded.

Create a Social Infrastructure

Considerable time was spent discussing the strengths and weaknesses of different government programs. An intergovernmental system has been developed to prepare for disasters like Floyd. The Federal Emergency Management Agency (FEMA) was generally acknowledged to be a model agency, but it cannot be a "911," or the automatic savior. There is a need to improve the linkage between local, state, and federal government entities and between governments and the many volunteer associations. Incorporating volunteer associations may be crucial to any disaster preparation plan since they are often the first to respond to the needs of disaster victims.

Bob Edwards put the problem in these words: "Each agency may be making a good faith effort to help, but people within each agency need to develop social infrastructures, so they will work together. But do agencies perceive the need to develop social infrastructures?" He continued, "If the agencies do not always work well together, why are we surprised that the public, especially the poorest among them, do not know how to network with these agencies?" Lastly, he posed the question, "Is there a model of a social infrastructure that could work in such disasters?"

As the conversation continued, it became more and more apparent that there is a great need for a *social* infrastructure or for a *series* of social infrastructures. When we talk about infrastructure, we think of road, sewage, and water systems. We need an equivalent social infrastructure to address the needs of our increasingly complex society.

Recommendations for Responding to the Needs of High-Risk Groups

Linking all members of a community together, especially those at high risk for being neglected during disaster relief, recovery, and preparation, is essential to creating a viable community that is able to quickly recover from the impact of natural disasters. To achieve this goal the following recommendations should be considered:

- To ensure that those at risk of not seeking or receiving aid are included, government officials must use alternative ways to communicate the details of the recovery assistance process.
- Create a system for effective communication among different government agencies and between government agencies and nongoverment organizations. This must include incorporation of volunteer associations because they will be crucial to implementation of any disaster plan.
- Create a Disaster Extension Service, modeled after the Agricultural Extension Service, which could initially be developed by East Carolina University.

About the Author: Dr. D'Antonio is currently a visiting research professor in the Department of Sociology, Life Cycle Institute, Catholic University of America, Washington D.C. He is also professor emeritus at the University of Connecticut. His primary areas of specialization include political sociology, race-ethnic relations, family, and religion.

Repeated Exposure to Hurricanes and Willingness to Evacuate: Implications from the Hurricane Floyd Experience

David N. Sattler

Introduction

Hurricane Floyd threatened the southeast coast and prompted the largest peacetime evacuation in United States history. More than two and a half million people in Florida, Georgia, South Carolina, North Carolina, and Virginia fled their homes to safer areas (American Red Cross 1999). At noon, 14 September 1999, South Carolina governor Jim Hodges declared a mandatory evacuation for Charleston, the barrier islands, and Myrtle Beach. Just one hour later, cars on the evacuation routes were stuck in traffic gridlock. It took many evacuees five hours to travel the first fifteen miles of Interstate 26 out of Charleston and sixteen hours to travel to cities that were normally reached within four hours. Many people did not have food or water or access to restroom facilities. Under threat of one of the largest and most powerful hurricanes of the twentieth century, evacuees were afraid and felt vulnerable to the storm (American Red Cross 1999; Munday 1999).

The westbound lanes of Interstate 26 that head inland from the city of Charleston were at a standstill; the eastbound lanes were virtually empty. Many residents believed that a lane reversal plan had been created after Hurricane Hugo, which devastated Charleston in 1989, and were upset when the eastbound lanes were not reversed in 1999. Watching correctional facility buses loaded with inmates drive by on a shoulder lane that they were not allowed to use added to their frustration and anger (Munday 1999).

In the days following the evacuation, many citizens were concerned about how the evacuation was handled. Not allowing use of the eastbound lanes of Interstate 26 was the most commonly cited problem. Anecdotal evidence and frequent media reports suggested that the Hurricane Floyd evacuation for many people was so upsetting and stressful that they would not be willing to evacuate in the future (Munday 1999). People questioned whether the Department of Transportation and state officials could successfully handle another evacuation. People said they would rather take their chances and stay at home than go through another evacuation. If these statements are accurate—if a significant number of people are not willing to evacuate for future hurricane threats—then many people could be at increased risk to the life-threatening impacts of future hurricanes (Langley 2000).

This paper examines experiences during the Hurricane Floyd evacuation in Charleston, South

Carolina, and considers how experience with prior hurricanes can influence the way people perceive and prepare for new hurricane threats. Experiencing multiple natural disasters may not be uncommon. At least one-third of natural disaster survivors may have experienced another disaster (Freedy et al. 1994), and population trends indicate that an increasing number of people are moving into regions that are vulnerable to recurring natural disasters (Phifer and Norris 1989). Being threatened repeatedly by or experiencing multiple disasters can influence the way that people perceive and prepare for disasters, experience psychological distress, and assist survivors (Lindell and Perry 1992; Sattler et al. 1995; Weinstein 1989). What lessons can people learn when a hurricane strikes? What lessons can people learn when hurricanes repeatedly threaten but do not strike their area? Do *near misses* lead people to discount future threats or to be prepared and vigilant? Would people risk staying in harm's way rather than endure another stressful evacuation? To begin answering these questions, this paper first considers how exposure to repeated hurricane threats might influence the way people perceive and respond to new disaster threats. Next, this paper examines experiences during the Hurricane Floyd evacuation in Charleston and people's willingness to evacuate for future hurricanes. Finally, this paper examines some of the lessons learned from Hurricane Floyd and the actions state governments have taken to facilitate future evacuations.

One Community's Experience: Charleston, South Carolina

Experiencing multiple hurricane threats

Charleston, South Carolina, has endured numerous hurricanes and one earthquake since its settlement in 1670. Hurricane Hugo was the most recent storm to make landfall. This category four storm, with sustained winds of 135 miles per hour, devastated the city and surrounding areas on 21 September 1989. Over half of the counties in South Carolina were declared disaster areas (Mullins and Morgan 1989). At the time, Hurricane Hugo was the costliest natural disaster in U.S. history. Property damage estimates were close to $7 billion. Charleston has been threatened seriously by four hurricanes since Hugo: Emily (September 1993), Bertha (August 1996), Fran (September 1996), and Floyd. Each of these storms was predicted to strike, and the National Weather Service issued hurricane watch and/or hurricane warnings for Charleston. Hours before they were predicted to make landfall, each storm changed course. Hurricane Emily struck Cape Hatteras, North Carolina; Hurricane Bertha and Hurricane Fran struck Wilmington, North Carolina; and Hurricane Floyd created devastating floods in North Carolina. Charleston's history of disaster threats since Hugo provided opportunities to investigate how the Hurricane Hugo disaster experience influenced the way people perceived and prepared for each subsequent disaster threat.

As Hurricane Emily threatened Charleston in September 1993, I conducted a study to examine whether experiences during Hurricane Hugo were associated with how people were preparing for Hurricane Emily and with their level of psychological distress as a result of the new threat. Residents completed a short questionnaire while the city was under National Weather Service hurricane watch and hurricane warning advisories. Two hundred and fifty-seven people participated in the survey (78 men, 179 women; the average age was 30 years). About two-thirds of the participants were living in Charleston when Hurricane Hugo struck. The response rate (i.e., the number of people approached who agreed to participate) was 80%. The results showed that individuals who were better prepared for Hurricane Emily were older, had higher incomes, experienced higher levels of psychological distress as a result of Hurricane Hugo, believed that their actions control what happens to them, believed that the new hurricane was a threat, and experienced higher levels of psychological distress during the hurricane threat. However, property loss as a result of Hurricane Hugo was not associated with preparation efforts for Hurricane Emily.

In September 1996, when Hurricane Fran threatened Charleston, my colleague Charles Kaiser and I replicated and extended the Hurricane Emily study. We conducted the study when Charleston was under a hurricane warning and when classes at local schools had been canceled. Many residents had begun to voluntarily evacuate. One hundred and eighty people participated in this survey (62 men, 118 women; the average age was 23 years). The response rate was 85%. About two-thirds of the participants were living in Charleston when Hurricane Hugo struck. The results showed that older adults and people who perceived a greater threat due to Hurricane Emily were better prepared for Hurricane Fran. But a person's past hurricane experience was not associated with preparing for Hurricane Fran. Why did hurricane experience predict preparation for Hurricane Emily but not for Hurricane Fran? Over time, distress symptoms tend to diminish (Freedy et al. 1993). It may be more difficult to recall past stressful experiences (Higgins, 1989), and distress symptoms may be less readily activated by appropriate stress cues (McFarlane and Papay 1992). In general, people tend to forget events that happened a long time ago, and memory biases may form.

Optimistic bias can influence people's perceptions of disaster threats. Additional findings from both the Hurricane Emily and the Hurricane Fran studies suggest that optimistic bias may have played a role in people's perceptions of these threats. In each study, almost 80% of the participants believed that the hurricane would strike and cause moderate to severe property damage to their house, yet almost 80% believed that the building in which they were living was safe and could withstand a hurricane. Although close to half of the participants were gathering supplies and making other preparation efforts, many denied the severity of the storm. These findings are consistent with other research. For example, Burton, Kates, and White (1978) interviewed individuals worldwide who live in areas that are at risk of experiencing a natural disaster. In several communities, over three-quarters of the participants denied the possibility that a natural disaster could occur in their lifetimes. This tendency is known as *unrealistic optimism*—an individual's belief that he or she is less likely than others to experience negative life events. Although unrealistic optimism may help reduce anxiety when an individual is threatened by a catastrophic event, it also may restrain people from taking precautionary or preventive actions.

The Hurricane Floyd evacuation experience

Two weeks after the Hurricane Floyd evacuation, I conducted a study to examine people's experiences during the evacuation, their willingness to evacuate in the future, and their trust in state government to handle future evacuations. The project was guided, in part, by Perry's evacuation behavior model. The model proposes that people are more likely to comply with an evacuation order when the warning source is perceived to be credible, reliable, and trustworthy. This model also suggests that possession of an adaptive plan, family context, and people's perception of their risk when a warning is received influence evacuation behavior (Lindell and Perry 1992; Perry and Mushkatel 1984). Frequent media reports and anecdotal evidence following Hurricane Floyd suggested that people had lost trust in governmental agencies to handle future evacuations (Langley 2000).

Participants were selected by randomly choosing telephone numbers from the Charleston telephone directory. There were 181 participants (69 men, 112 women; the average age was 40 years). The response rate was about 75%. The majority (83%) was Caucasian, 12% were African American, and 5% were of other ethnic groups. Most of the participants (55%) were married, 30% were single, 13% were separated, divorced, or widowed, and 2% were living together as a couple. About half were living in Charleston when Hurricane Hugo struck.

Almost three-quarters of the participants evacuated for Hurricane Floyd (Table 1). The average distance traveled was 240 miles, with a range from 45 to 780 miles. The average time on the road was ten hours, with a range from one to twenty-two hours.

One of the main questions addressed in this study was whether people would be willing to evacuate for a storm of similar size and strength to Hurricane Floyd. When Hurricane Floyd was threatening Charleston, it was a strong category four storm (131-155 mph winds) that bordered on a category five (greater than 155 mph winds). Table 1 shows that nearly three-quarters of the participants said they would evacuate for a future category four hurricane, 18% were not sure, and

Table 1. People's willingness to evacuate (n=181).

Did you evacuate for Hurricane Floyd?	
Yes	72%
No	28%
Would you evacuate if a category four hurricane is predicted to strike and an evacuation order is issued?	
Yes	70%
Not sure	8%
No	12%
Are you likely to evacuate if the governor reverses the Interstate 26 lanes heading into Charleston?	
More likely to evacuate	71%
Not sure	6%
No	23%

12% said they would not evacuate. This finding suggests that the Hurricane Floyd experience may influence people's future behavior. For example, 28% of the participants did not evacuate for Floyd, but 12% said they would not evacuate for the next storm. Of course, 18% said they were "not sure" if they would evacuate, and a portion of this group might not evacuate for the next storm. Future research should continue to examine reasons why people choose not to evacuate and to find ways to increase compliance with evacuation orders (Lindell and Perry 1992).

Table 2. Why people choose not to evacuate (n=51).

They did not want to sit in traffic	9%
They believed the hurricane might not hit	16%
They believed they would be safe at home	14%
They belived the evacuation would be too stressful	14%
They wanted to protect home and possessions	11%
They believed that damage to their home would not be that bad	9%
They did not want to spend money on hotel and gas	5%
They needed to take care of family that were unable to evacuate	4%
Their job required them to stay	4%
They could not travel/move around easily	1%
Other reasons	1%

One of the primary issues surrounding the evacuation was the decision to not open the eastbound lanes of Interstate 26 to facilitate the evacuation of the city. Seventy-one percent of the participants said they would be more likely to evacuate if the Interstate 26 inbound lanes were reversed (Table 1). However, an additional analysis revealed that most of the participants who indicated a likeliness to evacuate if the lanes were reversed were the same people who evacuated for Hurricane Floyd.

The participants who did not evacuate for Hurricane Floyd (28%) cited a variety of reasons for their decisions. The primary reasons cited were a desire to avoid sitting in traffic and a belief that the hurricane would not hit the city (Table 2).

Participants were also asked about their level of trust in state government agencies to handle future evacuations and their trust in local weather hurricane forecasts (Table 3). Half of the participants somewhat trusted the South Carolina Department of Transportation (DOT) to handle future hurricane evacuations, about one-tenth trusted the DOT quite a bit, but more than one-third did not trust the agency. More than half of the participants trusted local weather hurricane forecasts. Perceptions of governmental agencies and representatives can fluctuate over time and are influenced by many factors. Because participants were not asked before the hurricane threat about their degree of trust in these agencies, we do not know if people lost trust as a result of the storm or if these numbers reflect pre-Hurricane Floyd trust levels.

Table 3. People's level of trust (n=181).

Do you trust the South Carolina Department of Transportation to handle hurricane evacuations?	
Quite a bit	13%
Some	50%
Not at all	38%
Do you trust the South Carolina governor to handle future hurricane evacuations?	
Quite a bit	20%
Some	47%
Not at all	31%
Do you trust local television weather forecasts to predict hurricanes?	
Quite a bit	56%
Some	40%
Not at all	3%

Currently, I am replicating and extending the Hurricane Floyd study to examine if people's willingness to evacuate and their trust in government agencies to handle evacuations have changed. This is especially important because the South Carolina government created a special commission to examine why the Interstate 26 inbound lanes were not reversed. Just before the hurricane season began in June 2000, South Carolina governor Jim Hodges declared that a lane reversal plan had been approved and would be initiated during the next hurricane threat. It is possible that these appropriate measures may increase citizens' level of trust and willingness to evacuate.

Summary

The studies presented in this paper show that hurricane experience is associated with the way people perceive and respond to new hurricane threats. Psychological distress that resulted after Hurricane Hugo in 1989 was associated with people's preparation activities for Hurricane Emily in 1993, but not with Hurricane Fran in 1996. The Hurricane Floyd study found that about three-quarters of the participants evacuated. Despite the inconvenience and stress associated with the evacuation, almost three-quarters of the participants were willing to evacuate for a future hurricane of similar size and would be more likely to evacuate if plans allowed for all interstate highway lanes to carry evacuation traffic heading inland. These findings are consistent with previous research. Individuals who live in areas that are frequently threatened by natural disasters may be more likely to acknowledge that a threat exists (Lindell and Perry 1992), to take more preventative measures (Faupel et al. 1992), and to comply with warnings (Drabek and Boggs 1968) than individuals who are infrequently threatened by disasters.

Hurricane Floyd taught several important lessons, and many states have modified their evacuation plans. For example, South Carolina now has a plan to reverse at least 100 miles of Interstate 26 eastbound lanes between Charleston and Columbia. In May 2000, the Department of Transportation tested this lane reversal plan, including stationing public safety officers along the route. The plan was considered a success. Emergency message boards and enhanced communication networks also have been established to help emergency management officials stay informed about problems and issues that arise during an evacuation.

Part of the challenge in declaring an evacuation is knowing where a hurricane is heading. For example, a hurricane warning can be issued when a storm is twenty-four hours away, but the error rate can be about 100 miles. Because storms vary in size, damaging winds and rain can affect areas as far away as 50 to 150 miles from the center of the storm (Langley 2000). For these and other reasons, it is important for citizens to understand the dynamics of hurricanes, to know how the hurricane warning system works, and to be vigilant and prepared (Sattler et al. 1997). Fortunately, hurricane forecasting has improved significantly over the years, and more advancements are on the horizon.

References

American Red Cross 1999. American Red Cross relief workers continue to shelter thousands as Floyd now sweeps toward the Carolinas. <http://www.redcross.org/news/inthnews/99/9-15c-99.html>.

Burton, I., R. Kates, and G. White. 1978. The environment as hazard. New York: Oxford University Press.

Drabek, T. E., and K. Boggs. 1968. Families in disaster: Reactions and relatives. Journal of Marriage and the Family 30:443–451.

Faupel, C. E., S. P. Kelley, and T. Petee. 1992. The impact of disaster education on household preparedness for Hurricane Hugo. International Journal of Mass Emergencies and Disasters 10:5–24.

Freedy, J. R., D. G. Kilpatrick, and H. S. Resnick. 1993. Natural disasters and mental health: Theory, assessment, and intervention. In: Handbook of post-disaster interventions [Special issue], edited by R. Allen, Journal of Social Behavior and Personality 8:49–103.

Freedy, J. R., M. E. Saladin, D. G. Kilpatrick, H. S. Resnick, and B. E. Saunders. 1994. Understanding acute psychological distress following natural disaster. Journal of Traumatic Stress 7:257–273.

Higgins, E. T. 1989. Knowledge accessibility and activation: Subjectivity and suffering from unconscious sources. In: Unintended thought: Limits of awareness, intention, and control, edited by J. S. Uleman and J. A. Bargh, 75–123. New York: Guilford Press.

Langley, L. 2000. Area prepares for hurricane season, with lessons learned from Floyd. Post and Courier (Charleston, S.C.), 6 June.

Lindell, M. K., and R. W. Perry. 1992. Behavioral foundations of community emergency planning. Washington, D.C.: Hemisphere Publishing.

McFarlane, A. C., and P. Papay. 1992. Multiple diagnoses in posttraumatic stress disorder in the victims of a natural disaster. Journal of Nervous and Mental Disease 180:498–504.

Mullins, S., and K. Morgan. 1989. Massive cleanup begins in S.C.: Six deaths blamed on Hurricane Hugo. News and Courier (Charleston, S.C.), 22 September.

Munday, D. 1999. Remnants of Hurricane Floyd: Feelings of anger remain. Post and Courier (Charleston, S.C.), 26 September.

Norris, F. H., and K. Kaniasty. 1992. Reliability of delayed self-reports in disaster research. Journal of Traumatic Stress 5:575–588.

Phifer, J., and F. H. Norris. 1989. Psychological symptoms in older adults following natural disaster: Nature, timing, duration, and course. Journal of Gerontology 44:207–217.

Perry, R. W., and A. H. Mushkatel. 1984. Disaster management: Warning response and community relocation. Westport, Conn.: Quorum Books.

Sattler, D. N., M. G. Adams, and B. Watts. 1995. Effects of personal experience on judgments about natural disasters. Journal of Social Behavior and Personality 10:891–898.

Sattler, D. N., C. F. Kaiser, and J. B. Hittner. 2000. Disaster preparedness: Relationships among prior experience, personal characteristics, and distress. Journal of Applied Social Psychology 30:1396–1420.

Weinstein, N. D. 1989. Effects of personal experience on self-protective behavior. Psychological Bulletin 105:31–50.

Note: *Each study discussed in this paper has limitations that are common in disaster research. They employed samples that may not represent the population affected or threatened by disasters, and relied on self-report from the participants. Norris and Kaniasty (1992) note, however, that self-report disaster data appear to be reliable. For a complete description of the Hurricane Emily and Hurricane Fran studies, see Sattler et al. (2000).*

About the Author: David N. Sattler is a natural disaster researcher and a professor of social and environmental psychology in the Department of Psychology at Western Washington University in Bellingham, Washington. For several years he taught at the College of Charleston.

Looking into the Face of the Storm: The Shelter Experience

Robin Webb Corbett

Dr. Corbett is an assistant professor in the School of Nursing at East Carolina University. She has more than twenty years of experience in community health nursing. During Hurricane Floyd and the flooding aftermath, she managed a special needs shelter in her rural community in Edgecombe County.

I am from Pinetops, North Carolina, which is a very small town in the relatively poor county of Edgecombe—a region with limited resources. During the flooding, I went to help at a shelter in my home area. That's where I stayed for two and one-half weeks. My husband, by virtue of being married to me, also stayed there. I want to share with you how one community responded to this disaster.

Initially, the shelter had approximately 200 people, but we had to expand because of the extent and long duration of the flooding in our area. The people at the shelter were predominantly black with some whites and some Hispanics. Some of the people had been traveling when they were caught by the storm and were stranded in their cars before being rescued and brought to the shelter. People arrived by boats, helicopters, and jet skis. We were pretty much rescuing anybody, in any way that we could. Often they came to the shelter wet and cold. Sometimes they were being moved from one shelter to another. Some had been outside all day long in the hot sun, trapped when the floodwaters rose. These people had nowhere to go, so they were brought to the shelter.

The people volunteering at the shelter were wonderful. They worked very well together, though they often had to sleep on the floor. Generally, the external agencies that we were working with were extremely positive. I cannot speak highly enough about the National Guard, Department of Motor Vehicles, our churches, and FEMA. They went out of their way to do whatever needed to be done, although we ran into some problems with some other agencies. There were rules that had to be followed. What we learned from dealing with these various agencies was that it was important to identify one person in the shelter as the spokesperson. This person was involved in negotiations and acted as a representative for individuals. Rules are rules, but you need to be able to work with those rules to meet the needs of the people.

Because of the duration of the flooding, we ended up as a special needs shelter. We ended up with patients who had congestive heart failure, respiratory illnesses, people who had chronic obstructive pulmonary disease, and patients who had had strokes. We had a large population of diabetics, but only one blood-glucose glucomator. One machine to test for everyone. Needless to say we had to share.

Now recognize that in a small community, you're pretty much going to know everybody. You've gone to school with them. You've been married to somebody that they know, or your children go to the same school as their children. This was very beneficial. One of the things we identified very quickly was that most of the health-care professionals in the county knew each other. When I sought assistance from other health-care workers, I didn't have to demonstrate my credibility because it was already established. This was a great benefit throughout my time at the shelter. When I called the pharmacists, they worked with us. We also had a physician backup and a nurse practitioner because they knew me and vice versa. Very early in the process, we set up ground rules. The nurse practitioner came by and made morning rounds. Then she would come back by in the afternoon to make evening rounds. If I had an emergency, I would call her. One problem we had was being able to communicate. Our cell phones didn't work. Shoot them all, none of those blasted things worked. Because of the nature of where we were, so isolated, we ended up using the assistance of ham operators. One ham operator was just wonderful. He instructed me on the fine art of how to use that radio.

Our shelter also had church services. We were situated very close to where seven people drowned in a boating accident. The site was actually within sight of our particular shelter. So church services were very, very beneficial to our shelter community. I think one of the most important things I did, besides making connections for individuals with regard to health-care needs, was helping some of the survivors from the boating accident. One man would awaken in the middle of the night, and every night we would go back through the story of what had happened: how the boat capsized, how he couldn't reach his wife, how the children were outside of his reach, and how he was under the boat and couldn't get out. Over and over he would tell that story, and we would listen and try to help as he sobbed and grieved. There was a lot of closure when they were able to find the childrens' bodies. Somehow that made the community feel better.

A sea of mops await new owners in this Salvation Army Distribution Center in Wilson, N.C. The center served more than 300 families a day with food, clothing, water, and cleaning supplies. (Photo by Dave Saville, courtesy of FEMA News Photo)

When the people were able to leave the shelter, either to go home or to stay with family, some still came to the shelter to eat. When they were able to go back into their homes, one of the ladies was very clear about how she felt about leaving. She said, "I really looked forward to going home." But when she walked into her home, she got to her bedroom, looked in the bed, and there was a pig lying in the bed with its head on the pillow. She told me, "I looked at that pig and I said, 'This is my house.'" The pig raised up its head, looked at her, put down its head, and she said, "You're right, you can have it, it's no longer mine, it's yours, I don't want it that bad."

The most important point I want to make is that small communities truly can pull together. We were able to identify people in our particular community who were able to meet the needs of the community. We were able to identify volunteers. Many people wanted to do something, but didn't know what to do. If you contacted them and let them know what to do, they were willing to help. We also had a lot of people who came in from outside the community, public health nurses, physicians, nurse practitioners, and physician's assistants. But it was always crucial to have someone from the home community or someone connected to the shelter to coordinate activities. There should be someone from every community that is able to fulfill this role.

Public Perceptions of Economic Development and Technology After the Storms

Kenneth Wilson, Bob Edwards, Marieke Van Willigen, John R. Maiolo, and John C. Whitehead

Introduction

Between 1996 and 1999, a series of hurricanes (Bertha, Fran, Bonnie, Dennis, and Floyd) battered eastern North Carolina. These types of natural hazards are causing substantially more damage than in the past because of the extensive development and increasing population density in the coastal zone east of Interstate 95. The heightened vulnerability of eastern North Carolina to severe weather events reflects the gradual transformation of the region from one of sparsely populated rural and coastal communities to a region with a higher population density. In 1990, there were 2,554,135 people living in the forty-four counties impacted by Hurricane Floyd. By 1998, the population had grown to 2,927,021. Excluding Wake County, the population growth rate was slightly slower than the state as a whole (10.5% versus 13.8%), but this was still a substantial increase in less than a decade. A 1999 study indicated that there are over 96,000 businesses in the forty-four impacted counties (Wilson et. al. 1999a).

Before Hurricane Floyd, the counties most affected by the storms of 1999 were struggling to address the challenges that new technology and globalization have presented to rural America. In North Carolina, rural areas are at a particular disadvantage. They lack the social and economic infrastructure that has been carefully cultivated in urban regions over the last fifty years. Plants are closing. Schools are failing to prepare many students for the future technological challenges they will face. Governor Hunt worried, “We’re on the verge of becoming two North Carolinas. One is urban and thriving; the other is rural and struggling” (Rural Prosperity Task Force 2000). Without infrastructure, jobs, and an educated workforce, these rural areas will watch the gap between their quality of life and the quality of life of their urban neighbors widen (Vision 2030 1999).

The realities of life in rural North Carolina are important to understanding the recovery process after Hurricane Floyd. Eastern North Carolina was struggling before Floyd. Such a monumental event could easily break the spirit of the people, preventing them from improving their situation. Or, it could strengthen their resolve to provide a better life for their children. This paper examines whether people living in eastern North Carolina changed their basic attitude concerning economic development and technology after the fall of 1999.

Surveying the Perceptions of North Carolinians

Before the storms

This paper utilizes the results of two surveys. The first was a statewide survey of North Carolina conducted in August 1999, the month before Hurricane Floyd struck eastern North Carolina. The second survey replicated the original survey but was conducted only in the forty-four counties impacted by Hurricane Floyd. This survey was conducted a month after Hurricane Floyd, in November and early December 1999.

In 1999, Governor Jim Hunt initiated North Carolina's Vision 2030 Project to investigate the science and technology innovations that will drive the global economy over the next thirty years. One project goal was creating policies that will keep North Carolina's workforce and industry competitive in the new economy. As part of this project, the North Carolina Board of Science and Technology asked the East Carolina University Survey Research Laboratory to develop a survey to assess public perceptions of the role and importance of science and technology in the North Carolina economy. The fifty-six-question survey was designed to assess the extent to which the citizens of North Carolina thought that the economy was currently meeting the needs of people, whether they recognized the changes occurring in the economy, and whether they supported programs designed to strengthen the state's economy.

Survey Sampling, Inc. drew a random sample of telephone numbers from among households with telephones, which were then used in the telephone survey. This organization estimates that 91.1% of the households in eastern North Carolina have telephones, but only 78.7% have telephones that are listed in a telephone directory. In other words, the random digit dialing procedure assures better representation of households in North Carolina counties. Five hundred and twenty-two statewide interviews were completed, with a response rate of 71%. These data were weighted to insure that we had an accurate geographic distribution of survey results across the entire state.

The Vision 2030 survey questions measured the respondents' support for state programs designed to enhance economic development, their willingness to participate in training programs to prepare for better jobs, and whether their attitudes or behaviors were consistent with economic success and changes in the coming decades. Questions that assessed attitudes and behavior included determining whether the respondent had a computer, whether they had Internet access, if Internet access was available from their local library or community college, if they agreed that all citizens should have access to the Internet, and if the Internet represented a great opportunity for the people in their community.

The respondents were also asked a set of questions about their social and economic backgrounds. These variables included the respondent's gender (male or female), age, race (white, black, or other), education, work status (not full time or full time), marital status (not married or married), preschool children living at home (no or yes), and teenagers living at home (no or yes).

After the storms

Because the flooding caused by hurricanes Dennis and Floyd had such a tremendous impact on eastern North Carolina, the North Carolina Board of Science and Technology agreed to fund a follow-up study of the forty-four counties impacted by these storms and floods. While most storms severely impact a small geographic area, the hurricanes and rains of late 1999 impacted a large area. The forty-four affected counties cover all of eastern North Carolina from Raleigh to the coast (Wilson et al. 1999b).

In the Vision 2030 study, 202 of the 522 interviews were completed in the impacted counties. The follow-up study was designed to yield approximately 200 completed interviews. The same procedures used in the Vision 2030 study were followed, in order to make the results as equivalent as possible. However, the original fifty-six-question survey was revised. Four new questions were added at the end of the survey to briefly assess the respondents' experiences during the storms. These added questions assessed whether the respondent's home was damaged, whether someone lost a job as the result of the storms, whether the household suffered a reduction in income as the result of the storm, and whether someone moved into the household. During November and early December 1999, 214 interviews were conducted, with a response rate of 66%. These data were also weighted to insure an accurate geographic distribution across the impacted counties.

The details of the Vision 2030 study, including how measures were constructed and their reliability and validity, have been presented elsewhere (Wilson et. al. 2000a). Also, details of the statistical analyses of these surveys were presented at the In the *Aftermath of Hurricane Floyd* conference, and those interested in the statistical procedures should read the conference paper available at <http://www.ecu.edu/coas/floyd>.

Victims of the Storm

Overall, 25.7% of the respondents reported that their homes had been damaged by the hurricanes. The proportions ranged from roughly 30% in the moderately and severely affected counties to 15% in the counties that sustained minor damage. No information was collected on the extent of the damage, so it could range from leaks and lost shingles to total destruction. The probability of suffering some damage was roughly equal across a wide range of social and economic variables. This is consistent with earlier findings that hurricanes damage all kinds of people, and it is not until you examine the family's ability to recover from their losses that the role of social structures becomes clear (Maiolo et al. 1999).

Over 11% of the households reported that people moved in with them during this emergency. This ranged from almost 15% of the households in the counties with severe damage to 6% in counties with moderate damage. In counties with minor damage, almost 12% had people move into their households. The probability of having someone move in with you was roughly equal across a wide range of social and economic variables.

Table 1. Percentage of households whose resources were reduced by the presence of preschool or school-aged children.

	Reduced Income	One or More Lost Jobs
No Child Living at Home	9.9%	3.9%
Children 5 and Under	29.0%	15.2%
All Children 6 or Over	18.4%	2.0%

Respondents were also asked if the total income of their household was reduced by the hurricane. Overall, 15.7% reported a reduction in household income. This ranged from almost 22% in the severely impacted counties to 8% in the counties with minor damage. A household including preschool children was almost three time more likely to lose household income (29.0%) than were households with no children (9.9%). Households that only included school-age children were almost twice as likely to suffer a loss of household income (18.4%) (Table 1).

Almost 5% of the respondents reported that someone in their household lost a job because of the hurricanes and floods. None of the respondents from counties with minor damage reported a household member losing a job, but 8% of the households in the counties with severe damage reported a lost job. Households with preschool children were almost four times more likely to lose their job because of the hurricane than households with no children (15.2% versus 3.9%).

Perceptions of Economic Opportunities

How did the storms effect respondents' perception of their economic opportunities? Overall perceptions did not change after the fall storms. However, respondents in moderately impacted counties perceived more opportunities, while respondents in severely impacted counties perceived fewer opportunities after the storms.

This finding illustrates the importance of the understanding the social and economic context of people's perceptions. Most of the affected counties are rural, and their resources may have been stretched to the limit as they responded to the changing world economy and new technologies. For years their needs have been ignored while state leaders focused on developing a world class growth center in Research Triangle Park, near Durham. After the hurricanes and floods, politicians rushed to eastern North Carolina to have their pictures taken beside areas of extensive damage and pledged their support for a massive rebuilding effort.

Finally, people are paying attention. A serious rebuilding program could help these counties address some of their long-term problems. But people have to wonder if the serious rebuilding programs will materialize. When the follow-up poll was conducted, the extent of the relief and rebuilding efforts was not clear. These results suggest that people living in moderately impacted counties had greater confidence that the programs would meet their needs than did the people living in severely damaged counties.

Respondents were asked their opinions about the ability of various state government programs to enhance economic development. The storms and floods did not significantly change the people's support for particular types of programs.

If rebuilding is going to address some of the long-term problems facing these counties, then workers must be trained or retrained for jobs in growing industries. Most respondents were willing to participate in training programs that qualified them for a better job, and the storms did not affect their attitude. After the storms, 86.4% of the respondents were willing to get training at a local community college; 80.4% percent were willing to get training at a center set up in a local church; and 74.7% were willing to get training over the Internet.

The severity of the storms' impact did affect people's willingness to get training for a new job. In counties that had minor impacts, people were more willing to get training than were people living in severely impacted counties. While the decrease is statistically significant, a large majority of people still indicate a willingness to get training. After the storms, people living in counties with minor impacts were more willing than people living in severely impacted counties to get training at the local community college (94.0% versus 81.7%), a training center in a local church (86.3 versus 73.6%), or over the Internet (86.0% versus 68.6%). While there is still widespread willingness to invest in their own future, these results suggest that a number of people have become less optimistic.

Hurricane Floyd did not change the public's mind about the general nature of the modern economic system. Before the storms struck, most people recognized that people are rewarded more for their knowledge than for their physical labor and held similar opinions afterwards, with about 60% of the respondents from each survey reporting that knowledge was rewarded more than physical labor.

Perceptions of Technology

Did the fall storms affect people's willingness to adopt new technology? Respondents were more likely to have a home computer after Floyd than before (49.0% versus 57.8%), and this was not influenced by the severity of the damaged suffered by the respondent's county. More households were hooked to the Internet after the fall storms than before (31.0% versus 48.4%). The number of households in the counties that suffered severe storm impacts decreased slightly (41.2% versus 40.8%), but the proportion of homes with Internet access did increase significantly in counties that sustained minor (28.9% versus 58.9%) or moderate levels (22.8% versus 45.5%) of storm damage.

While home Internet access increased after Floyd, the level of public Internet access did not change. Both before and after the storms and floods, over 70% of the respondents reported having public access to the Internet at a local library or community college. The storms did increase public support for universal Internet access, with the proportion supporting universal Internet access increasing from 67.3% to 83.1%. About two-thirds of the respondents reported that telecommuting provided a great opportunity for the people in their area. This was not significantly influenced by the fall storms.

Summary

In a region of almost 3 million people, one person in four reported some damage to their home. Most of this damage was minor but served as a potent reminder of the thousands who had to leave their homes for months, for years, or forever. Over 11% of the households reported that people moved in with them during this emergency. Businesses reported that the storms or floods displaced a total of 30,000 employees. The storms and floods impacted all social classes. With thirty-nine of the forty-four counties having poverty levels that exceed a statewide rate of 13.1% and thirteen counties having poverty rates above 20%, many family budgets were stretched even thinner to make needed repairs.

Almost three-fourths of the businesses in eastern North Carolina reported that Hurricane Floyd disrupted their business (Wilson et. al. 2000b). While many businesses worked to protect their employees, almost one household in six suffered a significant loss of income. One household in twenty reported that someone lost a job. Businesses report that 31,000 jobs in eastern North Carolina were lost due to the hurricane and floods (Wilson et. al. 2000b).

These results reveal that the real tragedy of these storms is the impact on the children of eastern North Carolina. Families with preschool children were three times more likely to suffer a loss of income and almost four times more likely to have a family member lose a job. Almost one family in three that had a preschool child living at home suffered a reduction in their family income, and almost one in six had a family member who lost their job because of the hurricanes and floods.

These results illuminate the impact of the fall storms and floods on the people and families of eastern North Carolina. But the storms may have also had an impact on the zeitgeist of the region. Most of the counties hit by Hurricane Floyd were poor. Most were struggling to meet the challenges created by rapidly changing technology and globalization. This study showed that the people of these counties have a commitment to meeting these challenges, and that they are willing to undertake the required personal efforts necessary to better their family's economic situation. They are learning about and adopting computer technology into their lives.

After Floyd, the people in these counties heard the promises of a massive rebuilding effort. A year later the extent to which these promises are fulfilled was still unclear. Without rebuilding infrastructure, creating jobs, and educating the workforce, these counties will watch the gap between their quality of life and the quality of life of their metropolitan neighbors widen. Without a comprehensive redevelopment program, a disaster like Floyd could break the community's will to improve its situation. If the promises made in the aftermath of the storms and floods are fulfilled, this disaster could strengthen their resolve to provide a better life for their children.

Acknowledgments

The North Carolina Vision 2030 Project and the North Carolina Board of Science and Technology funded this project. The authors would like to thank Jane Patterson, Margie Boccieri, and Deborah Watts for their support and insights in developing this project and for their concern for the people of eastern North Carolina.

References

Delia, A., S. R. Brockett, and M. T. Simpson. 2000. North Carolina's Global TransPark: Comparisons of the past—Prospects for growth. Regional Development Services Survey Research Laboratory. Greenville, N.C.: East Carolina University.

Maiolo, J. R., A. Delia, J. C. Whitehead, B. Edwards, K. Wilson, M. Van Willigen, C. Williams, and M. Meekins. 1999. A socioeconomic impact analysis and hurricane evacuation impact assessment tool (methodology) for coastal North Carolina: A case study of Hurricane Bonnie. Final report to North Carolina Division of Emergency Management.

Rural Prosperity Task Force. 2000. Final Report. <http://ruraltaskforce.state.nc.us/finalreport/report.html>.

Vision 2030 Project. 1999. Forces for change—An economy in transition. <http://www.governor.state.nc.us/govoffice/vision2030/index.html>.

Whitehead, J. C., B. Edwards, M. Van Willigen, J. R. Maiolo, and K. Wilson. 2000. A socioeconomic impact analysis for hurricanes Bonnie, Dennis and Floyd. Progress Report to North Carolina Division of Emergency Management and North Carolina Sea Grant Program.

Wilson, K., P. Harrell, K. Arena, N. Johnson, R. Navarro, and H. Burguss. 1999a. Public perceptions of the importance of science and technology to the North Carolina economy. Regional Development Services Survey Research Laboratory, Greenville, N.C.: East Carolina University. <http://www.governor.state.nc.us/govoffice/science/projects/nc2030/survey/index.html>.

Wilson, K., J. R. Maiolo, J. C. Whitehead, M. Van Willigen, B. Edwards, P. Harrell, K. Arena, and G. Gunawardhana. 1999b. A socioeconomic hurricane impact analysis for Hurricane Floyd. Regional Development Services Survey Research Laboratory, Greenville, N.C.: East Carolina University.

Wilson, K., B. Edwards, M. Van Willigen, J. Maiolo, and J. C. Whitehead. 2000a. Hurricane Floyd's effect on public perceptions of economic development and technology. In: In the aftermath of Hurricane Floyd: Recovery in the coastal plain: Social, physical and economic impacts on groups and individuals. Available at conference web site <http://www.ecu.edu/coas/floyd>.

Wilson, K., J. Maiolo, B. Edwards, J. C. Whitehead, and M. Van Willigen. 2000b. Hurricane Floyd's impact on eastern North Carolina businesses. In: Eye of the storm: Essays in the aftermath, edited by E. Wood Rickert. Wilmington, N.C.: Coastal Carolina Press.

About the Authors: Dr. Kenneth Wilson is a professor in the Department of Sociology at East Carolina University and at the university's Survey Research Laboratory. His research interests include social psychology, development, and research methodology. Bob Edwards is an assistant professor and graduate director in the Department of Sociology at ECU. Marieke Van Willigen is also an assistant professor in the Department of Sociology, and Dr. John Maiolo is emeritus professor in the Department of Sociology at ECU and the planning committee chair of the Hurricane Floyd conference. Dr. John Whitehead is associate professor in the Department of Economics and chair of the Coastal and Marine Studies Program at ECU. Collectively, these researchers form the ECU team currently involved in hurricane evacuation and impact research.

Hurricane Evacuation Behavior of Coastal North Carolina Residents During Bonnie, Dennis, and Floyd

John C. Whitehead, Bob Edwards, Marieke Van Willigen, John R. Maiolo, and Kenneth Wilson

Introduction

In August of 1998 Hurricane Bonnie approached the North Carolina coast. On Monday, 24 August, the National Hurricane Center issued a hurricane watch that covered North Carolina. Shortly thereafter, state emergency managers recommended mandatory evacuations for more than a quarter million coastal North Carolina residents and vacationers. On Tuesday, 25 August, the hurricane warning was extended to cover North Carolina.

Hurricane Bonnie made landfall on the coast of North Carolina near Cape Fear, twenty miles south of Wilmington, on 26 August (Avila 1998). Based on the familiar Saffir-Simpson Hurricane Scale (Tropical Prediction Center 1999), Bonnie was a low category three hurricane when it made landfall, with 115 mile per hour winds. Quickly Bonnie diminished to a category one storm, and over the next two days a weakened Bonnie made its way up the entire North Carolina coast. Much of coastal North Carolina experienced Bonnie as a tropical storm. One out of every four North Carolina residents and thousands of vacationers evacuated the coast.

Hurricanes are a reoccurring experience for those living in North Carolina, and evacuations are a component of the hurricane experience. After Hurricane Bonnie, we realized that much was unknown about the dynamics of disaster evacuation behavior. Understanding hurricane evacuation behavior and the ability to make informed predictions based on that behavior is an important tool for emergency managers. The managers issue evacuation orders, reverse highway lanes, close bridges, and make other decisions that directly concern evacuees. Being able to understand why people behave the way they do and the economic impacts of their behavior is essential information as emergency policy decisions are made.

After the evacuation experience of Hurricane Bonnie, we wanted to determine how many people evacuated, why people did or did not evacuate, where they went, how far they went, and how much money they spent during their time away from home (Maiolo et al. 1999). During January 1999, with funding from the North Carolina Division of Emergency Management, we interviewed over 1,000 North Carolina coastal residents to better understand the evacuation process.

During the Bonnie survey, we also asked people what they would do if a hurricane approached North Carolina in 1999. Using the Saffir-Simpson Hurricane Scale, which ranges from a category one to a category five storm, participants were presented with one of the five possible hypothetical hurricane scenarios, with an approximately equal number of participants responding to each.

Based on the category of hurricane with which they were confronted, respondents were asked if they would evacuate, where they would go if they evacuated, and how far they would travel away from their home. We asked these questions so that we could try to predict the number of evacuees and the cost of evacuations in future storms.

During August of 1999, category one Hurricane Dennis approached the North Carolina coast, missed, stalled off the Outer Banks for two days, and then landed on the northeast North Carolina coast and quickly lost hurricane intensity (Beven 2000). Again, portions of the entire North Carolina coast received evacuation orders. Less than one month later, Hurricane Floyd approached North Carolina as a category four hurricane. It weakened as it reached North Carolina, landed near Wilmington as a borderline category three, and left the state the next day (Pasch et al. 2000). Hurricane Floyd led to massive evacuations along the entire southeastern coast of the United States. These two hurricanes provided us with an opportunity to compare evacuation behavior for three storms of different intensity and to determine the accuracy of the predictions made by the respondents to the Bonnie survey.

With funding from the North Carolina Division of Emergency Management and the North Carolina Sea Grant Program, we tailored the Bonnie evacuation survey so that it would be suitable for a hurricane Dennis-Floyd survey. In January and February 2000, we attempted to re-interview the original participants from the Bonnie survey. We asked participants questions that were very similar to ones asked in the original survey: Did they evacuate during hurricanes Dennis and Floyd; If they did, where and how far did they go; and How much money did they spend while away from home.

The Dennis-Floyd survey is unique because other hurricane evacuation research takes a single storm approach. In other words, people are interviewed after one hurricane and then forgotten. With a single storm study, we do not learn whether people behave differently when faced with storms of different severity. Yet, previous social science research suggests that the severity of storms should matter as people decide to evacuate (Baker 1991; Peacock and Gladwin 1992; Dow and Cutter 1997). The data that we collected allowed us to make a comparison between three storms of different intensity. Since we were able to re-survey respondents, we could compare the way people said they would behave in a hypothetical storm with the way they actually behaved. This is exactly the type of information emergency managers require as they make important hurricane evacuation decisions.

In this paper we present a summary of analysis presented in our preliminary report to the North Carolina Division of Emergency Management and the Sea Grant Program (Whitehead et al. 2000), and we describe the data from the Bonnie survey and the Dennis-Floyd follow-up survey. We also compare evacuation behavior and costs across the three storms. Then we present results of the type of people who evacuated during Bonnie, Dennis, and Floyd to see what differences emerge. Finally, we compare the hypothetical evacuation decisions that people said they would pursue with the actual decisions they made during 1999.

Conducting the Hurricane Evacuation Surveys

The data collected for both our Bonnie and Dennis-Floyd surveys were collected from telephone interviews. North Carolina residents who were affected by Hurricane Bonnie in the summer of 1998 were surveyed in January 1999 (Maiolo et al. 1999). The survey used a representative sample of households in eight North Carolina ocean counties: Brunswick, Carteret, Currituck, Dare, Hyde, New Hanover, Onslow, and Pender. Of the households contacted, 76% completed the interview. Almost 1,000 of the survey respondents gave enough information to be included in our study.

In January 2000, after hurricanes Dennis and Floyd, we attempted to contact the same member of the household that we contacted after Bonnie. Of the people who responded to the Bonnie survey, sixty-six had moved away from coastal North Carolina and 164 had either disconnected or changed phone numbers. Five hundred and sixty-five interviews were conducted, for a response rate of 68%. To ensure that the sample is identical for comparisons between the two surveys, we only considered those people who participated in both surveys.

An important difference between the full Bonnie sample (almost 1,000 respondents) and the Bonnie-Dennis-Floyd sample (565 respondents) is the number of people who evacuated. The overall evacuation rate from the Bonnie survey was 26%. But for the 565 Bonnie survey participants who responded to the Dennis-Floyd survey, the evacuation rate was only 22%. For the Bonnie survey participants that we were unable to contact, the evacuation rate was 31%. Thus, the Dennis-Floyd survey participants did not accurately represent the Bonnie survey participants, since a smaller proportion evacuated compared with the total survey results. In order to correct for the problem between the two survey samples and to compare our survey results, we applied an adjustment factor of 1.2 (i.e., 26/22 = 1.2) in our estimates of evacuation rates for Dennis and Floyd.

Other factors that help to describe response differences between the two surveys are the number of years spent at a residence and the distance of the residence from a river. Long-time residents were more likely to respond to both surveys. This is a typical characteristic of follow-up telephone surveys, especially when the period between calls is a year or more. It is always more difficult to contact people a second time by phone if they are likely to move from residence to residence.

People living within two miles of inland portions of rivers were less likely to participate in the follow-up survey. Much of the narrow, inland portions of eastern North Carolina's rivers flooded after

Hurricane Floyd. This suggests that inland flooding may help explain the lack of participation in the Dennis-Floyd survey. Households that were affected by flooding were more likely to move outside of coastal North Carolina and/or change their phone numbers after moving within a coastal county.

The Evacuations

The evacuation decision

The type of information people seek as a storm approaches and where they get that information are factors that help form their decision about whether to evacuate. We wanted to know if the type of information people sought and obtained was different between the three storms. Most of the surveyed coastal North Carolina residents watched weather reports very closely as each storm approached (80% for Bonnie, 70% for Dennis, and 80% for Floyd). The majority of survey respondents said that all of the information that was necessary to make a timely evacuation decision was provided as part of the hurricane watch and warning broadcasts (65% for Bonnie, 69% for Dennis, and 72% for Floyd). In general, as the intensity of an approaching hurricane increases, coastal North Carolina residents gather more information. During each of these storms, less than half of coastal North Carolina residents received either a voluntary or mandatory evacuation order (Bonnie 30%, Dennis 20%, and Floyd 31%) (Table 1).

Surprisingly few coastal North Carolina residents evacuate their homes during hurricanes (Table 2). But more people evacuate during stronger storms. Twenty-two percent of respondents evacuated for Bonnie and 14% and 34% evacuated during Dennis and Floyd, respectively. Applying the previously described 1.2 adjustment factor to these numbers increases the estimate of the percent of respondents who evacuated during Dennis and Floyd. Almost 6% of all respondents evacuated for Hurricane Dennis only, less than 1% evacuated for Tropical Storm Dennis only, and almost 7% evacuated for both Hurricane and Tropical Storm Dennis.

The decision to evacuate was not difficult to make. Thirteen percent of respondents had difficulty deciding to evacuate during Bonnie and during Dennis. Among those who received a mandatory evacuation order for Bonnie, whites and females found the evacuation decision difficult. For Dennis, only those who thought their home was at risk from wind or flooding had difficulty with the decision. During Floyd, 21% had difficulty deciding to leave. Households that were unsure whether they were covered by

Table 1. Percentage of respondents who received voluntary and mandatory evacuation orders.

	Bonnie	Dennis	Floyd
Voluntary	17.5%	10.2%	15.1%
Mandatory	12.5%	9.5%	15.4%

an evacuation order found the evacuation decision particularly hard. The evacuation decision was also difficult for smaller households (one or two people), those with pets, and those not in mobile homes. Similar to results for Bonnie, females had difficulty deciding to evacuate for Floyd, and like Dennis, households who were concerned about the wind risk found the decision difficult. It seems that the stronger the storm, the more difficult the evacuation decision is to make.

Table 2. Percentage of respondents who evacuated.

	Bonnie	Dennis	Floyd
Without Adjustment Factor	22%	14%	34%
With Adjustment Factor (1.2) Applied	26%	17%	41%

Table 3. What did the neighbors do?

	Bonnie	Dennis	Floyd
No Neighbors Evacuated	43%	48%	34%
Some Neighbors Evacuated	39%	35%	40%
Most Neighbors Evacuated	18%	17%	26%

The evacuation behavior of the survey respondents' neighbors also indicates that more people evacuate when the strength of a hurricane is high (Table 3). Fewer people had "no" neighbors leave the area during Floyd than during Bonnie or Dennis. More people had "most" of their neighbors leave the area during Floyd than during Bonnie or Dennis.

Most evacuees went to stay with friends or relatives while they were gone from home (Table 4). Overall, there are very few differences between the evacuation destinations when storm intensity differs.

Evacuation costs

Many factors contribute to the amount of money people spend for an evacuation. The number of people in the household, the distance traveled, and the days spent away from home each contribute to the total expense of evacuating. The average number of people in the household who evacuated is very similar for Bonnie, Dennis, and Floyd. However, the round trip distance traveled was very different—175 miles for Bonnie, 135 miles for Dennis, and 277 miles for Floyd. The increased mileage for Floyd is probably due to the high number of shelter and motel/hotel "no vacancy" signs encountered, which resulted from evacuees from more southern states fleeing to the north. Also, these numbers may reflect people's misperception that they are safer the farther they are from a strong storm.

The number of days spent away from home was also very different across storms. The average evacuee was gone from home 4 days for Bonnie, 6.5 days for Dennis, and 5.5 days for Floyd. The longer time away during Dennis is probably due to the length of time that Dennis stayed along the coast (almost seven days) and because some coastal residents evacuated twice. The number of days for Floyd likely resulted because inland flooding occurred after the hurricane. Many evacuees were unable to return to their homes quickly because high floodwaters closed roads.

Table 4. Where did people stay?

	Bonnie	Dennis	Floyd
Relatives or Friends	65%	71%	65%
Hotel or Motel	18%	17%	23%
Shelter	11%	6%	11%

Table 5. How much did an average household spend while away from home?

	Bonnie	Dennis	Floyd
Average Daily Cost	$29	$31	$38
Total Cost	$124	$131	$169

The evacuation costs incurred by coastal North Carolina residents for Floyd were higher than for Bonnie and Dennis, which were about the same (Table 5). Also, the evacuation cost per day was higher for Floyd than for the other storms, with the daily costs for Bonnie and Dennis being about equal.

The total evacuation cost is the sum of travel, food and beverage, lodging, entertainment, and miscellaneous costs. Food and beverages, the largest component of evacuation costs, account for more than 40% of total costs. While relatively few people choose to go to a hotel or motel, these costs are the next largest component, accounting for about 25% of the total. Reflecting the differences in round trip distance, automobile costs are significantly higher for Floyd than for Bonnie and Dennis. Automobile costs account for 22% of total costs for Bonnie and Floyd but only 15% for Dennis. Entertainment and miscellaneous costs are less than 5% and 10% for each hurricane.

With about 185,000 households in the eight North Carolina coastal counties, we estimate that about 32,000 evacuated during Dennis and 76,000 households evacuated during Floyd. These numbers bracket the 48,000 evacuated households that we estimated for Hurricane Bonnie (Maiolo et al. 1999). Multiplying the aggregate evacuation estimates by the household evacuation cost gives an estimate of the aggregate evacuation costs. Hurricane Bonnie cost North Carolina households $5.96 million, Dennis cost $4.19 million, and Floyd cost $12.79 million. Clearly, hurricane evacuations are an expensive endeavor.

The evacuees

One of the great mysteries of hurricane evacuation research is that some people who are at serious personal risk do not evacuate during a hurricane, and some people who are not at risk evacuate. It is important that emergency managers have a profile of the people likely to evacuate and those that are not likely to evacuate. Profiles can be used to develop educational programs and other strategies for matching risk and evacuation behavior.

The decision to evacuate during hurricanes Bonnie, Dennis, and Floyd depended on pet ownership, whether evacuation orders were received, residential characteristics, the risk that people thought they would face, and some demographic characteristics.

Coastal North Carolina residents who own pets are less likely to evacuate. This is because shelters, motels, and hotels typically do not allow pets. Protecting their pet was one of the main reasons pet owners gave for not leaving home.

It is encouraging that residents who receive mandatory and voluntary evacuation orders are likely to evacuate, since those who receive evacuation orders are clearly at higher personal risk during the storm than are others. However, all residents who received these orders do not evacuate. Mobile homes are at high risk to damage during a hurricane because they are unstable during high-force, tropical storm winds. While mobile home residents are likely to seek a safer structure to ride out the storm, not all residents of mobile homes evacuate.

There are only a few characteristic differences between those who evacuated during Bonnie and those who evacuated during hurricanes Dennis and Floyd. During Bonnie, females, those with more education, and those who thought that their homes were susceptible to flooding were likely to evacuate. During hurricanes Dennis and Floyd susceptibility to flooding and education level were not important characteristics of those who evacuated, but white residents were less likely to evacuate during Hurricane Dennis.

Can Hypothetical Evacuations Predict Actual Evacuations?

The Bonnie survey gave us a unique opportunity to compare projected behavior with actual actions. Recall that the Bonnie survey included questions relating to how participants would behave during future hurricanes of differing intensity. Participants were asked whether they would evacuate after a hurricane watch announcement, voluntary evacuation order, and mandatory evacuation order was issued. These personal predictions were made eight months before Dennis and Floyd threatened the North Carolina coast.

To facilitate the comparison between the way people said they would behave to the way they actually behaved, we assumed that people who were presented with category one and category two hypothetical storms were placed in a situation similar to Hurricane Dennis, which was forecast as a category one storm that could strengthen to category two. We assumed that respondents who were presented with category three, four, or five storm faced a situation similar to Hurricane Floyd, which was forecast as a category four storm that could strengthen to category five, but landed as a borderline category three.

Of those in the Hurricane Dennis comparison, the hypothetical evacuations correctly predicted 83% of the actual evacuations. The hypothetical evacuations correctly predicted 64% of the actual evacuations in the Hurricane Floyd comparison. The difference in the hypothetical and actual round trip distance traveled by evacuees was calculated for both the Dennis and Floyd sub-samples. For the Dennis group, the average difference in miles driven is high, 87 miles, but the typical difference is 0 miles. The result for the Floyd group is better. The average difference in miles driven is only 5.6 and the typical difference is 0 miles. Seventy-three percent of the Dennis group went to the same type of destination (e.g., hotel/motel) that they said they would. For the Floyd group, 60% went to the same destination.

In general, we find that hypothetical and actual behavior is not much different for these evacuation decisions. While preliminary, our results provide optimism about the usefulness of hypothetical survey questions in emergency management policy.

Summary

In our comparison of hurricane evacuation behavior among coastal North Carolina residents during hurricanes Bonnie, Dennis, and Floyd, we found several differences in the way people behaved. For example, fewer residents said that they closely watched weather reports during Dennis. Fifty-seven percent more residents evacuated for Floyd than for Bonnie, and 140% more residents evacuated for Floyd than for Dennis. Also, the decision to evacuate was more difficult to make during Floyd relative to Bonnie and Dennis. The comparison of the three storms did show that hurricane intensity could indicate when coastal North Carolina residents are more likely to evacuate.

There are also important differences in the household cost of evacuation, with evacuation costs generally increasing with increased storm intensity. When comparing Floyd to Dennis and Bonnie, the round trip distance traveled was over twice that of Dennis and 50% greater than Bonnie. The household evacuation costs and the daily evacuation costs for Floyd were also higher than for Bonnie and Dennis, due largely to the higher automobile costs during Floyd.

Hurricane evacuations are a great cost to coastal communities. Looking back at the 1999 hurricane season, evacuation was a good decision for some North Carolina coastal residents because Dennis and Floyd hit their area. For other evacuees along the Atlantic Coast, Hurricane Dennis and especially Hurricane Floyd were false alarms. Evacuation costs were incurred without a corresponding increase in personal safety. An understanding of evacuation costs for a household should be an important consideration of emergency managers.

As emergency managers plan for future storms they should also understand the reasons why people evacuate. The major determinants of whether someone evacuates were similar for the three hurricanes. The evacuation decision depends on pet ownership, whether evacuation orders are received, and if residents live in a mobile home. The risk of flooding, gender, and education were important evacuation factors for Bonnie, while for Dennis race was an important determinant. In general, households make evacuation decisions that are consistent from one hurricane to another and from one hurricane season to another. Unfortunately, not all residents in storm surge zones evacuate. And some residents who are not at risk from flooding evacuate their homes, clogging roads, shelters, and motels. Several changes could be implemented to ensure that those at highest risk evacuate. For example, pet friendly shelters and motels would allow many pet owners to feel more comfortable about leaving their home. Education about the risk of flooding would also improve the evacuation decision process.

Comparing the hypothetical hurricane behavior collected for the Bonnie survey with actual behavior during the 1999 hurricane season revealed that hypothetical and actual behavior is surprisingly similar for the likelihood of evacuation, distance traveled, and destination decisions. While preliminary, we are optimistic about the usefulness of hypothetical survey questions in providing important information for emergency management decisions. Little is known about how people would behave when confronted with a catastrophic event (e.g., a category five hurricane). Answers to hypothetical survey questions can provide insights about the impacts of these events and, therefore, aid in planning for them.

The overall goal of this research is to assist emergency managers in developing predictive models about behavior during an approaching hurricane. Good predictive models will help improve future emergency management decisions. We are currently working to build these models and use them to 1) develop a matrix of evacuation cost estimates for different storm categories and evacuation order scenarios; 2) investigate the reasons why evacuation decisions differ over the 1998 and 1999 hurricane seasons; and 3) explore the usefulness of hypothetical evacuation behavior to predict the impacts of catastrophic hurricanes.

References

Avila, L. A. 1998. Preliminary report: Hurricane Bonnie, 19-30 August 1998. National Hurricane Center. <http://www.nhc.noaa.gov/1998bonnie.html>.

Baker, E. J. 1991. Hurricane evacuation behavior. International Journal of Mass Emergencies and Disasters 9:287–310.

Beven, J. 2000. Preliminary report: Hurricane Dennis 24 August-7 September 1999. National Hurricane Center. <http://www.nhc.noaa.gov/1999dennis_text.html>.

Dow, K., and S. L. Cutter. Crying wolf: Repeat responses to hurricane evacuation orders. Coastal Management 26:237–251.

Maiolo, J. R., A. Delia, J. C. Whitehead, B. Edwards, K. Wilson, M. Van Willigen, C. Williams, and M. Meekins. 1999. A socioeconomic hurricane evacuation analysis and hurricane evacuation impact assessment tool (methodology) for coastal North Carolina: A case study of Hurricane Bonnie. Regional Development Services, Greenville, N.C.: East Carolina University.

Pasch, R. J., T. B. Kimberlain, and S. R. Stewart. 2000. Preliminary report: Hurricane Floyd, 7–17 September 1999. National Hurricane Center. <http://www.nhc.noaa.gov/1999floyd_text.html>.

Peacock, W. G., and H. Gladwin. 1992. Assessing the likelihood of evacuation next time: Some preliminary findings from the FIU Hurricane Andrew survey. The Institute for Public Opinion Re search, Miami, Fla.: Florida International University.

Tropical Prediction Center. 1999. The Saffir-Simpson hurricane scale. National Hurricane Center. <http://www.nhc.noaa.gov/aboutsshs.html>.

Whitehead, J. C., B. Edwards, M. Van Willigen, J. R. Maiolo, and K. Wilson. 2000. A socioeconomic impact analysis for hurricanes Bonnie, Dennis and Floyd. Progress Report to North Carolina Division of Emergency Management and North Carolina Sea Grant Program.

About the Authors: Dr. John Whitehead is associate professor in the Department of Economics and chair of the Coastal and Marine Studies Program at East Carolina University. His research focuses on natural resource and environmental economics. Bob Edwards and Marieke Van Willigen are both assistant professors in the Department of Sociology at ECU. Dr. John Maiolo is emeritus professor in the Department of Sociology at ECU and committee chair of the Hurricane Floyd conference. Dr. Kenneth Wilson is also a professor in the Department of Sociology at ECU and at the university's Survey Research Laboratory. Collectively, these researchers form the ECU team that is currently involved in hurricane evacuation and impact research.

Part II / Evaluating Disaster Response Strategies—A Community Perspective

Helping the Students of Pattillo A+ Elementary School Recover from the Flood Disaster

Carmen V. Russoniello, Thomas K. Skalko, Judy Baker, Jennifer Beatley, and Dana Bingham Alexander

Introduction

"We need recreational therapy," pronounced Dana Alexander, social worker at Pattillo A+ Elementary School in Tarboro, North Carolina, in a telephone conversation soon after Hurricane Floyd. She needed help providing support for 450 fourth and fifth grade students who had been displaced because of flooding. In response to this request, several faculty members from East Carolina University (ECU) arranged for ECU athletes to make weekly trips to the elementary school to engage the students in various activities. Also, individual faculty members specializing in counseling are helping students recover from the lasting effects of the disaster.

The Loss of a School

Located within one of the poorest counties (Edgecombe County) in North Carolina, Tarboro, an historic agricultural tobacco and cotton town, was hit exceptionally hard by the disaster. In the days, weeks, and even months following the flood, Tarboro would experience conditions reminiscent of war. Large sections of the town were evacuated. Helicopters seemed to fly over the town every fifteen minutes during the first days of the flooding. Four days after the hurricane, speaking in Tarboro, President Clinton observed, "... Hurricane Floyd has wreaked havoc in Edgecombe County ... dumping over 20 inches of rain and uprooting hundreds of trees with high winds ... Princeville Montessori and Pattillo School in Tarboro were severely damaged and are still under water."

A Pattillo A+ Elementary School student's drawing captures the drama of the flooding in Tarboro, N.C.

The waters rose quickly and enveloped

entire buildings. Pattillo A+ Elementary School was in the direct path of the floodwater. There was little warning. Students, teachers, administrators lost everything. In a matter of days, the familiar places where the children sat, learned, stored their belongings, and played were gone. No one predicted that the students would never be able to return to their school.

At home, many children were relocated to FEMA housing or temporarily stayed with relatives and friends. There were many changes and losses as a result of Hurricane Floyd, all of which greatly impacted the stability and security of the fourth and fifth grade students at Pattillo A+ Elementary School.

When students did return to school, approximately three weeks after the hurricane, it was to modular classrooms set up adjacent to the Tarboro Armory. The thirty-two makeshift modular classrooms, although adequate and comfortable, gave the school the look of a military compound. Tightly grouped together and connected by sidewalks made from pallets, the modular classrooms have few windows, and the windows that are present look directly at other classroom walls or at the armory parking lot. Two classrooms are separated from the main group of classrooms, leaving the children in these classes to face greater hardship because of additional separation from the rest of the school. A tank on the armory property is within site of the school, and there is currently no playground. There is little outdoor space for running, playing ball, and other physical activities. Overall, the "campus" grounds are crude and inadequate for the growth and developmental needs of grade-school children. The children's inability to participate in regular activities coupled by the devastation of the flooding certainly contributed to the dramatic increase in behavioral problems noted by teachers and administrators.

Pattillo A+ Elementary School after the flood.

Posttraumatic Effects at Pattillo A+ Elementary School

Elementary school children experience specific reactions to trauma associated with disasters. This trauma, or posttraumatic stress, includes withdrawal, apathy, anxiety, depression, somatization, hostility towards peers, parents, and others, decreased interest in activities, and insomnia (National Institutes of Health 1999). In addition, posttraumatic stress results in dysfunctional behaviors and decreased performance in school. It is measurable well beyond the event. Children show difficulty in concentrating, remembering, and controlling emotions. The cumulative effect can be seen as they do poorer on assignments and tests (American Academy of Pediatrics 1999; Sleek 1998; National Association for Social Workers 1999). Notably, children with preexisting risk factors, such as physical and psychological problems, are particularly vulnerable to the lasting effects from a disaster and should be sought out for intervention (American Academy of Pediatrics 1999).

Incredibly, children in elementary school often still believe that death and loss are forms of punishment. How cruel to think that any child might feel that they were responsible for a disaster. Left unattended, the symptoms of posttraumatic stress will continue to negatively affect a child's health and performance for an indefinite period of time. For example, in a landmark study conducted four years after Hurricane Andrew, posttraumatic stress was reported in 40% of the most affected children (Sleek 1998).

Approximately 50% of the children of Pattillo A+ lost their homes. Other children lost play areas and personal belongings. The children not directly affected at home lost their school, their "home away from home." Some students expressed survivor's guilt and empathy for classmates who were affected. Pictures drawn during one exercise immediately after students returned to school poignantly depict the sorrow and sadness of the children's losses. While many of these losses were material and can be replaced, others, like innocence and the sense of safety and security, will be difficult, if not impossible, to recapture. Given the vulnerable age of these children, the impact of Hurricane Floyd and its flooding may last a lifetime.

To begin recovering from the flooding disaster, Pattillo students were asked to draw some of their memories about the disaster.

The Intervention

Approximately one month after the crisis, a team consisting of ECU students and faculty were briefed on the situation at Pattillo A+. Using their own transportation, the ECU students drove fifty-four miles roundtrip from Greenville to Tarboro every Monday, Wednesday, and Friday afternoon. It is noteworthy that some of the ECU students involved in the relief project lost their homes and/or belongings in the flood. Their actions in this volunteer effort epitomize the sprit of altruism.

The ECU intervention teams immediately began to systematically work with one classroom at a time until all children had an opportunity to begin the healing process. The initial goal was teaching coping skills to assist the children to deal with stress and to facilitate the process of healing through a series of recreational and other biopsychological activities.

Shortly after this initial effort began, the ECU Department of Recreation and Leisure Studies and the School of Health and Human Performance suggested adopting Pattillo A+ Elementary. A committee consisting of faculty from Health Education, Exercise and Sport Science, and Recreation and Leisure Studies met and planned a multi-faceted approach to address the needs of Pattillo's children and teachers. The disaster relief project was granted the use of a van to transport students to and from Pattillo, and a graduate assistant was assigned to help coordinate the project. These two additions directly contributed to the expansion of the project and allowed more effective delivery of services.

A number of individuals and volunteer organizations assisted in the acquisition of recreational equipment, sportswear, and school supplies. These groups included the Recreation and Leisure Studies Student Society, other campus societies, and volunteer associations. One student group raised donations that enabled the children to enjoy a professional presentation of *Charlotte's Web.* One volunteer group delivered flowers, others provided prizes for those students that were impacted by the floods but were still excelling in school. Other activities included a stress management seminar for teachers and training sessions for student volunteers.

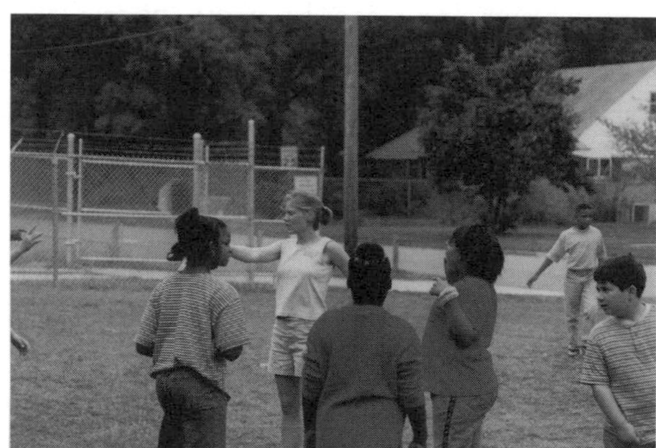
An ECU student organizes play activities.

Current Status of the Intervention

The disaster relief project

The disaster relief project for Pattillo A+ is a formal, three-tier volunteer program. Graduate and undergraduate students are currently delivering a comprehensive program of physical and social activities designed to promote cognitive, social, emotional, and physical development and to enhance strategies for coping with stress. The program, Children Overcoming Posttraumatic Stress Experiences (COPE), employs a biopsychosocial program strategy and includes a cognitive\behavioral stress control component. This type of program was found effective in increasing the use of appropriate coping strategies and self-concept of school-aged children (Henderson and Kelbey 1992). ECU students are leading classroom groups to help students identify and cope with stress (cognitive/behavioral). They also facilitate growth and development with recreational activities (biopsychosocial), which also decreases the negative symptoms associated with posttramautic stress. In addition, high-risk students, identified by a teacher rating scale developed from criteria outlined in the American Psychiatric Association's *Diagnostic and Statistical Manual IV*, were asssigned to undergraduate and graduate students for one-on-one and small group services.

Project materials and resources

As a result of a tremendous amount of work, numerous products have been developed for this relief project. We developed a disaster relief manual and a disaster relief rating scale. In addition, a web site accessed through the School of Health and Human Performance was created (<http://www.ecu.edu/rcls/pattillo/pattillo.htm>). The web page will eventually include disaster relief resources for children and adults, links to other disaster relief sites, on-going projects, and a section where children can share their experiences. In the near future, the Recreation and Leisure Studies Department will assist in the development and planning of a new playground. Recreational therapy faculty and students are committed to continuing the COPE program and other intervention services at Pattillo. Data on the impact of the COPE program will soon be analyzed to determine the program's effectiveness and if modifications are needed.

Summary

The Pattillo A+ project is the first of its kind. It demonstrates the effectiveness of a planned biopsychosocial intervention and provides a point of reference for future disaster relief efforts. The project has become a successful learn-and-serve project. ECU students are learning and practicing the recreational therapy process and reaping the benefits of altruism. The children of Pattillo A+ continue to learn how to effectively cope with the aftermath of a disaster and with general life problems. This project demonstrates that in spite of the pain caused by a natural disaster, many positive experiences can occur for those who need assistance and those providing assistance. Finally, the Pattillo project illustrates the practical application of recreational therapy and its contribution in the reduction of posttraumatic stress symptoms.

References

American Academy of Pediatrics, Work Group on Disasters. 1999. Psychosocial issues for children and families in disasters: A guide for the primary care physician. Elk Grove Village, Ill.: American Academy of Pediatrics. <http://www.mentalhealth.org/publications//allpubs/sma95-3022/sma3022.htm>.

American Psychiatric Association. 1994. Diagnostic and statistical manual IV. Washington, D.C.: American Psychiatric Association.

Kelbey, T. 1992. Effects of a stress-control program on children's locus of control, self-concept, and coping behavior. School Counselor 40(2):125–126.

National Association of Social Workers. 1999. Social workers offer tips for coping with stress from disasters.

Washington D.C.: National Association of Social Workers. <http://www.naswdc.org/practice/distips.htm>

Sleek, S. 1998. After the storm, children play out fears. American Psychological Association Monitor Online 29(6). <http://www.apa.org/monitor/jun98/child.html>

About the Authors: Dr. Carmen Russoniello is an assistant professor in the Department of Recreation and Leisure Studies at East Carolina University. His research interests include the science and ethics of recreational therapy, the medicinal benefits of recreation participation, biofeedback, and the psychophysiology of recreation, fun, and play. Dr. Skalko is professor and chair of the Department of Recreation and Leisure Studies, with research interests focusing on recreational therapy, public policy, and program evaluation. A lecturer in ECU's Department of Health Education and Promotion, Judy B. Baker, has studied volunteerism, community needs and services, and issues relating to alcohol and drug abuse, and mental health. Jennifer Beatley is currently an ECU graduate student working with Dr. Russoniello. Dana Bingham Alexander has been a school social worker in Edgecombe County for the past two years and involved in social work for over thirteen years.

Looking into the Face of the Storm: The Children

Lane Geddie and Lesly T. Mega

Lane Geddie is an assistant professor in the Department of Psychology at East Carolina University, specializing in pediatric psychology and child abuse. Dr. Mega is a professor of Child and Adolescent Psychiatry at the Brody School of Medicine, East Carolina University. Dr. Geddie and Dr. Mega directed an interdisciplinary project designed to meet the mental health needs of school-aged flood victims in the Pitt County school system.

Lane Geddie—

We're so excited to be able to discuss how the flooding impacted children in Pitt County. The schools were out for about two weeks after the flooding. Teachers and the children had no idea to what extent their schools were damaged or what had happened to individual students and teachers. The families of about 2,000 children suffered severe property damage, some completely lost their home—this represents about 10% of the total Pitt County school population. We know from other disasters that school systems frequently face drops in grades, increased absenteeism, problems with discipline, increased depression, panic attacks, and feelings of anxiety. So after students returned to school, school officials were really concerned about how to help the students. Unfortunately, in Pitt County, at that time, we had suffered some losses in our mental health center, with fewer folks available to provide therapy services, so we really didn't have a lot of extra services available to handle the influx that was expected.

With that in mind, the schools requested some assistance from East Carolina University (ECU) to try to help meet the mental health needs. The goal of our project is to evaluate the emotional needs for Pitt County's school children and to provide school-based and family-group interventions to help address those needs. The services are provided through ECU students and faculty. We have about forty people working with us from four different university departments: psychology, marriage and family therapy, nursing, and psychiatry.

We set into place a three-phase program. The first phase deals with group screening. Initially, we have six schools that chose to do a school-wide screening to try to determine the mental health needs of the students. We have five schools that chose to just screen the students that they know suffered some extensive damage. Now, school-wide screening may be a better approach because some research indicates that you can't really predict very well which kids are going to have a strong reaction to a disaster.

We know that with increased severity of exposure to the disaster, victims have a tendency to have more emotional problems. But many times children who are not severely impacted will have significant problems. Parents and teachers don't often predict those children very well. We were hoping to do as many school-wide screenings as we could. But there are many difficulties with this type of screening. First, we needed to get parental permission, and we know that it is very difficult to get permission slips returned. The numbers range pretty widely in our school-wide screenings, from about 40% to as high as 100%, depending on the number of children that were identified in the initial screening.

Lesly Mega—

Well, as we are putting some of our findings together, we were most impressed with what some of the children actually said. Basically, we have found what other people have found: our children are all worried, our children are nervous, they're experiencing emotional distress, and physical distress is resulting from the emotional distress. They are also sad. Some of them are sad about losing things. They want to know where their things are and if they will be found. Others are worried about what other people have lost. To this day some children even talk about suicide. Even though the event happened awhile back, they are still experiencing loss and are still upset.

Some kids are irritable and say so. Other kids don't express their irritation; they act it out. We have seen more children getting into fights and getting suspended from school than ever before. On the more positive side, some children have become more spiritual and some have gotten closer to their family. As an example of the range of the responses, consider what this six-year-old said:

> I was worried about Lucky my cat. After fourteen days of being separated from Lucky, I didn't know what happened to him, but there he was. He hugged us, and he was real happy to see us, and he was so hungry that we didn't know what to do to give him food, and we missed him so much.

Now her eight-year-old brother, on the other hand, worried about more adult-type things, like losing their home or his father losing his job. He was very, very concerned about the food they had to eat. He actually kept a diary of what they ate each day. Basic day-to-day needs were very important to him.

A seven-year-old boy described being afraid that another flood was going to happen. Every time it rains, he has this feeling. When he does talk about the flood, or when it rains, he gets a headache or a stomachache. Another seven-year-old also has physical symptoms. I'm not sure what to make of this because there were some bacterial viruses that people might have gotten from the floodwaters. But this child's mother reported that her child experienced more colds, more fevers, nausea, vomiting, headaches and stomachaches than she had seen before the storms, and that it seems to be related to wind.

Every time it's windy this child crawls into bed with her mother and will not get out.

A ten-year-old talked about toys she lost. After the flooding, when she got back into her home, although some things were salvaged, her material things were not. She couldn't remember they were lost. She would go up to her room, look for them, and then come back and feel very upset that her favorite doll and her favorite toy, which her grandmother had given her, were no longer there. She was very sad, particularly because the toy from her grandmother was not replaceable.

Older students also had problems. I'll share the experience of two teenagers, a brother and sister. One is fifteen and the other is eighteen. They suffered many losses, but they did not lose their home. Both of them describe difficulty falling asleep and both have nightmares. They worried another flood would come. They worried that they might die. The fifteen-year-old girl said she was getting into more fights in school, and her eighteen-year-old brother said that he did not feel accepted any more. He said, "I feel invisible." He and his sister said that they are worried about themselves, but they are more worried about other people, people who actually lost their homes. In general, they are worried about people who are worse off than they are. In psychological terms we call this survivor's guilt. This is something we have to help them deal with.

We did find that those who were exposed to more devastation did have more symptoms. Also, children had other pressures on top of dealing with the flood. One teenage girl delivered a baby while she was in a shelter. Obviously she doubled or tripled the amount of pressure in her life.

I want to end by describing some of the obstacles we faced in trying to help the children in Pitt County. Not only did we have difficulty getting permission from the parents to let us screen their kids, but we also had problems when we tried to intervene to help them in groups. Another problem was getting enough people into the schools to assess which students were in trouble and to help them. A third problem was with the overall school system. Our schools were pressured into worrying about end-of-school grades and achievement. I think that this stopped school personnel from trying to help us with some of the emotional problems we found, because they were under stress to meet performance expectations in addition to stresses related to the flood.

Hurricane Storm Surge: Cost-Effective Mitigation in Wilmington, North Carolina

Robert T. Burrus, Jr., Christopher F. Dumas, and J. Edward Graham, Jr.

Introduction

Hurricanes cause billions of dollars in property damage along the East and Gulf Coasts of the United States. Hurricane Hugo inflicted close to $8 billion in damage in South Carolina in 1989. Hurricane Andrew left an estimated $28.62 billion in property damage in south Florida in 1992, while Floyd caused $5.45 billion in damage in eastern North Carolina in 1999 (Hebert et al. 1997; N.C. Office of the Governor 1999). After accounting for changes in purchasing power, population, and wealth, Pielke and Landsea (1998, 1999) found that the average annual U.S. hurricane damage for the 73 years ending in 1997 was $5.2 billion; they also noted that increasing coastal development exacerbates potential damage

Much of this damage is attributable to storm surge. *Storm surge* is defined as the increase in sea level height above the average height, or mean sea level (MSL), due to storm-generated winds. Although extreme tropical weather rainfall may cause upstream flood damage (as was evidenced by Floyd), the primary flood threat in coastal areas is storm surge.

Storm surge-related costs are the sum of uninsured storm surge damages, flood insurance premiums, and the costs of any structural improvements undertaken to reduce potential damages. Homeowners minimize storm surge-related costs in two ways. First, they choose a deductible level for any flood insurance policy they purchase. Choosing a higher deductible decreases insurance premium costs but increases potential uninsured storm surge damage costs. Second, although coastal building codes are designed to protect property against storm surge flooding, owners may choose to make defensive structural improvements beyond code to provide added protection. Structural defenses for flood protection include elevation on fill or pilings, construction of levees and floodwalls, and house relocation.

Motivated by the recent series of hurricane strikes affecting Wilmington, North Carolina—Bertha, Fran, Bonnie, Dennis, and Floyd—we gather data on hurricane strike probabilities and intensities, storm surge flood depths associated with storms of various intensities, insurance premiums and deductibles, and types and costs of structural defenses for a hypothetical residential property in the region. Using these data, we calculate the cost-effective (i.e., cost-minimizing) combination of insurance deductible and structural defenses for the representative home over a thirty-year planning period.

The Residential Structure

We consider a hypothetical residential property representative of the Wilmington region. Rogers (1985, 1994) suggests that most residential structures in the region meet building codes; thus, we assume that the home conforms to the 1999 North Carolina building code.

The property is a new, 2,150 square foot, one-story, wood-frame residential structure with vinyl siding valued at $140,000. The structure includes three bedrooms, two bathrooms, and a two-car garage. The home's contents are valued at 70% of the structure's value, or $98,000. It is located within five miles of the ocean, but is far enough inland to escape direct wave action in the event of storm surge flooding. In addition, *the structure is not at risk for upstream flooding*, an assumption consistent with Wilmington's geography.

The ground elevation of the study property is 9 feet above MSL. This elevation is representative of several important locations in the region, including the downtown Wilmington waterfront, downtown Carolina Beach, and sections of downtown Wrightsville Beach. We also assume that the structure is raised on a 3-foot crawl space. The study property is located in a participating National Flood Insurance Program (NFIP) community. (Most eastern N.C. communities participate in NFIP.) Because the home is located within a Special Flood Hazard Area (flood zone A10), as identified by a Flood Insurance Rate Map (FIRM), it must be elevated above base flood elevation (10 feet above MSL) to qualify for NFIP insurance. Atop its crawlspace, the home rests 2 feet above base flood elevation; hence, NFIP flood insurance is available to the owner.

Potential Damages and the Homeowner's Mitigation Options

Storm surge damages

We use output from the National Weather Service's (NWS) Sea, Lake and Overland Surges from Hurricanes (SLOSH) model (Jarvinen and Lawrence 1985), calibrated for Wilmington, North Carolina, to estimate the relationship between tropical weather wind speed and storm surge for the study location. In general, as wind speed increases, storm surge levels increase at an increasing rate. Table 1 gives predicted storm surge levels by hurricane category for the Wilmington area.

The flood depth experienced within a structure depends on storm surge level, ground elevation, and whether any structural defenses for flood protection have been implemented. A *zero damage elevation* (ZDE) is the elevation above MSL at which floodwater first enters a structure. ZDE for the home is 12 feet—the 9-foot ground elevation plus the 3-foot crawl space. For the representative property, a 15.2-foot storm surge produces a 6.2-foot depth above ground elevation and a 3.2-foot flood depth within the home (above ZDE).

Table 1. Tropical storm categories with the associated wind speed ranges, storm surge height, and flood depth. The last column is the probability that each category storm will impact our hypothetical Wilmington, N.C., home in a given year (MSL = mean sea level; ZDE = zone damage elevation).

Saffir-Simpson Storm Category	Maximum Sustained Wind Speed (mph)	Midpoint Wind Speed (mph)	Storm Surge[1] (feet above MSL)	Flood Depth[2] (feet above ZDE)	Annual Probability[3]
Tropical Storm	39–73	56.0	1.9	0.0	0.15336
Category 1	74–95	84.5	5.0	0.0	0.02826
Category 2	96–110	103.0	7.6	0.0	0.00817
Category 3	111–130	120.5	10.6	0.0	0.00520
Category 4	131–154	143.0	15.2	3.2	0.00254
Category 5	155+	175.0	22.9	10.9	0.00010

[1]Based on NWS Sea, Lake and Overland Surges for Hurricanes (SLOSH) model
[2]Assumes Zero Damage elevation (ZDE) is 12 feet above MSL
[3]Source: Neumann 2000; based on the NWS's HURISK model

Flood depths are listed in Table 1 for each tropical weather category. Note that hurricane categories 1–3 (Hurricane Floyd was a borderline category three storm) do not flood the representative home. In the event of a category four or category five hurricane, both the structure and its contents suffer flood damage. Damage estimates are based on FEMA Actuarial Information System claims data (USCE 1993). The data allow for estimating the relationship between flood depth and the amount of damage to a structure and the value of its contents, expressed as a percentage. For a given flood depth, the percentage of contents damage is typically higher than the percentage of structural damage, because most valuable items in a home are close to the ZDE elevation (i.e., furniture and major appliances rest on the floor). Accordingly, we consider structure and contents damages separately. As an example, a 3.2-foot effective flood depth is expected to cause *structural* damage equal to 26% of a structure's value, or $36,400 (0.26 times the $140,000 home value). The same 3.2-foot flood depth is expected to cause *contents* damage equal to 32% of content value, or $31,360 (0.32 times the $98,000 contents value). Thus, a category four hurricane causes approximately $67,760 worth of total damage. As flood depth increases, each type of damage increases, but the incremental additions to damage get smaller and smaller. A 10.9-foot flood depth from a category five hurricane is expected to cause $126,980 worth of total damage, or 48% of structure value and 61% of contents value are destroyed.

Structural defenses

Property owners have several structural options *beyond building code requirements* to better protect their homes. A homeowner can choose to relocate a house, elevate it on fill or pilings, or build floodwalls and levees. (USCE 1993, 1997, 1998; FEMA 1998). Floodwalls do not harden the shoreline, but rather immediately surround and protect the home. Data on the costs of achieving various degrees of flood protection for each type of structural defense are found in Burrus, Dumas, and Graham (2000).

In general, costs are higher for structures built on slab foundations relative to crawl-space foundations. The case study structure has a crawl space foundation. Figure 1 shows the costs of various structural defenses for a house with this type of foundation.

The property owner calculates the least-cost method of achieving a given level of flood protection using defensive structural improvements. Figure 1 reveals that for a flood depth of 6 feet, adding fill dirt prevents flooding at a cost of $11.87 per square foot, elevating the house costs approximately $18.00 per square foot, relocating the house costs $27.00 per square foot, or building a 6-foot-high levee around the house costs $40.00 per square foot. In this case, the owner would choose fill dirt.

Least-cost structural defenses are the "lowest" points in Figure 1. Prior to construction, Figure 1 indicates that the least-cost flood damage reducing activity for low flood depths is simply to add fill dirt. However, the cost of raising an *existing* home on fill dirt is much higher. For an existing home, levees and floodwalls are the least-cost responses to the threat of low flood depths. For higher flood depths, raising the house on pilings and, for even higher flood depths, total relocation of the house are the least-cost options. Ruling out house relocation, raising the structure on pilings is the least-cost defense for higher flood depths. Work, Rogers, and Osborne (1999) support this conclusion; their study of coastal flood retrofit activities in North Carolina finds that a majority (77%) of survey respondents choose piling elevation. (Elevation on pilings also provides under-home parking and dry storage benefits.)

As expenditures on least-cost structural defenses increase, flood damages resulting from a given flood depth decrease more and more quickly. The reason is that moderate elevation protects only the *upper* portion of a house, where little value is located, whereas further elevation protects the *lower* portion of the house, where most contents value is located.

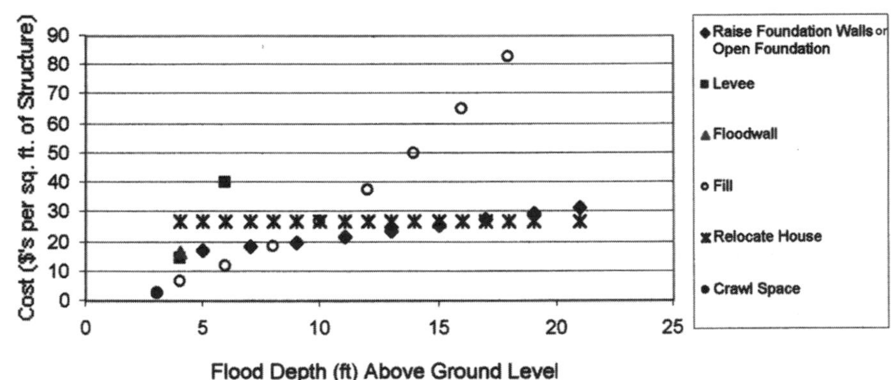

Figure 1. Costs of protecting a residential structure with a crawl space foundation against various flood depths for representative structural defenses that were designed to reduce flood damage.

Flood insurance

Although standard homeowner's insurance policies do *not* provide coverage against flood losses, the federal government offers subsidized flood insurance to homeowners through the National Flood Insurance Program (NFIP). When choosing flood insurance, the owner chooses a combination of an insurance premium and deductible. NFIP policies feature separate deductibles for the structure and its contents, each ranging from $500 to $5,000. Based on current combinations of premiums and deductibles, we estimate the relationship between the two and allow the owner to choose *any* deductible level up to the value of the home. As higher deductibles are chosen, premiums decrease. As is typical in the Wilmington region, we assume that if owners insure, they insure for the full value of the structure and contents and choose the same deductible for each.

Probabilities, Expected Damages, and Expected Storm Surge Costs

When choosing among various mitigation activities, homeowners estimate the likelihood of suffering hurricane strikes of various storm categories. Table 1 provides the National Weather Service's (NWS) HURISK computer model estimates of the annual probabilities of Wilmington experiencing hurricane wind speeds of various intensities. These estimates are current and consider all 1999 hurricane strikes including Dennis and Floyd. The annual strike probabilities reported in Table 1 are *lower* than many homeowners might expect. After factoring in Wilmington's rash of hurricane strikes over the last four years, the probability of the region experiencing severe wind speeds due to tropical weather is still quite small.

We assume that homeowners use these probabilities in their estimation of *expected* damage. Expected storm surge damages for any year are computed by multiplying the probability of a hit from a specific category hurricane by the damage caused by that category, and then summing these value over all the categories, given existing structural mitigation. For a home unprotected above building code guidelines, categories 1–3 cause no damage (Table 1). But damage does result from a category four storm, with a strike probability of 0.00254, and from a category five storm, with a strike probability of 0.0001. Thus, using the storm surge damage costs calculated previously for these two categories, the annual expected damages are (0.00254 x $67,760) + (0.0001 x $126,980), or $184.80. Expected damages are lower if the owner purchases structural defenses. The owner pays for damages up to the deductible amount.

Expected storm surge-related costs are the sum of uninsured expected storm surge damages, flood insurance premiums, and the costs of any structural defenses undertaken to reduce potential damages. We make the simplifying assumption that structural defenses last thirty years. Alternatively, both insurance premiums and expected damages are incurred on an annual basis.

Cost-Effective Allocation of Insurance and Structural Defenses

Using computer simulations, we calculate the combinations of insurance deductibles and least-

Table 2. The cost-minimizing values for four hurricane strike probability scenarios.

Variable	Hurricane Strike Probability Scenario: Table 1 Probability Data	1.69x Table 1 Probability Data	3.5x Table 1 Probability Data	3.98x Table 1 Probability Data
Structural Defenses ($/ft²)	$0	$0	$0	$0
Flood Insurance Premium ($/yr)	$0	$283	$322	$365
Flood Insurance Deductible ($/yr)	$238,000	$10,000	$5,465	$1,000
Value of Structural Defenses, Premiums and Uncovered Damages ($)	$2,407	$4,064	$4,626	$4,675

Table 3. The cost-minimizing values for four hurricane strike probability scenarios and tripled insurance premiums.

Variable	Hurricane Strike Probability Scenario: Table 1 Probability Data	5.1x Table 1 Probability Data	10x Table 1 Probability Data	11.94x Table 1 Probability Data
Structural Defenses ($/ft²)	$0	$0	$0	$0
Flood Insurance Premium ($/yr)	$0	$849	$921	$1099
Flood Insurance Deductible ($/yr)	$238,000	$10,000	$7,167	$1,000
Value of Structural Defenses, Premiums, and Uncovered Damages ($)	$2,407	$12,203	$13,773	$14,027

cost structural defenses that minimize all expected storm surge-related costs over a thirty-year planning period. Structural mitigation activities are purchased when $1 spent at the beginning of the thirty-year period prevents more than $1 in expected damages (discounted at 7%) over the entire period. Insurance is purchased when $1 spent on annual insurance premiums prevents more than $1 in annual uninsured expected damage. We consider several scenarios defined by alternative hurricane strike probabilities and insurance rates.

Given current hurricane strike probabilities, Table 2 reveals that the cost-minimizing property owner purchases no structural defenses or flood insurance. In fact, the second column of Table 2 shows that hurricane probabilities must be increased by 69% (1.69 times the probability data for a category four and five storm listed in Table 1) to encourage the cost-minimizing homeowner to buy a $10,000 deductible flood policy. Even in that case, no structural defenses are purchased. With hurricane strike risks increased 3.5-fold, only flood insurance, albeit with a deductible of "only" $5,465, is purchased. No structural defenses are utilized. Hurricane probabilities must

Table 4. The cost-minimizing values for three hurricane strike probability scenarios, with no insurance available.

Variable	Hurricane Strike Probability Scenario: Table 1 Probability Data	17.49x Table 1 Probability Data	167x Table 1 Probability Data
Structural Defenses ($/ft²)	$0	$18.50	$25.39
Flood Insurance Premium ($/yr)	n.a.	n.a	n.a
Flood Insurance Deductible ($/yr)	n.a	n.a	n.a
Value of Structural Defenses, Premiums, and Uncovered Damages ($)	$2,412	$41,995	$54,588

n.a= not available

increase 3.98 times to justify paying the high flood insurance premiums necessary to purchase the minimum combined deductible of $1,000. Under these increased strike probabilities, the present value of all expected costs increases to $4,675, but this is inadequate to justify a structural defense purchase.

Table 3 presents the results of a second set of simulations in which flood insurance rates are tripled. In this case, insurance is not purchased until the risks of hurricane flooding increase 5.1 times. The last two columns of Table 3 reveal that no structural defenses are purchased, even under greatly increased hurricane risks and higher insurance rates. The present value of hurricane costs increases to $14,027 and includes an annual insurance premium of $1,099.

Table 4 presents results for a final set of simulations in which flood insurance is completely unavailable. We find that the cost-minimizing homeowner denied flood insurance begins to purchase structural defenses only when strike risks increase almost eighteen-fold. Although the present value of expected damages increases greatly without insurance, the high costs of structural defenses preclude their cost-effective purchase until the probability of a storm surge increases greatly. However, this set of simulations demonstrates that the cost-minimizing homeowner *will* buy structural defenses if expected damages increase sufficiently.

Summary

The decisions of individual homeowners regarding insurance and defensive home improvements impact regional hurricane damages, insurance industry liability, construction demand, and coastal property values. Given existing insurance options and hurricane strike probabilities, the purchase of structural defenses *beyond building code requirements* for a representative property in the Wilmington, North Carolina, region is not cost-effective. Though Hurricane Floyd caused enormous upstream flooding, Floyd's impact on annual storm surge probabilities (Table 1) was minimal. Floyd does not significantly alter the cost-effective storm surge mitigation decision for the representative coastal property owner.

Under higher strike probabilities, insurance purchases are a better dollar-for-dollar value than additional structural defenses, even if insurance premiums are tripled. Only if flood insurance is unavailable does the cost-minimizing owner purchase structural defenses. We suspect that structural defense purchases observed "in the field" may be explained by either 1) differences between actual hurricane strike probabilities and strike probabilities as perceived by homeowners or 2) homeowner risk aversion. The authors are currently investigating this issue.

These findings suggest that government insurance subsidy programs, such as the NFIP, reduce the effectiveness of government structural mitigation programs, such as some components of FEMA's Project Impact. In addition, both programs likely distort homeowner choices in ways that raise the total costs of hurricane defense. On the other hand, government *research and education* programs (such as other components of Project Impact) that provide information on 1) hurricane strike probabilities; 2) expected damages; and 3) reductions in expected damages due to specific mitigation activities, would likely improve the efficiency of homeowner choices and reduce overall defense costs.

The results presented here are illustrative but are not necessarily germane to all property types, locations, or individuals. Cost-effective combinations of insurance and structural defenses likely differ from region to region. As well, some owners are willing to incur considerable costs to preserve property for its sentimental value. The "best" response to any risk must include consideration of such personal factors in addition to monetary costs.

Acknowledgements

We thank an anonymous reviewer for comments that improved the quality of our paper. This research was funded in part by grants from the Center for Applied Real Estate Education and Research, University of South Carolina, and the Charles L. Cahill Faculty Research and Development Award Program, University of North Carolina at Wilmington. This paper is a contribution to the UNCW Cameron School of Business Working Paper Series (No. 2000-02-006).

References

Burrus, R., C. Dumas, and E. Graham. 2000. Reducing expected hurricane damage costs: A microeconomic perspective. UNCW Cameron School of Business Working Paper Series No. 2000-02-001.

Hebert, P. J., J. D. Jarrell, and M. Mayfield. 1997. The deadliest, costliest and most intense United States hurricanes of this century (and other frequently requested hurricane facts). NOAA Technical Memorandum. NWS TPC-1. Miami, Fla.: National Hurricane Center.

Jarvinen, B. R., and M. B. Lawrence. 1985. An evaluation of the SLOSH storm-surge model. Bulletin of the American Meteorological Society 66:1408–1411.

Neumann, C. 2000. Personal Communication with first author. National Hurricane Center, Miami, Fla.

North Carolina Office of the Governor. 1999. Governor Hunt calls special session for flood relief. Press release 8 December 1999. Raleigh, N.C.: North Carolina Office of the Governor.

Pielke, R. A., Jr., and C. W. Landsea. 1998. Normalized Atlantic hurricane damage, 1925–1995. Weather Forecasting 13: 621-631.

Pielke, R. A., Jr., and C. W. Landsea. 1999. La Niña, El Niño and Atlantic hurricane damages in the United States. Bulletin of the American Meteorological Society, Boston. October.

Rogers, S. M., Jr. 1985. Hurricane Diana: Impact on coastal development. Coastal Zone 2:2468–2486.

Rogers, S. M., Jr. 1994. Hurricane Andrew and the south Florida building code: Relevance to the North Carolina building code. Raleigh, N.C.:University of North Carolina Sea Grant.

U.S. Army Corps of Engineers (USCE). 1993. Flood proofing: How to evaluate your options. U.S. Army Corps of Engineers, National Flood Proofing Committee. Washington, D.C.

U.S. Army Corps of Engineers (USCE). 1997. Flood proofing: Techniques, programs and references. U.S. Army Corps of Engineers, National Flood Proofing Committee. Washington, D.C.

U.S. Army Corps of Engineers (USCE). 1998. Flood proofing performance: Successes and failures. U.S. Army Corps of Engineers, National Flood Proofing Committee. Washington, D.C.

U.S. Federal Emergency Management Agency (FEMA). 1998. Homeowner's guide to retrofitting: Six ways to protect your house from flooding. FEMA 312. Washington, D.C.: Federal Emergency Management Agency.

Work, P. A., S. M. Rogers, Jr., and R. Osborne. 1999. Flood retrofit of coastal residential structures: Outer Banks, North Carolina. Journal of Water Resources Planning and Management 125(2):88–93.

About the Authors: Dr. Robert Burrus is an assistant professor of economics in the Cameron School of Business, Department of Economics and Finance at the University of North Carolina at Wilmington. In addition to his research on the economics of hurricanes, Dr. Burrus also studies the economics of illicit drug policy. His colleague, Dr. Christopher Dumas is an assistant professor of economics, with research interests in environmental and natural resource economics and applied microeconomics, while J. Edward Graham, professor of finance, studies real estate investment analysis. Both are also on the faculty of the Cameron School of Business, Department of Economics and Finance at UNCW.

A Dialogue: Responding to the Long-Term Recovery Needs of Disaster Victims

Marieke Van Willigen

Starting the Dialogue

The Questions: *How do community-level impacts from extreme weather events, such as Hurricane Floyd, change over an extended time period? Based on the experiences associated with Hurricane Floyd, should we reexamine the current recovery assistance protocols used for dealing with natural disasters?*

The discussion was guided by **Glenn Woodard**, Director, Response Recovery Division of the Federal Emergency Management Agency (FEMA), and **Chris Coudriet**, a planner in the Nartural Hazards Planning division of the North Carolina Division of Emergency Management. The audience participants were a diverse group, ranging from hazards experts, interfaith fellowship representatives, rescue team members, and banking representatives to flood victims and state emergency management officials.

Introduction

Hurricane Floyd and the floods that followed left scores of households and business owners still struggling to get back on their feet months after the hurricane. The long-term impact of these events is uncertain. But the long-term impacts are likely to be significant if effective, thorough, and continuous monitoring and assistance are absent.

Assistance programs were designed to help victims recover material losses, but were people effectively assisted by these programs? Do these programs adequately address the potential long-term impacts of the hurricane? In order to meet these challenges, programs must be dynamic and responsive to identified needs. The participants in this dialogue discussed some of the changes and improvements that would make the process of receiving recovery assistance easier and more efficient. Some participants also took the opportunity to ask emergency management personnel questions regarding the recovery programs currently in place. This is a summary of participants' direct comments and suggestions, as well as the common themes of the questions asked.

We began by looking at the obstacles in the aid-application process. We also discussed obstacles in the repair of damaged homes, the need for permanent housing for victims left homeless, and the strains of small business owners. Most importantly, we discussed the need of all assistance groups, both public and private, to recognize that the needs of the hurricane and flood victims persisted long after the downed trees were removed and the floodwaters receded.

The Process of Applying for Aid

Many participants identified the recovery assistance process as bureaucratic and confusing. Application forms for obtaining aid are unnecessarily confusing. The terminology associated with recovery assistance, including the names of programs, forms, and verbal communication, must be easier to understand. Programs need names that make sense to those who are seeking help. After a disaster, people are often traumatized and in no condition to wade through complicated paperwork. The process is particularly confusing for those with little education, those who are not fluent English speakers, or those with no previous experience dealing with bureaucracies. As a result, it may take longer for victims to complete paperwork, which would extend the recovery assistance process, increase operation costs, and delay the receipt of aid.

Participants also suggested a clearer organization of disaster application centers and clear identification of the individuals responsible for the different forms of assistance. While participants identified organization as a problem, they also suggested that the entire relief application process needs a more sympathetic face. Several suggestions were offered. Interfaith or other volunteers could be used as a visible presence in the application centers, greeting victims, pointing people in the appropriate direction, and offering a sympathetic ear. Another participant suggested that FEMA and other agencies could more effectively meet victims' needs by providing caseworkers for one-on-one assistance.

These suggestions would also assist victims to have a clearer understanding of the steps they will need to take to receive assistance. Caseworkers should create individualized plans, outlining for each victim the assistance for which they qualify and which they should pursue. This should include the names of the agencies they need to contact and forms they need to complete.

Finally, participants discussed the issue of disclosing case information to victims. Victims need better information about how damage estimates are made, and what decisions are being made on their behalf. Victims are uncertain of their rights to access the information in their recovery assistance files. Without full information about their case, victims cannot effectively pursue the assistance they need.

Receiving Aid

Once recovery assistance has been approved, a problem results when assistance from different sources comes at different times. This makes it difficult for victims to move forward in the recovery process. Repairs are delayed because the funds from all sources are needed before work can begin. Victims may be forced to use recovery assistance funds for short-term needs rather than long-term recovery. The length of time needed to obtain aid must be reduced. As one participant stated, buyouts from Hurricane Fran, which impacted eastern North Carolina in 1996, still have not been completed. To address the timing problem, the application process should be streamlined. Permanent disaster assistance offices could be established in areas where natural disasters are common events. Participants recognized that disasters vary greatly and that no one plan will work for all disasters. However, permanent recovery personnel could review previous programs and develop future recovery strategies, with the assistance of local, state, and federal agencies, as well as private, nonprofit groups. Such planning could lead to more regionally tailored disaster-education literature and programs.

Making Needed Home Repairs

Even after victims received funds, they often could not get work done on their homes, or the cost estimates they received seemed excessive. Available repair services (e.g., roofers, electricians, plumbers, contractors, carpenters, etc.) were inadequate to meet the demands of flood and hurricane victims. This shortage in repair services could be lessened if out-of-state repair crews were allowed to work in the state during times of extreme need, like after a disaster. Presently, recognizing out-of-state licenses is against the law, so it is imperative that the law be changed. The new law would stipulate that this waiver of in-state licensing would only occur for federally declared or state-declared disaster areas. Also, repair crews would be more likely to come to a disaster area if they were assured housing. It was proposed that empty FEMA trailers could be used. However, it is currently against government policy to use FEMA trailers for this purpose.

Long-term Housing Needs

Emergency management personnel identified their top priority as the continued provision of housing for victims not yet in permanent homes. Many victims whose homes were deemed uninhabitable remain in the FEMA-provided emergency trailers and mobile homes. However, as the questions of several participants indicated, victims and service providers worry about what will happen when the eighteen-month housing assistance period is over. It was recommended that the deadline be extended. The FEMA representative stated that the disaster victims would not be ejected from the emergency trailer parks at the end of the eighteen-month period.

However, extending the emergency housing is not a permanent solution to the housing problem.

Both the participants and discussion leaders agreed that housing families in temporary circumstances for extended periods of time will likely lead to additional problems and slow down individuals' recovery processes. One suggestion was to encourage more victims to purchase FEMA mobile homes through a more aggressive selling program than is currently in use, and at lower prices. However, this strategy might lead to greater difficulties down the road by increasing the number of families in mobile homes, which are particularly at risk to damage during disasters. Speeding up recovery assistance would have the greatest impact on moving families into permanent housing. Participants also underscored the importance of trying to maintain the social networks established within neighborhoods and communities. One participant suggested that finding a means by which entire groups of households could be offered the opportunity to relocate as a block, perhaps through a grouping of resources, could facilitate a timely and permanent relocation.

Finding New Jobs and Helping Small Businesses

Many participants felt that the impact of job loss and business losses had been underappreciated. People who lose jobs due to a natural disaster are obviously at a great economic disadvantage, but they are also doubly disadvantaged in trying to navigate the recovery process. Business assistance programs could also serve indirectly as individual victim assistance. Recovery programs must prioritize keeping distressed businesses in operation so that job losses are minimized and individuals are assisted with getting back to work as quickly as possible.

Participants perceived that small businesses are at particular risk after a disaster and that their needs are not being met. Small business owners do not have the resources to ride through a loss of revenues for even a relatively short period of time. They may be forced to let employees go or even to shut down. New businesses are particularly disadvantaged in the Small Business Administration's (SBA) loan program because they do not have the track record to establish an ability to repay a loan. Participants suggested that some businesses might need relief from debt payments during a shut-down period. Immediate, low-interest SBA loans might help to stave off the need for more extensive financial assistance later. Finally, new business owners should be granted some leeway in establishing financial viability. Plans to assist people who suffer job or business losses need to be undertaken in order to facilitate long-term recovery and continued regional development. Participants expressed concern over how impacts on businesses might effect long-term growth.

Future Construction

There is a critical need to evaluate where new homes and businesses are constructed. Some participants suggested not permitting rebuilding in an area with a history of flooding. Some recommended a moratorium on building in the floodplain in eastern North Carolina. There was a strong consensus that public housing needs to be relocated out of the existing floodplains. Families in these housing units are already at great economic risk and cannot afford the added risk of flood damages. Current city, regional, or county land-use plans should be reevaluated and changed to move construction out of the floodplain. This should be done in conjunction with a remapping of the floodplain boundaries.

Education Programs Can Prepare People for Disasters

Dialogue participants agreed that people living in a disaster-prone region must have a clearer understanding of how a disaster could impact their lives and community. Despite the concerns that the participants identified about the recovery assistance process, they also recognized that the public's sometimes unrealistic or uninformed expectations could lead to stress for both victims and recovery personnel. Emergency management personnel underscored the fact that recovery programs cannot realistically be expected to compensate individuals for all of their losses. Yet, the public expects the government to get them "back on their feet." Unrealized expectations can often add to the emotional stress victims have already endured from losses suffered after a disaster. For example, victims of the floods were confused when they were informed that buyouts did not apply to people not living in a floodplain. Those working at assistance centers should identify the public's expectations for assistance. People should then be educated and informed about what they should realistically expect as the assistance process proceeds.

In eastern North Carolina, the essential first step is to educate people on their realistic risk to flooding. For instance, people who need flood insurance often do not buy it; and many low-income families cannot afford it. Second, whether or not they live in the designated flood zone, people should be informed on how they should document their possessions and important papers. After a disaster hits, the paperwork needed to start the assistance process may simply be gone. If a permanent, regionally based emergency management office were established, these personnel could work with local agencies and nonprofit groups to get disaster preparation messages to their constituencies. One participant suggested that a professional, disaster preparation and response video be developed and shown regularly on public television and to community and faith groups. Participants also suggested that school programs should be developed to educate school-aged children about hurricanes, flood risk, and on how to prepare and recover from these types of disaster. There are specific groups who often do not receive disaster-education information. These vulnerable groups must be identified and specific education strategies that match the needs of that group should be developed. A permanent planning and response office would assist in identifying these groups and the strategies that best meet their needs.

Recommendations for Improved Recovery Response for Disaster Victims

The following recommendations were consistently repeated throughout the session and exhibited consensus:

- Communication between different agencies and between agencies and the public must be improved. People do not always receive the message that different agencies attempt to convey—no matter how hard they try or how much they believe the message was received. Interfaith and other volunteers could be utilized at application centers to help guide victims to needed resources and to put a more sympathetic face on the recovery assistance process. The entire application process should be streamlined, and the names of programs and forms should be changed so they make sense to those seeking help. FEMA caseworkers could be provided for one-on-one assistance.
- The groups that are responsible for creating long-term plans, whether city, country, state, or federal, should be identified and the specific responsibilities of each should be clearly defined. Perhaps a centralized management and planning office could serve to integrate the responsibilities of each group. After a disaster, personnel at a permanent disaster assistance office could assist victims. Before a disaster, they could review current programs and develop future recovery strategies and education programs.
- Individuals need to be empowered to protect themselves from losses. People should be aware of their realistic risk to flooding. Disaster preparation and response videos could be shown regularly on television. School programs could educate children about hurricanes and flood risk. Also, there are many different types of communities in eastern North Carolina, and the education methods that are effective for one group many not be effective for another. Many alternatives for public education on disaster preparation and recovery must be developed.
- Housing needs, both relocation and repairs, are an important piece of the recovery process. Out-of-state repair crews should be allowed to work in the state after a state-declared or federally declared disaster. For victims who face finding a new home, it is important that social networks be included in their recovery. This could involve a joint relocation to a group of households or an entire block, so that victims retain a sense of community and continuity.
- To decrease job losses and small business failures, temporary debt relief could be available to new business owners who have yet to establish the financial profile that is required to secure a low-interest loan.
- There is a need to develop sound, long-term plans that will decrease the impacts of future hurricanes and related disasters on the people of eastern North Carolina. These plans should include

disaster preparation, response, and land-use and growth plans. Preferably, land-use plans should locate homes and business out of the floodplain.

About the Author: Marieke Van Willigen is an assistant professor in the Department of Sociology at East Carolina University. Her research focuses on the impact of volunteer work and social inequality on individuals' physical and psychological well-being. As part of the ECU Social Science Hurricane Research Team, she is currently studying the impacts of Hurricane Floyd on rates of distress and mortality among residents in eastern North Carolina, with a particular emphasis on how these effects vary by gender.

Part III / Dynamics of Hurricanes and Floods: Achieving New Insights—Historical Reflections

Disasters by Design

Dennis S. Mileti

Professor Dennis Mileti is the chair of the Department of Sociology and the director of the Natural Hazards Research Applications and Information Center at the University of Colorado at Boulder. He recently completed the coordination of a national effort to assess knowledge, research, and policy needs for natural and technological hazards and disasters in the United States from a sustainable development viewpoint. He is the author of over 100 publications, primarily focusing on the societal aspects of emergency preparedness and hazard mitigation. Dr. Mileti has a variety of practical, hazard mitigation experiences, including developing emergency response plans for nuclear power plants and serving on the California Seismic Safety Commission. He has been chairman of the Committee on Natural Disasters at the National Academy of Sciences, a member of the Advisory Board on Research at the U.S. Geological Survey, and chair of the Board of Visitors at the Federal Emergency Management Agency's Emergency Management Institute. Dr. Mileti gave a plenary presentation at the conference and was introduced by Dr. Stephen Culver, chair of the Department of Geology at East Carolina University.

Introduction

It has become clear that natural and technological disasters are not problems that can be solved in isolation. Rather, the occurrence of a disaster is a symptom of broader and more basic problems. Often society creates its own disasters. Sometimes this participation is obvious, such as with technological disasters that result from human-created hazards—accidents at nuclear power plants (e.g., the Chernobyl and Three-mile Island disasters), spills of environmentally dangerous toxic pollutants, or the failure of flood-control structures to protect property and people. But human activities also directly increase the impact of natural hazards, both climatological (e.g., hurricanes, droughts, floods, fires, etc.) and geophysical (e.g., earthquakes, volcanoes, landslides, etc.).

Since 1994 a team of over 100 expert academics and practitioners, including members of the private sector, have assessed, evaluated, and summarized knowledge about natural and technological hazards in the United States from the perspectives of the physical, natural, social and behavioral, and engineering sciences. This paper and the report on which it is based (Mileti 1999) reflect the efforts of these experts to take stock of Americans' relationship to past, present, and, most importantly, future hazards. The major thesis of the findings is that losses resulting from hazards, and the fact that there seems to be an inability to reduce losses, are the consequences of narrow and short-sighted development patterns, cultural premises, and attitudes toward the natural environment, science, and technology. The contributions from this collaboration were used to outline a comprehensive approach to enhancing society's ability to reduce the costs of disasters. We propose a way for people and the nation to take responsibility for disaster losses, to define future, acceptable levels of loss, and to link plans for minimizing impacts from disasters with sustainable development.

Recognizing the Problem

A quarter-century ago geographer Gilbert F. White and sociologist J. Eugene Haas published a pioneering report on the United States's ability to withstand and respond to natural disasters (White and Haas 1975). At that time, physical scientists and engineers dominated research on disasters. As White and Haas pointed out in their *Assessment of Research on Natural Hazards*, little attempt had been made to tap the social sciences to better understand the economic, social, and political dimensions of extreme natural events.

White and Haas attempted to fill this void. But they also advanced the critical notion that rather than simply picking up the pieces after disasters, the nation could employ better planning, land-use controls, and other preventive measures to reduce the toll in the first place. Today, at long last, public and private programs and policies have begun to adopt this approach as the cornerstone of the United States's policy for addressing natural and technological hazards. The 1975 report also had a profound impact by paving the way for an interdisciplinary approach to research and management, giving birth to a "hazards community"—people from many fields and agencies who address the myriad aspects of natural disasters. Hazard research now encompasses disciplines such as climatology, economics, engineering, geography, geology, law, meteorology, planning, seismology, and sociology. Professionals in these and other fields have continued to investigate how engineering projects, warning announcements, land-use management, planning for response and recovery, insurance, and building codes can help individuals and groups adapt to natural hazards, as well as reduce the resulting deaths, injuries, costs, and social, environmental, and economic disruption. These people have improved our understanding during and after disasters. Yet troubling questions remain about why more progress has not been made in reducing dollar losses.

One central problem to curtailing losses due to hazards is that many of the accepted methods for coping with hazards are based on the idea that people can use technology to control nature and make themselves safe. What's more, most strategies for managing hazards have followed a traditional planning model: study the problem, implement one solution, and move on to the next problem. This approach casts disasters as static and problem solving as a one-size-fits-all process. But the impact of a disaster varies with the hazard type and intensity. A single solution cannot be applied across the range of disasters.

To redress this shortcoming, there must be a link between wise management of natural resources and local economic and social needs. In the hazards community the term "sustainable hazard mitigation" is used to describe this link. But understanding the term mitigation is often not easy. Hazard mitigation is an action. This action involves avoiding, minimizing, recovering, and reducing or eliminating the impact of natural and technological hazards. In this volume, David Godschalk provides a more detailed definition and description of hazard mitigation and the concept of sustainability. However, it's sufficient to state that sustainable mitigation activities last over the long term without adversely affecting resources that are necessary to support the same activities in the future.

Disaster Losses are Growing in the United States

From 1975 to 1994, natural hazards killed over 24,000 people and injured some 100,000 in the United States and its territories. About one-quarter of the deaths and half the injuries resulted from events that society would label as disasters. The rest resulted from less dramatic but more frequent events such as lightning strikes, car crashes owing to fog, and localized landslides.

The United States has succeeded in saving lives and reducing injuries from some natural hazards, such as hurricanes, over the last two decades. However, casualties from floods—the nation's most frequent and injurious natural hazard—have failed to decline substantially. And deaths from lightning and tornadoes have remained constant. Meanwhile injuries and deaths from dust storms, extreme cold, wildfire, and tropical storms have grown.

The dollar losses associated with most types of natural hazards in the U.S. are rising. A conservative estimate of total dollar losses during the past two decades is $500 billion (in 1994 dollars). More than 80% of these costs stemmed from climatological events, while around 10% resulted from earthquakes and volcanoes. Only 17% were insured. Determining losses with a higher degree of accuracy is impossible because the United States has not established a systematic reporting method or a single repository for the data. Further, these numbers do not include indirect costs such as downtime for businesses, lost employment, environmental damage, or the emotional effects of disaster victims. Most of these losses result from events too small to qualify for federal assistance, and most are not insured, so victims must bear the costs.

Seven of the ten most costly disasters in the U.S. history (based on dollar losses) occurred between 1989 and 1994. In fact, since 1989 the nation has frequently entered periods in which losses from catastrophic natural disasters averaged about $1 billion per week. The dramatic increase in disaster losses is expected to continue. Many of the harshest recent disasters could have been far worse: if Hurricane Andrew had been slower and wetter or torn through downtown Miami, for example, it would have wreaked devastation even more profound than the damage it did inflict. And the most catastrophic likely events, including a great earthquake in the Los Angeles area, have not yet occurred. Such a disaster would cause up to 5,000 deaths, 15,000 serious injuries, and $250 billion in direct economic losses.

The Roots of the Problem

Many disaster losses, rather than stemming from unexpected events, are the predictable results of interactions among three major systems: the physical environment, which includes hazardous events; the social and demographic characteristics of the communities that experience them; and the buildings, roads, bridges, and other components of the human-built environment. Growing losses in the United States result partly from the fact that the nation is becoming wealthier, but they also stem from the fact that all these systems, and their interactions, are becoming more complex.

Three main influences are at work. First, the earth's physical systems are constantly changing—witness the current warming of the global climate. Scientists expect a warming climate to produce more dramatic meteorological events such as storms, floods, drought, and extreme temperatures. Second, recent and projected changes in the demographic composition and distribution of the U.S. population mean greater exposure to many hazards. The number of people residing in earthquake-prone regions and coastal counties subject to hurricanes, for example, is growing rapidly. The worsening inequality between the rich and the poor makes some people more vulnerable to hazards and less able to recover from them. Third, the human-built environment—public utilities, transportation systems, communications, and homes and office buildings—is growing in density, making the potential losses from natural forces larger.

Settlement in disaster-prone areas has also destroyed local ecosystems that could have provided protection from natural hazards. The draining of swamps in Florida and the bulldozing of steep hillsides for homes in California, for example, have disrupted natural runoff patterns and magnified flood hazards. And many efforts to prevent disaster-related damage can degrade the environment and thus contribute to the next disaster.

Another major problem that has become clearer over the past twenty years: some efforts to head off damages from natural hazards only postpone them. For example, existing dams and levees were designed to prevent flooding of specific communities. But communities grow, so if these structures fail, there is greater property lose than was anticipated when the structures were built. Such a situation contributed to catastrophic damage from the 1993 floods in the Mississippi basin. And many of the U.S.'s dams, bridges, and other structures are approaching the end of their designed life, revealing how little forethought their backers and builders gave to future events. Similarly, by providing advance warnings of severe storms, the U.S. may well have encouraged more people to build in fragile coastal areas. Such development, in turn, makes the areas more vulnerable by destroying dunes and other protective natural features.

Who is at Risk?

Research has shown that people are typically unaware of all the risks and choices they face. They plan only for the immediate future, overestimate their ability to cope when disaster strikes, and rely heavily on emergency relief.

Hazard researchers also recognize that demographic differences play a large role in determining the risks people encounter, whether and how they prepare for disasters, and how they fare when disasters occur. For example, nonminorities and households with higher socioeconomic status fare better, while low-income households are at a greater risk mainly because they live in lower-quality housing and because disasters exacerbate poverty.

The residents of this Kinston, N.C., neighborhood may not have been fully aware of their flood risk before the waters of the Neuse River quickly rose. Public education programs and sound land-use use plans could help prevent or lessen the impacts of future floods. (Photo by Dave Saville, courtesy of FEMA News Photo)

The need for disaster planning and response efforts that acknowledge the demographic differences among U.S. citizens will become even more critical as the U.S. population becomes more diverse. Research is also needed to shed further light on how disaster preparedness programs, ranging from public education to disaster relief, can be rendered equitably.

A New Approach to Living with Natural Disasters

Researchers and practitioners in the hazards community need to shift their strategy to cope with the complex factors that contribute to disasters in today's, and especially tomorrow's, world. The following issues are the main guidelines for improving our ability to mitigate the impact of disasters.

Adopt a global perspective

Rather than resulting from surprise environmental events, disasters arise from the interactions among the earth's physical systems, its human systems, and its human-built infrastructure. A broad view that encompasses all three of these dynamic systems and the interactions among them can enable us to find better solutions.

Accept responsibility for hazards and disasters

Human beings, not nature, are the cause of disaster losses, which stem from choices about where and how human development will proceed. Nor is there one final solution to natural hazards, since technology cannot make the world safe from all the forces of nature.

Anticipate ambiguity and change

The view that hazards are relatively static has led to the false conclusion that any effort to decrease their impact is desirable and will, in some vague way, reduce the grand total of future losses. In reality, change can occur quickly and randomly. Human adaptation to hazards must become as dynamic as the problems presented by hazards themselves.

Reject short-term thinking

Mitigation, as it is frequently conceived, is too shortsighted. In general, people have a cultural and economic predisposition to think primarily in the short term. Sustainable mitigation will require a long-term view that takes into account the overall effect of mitigation efforts on this and future generations.

Account for social forces

Societal factors—such as how people view both hazards and mitigation efforts or how the free market operates—play a critical role in determining which steps are actually taken, which are overlooked, and thus the extent of future disaster losses. Because such social forces are now known to be much more powerful than disaster specialists previously thought, simply having a better understanding of physical systems and improving technology cannot suffice. To effectively address natural hazards, mitigation must become a basic social value.

Embrace sustainable development principles

Disasters are more likely where uncontrolled development occurs. Development that allows economic growth while allowing for protection of environmental quality is sustainable development. It ensures that future generations enjoy a quality of life similar to that of the current generation. Disasters can hinder movement toward sustainability because they degrade the environment and undercut the quality of life. There needs to be a stable, reinforcing relationship between human activities and the natural world.

Creating a Resilient and Sustainable Community

A sustainable community is a locality that can tolerate and overcome damage, diminished productivity, and reduced quality of life from an extreme event without significant outside assistance. A sustainable community is resilient because it is able to quickly rebound after a disaster. Five years after a disaster the effects of the disaster—damaged buildings, empty storefronts that represent closed businesses due to a disaster, disaster-related unemployment and social problems—are not present in a resilient community. To achieve resiliency and sustainability, communities must take responsibility for choosing where and how development proceeds. In his discussion of the creation of resilient, sustainable communities in eastern North Carolina, David Godschalk (this volume) outlines the steps required to stop the trend toward increasing catastrophic losses from natural disasters. In essence, each locality must evaluate its environmental resources and hazards, choose future losses that it is willing to bear, and ensure that development and other community actions and policies adhere to those goals.

Settlements in disaster-prone areas, like this coastal North Carolina community, often destroy the local ecosystems that could have provided protection from natural hazards. In the event of a strong hurricane, this community will not be self-reliant. Recovery will most likely require federal and state funds.

Required Tools for Reducing the Impact of Disasters

Over the past few decades an array of techniques and practices has evolved to reduce and cope with losses from disasters. These and other tools will be vital in pursuing sustainable hazard mitigation.

Develop land-use plans that keep people and property away from hazards

Wise land-use planning that limits expansion into sensitive areas is essential to sustainable hazard mitigation. Unfortunately, no overarching guidance directs development in hazard-prone areas of the United States. Instead, a patchwork of innumerable federal, state, and local regulations creates a confusing picture and often reduces short-term losses while allowing the potential for catastrophic losses to grow. This scattershot approach, as well as the federal and state trend to cut risk and assume liability, have undermined the responsibility of local governments for using land-use management techniques to reduce exposure to hazards.

Provide a uniform system for delivering hazard-warning announcements

Since White and Haas's first assessment was completed, significant improvements in short-term forecasts and warnings (hours to days ahead of a hazardous event) have dramatically reduced loss of life and injury in the United States. Yet many communities lag in their ability to provide citizens with effective warning messages. The nation needs to make local warning systems more uniform, develop a comprehensive model for how they work, and provide this information to local communities along with technical assistance. Better local management and decision making are more critical than most future advances in technology.

It is also important to remember that short-term warning systems do not significantly limit damage to the human-built environment, nor do they mitigate economic disruption from disasters. Long-range forecasts that help define the risks to local communities years to decades ahead of potential hazards could assist local decision makers in designing their communities to endure them.

Create and enforce appropriate engineering and building codes

The ability of buildings and structures to withstand the impacts of natural forces plays a direct role in determining the casualties and dollar costs of disasters. Disaster-resistant construction of buildings and infrastructure is therefore an essential component of local resiliency. Engineering codes, standards, and practices have been promulgated for natural hazards. Local governments have also traditionally enacted building codes. However, investigations after disasters have revealed shortcomings in construction techniques and code enforcement. Existing building codes, standards, and practices must be reevaluated in light of the goal of sustainable mitigation, and communities must improve adherence to them.

Define a new and proactive role for the insurance industry

The public increasingly looks to insurance to compensate for losses from many types of risk-taking behavior. However, most property owners do not buy coverage against special perils, notably earthquakes, hurricanes, and floods. For example, nationwide only about 20% of homes exposed to floods are insured. Many people assume that federal disaster assistance will function as a kind of hazard insurance, but such aid is almost always limited. And even when larger amounts are available, they are usually offered in the form of loans, not outright grants.

Insurance does help minimize some disruption by ensuring that people with coverage receive compensation for their losses as they begin to recover. The insurance industry could facilitate the lessening of disaster impacts by providing information and education, helping to create building codes, offering financial incentives that encourage prevention and preparation, and limiting the availability of insurance in high-hazard areas.

The industry already has problems providing insurance in areas subject to catastrophic losses because many insurers do not have the resources to pay for a worst case disaster. Furthermore, the current regulatory system makes it difficult for an insurance company to aggregate adequate capital to cover low-frequency but high-consequence events.

Use the latest technology for disaster preparedness

Computer-mediated communication systems, geographic information systems (GIS), remote sensing, electronic decision-support systems, and risk-analysis techniques have developed substantially during the last two decades and show great promise for supporting sustainable hazard mitigation. For example, GIS models enable managers to consolidate information from a range of disciplines, including the natural and social sciences and engineering, and to formulate plans accordingly. Remote sensing can be used to make land-use maps and show changes over time, feed information to GIS models, and gather information in the wake of disasters. Finally, decision-support systems can fill a gap in hazards management by analyzing information from core databases, including data on building inventories, infrastructure, demographics, and risk. The systems can then be used to ask "what-if" questions about future losses to inform today's decision making. Such systems are now constrained by the lack of comprehensive local data, but they will become more important as the process of evaluating and managing risk grows in complexity.

Involve the entire community in emergency preparedness and recovery

Even if encouraged by more holistic state and federal policies, sustainable hazard mitigation will never eliminate the need for plans that address the destruction and human suffering imposed by disasters. In fact, one way to progress toward sustainable hazard mitigation is to create policies for disaster preparedness, response, and recovery that support that goal.

Studies have found that pre-disaster planning can save lives and prevent injuries, limit property damage, and minimize disruptions, enabling communities to recover more quickly. Recovery, although once viewed as a linear phenomenon, with discrete stages and end products, is a process that entails decision making and interaction among all affected people—households, businesses, and the community at large. Research has also shown that recovery is most effective when community-based organizations assume principal responsibility, supplemented by outside technical and financial assistance. An even further shift—away from an exclusive focus on restoring damaged structures and toward effective decision making at all levels—may be needed. Outside technical assistance can help strengthen local organizational and decision-making capacity.

Adopt a consensus building approach at the local level

A sustainable community selects disaster-planning strategies that evolve from full participation of the entire community. The participatory process itself may be as important as the outcome. A long-term, comprehensive plan for averting disaster losses and encouraging sustainability offers a locality the opportunity to coordinate its goals and policies. A community can best forge such a plan by tapping businesses and residents as well as experts and government officials. And while actual planning and follow through must occur at the local level, a great deal of impetus must come from above. Nothing short of strong leadership from state and federal governments will ensure that planning for sustainable hazard mitigation and development occurs. Local leaders, too, often fail to take advantage of the recovery period to reshape their devastated communities to withstand future events.

Most local disaster plans need to be extended not only to explicitly address recovery and reconstruction but also to identify opportunities for rebuilding in safer ways and in safer places. Fortunately, revisions to disaster legislation in the last several years have allowed a greater percentage of federal relief monies to fund mitigation programs. Pre-disaster planning for post-disaster recovery is vital to communities' ability to become disaster resilient.

Essential Steps for Building a National Sustainable Community

The shift to a sustainable approach to hazard mitigation will require extraordinary actions. Here are several essential steps: (Many initial efforts are already under way in the United States.)

Create supportive hazard mitigation networks

Today, hazard specialists, emergency planners, resource managers, community planners, and other local public and private agencies seek to solve problems on their own. An approach is needed to forge local consensus on disaster resiliency and nurture it through the complex challenges of planning and implementation. One potential approach is to create in each of the nation's communities a "sustainable hazard mitigation network." Each network would engage in collaborative problem solving and produce an integrated, comprehensive plan linking land-use, environmental, social, and economic goals. An effective plan would also identify hazards, estimate potential losses, and assess the maximum population size and development that can be supported by the region's resources (i.e., the environmental carrying capacity). The network especially needs to determine the amount and kind of damage that those who experience disasters can bear. These plans would enable policymakers, businesses, and residents to understand the limitations of their region and work together to address them. Full consensus may never be reached, but the process is key because it can generate ideas and foster the sense of community that is required to decrease hazards.

Federal and state agencies could provide leadership in this process by sponsoring, through technical and financial support, a few prototype networks, such as model communities or regional projects.

But most importantly, the process will advance the idea that each locality controls the character of its disasters, forcing them to take responsibility for natural hazards and resources and realize that the decisions they make today will determine future losses.

Establish a holistic government framework

All policies and programs related to hazards and sustainability should be integrated and consistent. One possible approach toward this goal is a conference or series of conferences that enable federal, state, county, and city officials to reexamine existing statutory and regulatory foundations for hazard mitigation and preparedness, in the context of the principles of sustainable mitigation. Potential changes include limiting the subsidization of risk, making better use of incentives, setting a federal policy for guiding land use, and fostering collaborations among agencies, nongovernmental organizations, and the private sector.

Other efforts to foster a comprehensive government framework could include a joint congressional committee hearing, a congressional report, a conference by the American Planning Association to review experiences in sample communities, and a joint meeting of federal, state, and professional research organizations.

Conduct a nationwide assessment of hazards and risk

Not enough is known about the changes in or interactions among the physical, social, and human-built systems that are reshaping the nation's hazardous future. A national risk assessment should meld information from those three systems so hazards can be estimated, interactively and comprehensively, to support local efforts toward sustainable mitigation.

Local planning will require multi-hazard, community-scale risk assessment maps that incorporate information ranging from global physical processes to local resources and buildings. This information is not now available, and will require federal investment in research on risk-analysis tools and dissemination to local governments.

Build national databases

The nation must collect, analyze, and store standardized data on losses from past and current disasters, thereby establishing a baseline for comparison with future losses. This database should include information on the types of losses, their locations, their specific causes, and the actual dollar amounts, taking into account problems of double-counting, comparisons with gross domestic product, and the distinction between regional and national impacts. A second database is needed to collate information on mitigation efforts—what they are, where they occur, and how much they cost—to provide a baseline for local cost-benefit analysis. These archives are fundamental to informed decision making and should be accessible to the public.

A central repository for hazard-related social science data is also lacking. This third central archive would speed development of standards for collecting and analyzing information on the social aspects of hazards and disasters.

Provide comprehensive education and training

Today hazard managers are being called upon to tackle problems they have never before confronted, such as understanding complex physical and social systems, conducting sophisticated cost-benefit analyses, and offering long-term solutions. Education in hazard mitigation and preparedness should expand to include interdisciplinary and holistic degree programs. Members of the higher education community will have to invent university-based programs that move away from traditional disciplines and toward interdisciplinary education that solves the real-world problems entailed in linking hazards and sustainability. This will require not only new degree programs but also changes in the way institutions of higher education reward faculty, who now are encouraged to do theoretical work.

Measure progress

Baseline information for measuring sustainability should be established so the nation can gauge future progress and interim goals for mitigation. Other aspects of managing hazards should be defined and progress in reaching those goals regularly evaluated. Also important is evaluating hazard-mitigation efforts already in place before taking further steps in the same direction. For example, the National Flood Insurance Program, which combines insurance incentives and land-use and building standards, has existed for thirty years, yet its effectiveness has never been thoroughly appraised.

Each disaster yields new knowledge relevant to hazard mitigation and disaster response and recovery, yet no entity collects this information systematically, synthesizes it into a coherent body of knowledge, and evaluates the nation's progress in putting knowledge into practice. Systematic post-disaster audits, called for in the 1975 assessment by White and Haas, are still needed.

Share knowledge internationally

The United States must share knowledge and technology related to sustainable hazard mitigation with other nations and be willing to learn from those nations. In the U.S. and abroad, disaster experts also need to collaborate with development experts to address the root causes of vulnerability to hazards, including overgrazing, deforestation, poverty, and unplanned development. Disaster reduction should be an inherent part of everyday development processes, and international development projects must consider vulnerability to disaster.

The Key Role of Researchers for Hazard Mitigation

To support sustainable mitigation, researchers and practitioners need to ask new questions as well as continue to investigate traditional topics. Important efforts will include interdisciplinary research and education, and the development of local hazard assessments, computer-generated decision-making aids, and holistic government policies.

Future work must also focus on techniques for enlisting public and governmental support for making sustainable hazard mitigation a fundamental social value. Members of the hazards community will play a critical role in initiating the urgently needed national and global conversations on attaining that goal.

Acknowledgments

This paper was funded by the National Science Foundation under Grant Number CMS93-12647, with supporting contributions from the Federal Emergency Management Agency, the U.S. Environmental Protection Agency, the U.S. Forest Service, and the U.S. Geological Survey. The support of these agencies is greatly appreciated; however, only the author is responsible for the information, analyses, and recommendations in this paper.

References

Mileti, D. S. 1999. Disasters by design: A reassessment of natural hazards in the United States. Washington, D.C.: Joseph Henry Press.

White, G. F., and J. E. Haas. 1975. Assessment of research on natural hazards. Cambridge: MIT Press.

Coping with Floyd: Patterns of Impact, Assistance, and Community Response

Holly M. Hapke, Deborah Dixon, and Dennis McGee

Introduction

We investigated the impacts of Hurricane Floyd on the staff of East Carolina University (ECU) to determine the nature and extent of damages suffered by different groups of ECU staff. ECU is the third largest university in North Carolina, with a student population of 18,000. The east campus is located adjacent to the Tar River in downtown Greenville, in northeastern North Carolina. The Tar River, like many of the region's waterways, flooded for an extended period in the aftermath of the hurricane, inundating hundreds of homes and businesses, including the east campus of ECU and the surrounding neighborhoods.

The population sampled in this study is relatively small, but the economic and racial diversity of the ECU staff allowed us to examine if susceptibility to flood damage and distribution of recovery resources varied with income level (i.e., class) and ethnicity. Environmental hazard literature has linked class and race to the concept of "vulnerability," where groups who are socially marginalized because of their income level or due to active racial discrimination in housing and employment suffer more from disaster events than other citizens. These vulnerable groups may lack resources to prepare adequately for such events, or they may not have access to the information that is broadcast on television or radio, which typically issue warning of an approaching severe weather threat. Furthermore, low-income groups, usually nonwhite, are constrained to live in particularly hazard-prone areas because they either cannot afford to relocate or have historically been barred from doing so by racially discriminatory practices (Hewitt 1983;Watts 1983a, 1983b; and Emel and Peet 1989). However, these studies have tended to ignore the ways that vulnerable groups link together to either prepare for disasters or to help each other recover from a disaster's damaging effects. These links are often informal, such as membership in a church or participation in voluntary organizations like the Red Cross. Although these activities are short-term, they are of great practical and emotional significance to people trying to recover from a major disaster.

We studied the impacts of the hurricane and floods on the staff of ECU to better understand not only the character and degree of damage suffered by particular groups but also to reveal the many positive ways that people coped with the flooding disaster. We used a survey distributed to the non-faculty staff to determine if structural damage and emotional stress disproportionally impacted low-income and nonwhite employees. Because planning and preparation can reduce the severity of disaster impacts, we also determined if disaster preparedness, defined by factors such as insurance coverage and personal perception of risk, mediated the level of impact on particular groups. The pattern of recovery assistance and community response to the flood, both institutional and voluntary, was examined to see how much and what forms of assistance people received. We also wanted to gauge the effectiveness of governmental and institutional assistance programs.

Profile of the Sample Population: ECU Staff

The survey

A survey was distributed via campus mail to a randomly selected sample of 1,100 non-faculty staff persons at ECU, which represents about half of the non-faculty staff. The survey was administered in early January 2000. We originally intended to exclude faculty in our selected sample but because of the way that the Human Resources Office categorizes staff persons, faculty department heads were included.

Three hundred and twenty-two surveys (29%) were returned. Since a typical return rate for mail surveys with multiple mailings is between 30% and 40% (Yegidis and Weinbach 1991), we consider the rate of response to be very good. Although our sample size is relatively small, it closely parallels the ECU staff and thus may be considered adequate for the purpose of a preliminary analysis of the flood impact.

We choose to sample ECU staff for two reasons. First, ECU's staff encompasses a wide range of occupations and levels of household income. Second, since ECU is one of the largest employers in the region, its staff constitutes a significant subgroup of the general population. Understanding the flood's effect on ECU staff can provide insight into how the larger community was impacted.

The survey covered the following topics: level of property damage, evacuation behavior, relocation problems, insurance coverage, level of assistance received, the information and support networks used, personal perception of risk, disaster preparedness, effectiveness of institutional preparation and recovery agencies, and volunteer activities. We analyzed the results to identify the patterns of impact, assistance, and community response.

As with any mail survey, how well the respondents represent the larger population (i.e., the entire ECU non-faculty staff) is uncertain. One possible response bias in this study is that those who were most adversely affected by the disaster returned the survey at a lower rate than others did. We know, for example, that the housekeeping staff was the subgroup most adversely affected by the flood.

Their response rate to the survey, however, was significantly lower (about 16%) than the staff as a whole; therefore, our assessment of factors related to those experiencing the highest levels of damage may not be completely representative.

Population profile

The profile of our sample population closely represents the profile of the entire ECU staff. Of the 322 respondents, 79% are white, 20% are African American, and 2% are Hispanic, Asian, or other. The entire ECU staff is 77% white, 21% African American, and 2% Hispanic, Asian or other. However, women are somewhat disproportionately represented in our sample population, constituting 75% of the respondents but comprising only 67% of ECU's non-faculty staff. The mean age of our respondents is forty-one years, with the highest number of respondents in the 40–49 age category.

In terms of occupation, 24% of respondents work in clerical positions, 14% in janitorial, 8% in a trade, 31% in an academic/professional position, 19% are medical personnel, and 1% work in an unspecified "Other" occupation, again closely paralleling the occupational profile of ECU's staff.

A majority of respondents have an income in the $40,000–$69,000 range. However, income distribution by race is very uneven (Table 1). Seventy-one percent of black respondents occupy the lowest household income categories (less than $25,000) compared to only 15% of white respondents. Only 10% of black respondents reported annual household incomes above $40,000, compared to 65% for white respondents. This income disparity is likely due to the disproportionate number of black staff persons concentrated in "support services" (62% of black respondents are employed in support services). Among the entire ECU staff, 75% of the service and maintenance staff are black, while less than 5% of professional, academic, executive, or administrative employees are black.

Table 1. The percentage of white and black survey respondents in each income bracket. These results do not include the thirty-four respondents that were grouped in the ethnic category "Other."

	<15,000	**$15,000–24,999**	**$25,000–39,000**	**$40,000–69,000**	**$70,000–99,000**	**$100,000+**
White	0%	14%	20%	35%	22%	8%
Black	14%	59%	18%	8%	2%	0%

Patterns of Impact

Structural damage

Most respondents experienced no property damage (58%), while 41% indicated that they had sustained some type of damage. Damage was grouped into four categories: 1) no damage; 2) minor damage—damage repairable while occupants remained in the house; 3) major damage—damage that required repair before occupant(s) could return home; 4) condemned or permanent damage—condemned homes or homes with damage that prevented respondents from ever moving back. Most damage suffered by ECU staff was minor, but 4% of the survey respondents sustained major damage, and 6% had their homes condemned or suffered damage that prevented them from ever moving back.

Of the ten people that experienced major damage, 70% have household incomes of less than $50,000. Thirty percent are African American households with an income of less than $25,000 a year. For the individuals with condemned or permanently destroyed homes, 61% are African Americans with household incomes of less than $25,000. Only one African American household in this category has an income between $25,000 and $39,000. The remaining 34% are white with incomes in the lower-middle and middle-income categories ($25,000–$39,999 and $40,000–$69,999).

Perception of risk

Prior to Floyd, 86% of the respondents felt their risk of flood was low; 9% felt their risk was medium; and only 3% of the respondents indicated a high level of flood risk. Table 2 illustrates the relationship between perception of risk prior to the flood and the actual level of damage sustained. Of the twenty respondents having condemned or permanently damaged homes, 75% believed their risk of flood was low, as did 75% of those who experienced major damage. This indicates a relatively low level of preparedness.

Table 2. A comparison between people's perception of their risk to flooding and the level of actual damage sustained due to flooding.

Level of Damage	Moderate or High Risk	Low Risk
No Damage	8%	92%
Minor Damage	14%	86%
Major Damage	25%	75%
Condemned/ Permanent Damage	25%	75%

Patterns of Assistance

Flood insurance

Seventy-five percent of survey respondents had some form of homeowner's or renter's insurance, but only about 24% had insurance that covered flooding. Of those that experienced major damage or had condemned or permanently damaged homes (i.e., thirty-two respondents), only 25% reported having insurance with flood coverage. Although race is closely correlated with homeowner's and renter's insurance (53% of African American respondents reported having no insurance coverage of any kind, compared to 17% of whites), neither race nor income was a statistically significant factor in predicting flood insurance coverage. Also, the majority of respondents (44%, or 133 individuals) estimated that insurance would cover less than 25% of their damages.

Sources of assistance

Because race, income, and level of damage are highly correlated, we looked at the relationship between the sources of assistance received and the level of damage suffered (Table 3). People who experienced the least amount of damage (damage that could be repaired without leaving the home), often reported receiving no assistance. When this group did receive assistance, informal networks of support (i.e., friends, family, co-workers, church members) were the most important assistance source. For people that suffered major damage, informal networks, FEMA (Federal Emergency Management Agency), and relief organizations, such as the Red Cross and the Salvation Army, were the most cited sources of assistance. Those having homes that were condemned or damaged beyond repair obtained assistance from the entire range of both formal and informal sources. The ECU Relief Center was a significant assistance service, but informal networks and the Red Cross and the Salvation Army were also very important. Interestingly, only six people (30%) that suffered severe damage reported receiving assistance from FEMA.

Table 3. The different forms of assistance received by respondents. Infromal networks include friends, family, co-workers, and church members. (FEMA is the Federal Emergency Management Agency and ECU is assistance services available from East Carolina University.)

Level of Damage	No.	None	Informal Networks	Red Cross or Salvation Army	FEMA	ECU	Other
Minor Damage	101	60%	13%	4%	12%	6%	3%
Major Damage	12	8%	20%	24%	50%	25%	12%
Condemned/ Permanent Damage	20	10%	44%	38%	30%	65%	10%

Table 4. Survey participants' rating of the effectiveness of institutions providing assistance after the floods

Institution	Very Effective	Effective	Somewhat Effective	Not Effective	Don't Know
Federal	16%	24%	23%	9%	18%
State	22%	33%	20%	3%	11%
County	28%	33%	17%	3%	8%
Utilities	51%	19%	11%	2%	6%
ECU	26%	29%	18%	8%	8%

Few of the respondents to the survey rated the various government and other institutions that dealt with the impact of Floyd and the flooding as "not effective" (Table 4). Local utility commissions were perceived to be the most effective in dealing with the flood. The county government came in second with a majority of respondents ranking it as either "very effective" (28%) or "effective" (33%). Fewer individuals ranked the state government and ECU as very effective or effective, and only 16% of respondents felt the federal government was very effective, while 24% ranked it as "effective."

Patterns of Community Response

We assessed the community response to the hurricane and floods in terms of the volunteer activities of the ECU staff surveyed and their rating of the effectiveness of institutions providing assistance. ECU staff volunteered over 5,000 hours during and after the floods. Fifty-two percent of survey respondents performed volunteer work, and thirty hours was the average number of hours worked. Most people volunteered in church-related activities (44%) or at a Red Cross Distribution Center (32%). Fourteen percent reported volunteering at the ECU Relief Center, and approximately 12% offered assistance both in flood shelters and at the Salvation Army. Fewer individuals participated in cleanup programs, assisted the Humane Society, and/or local business efforts. Of those individuals who volunteered during the flood, 66% participate in church-related groups and 22% in some other community organization on a regular basis, at about 6.6 hours per week.

Summary

Nearly half of our sample population sustained some form of damage, emphasizing the extent of the crisis from the inland flooding that followed Hurricane Floyd. Fortunately, most of the damage could be repaired while the residents remained in their homes. However, our survey highlights the uneven distribution of damage along ethnic and economic lines. Low-income groups and African Americans were disproportionately represented among the individuals that experienced severe property damage.

Furthermore, the survey emphasizes that flooding was very much unexpected. Respondents, including those who lost their homes entirely, overwhelmingly perceived that their risk of flooding was very low. Consequently, people's homes were underinsured for flood damage. Only 25% of those that lost their homes had insurance that included coverage for flooding. Our findings reinforce the notion that disasters, whether natural or technological, have a differential impact on a population. The groups that are already marginalized through income or race are hardest hit and the least prepared.

Our survey also revealed a host of coping strategies that are adopted by these same groups. In general, the type of assistance received differed according to the level of damage sustained. Those with low levels of damage relied on informal networks for assistance, while those who experienced more serious damage received assistance from a wide range of both formal and informal sources. Of these, the Red Cross, the Salvation Army, and the ECU Relief Center were the most important formal sources. Few of those most severely affected by the flood received assistance from FEMA (six out of the twenty who lost everything).

Because most people utilized local and regional institutions in the aftermath of the flood, it is not surprising that these same institutions received the highest approval ratings. People's use of informal assistance networks is far more noteworthy. A large number of ECU staff volunteered in flood relief efforts (52%), which is likely due to their regular participation in church-related groups or other community organizations. In addition, the extensive local TV coverage led many people who had never volunteered before to offer help. As the floodwaters began to force thousands of people out of their homes, many staff (and students) helped friends and neighbors evacuate, or assisted at the many informal shelters, which were often the first source for aid. Based on the experience of Greenville residents, we conclude that it is the character and strength of local social networks—sustained through the media, church, school, kinship, or just plain neighborliness—that are of primary importance to those left to cope with the aftermath of a disaster like the events that followed Hurricane Floyd.

Acknowledgements

This research was funded by a grant from the Natural Hazards Research and Applications Information Center, University of Colorado, Boulder. We would like to thank the organizers of the flood conference for their support of our contribution to this volume and to the anonymous reviewer for comments on an earlier draft of this paper.

References

Emel, J., and Peet, R. 1989. Resource management and natural hazards. In: New models in geography, vol. 1, edited by R. Peet and N. Thrift, 49–76. London: Unwin Hyman.

Hewitt, K. 1983. The idea of calamity in a technocratic age. In: Interpretations of calamity, edited by K. Hewitt, 3–31. Boston: Allen and Unwin.

Regidis, B. L., and Weinbach, R. W. 1991. Research methods for social workers. New York and London: Longman.

Watts, M. 1983a. On the poverty of theory: Natural hazards research in context. In: Interpretations of calamity, edited by K. Hewitt, 23–62. Boston: Allen and Unwin.

Watts, M. 1983b. Silent violence: Food, famine and peasantry in northern Nigeria. Berkeley, Calif: University of California Press.

About the Authors: Dr. Holly Hapke is an assistant professor in the Department of Geography at East Carolina University. Her research is focused on issues relating to political economics, rural development, the environment, and feminist theory. Dennis McGee is currently a graduate student in the Department of Sociology at ECU, while also working as a supervisor in the university's Housekeeping Department. Dr. Deborah Dixon is a lecturer at the Institute of Geography and Earth Sciences at the University of Wales and a former assistant professor in ECU's Department of Geography.

Looking into the Face of the Storm: African Americans

N. Yolanda Burwell

Dr. Burwell is an associate professor in the School of Social Work at East Carolina University. She has a special interest in researching early social-welfare leaders and the social activities of African American communities.

There were many, many days during and after the flooding when people felt like they were living in eastern North Carolina during the 1940s and 1950s. In the midst of growth, modern advances, and technology, there were visible signs of another day and time. No matter how many times I tell people what the floods were like, those not living in eastern North Carolina will never have an idea of how really bad it was and how difficult it was for so many people. Whether you were running from the water, or on high ground, whether you lived over the river, or you were in some other area in the region, the days of flooding were difficult moments in all our lives.

Having said that, I also want to discuss how in coming together we began to see a whole different layer of the community emerge. There's a bigger picture than just the individuals that suffered losses, so rather than focusing on those who were victimized I want to show how we were able to see people's capabilities and willingness to help. At the community level, particularly for African Americans, we saw a vital infrastructure emerge, where leaders, organizations, and institutions rallied behind anyone and everyone in need. The African American response to this disaster demonstrated capabilities and strengths. The mobilization of African Americans as volunteers, philanthropists, and professionals and as part of organizations, churches, and media outlets remained vital throughout the immediate response to the disaster, and we need them to continue their involvement as we recover.

Unfortunately, sometimes traditional assistance helpers have a low regard, or no value, for what African Americans can offer. Often there can be a disconnection or a mismatch between the African American community's helping systems and larger assistance organizations. It is important to recognize the wide array of services available and the different type of people that we need to touch. But as we help people to rebuild, to find new homes, and to restore communities, it is also important to keep in mind that many people—whites, African Americans, Hispanics—live on a fixed income, public assistance, limited budgets, social security, or day wages. This is a region that has a stubborn and intentional level of poverty. New homes, modern structures, new electronic devices, and energy-efficient appliances are expensive. For many older adults, low-income families, and working class people the most modern conveniences cost more to maintain than the older equivalent. Also, these groups know that some of these benefits come with strings attached—in the form of a loan or some other long-term involvement. This is very frightening for many people.

One problem that arose after Hurricane Floyd was the chaos and confusion associated with receiving accurate, timely, and relevant information. This problem exacerbated issues of inequity for African Americans. The agencies said one thing, the newspaper said something else, and word-of-mouth said something totally different. If there was distrust before the flood, it's higher now. For many people, one turndown from a government assistance program and they don't come back. Getting what you rightly deserve as a citizen in North Carolina requires an enormous amount of perseverance and assertiveness. It wasn't simply the storm that broke spirits, but the treatment received by those who said they really wanted to help. It's tiring sometimes to negotiate the dance of power and race, so some people just stop trying.

African Americans live in all of the counties affected by the flooding. As historically and culturally significant as Princeville, North Carolina, is, it is not the only settlement where African Americans reside. The legacies of residential segregation are very much alive in the region. There are numerous places, townships, hamlets where the home or the home place is now gone. The impact of dislocation and alienation will have short-term and long-term consequences for children, adults, and elders, particularly with regard to health care needs, school matters, and family life. The many African Americans who migrated north for better jobs and a chance of dignity, now have nowhere to go when they return. I think that this is a very important fact that we need to recognize.

But I want to end with this comment, that in the face of depression, the African American community displays resilience and hardiness. The power of faith sustained many African Americans. In the face of fear, I have seen perseverance, and in the middle of sadness, I have also seen pride and dignity. This is a population that has given their life-blood and tears and helped this region to be what it is. They have an amazing sense of goodness. I hope that we can invite them to the table to help as we design a better way of life in eastern North Carolina.

Facing the Historic Needs of Rural North Carolina as We Recover from Hurricane Floyd

Billy Ray Hall

Mr. Hall is the founding president of the thirteen-year-old Rural Economic Development Center. The Center is recognized nationally as a leader in innovative rural, economic-development programs and policies. National initiatives, such as the Microenterprise Lending Program and the Public School Tech Prep Program, were developed by the Center. It won President Clinton's award for excellence in microenterprise development. Prior to heading the Center, Mr. Hall served four North Carolina governors in policy positions, ranging from Policy Director to Deputy Secretary for the Department of Natural Resources and Community Development. In September 1999, Governor Hunt appointed him as the director of the Hurricane Floyd Redevelopment Center. Mr. Hall is a lifelong resident of rural North Carolina and received his bachelor and master's degrees from North Carolina State University. Mr Hall gave a plenary presentation at the conference and was introduced by Dr. Ron Mitchelson, chair of the Department of Geography at East Carolina University.

Introduction

If you flew at about 10,000 feet and looked at Floyd's flood, which engulfed an area the size of Maryland, took 52 lives, damaged 55,000 homes, put 17,000 people in uninhabitable homes, and destroyed 7,000 homes, then you'd begin to get a feel for what a flood can do. If you flew at that level, you would've seen some of the 30,000 livestock and two million poultry that drowned, the $538 million worth of crops that were flooded, and the $280 million worth of farm structures and equipment standing underwater. That's what I saw while flying in a helicopter over this region of eastern North Carolina shortly after I was pulled into the Hurricane Floyd recovery efforts.

These houses in East Meadowbrook are among the 55,000 homes that were damaged in the floods. The floodwaters are receding but high water marks are clearly visible, and the rain continues to fall. (Courtesy of the city of Greenville, N.C.)

When Hurricane Fran hit this region of the

state three years ago, it was our biggest disaster since 1954. The Governor created, for only the second time in the state's history, a redevelopment center. I headed that effort for the governor. Three years and ten days later, Hurricane Floyd came, and to my surprise I was reenlisted to work on the recovery efforts for this disaster.

During that helicopter ride, I had a bird's eye view of the magnitude of the flood's impact. But when I moved to the ground level I saw the individuals. And when I looked closely at the individuals who were most impacted by the flood, I saw the history of how North Carolina was developed. I saw that the lowlands, the floodplains, are generally where the poor and many minorities live.

Land in the floodplain is cheap land. A lot of the small businesses and some municipalities that needed to find cheap land set up shop or built public facilities in the floodplains. Public facilities that were built in the lowlands were not required to meet all the normal building regulations, and housing construction was often substandard, increasing their vulnerability to the impact of a disaster like the floods that followed Hurricane Floyd. History reveals a lot about who we are. When we see the damage caused by the hurricane and flood, we are looking at damage that we all allowed to happen.

One of my responsibilities as the director of the Hurricane Floyd Redevelopment Center (HFRC) has been to work with state agencies and the Federal Emergency Management Agency (FEMA) to secure funds and deliver grants and loans as quickly as possible to disaster victims. This paper will discuss the status of these recovery efforts. But recovery and redevelopment cannot be discussed only in terms of North Carolina's needs that resulted from the Floyd disaster. North Carolina has been struggling for years with many social and economic problems. There are also many new issues we must address, as we simultaneously start the recovery process after the hurricane and floods and struggle with changes in our economy. This paper outlines both the enduring historical issues and the emerging issues that North Carolina confronts as it attempts to recover and change after Hurricane Floyd.

The Status of the Recovery Efforts

When considering the recovery effort, the response to the effort, and the individuals who were affected by the disaster, it's essential to look at the resources available for recovery. It's important for anyone involved with disaster preparation and recovery to understand the type of resources that are needed to respond to a disaster like Hurricane Floyd. It is also important to know where and how these resources can be obtained. This knowledge is important because in the future it may be much harder for the state and federal government to come to the help of those affected by a disaster. (See Rutherford Platt's paper in this volume for a detailed summary of federal recovery resources.)

When I reported to the general assembly the monetary figures that would be required for recovery from Hurricane Floyd, I reported a figure that we would be requesting from the federal government under the Stafford Act. Working with FEMA, we estimated that about $1 billion will be spent cleaning up after Hurricane Floyd. This is actually a low estimate. As of May 2000, we've spent over $930 million under the Stafford Act. We have $222 million worth of hazard mitigation grant requests; add to this the grants that we have yet to review and the total figure will be well over $1 billion—one billion dollars worth of recovery efforts.

One requirement of the Stafford Act is that the state provide matching funds (about 25% of the amount requested). This is an important fact when you consider the amount of money needed. Each time a new grant is discussed, whether it's the town of Princeville's grant or the recent grant issued to the city of Greenville, taxpayer dollars support a segment of that grant money.

While the Stafford Act is a good piece of federal legislation, it does not meet the disaster recovery needs of the nation. If the disaster need was met, then Congress wouldn't be required to make a special appropriation to add to the Stafford Act three to four times a year. This occurs because disaster relief isn't lobbied for unless a state is confronted with immediate, disaster-recovery needs. If the states that are most frequently engaged in disaster recovery helped rewrite the Stafford Act, I think that the need for disaster-specific lobbying would not exist. In order to make the process of receiving needed resources after a disaster efficient, those engaged in disaster work will need to get their message to the federal government *before* the next disaster.

As a result of HFRC and the governor's lobbying efforts, Congress agreed to provide $1 billion worth of additional assistance. But it's important to note that half of this money is for low-interest loans. Also, of the $1 billion secured under the Stafford Act, over $400 million is for loans that will be issued under the Small Business Administration. So when we think about the funds helping folks, keep in mind that that money generally comes in the form of loans. To date, of the $1 billion, about $200 million has been made available to flood and hurricane victims.

After we looked at the Stafford Act and the funds that we were able to get from Congress, we realized that a disaster of this size was going to require significant additional investments. And so we put together a state plan. In the months that followed the disaster, the Department of Commerce and other state agencies formed fifteen brand-new state programs. Those fifteen programs joined the five existing programs that were already receiving recovery money.

At one point, a one-cent tax increase, or a temporary income tax increase, was proposed. But I've been in Raleigh long enough to know how to count votes, and when you're going to lose, you're wasting your time. Alternatively, three state agencies (the Department of Commerce, the Recovery Office, and HFRC) put together a $836 million proposal to take to the leadership of both houses. Our proposal included the use of the "rainy day fund," which seemed to be appropriately named, at about $250 million. We then went to the state agencies and pulled $500 million out of their budgets. In the future, university officials will likely talk about shortages in their resources, or mental health or other programs will mention reductions in their budgets. These budgetary decreases are due to Hurricane Floyd. The impact of this disaster will have long-lasting impacts for all state agencies, because the critical resources needed to address disaster planning, preparation, and program development or redevelopment have not historically been available before we feel the impacts of a disaster. On 17 December the legislature appropriated our $836 million request.

Resources are critical to disaster response, as is brainpower for disaster planing and development, and legislation is for providing the funding for recovery activities. And so, those who head the recovery and redevelopment programs created after Floyd will continue to look for resources. We have representatives in Washington, watching the Senate and the House, negotiating to bring in between $250 million and $300 million out of a federal supplemental bill. But we still will not be able to attain the kind of resources needed to make hurricane and flood victims feel whole. In fact, the funds that we have secured for redevelopment after Floyd *cannot* make everyone whole. What the funds described here will do is help to make life bearable and livable again for many of the folks that have suffered the most after this disaster.

Facing Recovery: Emerging Issues

Just before Hurricane Floyd impacted eastern North Carolina, the Rural Economic Development Center had completed a fourteen-month long effort to reach out to business leaders, local leaders of faith communities, local groups, local government associations, and others in an effort to define the key issues that are going to confront rural North Carolina in the coming decades. We listed several areas that we thought were key to long-term development of these regions. I find it interesting that the economic challenges that we identified in rural communities are the same challenges that eastern North Carolina faces for long-term recovery after Floyd.

North Carolina has experienced dramatic changes in two historically important sectors of its economy: agriculture and manufacturing. Future long-term redevelopment in this state must recognize the changes that have occurred in agricultural production. Tobacco will no longer be king in North Carolina; it's not king now. Of the $8 billion generated from farm products in this state, tobacco accounts for $1 billion. And tobacco farming will become a smaller and smaller part of our economy. Agricultural technology will also change dramatically. The realities of agriculture production are nested in the three years of low commodity prices, increased international trade, and a nationwide shift to biotechnology. In any type of long-term redevelopment plan, we have to address an agricultural industry that requires, on average, $750,000 a year in loans that are applied toward product development.

Until recently, much of North Carolina's economy was in manufacturing. Presently, about 12% to14% of the state's economy is based in this sector. As we face the future we must ask: What will happen to manufacturing as we shift to high-technology industries in order to become more competitive worldwide? A technology-based economy requires highly skilled workers. Our universities and community colleges must discuss how the state will face the need for skilled employees. We have to be able to produce a labor force that is competitive, not just with South Carolina and Georgia, but with the world. In July 1999, Governor Hunt assembled a task force to look at the potential for future prosperity in rural North Carolina. One of the recommendations of the North Carolina Rural Prosperity Task Force was the need to bridge the digital divide in our state, which is most evident in rural areas. The issue becomes very simple: The Internet is the highway of the future, and without highways, we're not going to be connected.

Although the plan for North Carolina's economic future is grounded in technology, many of the state's current industries and developing industries are in the service sector. There is a lot of talk about the service industry as the place for new jobs. But as someone involved with rural communities in this state, I can provide insight into the role that service industries have in these communities. If you're in a rural county that does not have a city with a population over 50,000, which is most of the rural counties (84 out of 100), one of the things you realize is the disproportionate share of low-wage service jobs that are found there. If a county designs its economy to provide low-wage service jobs and service industries are the fastest growing segment of its economy, then the economy of that county is destined to be low income. Economic development in rural areas and a plan for long-term redevelopment after Floyd must include an effort to move high-end service jobs, such as health care service or banking jobs, to rural areas.

Finally, we cannot ignore environmental issues, particularly in the context of redevelopment after Hurricane Floyd. This point is illustrated with an interaction I had with a state cabinet member. We were discussing water-related issues that affected rural communities. In the course of our research, we discovered that one of our aquifers dropped 150 feet in five years. That was a heck of a drop. In fact, the cabinet member didn't believe it. We had to take him to the site and show him the data. The point of this story is pretty simple: We have to be acutely aware of our available natural resources, and we must be involved in environmental protection of these resources. Environmental issues will involve balancing environmental and production needs—for example, the impact of hog lagoons with the need for pork production and the consequences of building in our floodplains with the economic needs of eastern North Carolina.

Facing Recovery: Enduring Historical Issues

Although North Carolina will need to address many of the new emerging issues outlined above, this state has many old issues that we have not adequately addressed. One of the things we have to do as a state is to go to this next step, and take a look at our enduring issues. And I want to lay this out as a challenge—a challenge we face at the Rural Economic Development Center and a challenge in redevelopment, too. We need to deal with enduring issues that historically we have liked to ignore, including education, financial realities in rural communities, poverty, racism, sexism, and localism.

Many of us talk a great game about our commitment to education, as parents, as grandparents, as communities. But we are not doing a very good job to improve the education of people in rural communities. There's been a lot of discussion about improving education, and its essential role in the success of our state's economic future. But the truth is, half of the state's population and nearly half of all high school graduates live in rural areas. On SAT tests, rural high school students generally perform 50 to 100 points below the students in urban areas. A higher quality education that is accessible across communities in North Carolina must be addressed as we design a long-term recovery plan.

The fiscal resources needed in rural areas are huge. Travel through a rural area and these needs will become obvious. In fact, there are a billion dollars worth of needs out there—health facilities; water, sewer, and other infrastructure; roads; to name just a few. Property taxes are the primary mechanism for financing local infrastructure improvements. And those living in rural areas pay a higher property tax than do those living in urban areas. For the ten counties with the lowest income, all of which are rural, the average tax rate is 83 cents per dollar, while in the top ten urban counties, the tax rate is, on average, 62 cents per dollar. That's the effective tax rate, manipulated to make them comparable. Rural counties have a greater financial need than do more populated counties, and they face this need with less property tax, which is the major source of their local revenue (60% to 70%). It is difficult to imagine how these financially stressed rural communities are expected to participate in a proposed long-term recovery effort—an effort that will involve wonderful new infrastructure to make us globally competitive and investments in our education systems so that the next generation is globally competitive—when many of the basic needs of these communities are not available. This is the challenge for rural North Carolina.

When I started working in public life, the war on poverty was underway. Well I'm here to tell you that we lost the war. Whatever we're doing isn't working. In North Carolina, there were 850,000 people designated as living in poverty in 1990. As we move into this decade, there are now about 900,000 living in poverty, and over half of them live in rural areas. Some counties have 30% poverty. One in four children in eastern North Carolina is growing up in poverty. Incongruity exists between these facts and a redevelopment effort that is based on creating a globally competitive economy. Our children are not going to schools where new technology is available. Our children are going to school with empty stomachs.

We also like to talk a good game about combating racism. That was a big issue in the 1960s, and it's with us to this day. We haven't figured out how to solve this problem. The challenge for every generation that follows those that fought against racism out in the streets will be whether or not we will com-mit to a future that effectively addresses the issue of racism. We must put our words into action.

Similar to our lingering problems with racism, is the issue of sexism. Laws and the prevailing social climate may result in a public perception, particularly among white males, that things have improved with regard to these issues. But this perception is not easy to embrace when minorities are earning two-thirds for the same job as whites or when women are earning two-thirds of that earned by a white male performing the same job. The specific needs of working women, like childcare and alternative work schedules, should be addressed.

The final issue I want to discuss is the effect of localism. As much as we have talked in this state about working together on a regional basis by expanding development efforts beyond county and township borders, our attempts at making this change have failed. The Global Transpark, which was established to attract a variety of businesses to the eastern region of the state, is a great idea. It is the one project that is regional. But how effectively are local governments pulling together to develop regional water and sewer systems? How well are communities pulling together to develop regional business packages? Not very well. Many people may argue that North Carolina is doing well with regard to regionalism. But if we're doing so well, why don't we have any legislation on our books that provides a *region* with a property tax benefit when an industry locates to an area rather than giving an *individual county* this benefit?

Finding Solutions and Making Changes

The picture that I have painted may seem pretty dismal. There is no use in painting such a picture unless ideas are presented to address the problems that I've outlined. I want to discuss how I think we're going to begin to resolve some of these problems. Before I leave the office of the Hurricane Floyd Redevelopment Center, I am going to give the governor my recommendations on how we ought to approach many of these issues. First, we *all* have to be engaged in leadership. We can no longer just put together citizens' advisory groups, or assemble key groups who typically come and participate, while the majority of landowners and wealthy folks, who do have a great deal of influence on our future, disengage. We have to find a way to engage the community grassroots leadership, and we have to find a way to engage the people in the boardrooms. Without those two groups coming together, or a range of people coming together, we cannot create or implement an effective plan for redevelopment after Floyd. My recommendation to the governor is that we find a vehicle to make that happen. Historically, it's been blue-ribbon panels. The Rural Prosperity Task Force is the type of commission that should be organized—joining citizens, community leaders, experts, and legislators to meet a common goal with a specified deadline for making recommendations. We don't need more reports sitting on our shelves gathering dust. We need feasible solutions to our problems.

At the local and state level we need to create legislation that eliminates danger in disaster-prone regions of the state, like homes and businesses in the floodplains. We need to improve floodplain legislation. We need to create programs that get local governments involved in outreach education programs, informing citizens of the risks of living in or near a floodplain. For example, those living in Princeville have been flooded six times in the last forty years. But only about seven households out of 700 had flood insurance during Floyd. Flood insurance assistance has been offered to local governments for the last twenty-six years. I know because twenty-six years ago I headed an advocacy program for flood insurance in the Division of Community Assistance. We went to communities and worked with them and with the federal government to generate floodplain maps, which could then be used to write appropriate insurance ordinances. However, in many communities these ordinances and the purchase of flood insurance did not happen, and it is still is not happening. We have fallen short on reaching local communities and discussing issues related to disaster preparation, like the provision of flood insurance. We look very bad when we go to Washington and ask for money. Inevitably the people in Washington ask, "What have you done for yourself?" If we shrug our shoulders or talk about our intentions and not about our actions, we will leave Washington with empty pockets.

We must also use the knowledge of people like Dr. David Godschalk, or other planners, sociologists, geographers, and political scientists who have taught us about citizen participation. We must find a way to engage the citizens in the redevelopment planning process. Citizens must feel that they play an integral role in this process. If we all don't feel included in redevelopment planning, it will not happen.

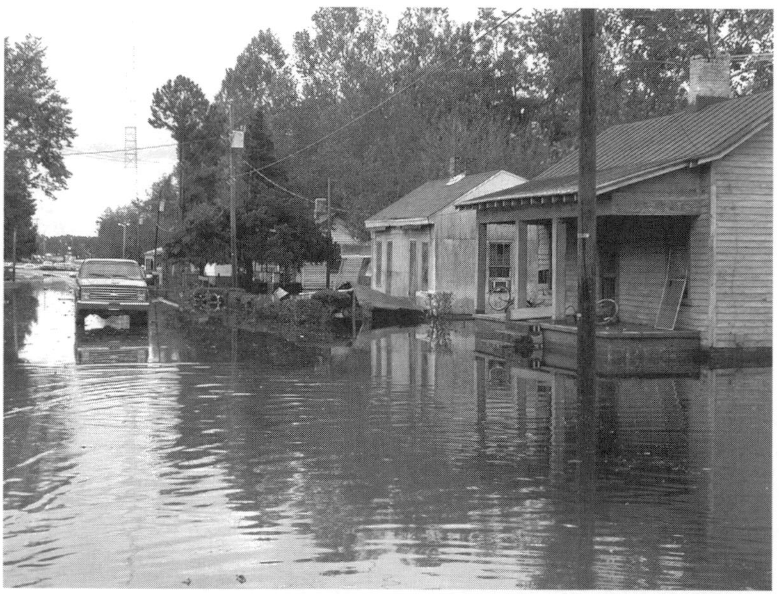

The muddy deserted streets of flood-ravaged Princeville, N.C., stand in silent testimony to the destruction wrought by the Tar River. Although the waters have dropped considerably, the town was off limits to residents due to health concerns. (Photo By Dave Saville, courtesy of FEMA News Photo)

Finally, we have to figure out a way to do something we don't do very well. To staff the redevelopment efforts in eastern North Carolina, we must merge the brilliance in our university system with the brilliance in our rural communities. Often, we engage one group to do academic thinking, the other group to do the planning for this next year's budget, and the twain never come together. We have to figure out a way to join these two groups. I'm going to recommend to the governor that we approach the university system to engage in this effort, perhaps providing an approach for participation that those in the universities have never experienced before.

Hurricane Floyd and the devastating floods that followed have been called the storm of the century, leading us to believe that it will be another one hundred years before we ever experience a disaster like this again. But there are many that propose, and I agree, that we are going to see some significant hurricane events in the coming years. North Carolinians face many challenges in our future. But perhaps our biggest challenge will be to lessen the impact of the next natural disaster by looking at our history, making changes, and having foresight as we prepare for the future.

Resources

Rural Prosperity Task Force. 2000. Final Report. <http://ruraltaskforce.state.nc.us/finalreport/report.html>.

Hurricane Floyd Redevelopment Center <http://www.ncredevelopment.org/>.

Looking into the Face of the Storm: Farmers

Scott Marlow

Mr. Marlow is director of the Disaster Recovery Program for the Rural Advancement Foundation International-U.S.A. He is also the director of the Peanut Project, which since 1995 has assisted farmers in rural North Carolina in their use of chemical pesticides through research and information sharing.

According to the North Carolina Department of Agriculture, the cost of agricultural losses from the hurricanes and flooding is about $813 million. As dynamic as the photos of the floating hogs were, livestock losses were only $13 million of this total. By far the largest component was crop loss, which accounted for $559 million. The farmers we worked with were just happy to be alive, and they had a really hard time complaining about the loss of a cotton crop when other people had lost homes, possessions, and family members.

Like other flood victims, farmers were very confused by the federal and state assistance programs. There was also a great deal of conflicting and often incorrect information. For instance, in December the state assistance program for crop loss announced that when farmers applied for assistance, checks would be quickly cut for half of the money they were due. They would receive the second half very soon after the sign-up period ended on 28 February 2000. Many of the farmers I work with have yet to see a check. While I understand that these agencies are dealing with situations with which they have little previous experience, this year many farmers received financing to provide operating capital based on that expected funding. But we are now coming to the end of planting season and if that funding doesn't come soon, it rapidly becomes irrelevant.

What I would like to point out is that a huge percentage of the disaster funds available for farmers were in the form of low-interest loans, and while low-interest money is great, it's still a loan. Those loans have to be paid back. Most of the farmers were already riding a very high level of debt before they entered the 1999 season. They had yet to pay off the debt from 1998 and their operating debt from 1999. They have to get loans for operating capital again this year. This sets them up in a situation where they are heavily financed. Basically, they will need a home run in crop production in order to stay on their land. The flood added a natural disaster to what was already a disastrous agricultural economy. North Carolina farmers came into 1999 riding three years of record low commodity prices, and over the last couple of years there was a 48% drop in the tobacco allotment.

We are currently in the middle of a huge, huge restructuring of North Carolina agriculture. For many people, the photographs of floating hog carcasses and poultry that were taken after the flood created a huge outcry against industrial agriculture, which has taken over agriculture production in eastern North Carolina. We've heard a lot of people say at this conference that we need to actively shape the type community in which we want to live. In agriculture, that choice has been made. That choice was made twenty years ago. The plan is already in motion. If anything, the impact of this flood sped up the rate of industrialization of agriculture in eastern North Carolina.

By some estimates, we lost about 10% percent of family farms in 1999. While this situation is fairly new for us, it's not new across the country. Other communities in other states have gone through all of this before. We know a lot about what happens in a farm crisis like the one that we are currently facing. We know that for about every seven farms that are lost, another main street business fails. We know that as more farms are lost, the rate of accidental deaths and accidental injuries increases, as does the rate of self-medication, including drugs and alcohol. Incidences of spousal abuse, child abuse, divorce, and suicides rise. We also know that farmers are among those in a community that are least likely to take advantage of mental health care. One study that I read found that individuals who had lost their family farm still showed very high rates of depression five and ten years after the loss, even though they had an increased standard of living and an increase in almost all of the quality of life indicators measured. By all the empirical measurements, their lives had gotten better, but rates of depression were still high. Most said that they would immediately move back to the farm if they had the opportunity.

I want to close with two things. When I worked at a university, it was very easy for those of us there to say, "Well, you know things would be a lot better if all of these people would just listen to us and do things the way we tell them." I find that it is very difficult for those of us who receive a salary to judge the decisions of people who risk all that they own, and all their families have created, each time they make a decision. I would suggest that the farmers, those folks who are out there making tough decisions, should pull together to create the kind of community impact discussed at this conference. Farmers must have a place at the table as decisions and proposed solutions are made. Any discussion of recovery and redevelopment after Floyd must include the economic realities that farmers face.

Part III / Dynamics of Hurricanes and Floods: Achieving New Insights—Improving our Understanding of Natural Systems

Inland Flooding in North Carolina due to Hurricanes Dennis and Floyd

Len J. Pietrafesa, Lian Xie, David A. Dickey, Kermit Keeter, and Steve Harned

Introduction

While North Carolina has experienced eighty-three named tropical storms and thirty-one hurricanes from 1887 to the end of 1999, no previous storm has had the environmental impact that followed Hurricane Floyd in September 1999. The question is, why? Admittedly, there has been enormous population growth and development in eastern North Carolina, and the subsequent costs of the flooding events can be partially attributed to these factors. Nonetheless, the magnitude of the precipitation and subsequent flooding in September and October 1999 were environmental in nature and must be understood independent of their economic impacts. This study addresses the environmental factors that resulted in the flooding.

Prior to Hurricane Floyd's arrival, we generated a potential flooding scenario for the storm using the time sequenced output from the Xie and Pietrafesa (1999) model. But the model predictions were inadequate and did not predict the subsequent event. This follow-up study documents the events preceding Hurricane Floyd's arrival in North Carolina and the events that occurred during and following Floyd's passage. We conclude by offering an improved model prediction scheme for forecasting inland flooding in North Carolina's coastal plain.

Reexamining the Data to Improve Flooding Predictions

Varying types of time series data were used in this study, collected from multiple sources. Data were collected for the time period beginning just prior to the North Carolina arrival of Hurricane Dennis and ending soon after Hurricane Floyd's departure. We collected data for three regions in the vicinity of the Pamlico and Albemarle sounds: the mouth of the Tar-Pamlico River (at Washington, North Carolina), an open ocean site located near Duck, a small Outer Banks village, and a site within Pamlico Sound, located at a marina to the north of Oregon Inlet.

Precipitation data were obtained from the National Weather Service (NWS). River discharge and water level at Washington were obtained from the U.S. Geological Survey (USGS) Raleigh Office.

Open-ocean, coastal sea level and sound-side water levels were obtained from the National Ocean Service (NOS). The National Climate Data Center (NCDC) provided wind speed and direction time series data, which NWS collected from the CMAN station at Cape Lookout, N.C., and at the Kinston, N.C., airport. Sea surface temperature data were downloaded at North Carolina State University (NCSU) facilities directly from the National Ocean and Atmospheric Administration's (NOAA) polar orbiting satellites. Sea surface and cloud color data were downloaded directly at NCSU from NASA's SeaWifs satellite (with permission of Orbitron Inc.). In order to calculate changes within the sound, NCSU scientists involved in this study collected water flow and salinity time series from Oregon Inlet.

The numerical scheme used to model the North Carolina system was originally described in Pietrafesa et al. (1997). This model focused on the inshore network of waters of the Pamlico and Albemarle sounds. However, Xie and Pietrafesa (1999) presented a more extensive approach in which a coupled coastal ocean-inshore waters system was developed. This coupled model utilizes the Princeton Ocean Model (Mellor 1993) at a horizontal resolution of 1 kilometer with eighteen levels in the vertical, whatever the depth and is the backbone of the next generation model.

Making a New Prediction for September 1999

North Carolina is broken up into eight "precipitation zones" (Figure 1). Precipitation data are available from the North Carolina Department of Conservation, either for the entire state or for each of the eight zones. These zones were established to determine the strongest relationship, or rather the highest correlation, between the water discharge (measured in cubic feet per second) in a watershed to the measured precipitation in a given river basin. The Neuse and Tar-Pamlico rivers are in zone 7, and the rivers flowing into the Abermarle Sound are in zone 8.

The data collected for zones 7 and 8 show that September 1999 registered the highest total monthly amount of precipitation in seventy years of recorded history (actually the entire 105-year record of the NWS). The monthly streamflow data for the Neuse and Tar-Pamlico rivers also had the highest discharges in each of the seventy years that data have been recorded for these rivers.

The precipitation and river discharge records for these precipitation zones occurred in September, but the flooding story really began on 30 August. On this date, Hurricane Dennis arrived along the North Carolina coast. It became stationary for several days off the coast to the northeast of Cape Hatteras, and on 3 September it moved due south and then turned due northwest. It finally left the area on 6 September. Thus, Dennis was present on this region of the coast for approximately seven days. This was not an insignificant visit.

To help explain the flooding events, we examined the time series records of the water levels at the open ocean, the sound side, and the river mouth site as well as the coastal wind levels. Figures 2a-c show the water levels at the open-ocean site (Duck, N.C.), the sound-side site (Oregon Inlet), and the river mouth site (Washington, N.C.) for the period preceding the arrival of the two hurricanes 25 August (Julian Day 237) to the point following the passage of both events on Julian Day 264, or 21 September. (Dennis arrived on Julian Day 240, or 30 August, and Floyd arrived on Julian 259, or 16 September.) These data are shown in low passed form, that is, the reversing tides are not shown explicitly. This follows Pietrafesa et al. (1976), which invoked a Lanczos 40-hour, half-power point filter, because we considered residual or subtidal hydrodynamics. The ranges of the astronomical tides are of the order of a meter at Duck and of the order of 30 centimeters (cm) at both the Oregon Inlet marina and Washington sites. Figure 3 shows the wind vector data collected at Cape Lookout during this same period, where northeastward winds are positive values and southwestward winds are negative.

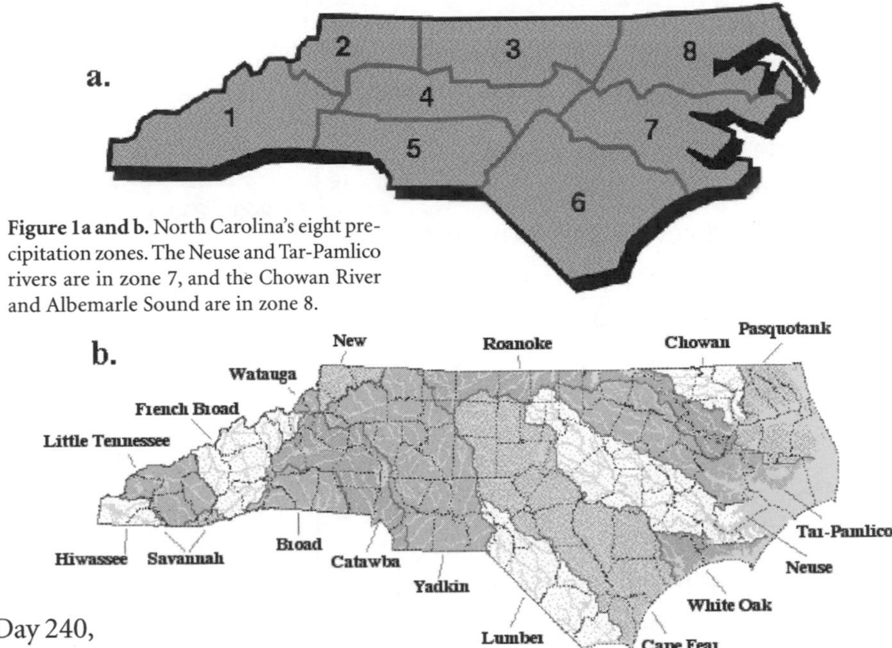

Figure 1a and b. North Carolina's eight precipitation zones. The Neuse and Tar-Pamlico rivers are in zone 7, and the Chowan River and Albemarle Sound are in zone 8.

The rise and fall of water levels at the three sites is very tightly coupled to the direction of the wind. When the winds blew from the north and northeast, water levels rose on the open-ocean side of the North Carolina coast, fell in the northern end or upper Pamlico Sound, and also rose in the upper Tar-Pamlico River. In fact, the water levels at Duck and the Oregon Inlet marina, and at Washington and the marina were essentially out of phase over the entire period of time extending from 25 August to 20 September. The rises and falls (Figures 2 a-c) are clearly very tightly coupled to the northeast-southwest component (Figure 3) of the total wind-field (not shown). The difference in water levels was most dramatic from 30 August (Julian Day 242) to 6 September (Julian Day 249), which is coincident with the presence and eventual passage of Hurricane Dennis.

Figure 3 shows that the southwestward blowing winds, resulting from the western or shoreward side of Dennis's eye on 30 August (Julian Day 242), contributed to a 98 cm rise in the water level at Duck, a 21 cm rise at Washington, and a 22 cm drop at the Oregon Inlet. What this indicates is a quick response time of the entire Pamlico Sound to winds blowing along the axis of the sound. Pietrafesa et al. (1986) reported that water levels respond to strong winds that blow along the axis of the Pamlico Sound within two hours and forty-five minutes. Water levels in the southwest end of the sound (e.g., the Washington site) will set up or rise and water levels in the northeast end of the sound (e.g., marina at Oregon Inlet) will set down or drop—somewhat like a teeter totter with the fulcrum likely located in the middle of Pamlico Sound in the vicinity of Bluff Shoals. The rise in the southwest corner that resulted due to Hurricane Dennis essentially blocked the flow of water at the mouths of both the Neuse and Tar-Pamlico rivers. When the downstream flow route was blocked, water levels rose upstream. As Dennis wobbled off the coast, the relative wind field intensity changed with time, while five to eleven inches of rain was deposited over the coastal region and water levels fluctuated. On 5 September (Julian Day 248), the water level at Duck peaked to 196 cm higher than the water level recorded prior to Dennis's incursion. Washington water levels reached 109 cm higher, and at the inshore Oregon Inlet marina site water levels were approximately 177 cm below coastal water levels and 85 cm below Washington water levels. Then as

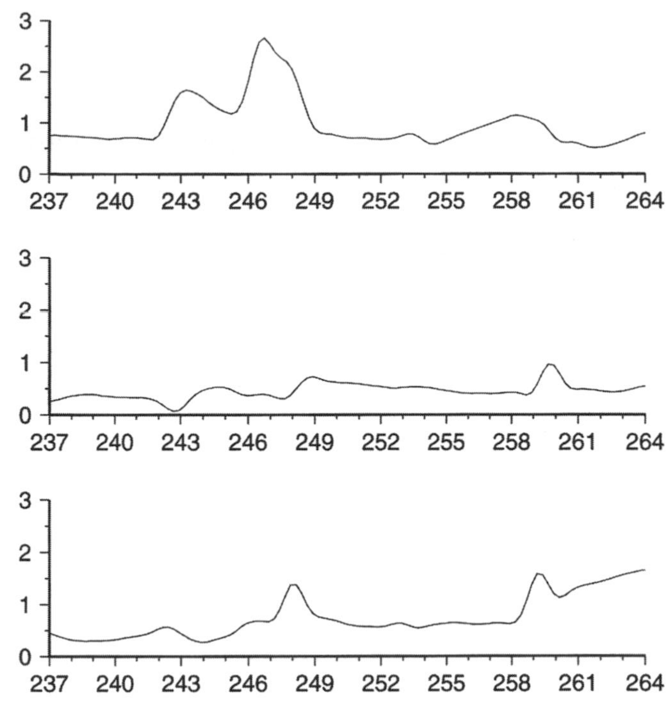

Figure 2. a. Sea level at Duck, N.C.; **b.** Oregon Inlet; **c.** and at Washington, N.C. for the period 25 August (Julian Day 237) to 21 September (Julian Day 264) 1999. Hurricane Dennis arrived on Julian Day 240, or 30 August, and Hurricane Floyd arrived on Julian 259, or 16 September.

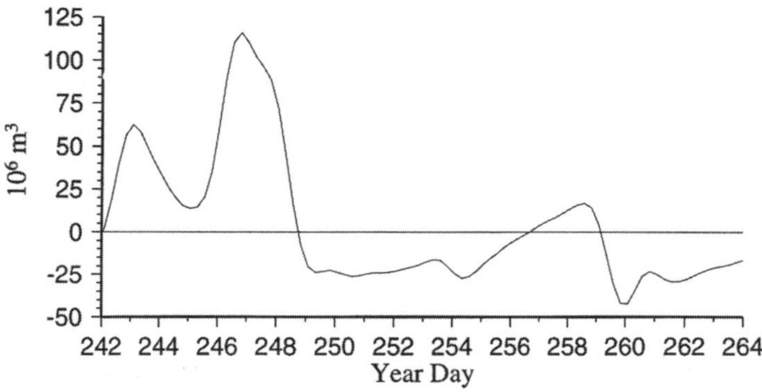

Figure 3. The wind speed and direction measured at Cape Lookout, N.C., for the period 25 August (Julian Day 237) to 21 September (Julian Day 264). Northeastward winds are positive values and southwestward winds are negative. Hurricane Dennis arrived on Julian Day 240, or 30 August, and Hurricane Floyd arrived on Julian 259, or 16 September.

Dennis moved across and finally departed the state on 6 September (Julian Day 249), offshore coastal and upstream river water levels began to return to previous levels.

Because water flow and sea level slope are very tightly coupled (there is a 43 cm per second per meter [cm/sec/m] and a 16.2 parts per thousand [ppt] per meter relationship between the two), we can use these very stable transform functions to compute the volumetric flux of water and the flux of salt through the Oregon Inlet. We used a cross-section value of 7,000 square meters (Nichols, 1991) to compute the time series of the volumetric flux, the cumulative flux of water either in or out of the sound, and the addition or loss of salt at the inlet from 30 August to 21 September. In Figure 4, we see that following the onset of Dennis, coastal waters began to flood Pamlico Sound via the Oregon Inlet on 30 August (Julian Day 242) and continued doing so until the 6 September (Julian Day 249).

During this time period, the flux of shelf water into the sound reached an amount of nearly 1.4 x 10^9 (1,400,000,000) cubic meters, with salinity values up to 30 ppt. Using the water level records and the estimates of the size of the sound proper (Pietrafesa et al. 1986), we calculated that the amount of water present in Pamlico Sound at the end of the month of August was approximately 1.86 x 10^9 cubic meters. Thus, the amount that entered the sound over the six to seven day period when Dennis was present increased the total amount of water in Pamlico Sound to 3.26 x 10^9 cubic meters of water—an increase of 75% more water than what was there prior to Dennis. Following Dennis's departure, the system began to drain, likely through all three barrier island inlets. The total volume of water dropped by about 0.8 x 10^9 cubic meters, but the sound still retained 2.46 x 10^9 cubic meters on 13 September (Julian Day 256). However, on 14 September the waves began to rise again as Floyd approached. (Hurricane Floyd was present from 15–17 September.) By 16 September an additional 0.1 x 10^9 cubic meters of water were added to the system, and the water level reached of 2.56 x 10^9 cubic meters by 16 September. This water level was still 38% higher than the water level in the sound prior to the arrival of either Dennis or Floyd. Subsequently, the water level gradually fell (i.e., the system drained). By 21 September the volume of water in Pamlico Sound proper had dropped to 2.25 x 10^9 cubic meters, or 22% more water than was present on 30 August.

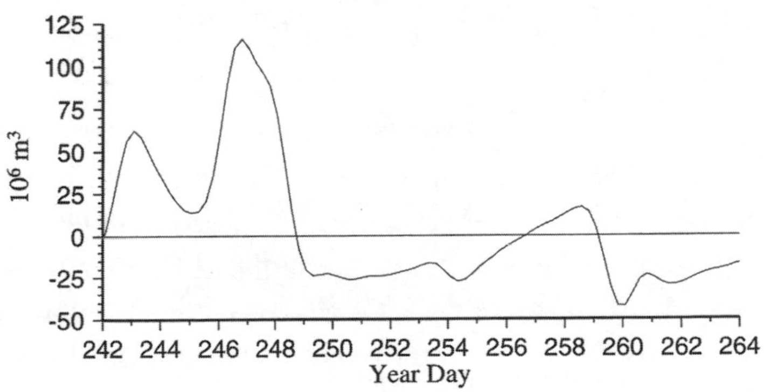

Figure 4. Fluctuation in the volume of water flowing into and out of Oregon Inlet during 30 August-21 September 1999.

Sea surface temperature data also supports the scenario that coastal water flooded into Pamlico Sound. Using satellite images taken on 18 August, the water temperature in the entire sound system was 27–28°C (80–83°F) and was 24–26°C (75–79°F) along the coast. By 9 September, water in the sound was 25°C (77°F), indicating a mixing of the colder ocean water with the warmer water in the sound. In fact, the 23 September SeaWifs image of the sound region strongly suggests that the highly turbid river waters have not yet made it to the Pamlico Sound, though they are present in the rivers (Figure 5). It is likely that some water cooling occurred during the passage of the hurricanes, particularly during Hurricane Floyd but that effect was not assessed.

The data and the satellite imagery strongly suggest that when Hurricane Dennis sat off the North Carolina coast, it created conditions favorable for the flooding of the Pamlico Sound with coastal waters. The enormous amount of highly saline coastal water that entered the system added 75% more water to what was already present. Now it might be assumed that this excess water could have flowed out of Hatteras and Ocracoke inlets to the south. However, the output flow data derived from the numerical model of Xie and Pietrafesa (1999) suggest otherwise. The flow essentially streamed past Hatteras Inlet, making it a neutral inlet. While surface flows did exit at Ocracoke Inlet, bottom flows moved into the sound. Thus, Ocracoke Inlet was only somewhat compensatory during Dennis's presence. Following Dennis's departure all three inlets likely began to drain, driven by the increased pressure gradient between the inside and outside areas of the sound.

The water level data (Figures 2 a-c) and satellite images from Hurricane Dennis suggest that Pamlico Sound acted like a bathtub that was filled to capacity. This overfilled bathtub may have blocked the mouths of the river-estuary tributaries, including the Neuse and Tar-Pamlico rivers. The series of dams built on the upper Neuse and Tar-Pamlico rivers may have also prevented Dennis's precipitation from discharging quickly down the rivers and into the sound. As Dennis moved across and finally departed the state on 6 September (Julian Day 249), offshore coastal and upstream river water levels began to return to their prior condition. But the entire system was still backed up or was in a "storage mode." The region's soils and vegetation were still highly saturated. Just as the system struggled toward the conditions that were present prior to Dennis, along came Hurricane Floyd. Floyd dropped an historic record amount of rain over a large swath of North Carolina's coastal and middle interior. The waters in the sound very likely were not able to drain to the sea quickly enough, causing blockage of the river mouths and upstream flooding, with water swelling over the riverbanks and literally drowning the coastal plain. To assess this possible scenario, we looked at

Figure 5. 23 September 1999, SeaWifs satellite image showing surface color following Hurricane Floyd. Notice the waters in the sound are visually different from those in the Neuse and Tar-Pamlico rivers.

the actual daily time series of streamflow data from both the Neuse and the Tar-Pamlico rivers.

Daily stream-flow data from both the Neuse and the Tar-Pamlico rivers show the dramatic combined effect of the two hurricanes. During most of Hurricane Dennis (30 August to 4 September, or Julian Day 242 to 247), the flows in both rivers actually dropped (not shown). The flux accelerated from 16–17Sep-tember (Julian Day 259-260); then the flows exploded. The individual and cumulative volumetric discharges from the two rivers are shown in Figure 6. By 19 September (Julian Day 262), the total discharge from the two rivers had reachedthe water level that entered the sound from offshore during the coastal flooding caused by Dennis. Therefore, there is clear evidence that Dennis and Floyd together, acting in concert, caused the extensive flooding of September 1999.

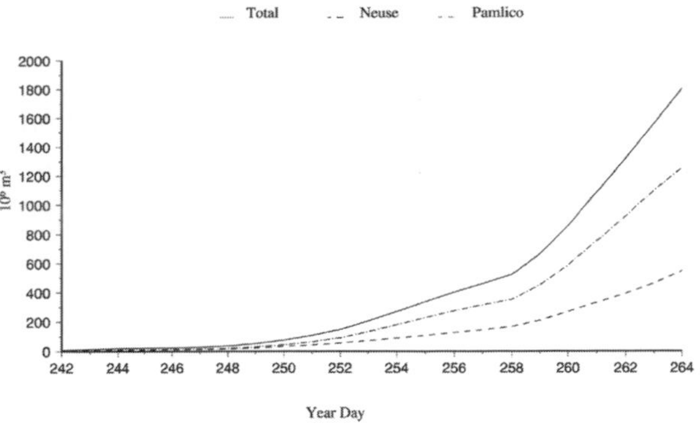

Figure 6. Total fluctuation in the volume of water draining into the Pamlico Sound from the Neuse, Tar-Pamlico, and the combined volume from both rivers from 25 August–21 September 1999. Hurricane Dennis arrived on Julian Day 240, or 30 August, and Hurricane Floyd arrived on Julian 259, or 16 September.

Does the statistical study support the above scenario? We again turn to the work of Dickey, Pietrafesa, and Xie (2000). Using current and past rainfall events, the model for the Neuse River discharge as a function of time, N(t), at time t, predicted the discharge in three precipitation zones (3, 4, and 7). The model for the Tar-Pamlico River discharge was predictable from precipitation zones 3 and 8 only. One result of the statistical study suggests that the Neuse River discharge displayed a very clear phase delay to the Floyd event, with the discharge lasting well beyond October, while the Tar-Pamlico River discharge responded more rapidly. These statistics are found to be very stable and strongly suggest that the southern basin of Pamlico Sound took a longer time to drain through the Hatteras and Ocracoke barrier island inlets then did the northern basin through Oregon Inlet. Perhaps Oregon Inlet is more effective as an outlet than are the other inlets. This could be related to the condition of coastal ocean sea level at that time, or it may suggest that the Tar-Pamlico watershed does not retain water as long as the Neuse watershed does.

Summary

Can the flooding attributed to events like hurricanes Dennis and Floyd be predicted in the future? Hydrodynamically speaking, the answer is "yes."

After looking at the many types of data collected around these two storms, we determined the physical processes that accompanied hurricanes Dennis and Floyd. The following is a summary of the sequence of events that led to the flooding disaster in eastern North Carolina:

- Dennis brought copious amounts of precipitation.
- Dennis's winds mechanically drove coastal waters towards the coast. Within eight hours a wall of water was built up along the offshore side of the coast. These same winds simultaneously drove inshore sound waters from the northeast end of Pamlico Sound towards the southwest end within three hours, thereby blocking the flows at the mouths of the Neuse and Tar-Pamlico rivers .
- Pamlico Sound was flooded by relatively salty coastal ocean waters, eventually bringing waters though Oregon Inlet with salinities reaching 30 ppt.
- The amount of ocean water that entered the sound system during Dennis was about a 75% addition to the water volume already present in the sound.
- The enormous amount of water in Pamlico Sound blocked the flows from the Neuse and Tar-Pamlico rivers. The two rivers acted more to store water than to move it. This created a backup of water toward the head of each river, thereby causing lateral flooding.
- After Dennis's departure, the waters in the sound began to discharge through the three barrier island inlets, but before the waters could drain, along came another hurricane.
- Hurricane Floyd brought a record amount of rain, which fell on an already saturated and still flooded environment.
- After Floyd, the rivers, still blocked as a result of Dennis, had nowhere to go but over the riverbanks.
- Following Floyd's departure, the system began to drain and continued doing so for several months.

A suite of hydrodynamic conditions, which can all be accounted for by the hierarchical systems modeling approach defined by Xie and Pietrafesa (1999), can model this entire scenario in the future. Further, the statistical technique developed by Dickey, Pietrafesa, and Xie (2000) can be used for predictions of future discharges based on forecasts or direct measurements of rainfall. These predictions can then be inputted to the Xie and Pietrafesa (1999) model as interactive boundary conditions and as surface input conditions. This new approach should improve the operational forecast methodology employed by the NWSO and NCSU collaborators.

Acknowledgments

The authors wish to thank Mr. James M. Epps for producing the data time series plots and remotely sensed satellite images used in the study. He also contributed in other important aspects of this study. Also, the authors thank Dr. M. Strobel of the USGS, who supplied the time series of river discharge, and Dr. J. Bales of the USGS for making the water level and streamflow data from Washington, N.C., available. This study was supported by a grant from NOAA's Charleston Coastal Services Center, Charleston, S.C.

References

Dickey, D., L. J. Pietrafesa, and L. Xie. (2000) On the statistical relationships between precipitation and river discharge for two North Carolina coastal systems. Bulletin of the American Meteorological Society (submitted).

Mellor, G. 1993. User's guide for a 3-D, primitive equation numerical ocean model. Report 35 Princeton University Atmospheric and Ocean Sciences Program.

Pietrafesa, L. J., G. S. Janowitz, T. Y. Chao, and R. H. Weisberg.1986. The physical oceanography of Pamlico Sound. NOAA UNC Sea Grant Publication WP-86-5.

Pietrafesa, L. J., L. Xie, J. Morrison, G. S. Janowitz, J. Pelissier, K. Keeter, and R. A. Neuherz. 1997. Numerical modeling and computer visualization of the storm surge in the Albemarle-Pamlico estuary system during the passage of hurricane Emily, August 1993. Mausam 48(4):567–578.

Xie, L., and L. J. Pietrafesa. 1999. Systemwide modeling of wind and density driven circulation in the Albemarle-Pamlico estuary system and the coastal ocean. Journal of Coastal Research 15(4):1163–1175.

About the Authors: Dr. Len Pietrafesa is director of the Office of External Affairs in the College of Physical and Mathematical Science and a professor in the Department of Marine, Earth and Atmospheric Sciences at North Carolina State University at Raleigh. He is active on many research and policy committees that deal with coastal and ocean issues, including the Steering Committee of Office of Environment and Health Research (DOE), chair of the Board of Governors and Executive Council of the Consortium on Oceanographic Research and Education (CORE), and a member of the U.S. Weather Research Program Prospectus Development Team 2, to name only a few. Dr. Xie is a professor in the Department of Marine, Earth and Atmospheric Sciences at NCSU and is the director of the Coastal Fluid Dynamics Laboratory. Also at NCSU, Dr. David Dickey is a professor in the Department of Statistics. Mr. Keeter is the Science Operations Officer and S. Harned is the Meteorologist-in-Charge at the Raleigh office of the National Weather Service.

A New Method for Mapping the Extent of Flooding in the Tar River Basin

Yong Wang, Jeffrey D. Colby, and Karen Mulcahy

Introduction

In response to an extensive flooding event like the one that occurred in eastern North Carolina in September 1999, it is important to quickly determine the extent of flooding and the types of land use and land cover that are under water. Access to this type of information can greatly assist comprehensive relief efforts (Corbley 1993). Capturing the extent of flooding in an efficient manner is essential for response, recovery, and mitigation activities during and after extreme flooding events. This paper describes a method for mapping flooding extent using data that is relatively easy to process, as well as being accessible in terms of cost and ease of acquisition. We integrated river gauge data and digital elevation model (DEM) data to map the flood extent on the portion of the Tar River Basin within Pitt County, North Carolina.

DEM data have been used in various ways to aid in flood mapping and modeling. DEM provides a digital representation of the topographic surface of the land, minus buildings, land cover, or any other features. Digital representations of topography in the form of DEMs have been used as an integral part of geographic information system (GIS) databases that are applied to hydrologic flood modeling efforts (e.g., Correia et al. 1998). In addition, the delineation of floodplains and the development of flood inundation maps have relied on DEMs (e.g., Jones et al. 1998). The recognition of the error inherent in DEMs is an important concern. However, it has been investigated (Brown and Bara 1994), and specific examples have been provided in the literature that are applicable to floodplain mapping (e.g., Hunter and Goodchild 1995).

In this paper, we present a method for mapping flood extent in a coastal floodplain through the integration of river gauge and DEM data. We then present the results of using this method to map flooding that occurred in the Tar River basin within Pitt County during September 1999. We also discuss potential limitations and cautions for applying this flood mapping method in coastal floodplains.

Study Area and Ground Observations

Most of eastern North Carolina lies within the Atlantic Coastal Plain Province. It extends 60 to 120 kilometers from the Piedmont Province (situated in the center of the state) to the coast, with an elevation drop of about sixty meters. Four large elongated river systems drain this province in a northwest-southeast direction. Flat, broad floodplains are usually located on the northern side of the rivers with higher ground on the southern side. Pitt County, with a population of about 126,000 (estimated in 1998), is located at the approximate center of the eastern coastal plain. Greenville, the largest city in the county, has a population of approximately 60,000 (estimated in 1998). Additional residents in the county are spread throughout rural towns.

In Pitt County the majority of the 1999 flooding occurred north of the Tar River, and some 6,000 homes were flooded. The city of Greenville suffered flooding to its airport, water treatment facility, power transmission substation, and numerous residential and industrial sites (Figure 1). Figure 1 clearly shows the flood and nonflood boundaries on both sides of Tar River.

Figure 1. Aerial photo of a portion of the city of Greenville, North Carolina, taken on the 23 September 1999. The major part of Greenville is on the south side of the Tar River. The flooded/nonflooded boundaries were easily identified.

Our study area consists of the portion of the Tar River basin that is within Pitt County (see Figure 2 for the location of the study area), which covers an area of 97,526 hectares (975.3 square kilometers). The study area comprises 57.5% of the total area of the county (1697.1 square kilometers). Once the floodwaters had completely subsided, but before high water marks faded, ground truth information was gathered in the field. Areas both north and south of the Tar River were examined for the extent and depth of flooding.

Using DEM and River Gauge Data

DEM data for Pitt County were obtained from the United States Geological Survey (USGS). The DEM has a 30-meter by 30-meter resolution in the horizontal, x, and vertical, y, direction. Within the study area, the elevation (or height) interval, z, is 0.30 meters, or 1 foot. A height of one half of the contour interval on the corresponding USGS topographic sheet represents the accuracy of the DEM data. The contour interval for topographic sheets in Pitt County is 2 meters (i.e., most errors occur within plus or minus 1 meter). Twenty-two 7.5-minute topographic quadrangles were mosaiked to cover Pitt County. A mask of the Tar River basin within Pitt County was used to extract the basin (see Figure 2).

Table 1. Total size of basin and size of flooded area for areas greater than 100 hectacres within each land-use and land-cover type in the Tar River basin of Pitt County (N.C.).

Land-Use and Land-Cover Type	Size of Basin (hectares)	Size of Flooded Area (hectares)
High-Intensity Developed	766	127
Low-Intensity Developed	1,033	110
Cultivated	33,856	4,407
Managed Herbaceous Cover	2,376	534
Managed Herbaceous Cover-Upland	258	2
Evergreen Shrubland	10,487	1,222
Deciduous Shrubland	1,054	152
Mixed Shrubland	1,539	90
Bottomland Forest/Hardwood Swamps	22,158	7,036
Southern Yellow Pine	20,553	1,189
Mixed Hardwoods/Conifers	2,440	541
Water Bodies/Rivers	927	503

We gathered data from two gauge stations on the Tar River. The first is located in the city of Tarboro in Edgecombe County, about 10 miles upstream along the Tar River. The second site is the gauge station on the Green Street Bridge in Greenville (Figure 1). At the Tarboro gauge station, the highest river reading was 39.59 feet on 21 September 1999 (averaged over the entire day), while the reading was 4.78 feet on 1 September, before Hurricane Dennis made landfall. At Greenville, the Tar River crested at 29.74 feet on 21 September, and on 1 September the water surface height at nonflood stage was 4.49 feet. Therefore, the elevation ranges that represented flooded areas on 21 September for the Tarboro area was 34.81 feet (39.59 feet minus 4.78 feet) and was 25.25 feet (29.74 feet minus 4.49 feet) near Greenville. There are no other gauge stations on the Tar River downstream from Greenville (to Washington, N.C.). Thus, the ranges in water levels at Tarboro and Greenville between 1 and 21 September were used to classify elevation values for the Tar River basin within Pitt County into the following categories: water bodies/rivers, flooded areas, and nonflooded areas.

North Carolina Land-Cover and Land-Use Data

The North Carolina Center for Geographic Information and Analysis (NCCGIA) contracted Earth Satellite Corporation (EarthSat) to generate comprehensive land-cover data for North Carolina (Earth Satellite Corporation 1997). These data were created to assist governmental agencies and others in making resource management decisions through the use of a GIS. There are twenty-one land-use/land-cover type categories in the entire state data layer. For Pitt County, there are seventeen categories, with twelve categories exceeding 100 hectares in size. The categories range from highly developed areas to water bodies/rivers (Table 1). Bottomland forest/hardwood swamps and cultivated land were the two land-use/land-cover categories most affected by the flood. Bottomland forests/hardwood swamps are areas where deciduous, dominant, woody vegetation is above 3 meters in height and occurs in lowland and wet areas. Tree crown density in these areas is at least 25%. Cultivated lands are areas occupied by row and root crops that are cultivated in distinguishable rows and patterns. Two other important categories were high- and low-intensity developed areas, which contain the housing and infrastructure for the majority of the human population in the area.

Mapping the Flood Using Topographic Data

The goal in flood mapping was to identify areas that were either flooded or were not flooded in September 1999. There were two steps to this process. First, we identified areas where water occurred (water areas) versus the areas where water did not occur (non-water areas) prior to the flood and during the flooding. Second, we compared the areas classified as water or non-water on two dates to determine the areas that were flooding. The preflood date was 1 September 1999 (before Hurricane Dennis), and the flood date was 21 September 21 1999, when the Tar River crested in the study area.

Based on the gauge data at Tarboro and Greenville on 1 September, we interpolated the river height between the two stations. If the elevation on the DEM of an area between the two stations is equal to or less than the interpolated elevation value, the area was classified as water or river channels. Otherwise, the area was classified as non-water. Since there is no gauge station downstream from Greenville to Washington, the gauge readings of Tarboro and Greenville on 1 September were extrapolated to estimate the river height from Greenville to the downstream. Again, if the elevation of an area within the basin was equal to or less than the extrapolated value, the area was classified as water. Otherwise, the area was classified as non-water or dry land. This method of analysis was carried out for the Tar River Basin in Pitt County for 21 September.

For this study, the Tar River basin within Pitt County was divided into fourteen segments, with each segment having a roughly equal distance measured along the Tar River. Each segment was independently inundated with interpolated river height values both prior to and during the flooding. Thus, if an area was classified as water before and during the flood event, it was not considered to be flooded. These areas represented the regular river channels. If an area was classified as dry or non-water on the preflood date, and the area was classified as water during the flood, the area was considered to be flooded. Finally, if an area was dry on both dates, the area was not flooded.

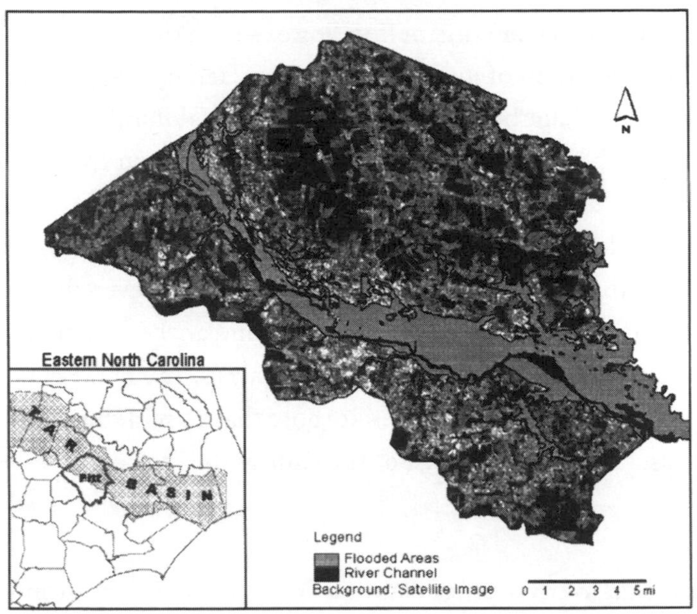

Figure 2. Flood map of the Tar River basin within Pitt County in September 1999 derived from river gauge data and topographic data.

The Extent of the Flooding

The flood map

Using river gauge data, DEM data, and the method described above, a map representing flooded areas in the Tar River basin of Pitt County on 21 September 1999 was created (Figure 2). The regular river channel is shown in black, and the flooded areas in gray. The nonflooded area is represented by satellite data to indicate ground features. The flooded area covered 15,931 hectares or 16.3% of the Tar River basin within Pitt County.

Area flooded by each land-use and land-cover type

After comparing the flooded areas on the land-use/land-cover data layer obtained from the NCCGIA, we found that the flooded areas of the Tar River basin within Pitt County (Table 1) were primarily bottomland forests/hardwood swamps (7,036 hectares), and cultivated land (4,407 hectares). Also, 127 hectares of the high-intensity developed areas and 110.1 hectares of the low-intensity developed areas were flooded in September 1999, which is where most homes and buildings were damaged.

Significance of the Results

There are several advantages to using river gauge data to inundate the DEM in flood extent mapping. In the U.S., government agencies operate many gauge stations on the rivers (e.g., the U.S. Geological Survey), and the data are available to the public. The DEM data, which do not change seasonally or yearly, are also widely available.

Most of the bottomland forest and hardwood swamps in the floodplain are located in places of low elevation or along the banks of rivers. By using river gauge data to inundate the DEM, one can map the flood underneath tree canopies in the bottomland forest and hardwood swamps. This is significant for flood mapping in forested environments. Due to the dense or continuous canopy coverage in bottomland forest/hardwood swamps, and due to the lack of canopy penetration of optical remotely sensed satellite data (e.g., U.S. landsat thematic mapper, TM, data), flooded areas under the canopies cannot be detected, as is found in our ongoing research. The underestimation of flooding extent in these areas was verified through ground truthing and visual interpretation of low-altitude oblique aerial photos taken during the 1999 flood. This underestimation is important because floods in the coastal floodplains of North Carolina, as well as the entire East Coast and the coast of the Gulf of Mexico, often occur from the mid-summer to fall, when trees in the floodplain are in full leaf.

Radar data (especially radar data from a long wavelength system) can penetrate even dense canopies and identify whether the areas underneath the canopies were flooded or not. However, due to the limited availability of the radar data and the more specialized data processing and analysis methods required, it may be inconvenient to incorporate radar data into flood mapping analysis. The DEM data, however, works well for flood mapping in areas of relatively flat terrain, like those that exist in this study area and other coastal floodplains along the East Coast and the coast of the Gulf of the Mexico.

Limitations of the method

Although the results derived from the integrated river gauge data and DEM data were very promising, we would like to offer three cautions. Away from river channels and at higher elevations, the flood mapping based on the river gauge and DEM data suggested that these areas were dry or were not flooded. However, based on ground observation and analysis of remotely sensed satellite data, there were flooded areas scattered in the northern and southern parts of the study area at high elevations. In another words, water bodies and/or flooded areas at higher elevations were not identified using the DEM data and the methods applied in this study.

Flooding of the DEM only works for a reasonable distance from the river gauge stations from which measurements of river stage height are taken. This can be a large distance in areas with low relief such as the coastal plain of eastern North Carolina. To work in an area of larger spatial extent or large topographic variation, stage height from other river gauges should be incorporated, and an interpolation (and/or extrapolation) method should be developed to provide a continuous representation of flood elevations upstream and downstream. In areas where few river gauges exist, estimates have to be made.

USGS-created DEM data have an estimated accuracy of one half the interval of the contour lines in the USGS topographic sheet. The contour interval of the topographic sheets in the study area is 2 meters. The potential plus of minus 1 meter variation in accuracy of the DEM data may affect the estimated flooded areas due to the low topographic relief in the study area. In this study, we used ground observation and aerial photos taken during the flood to determine flood extent in addition to using the river gauge readings to inundate the DEM data. Thus, the ground observation and aerial photos helped to "calibrate" the flood mapping method that is introduced here.

Summary

By integrating river gauge data and digital elevation model (DEM) data, or topographic data in digital format, we presented a simple and efficient method for mapping flood extent in a coastal floodplain. The integration was straightforward and efficient. Furthermore, based on our limited ground observation and analysis of aerial photos taken in the study area during the flood, the results were reasonably accurate and reliable. This method could be used in the other coastal floodplains (e.g., the East Coast, and the coast of the Gulf of the Mexico of the U.S.). This study also demonstrated that this method should work well for areas of large spatial extent if the (local) topography is relatively flat.

Inundation of the DEM, based on river gauge data prior to and during the flood event that was coupled with ground observation and examination of aerial photos taken during the flood, provided important results for the extent of flooding for the Tar River basin within Pitt County in the September 1999 flood. Quickly accessing this type of information can greatly assist future relief efforts by allowing emergency personnel to identify areas that require response, recovery, and mitigation activities during and after extreme flooding events. Although there were many advantages of using river gauge data to inundate the DEM, there are limitations. Additional sources of data would be needed to identify whether areas were flooded or not, because it's difficult to identify flooded areas away from river channels and at high elevation. There is also a need to interpolate and/or extrapolate the readings along rivers to achieve a reliable result. Variations in the DEM data due to error is also a limitation because it could lead to a possibly significant discrepancy between observed and derived flood extent. Again, ground observation and other means of verification were critical to assessing the accuracy of the derived flood map. The U.S. Army Corp of Engineers is currently surveying high-water marks from flooding in this area, and once the data becomes available, the authors intend to use the data to assess and further study the accuracy of the DEM in modeling flood extent.

References

Brown, D. G., and T. J. Bara. 1994. Recognition and reduction of systematic error in elevation and derivative surfaces from 7.5-minute DEMs. Photogrammetric Engineering and Remote Sensing 60:189–194.

Corbley, K. 1993. Remote sensing and GIS provide rapid response for flood relief. Earth Observation Magazine September, 28–30.

Correia, F. N., F. C. Rego, M. D. S. Saraiva, and I. Ramos. 1998. Coupling GIS with hydrologic and hydraulic flood modeling. Water Resources Management 12:229–249.

Earth Satellite Corporation. 1997. Comprehensive land cover mapping for the state of North Carolina: Final report. March 1997, Rockville, Md.

Hunter G. J., and M. F. Goodchild. 1995. Dealing with error in spatial databases: A simple case study. Photogrammetric Engineering and Remote Sensing 61:529–537.

Jones, J. L., T. L. Haluska, A. K. Williamson, and M. L. Erwin. 1998. Updating flood inundation maps efficiently: Building on existing hydraulic information and modern elevation data with a GIS. U.S. Geological Survey Open-File Report 98–200.

About the Authors: Dr. Yong Wang is an assistant professor in the Department of Geography at East Carolina University. His research involves changes in land cover types and land uses caused by nature and human disturbance, as well as the responses of shorelines and coastal wetlands to sea-level rise. Dr. Jeffrey D. Colby is an assistant professor in the Department of Geography, where he researches remote sensing, watershed and environmental modeling, and water resources. Karen Mulcahy is an associate of the Center for Health Services Research and Development, Division of Health Sciences at ECU and an assistant professor in the Department of Geography. She specializes in cartography, map projections, and geographic information science.

A Dialogue: Lessons in the Floodplain—Finding a New Approach to Floodplain Management

Len J. Pietrafesa

Starting the Dialogue

The Question: *What are the required adjustments to our historical approach to floodplain management as we face continued, rapid population growth in eastern North Carolina?*

The discussion was guided by **Phillip S. Lesinger**, Branch Manager, North Carolina Division of Emergency Management and **Abdul Rahmani**, Project Manager, Hydraulics Design Unit, North Carolina Department of Transportation. Participants in the discussion were concerned professionals, including a representative from a city planning department, several individuals from state and federal emergency and resource agencies, academic researchers, and a lawyer for a nonprofit wetland protection group. Other participants included farmers, interfaith fellowship representatives, those concerned with issues affecting the disabled, and students.

Introduction

Our discussion on floodplain issues started slowly. Perhaps this was due to the myriad of tangential, and often emotional, issues associated with society's relationship to rivers and the land that surround them. Families have farmed for generations along the rivers and streams in eastern North Carolina. Communities like Princeville were born, grew, and created a common history along the banks of the Tar River. Floodplains are linked to commerce, recreation, wildlife viewing, and many other human activities.

Ultimately, it was a question from a hog farmer that launched the discussion. In all the years that he, his father, and grandfather farmed their land, it never flooded. But the floods after hurricanes Dennis and Floyd left a good part of his land under water. The farmer wanted to know why he wasn't allowed to remove debris that obstructed a stretch of river adjacent to his property, which he identified as the reason for the flooding of his land. As state and federal agency representatives addressed his question, it became clear that many of the agencies' decisions and regulations are not explained or made available to the people they most affect. For instance, floodplain managers explained that presently they are moving away from the creating straight-sided channels that maximize flow and towards allowing for a more natural configuration of waterways. If the farmer had removed the large debris from the river it might have increased the amount of flooding downstream, and it might not have reduced the flooding on his land.

As our discussion progressed it was indisputable that the extreme events that occurred during and following the passages of hurricanes Dennis and Floyd revealed serious deficiencies in floodplain management policies and procedures. We identified four issues of high priority for changing floodplain management in eastern North Carolina. A common theme for each issue was the need to share information and knowledge.

Extreme environmental events are perturbations of ambient conditions, and can be highly disruptive to the affected social and environmental systems. But sufficient planning, policies, and procedures exist to help society deal with such naturally occurring events. Proper planning, the dissemination of information, and good floodplain management practices should help reduce the losses of life, property, other economic impacts, and societal disruptions. While loss of life due to an extreme natural event is inevitable, large losses are avoidable. The billions of dollars in economic losses, the irreversible environmental damage, and the degradation of environmental stability that resulted from the hurricane and floods of 1999 can all be reduced in the future.

The increased role of extreme events for those living in coastal communities presents a great opportunity and an urgent need to rethink integration, application, dissemination, and evaluation of information and knowledge.

Improving Communication between Government Agencies and the Public

As was evident from the question posed by the hog farmer, there is a need to clearly define the allowable maintenance of stream and river channels. There is no obvious, single governmental body or agency to turn to with questions relating to stream channel maintenance. There should be a simple method by which people learn which agencies require notification of a proposed activity and which agencies issue permits, if required. There is a great deal of confusion about who is responsible for issuing permits, which activities are allowable and which are unlawful.

The public also needs to understand the interrelationship between the federal, state, and local agencies responsible for floodplain management. This information should include who is responsible for enforcement of floodplain regulations.

Creating Floodplain Education Programs

In general, people living near streams and rivers lack adequate knowledge about the normal and natural changes that occur in these aquatic ecosystems. People should comprehend what it means to live in or near a floodplain. Grade-school students learn about the planets in the universe, but they know very little about the river that they may see every day on their way to school, or about the floodplain on which their home or school is built. Floodplain education should be integrated into the curriculum of primary and secondary schools in eastern North Carolina. Information on living in a floodplain should also be made available to the entire public.

Providing Current and Reliable Information about Flood Insurance

Changes in national floodplain insurance and reinsurance rules and regulations are not generally known. Information that clearly defines the regulations for flood insurance requirements should be made available. This information should be written in a style that is understandable to the majority of the public. Often, confusion and misinformation result from the inability of property owners or renters to decipher the legal and technical language of insurance information material. There must be an easy means to answer questions such as: "Do I need flood insurance?" and "What is covered by flood insurance?"

Requiring Mandatory Disclosure of Flood Risk

A reoccurring statement made by many residents affected by the flooding was, "I didn't even know my home was in a floodplain." There should be a federal, state, and local government requirement for mandatory disclosure of all structures that are in the watershed of a particular river. A watershed is the total land area from which water flows into a river or stream. Many structures are located in an identifiable watershed, but not all structures are located in a floodplain. So all individuals should know, where within a specific watershed, a structure is located. This should include a person's home, place of employment, place of recreation, shopping center, etc.

Although the home-buying process does include disclosure of where a property is located relative to the 100-year flood line, one agency representative stated that this often occurred very late in the process. He recalled receiving calls from friends as they sat at the bank finalizing the purchase, asking him whether they should be worried about flooding. Greater time and attention should be given to explaining to potential buyers what the phrase "100-year flood" means. As was often repeated during the discussion, this does not mean that flooding will occur only once in a hundred years. This represents an average probability. For a homebuyer with a thirty-year mortgage, this translates into a 30% probability of his home experiencing severe flooding during the lifetime of the mortgage. And of course the probability increases when the discussion concerns a 50-year or 10-year flood event.

Recommendations for Changing Floodplain Management in Eastern North Carolina

In addressing the four high-priority issues relating to floodplain management outlined above, several problems, which apply to multiple issues, were identified. For example, floodplain maps are generally outdated, unavailable, and at times completely useless. Also, there is not a good, easily understandable definition of what constitutes a floodplain, or what is meant by the phrase "a 100-year flood."

Scientific knowledge and technological innovation offer new possibilities for understanding, anticipating, mitigating, and responding to the impacts of extreme events. Recent innovations and current knowledge must be incorporated into floodplain management strategies. Integrated models of natural and human systems, coupled with sophisticated computational technologies, promise powerful new insight into and understanding of event causation, probabilities, and impacts. These include remote sensing, geo-information systems and satellite imagery, and modern high-performance computing modeling of watersheds. These advances, combined with innovations in communication and information systems, can improve disaster warning and response strategies. Research that places disaster-related decision making in the context of uncertainty, complexity, and risks contributes a crucial perspective to improving the understanding of the causes and consequences of extreme events in the coastal plain. Lacking, however, is an effective integration of these disparate efforts with each other and into the broader context of societal needs. Because society and the environment are increasingly vulnerable to extreme events, achieving such integration is crucial.

Decisions that place societal needs and the environment at risk require reevaluation. This Greenville, N.C., electric substation and the surrounding neighborhood were flooded after Hurricane Floyd, and will be at risk in future floods. (Courtesy of the city of Greenville)

Several recommendations are proposed to begin the process of integrating knowledge and technology and to address the other problems we identified. These recommendations are one attempt at changing North Carolina's approach to floodplain management.

- The federal, state, and local government agencies that are responsible for creating and updating floodplain maps must be identified and encouraged to make these maps easily attainable. The maps should contain clear and easy-to-understand cartographic and topographic information with GIS (geographic information system) overlays that delineate the 10-year, 30-year, 50-year, 75-year, and 100-year flood line for a region. The maps and other information should be available in hard copy, at cost of reproduction, as well as on each agency's Internet web site.

- Provide a clear definition of the 10-year, 30-year, 50-year, 75-year, and 100-year flood for a specific community. This information should be in the form of easily obtainable packets and provided to all homeowners and renters. This could be sent to people as a part of the documents they receive for annual property tax statements, or they could be available at local post offices and libraries, similar to way that tax forms are available at these public facilities.
- Provide flood insurance information. This information should include: the name of the companies providing insurance for a particular region; stepwise guidelines that help people determine if they need flood insurance; a list of what is and what is not covered by different levels of insurance; and the name of the organization that underwrites the insurance.
- Provide information regarding the activities that can and cannot be implemented to maintain streams. Include a profile of the agencies that oversee regulations of activities in streams and floodplains. This information could be made available to the public at post offices and libraries and distributed in the annual tax statements received by public and private property owners.
- Disclosure statements indicating where a given structure is located within a watershed should be posted in public and private buildings. This information could be displayed in the main entrance. In a home or apartment complex or other forms of housing, the information should be provided in the annual tax statement with a requirement that the information be disseminated to all building occupants.
- The public must know what federal, state, and local agencies are responsible for floodplain management. This information should be disseminated in agency offices, in post offices, listed in phone directories, and made available on the Internet.
- The public must know which agencies are responsible for enforcement of floodplain regulations. This information should be disseminated in agency offices, in post offices, listed in phone directories, and made available on the Internet.
- Create educational materials written at a level that is understandable across age groups (i.e., a fourth-grade reading level). The publication could be titled "Living in a Floodplain" and be distributed at primary and secondary schools, to civic groups and public employees, and made available to the public at post offices, libraries, and other public places.
- Public informational meetings, perhaps a town-hall-type meeting, should be held to discuss all the issues that relate to floodplains. These meetings should be led by those federal, state, and local government officials responsible for floodplain management.

- Public hearings should be held to discuss the status of floodplain management rules and regulations and to identify problems and discuss reform. All federal, state, and local agencies with jurisdiction should attend the meetings, which should also be open to the public and advertised widely in local newspapers and on radio and television stations.

About the Author: Dr. Len Pietrafesa is director of the Office of External Affairs in the College of Physical and Mathematical Science and a professor in the Department of Marine, Earth and Atmospheric Sciences at North Carolina State University at Raleigh, N.C. He is active on many research and policy committees that deal with coastal and ocean issues, including the Steering Committee of Office of Environment and Health Research (DOE), chair of the Board of Governors and Executive Council of the Consortium on Oceanographic Research and Education (CORE), and a member of the U.S. Weather Research Program Prospectus Development Team 2, to name only a few.

Sedimentation on the Tar River Floodplain During the Flood of 1999

Scott A. Lecce, Patrick P. Pease, Paul A. Gares, and Catherine A. Rigsby

Introduction

Large floods are hydrologic events that are infrequently observed first hand and are difficult to recognize as discrete units in stratigraphic records (i.e., the layers of sedimentary material that are deposited through time). Consequently, few studies have examined the impacts of individual, large flood events on the deposition of sediment on floodplains. Because large floods exert the largest forces on the landscape and have the greatest capacities to transport sediment, it is reasonable to assume that they have the potential to produce the most significant modification of floodplains and the most lasting stratigraphic records. A considerable amount of research, however, has demonstrated that floods of moderate magnitude exert a dominant control over the transport of sediment and the morphology of river channels (Wolman and Miller 1960). Nevertheless, the role of large floods in landscape modification and the evolution of floodplains is uncertain (Magilligan et al. 1998). In some cases large floods have produced catastrophic impacts by scouring channel and floodplain surfaces and/or depositing large amounts of sediment (e.g., Schumm and Lichty 1963). In other cases only minor geomorphic changes occur (Gomez et al. 1995).

The flooding in eastern North Carolina that followed intense rainfall from hurricanes Dennis and Floyd in September of 1999 provides an unusual opportunity to address a central question in geomorphology and sedimentary geology: What is the impact of a very large, rare flood on floodplain sedimentation? Although the Coastal Plain Province of North Carolina has long been considered a slowly eroding landscape, recent research suggests that soil erosion may be more significant than previously believed (Slattery et al. 1998). Upland soil erosion and sediment yields of many streams confined to the coastal plain may equal or exceed those rivers located in the plateau region of the state (i.e., the Piedmont Province) (Phillips 1992), which extends from the base of the Blue Ridge Mountains to the coastal plain region. Phillips (1992, 1995) has also shown that sediment dynamics in the upper portion of piedmont-draining rivers are effectively decoupled from the lower basin so that little piedmont-derived sediment reaches the lower coastal plain. Nevertheless, little is known about the transport, storage, and ultimate fate of the eroded soil (Phillips et al. 1993). Because hydraulic characteristics favorable to deposition tend to be associated with wide, low gradient valleys (Lecce 1997), and because most of the soil eroded in watersheds is stored in sedimentary deposits before reaching the basin outlet (e.g., Trimble 1977; Simmons 1988), it is reasonable to expect that the 1999 flood produced relatively high rates of sedimentation along the Tar River. This paper tests this hypothesis using preliminary field observations of the magnitude and spatial variability of floodplain sedimentation along the lower Tar River in eastern North Carolina.

Study Area and Data Collection

a.

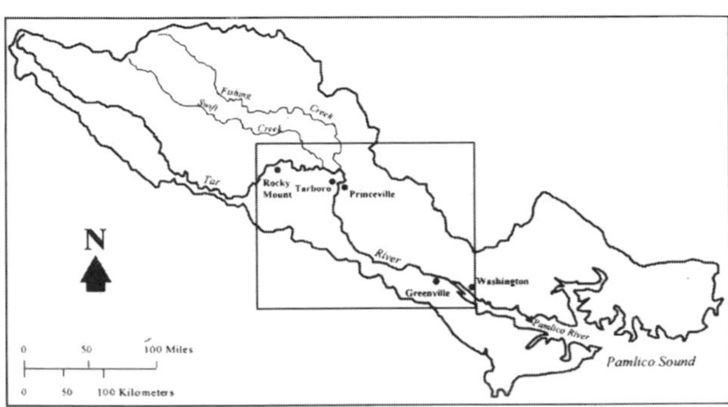

b.

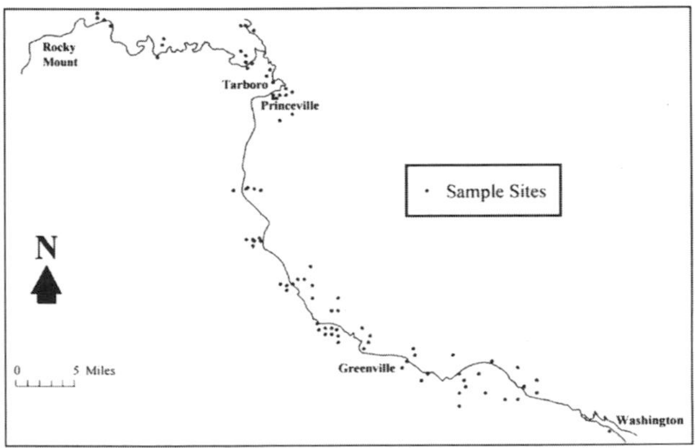

Figure 1. a. Location of the study reach (inset box) within the Tar River basin. b. Location of sample sites along the study reach.

A field survey of floodplain sedimentation was conducted on the lower Tar River between Rocky Mount and Washington, North Carolina (Figure 1). Field work was conducted soon after the floodwaters receded and winter snow had melted (January–February 2000) in order to distinguish the flood sediments from the preflood soil and to minimize modification of the sediments by organisms or human activities. The selection of sampling locations was, to some extent, controlled by access to the river and private property. Nevertheless, we sampled eighty-five sites that provided reasonably complete coverage of the study reach (Figure 1b). Because sedimentation rates might systematically decrease with increasing distance from the river channel, sites were selected at a variety of distances from the channel. Five sediment samples were collected at each site to account for small-scale variations in sedimentation rates.

The sediments deposited by the flood were easily recognizable in most field situations. The typical preflood soil surface consisted of well-decomposed plant litter and mineral soil. A layer of undecomposed leaves that had accumulated on top of this surface was associated with the high winds of hurricanes Dennis and Floyd as well as leaves carried by the floodwaters. Flood-transported sediments were often found as thin layers on top of the undecomposed leaf layer, or dispersed among the leaves and other flood debris. The top of the sequence contained leaves related to postflood leaf-fall in autumn. The frequent intermingling of small quantities of flood sediments with large amounts of plant litter made it impossible to separate the two in the field and required the collection of all material above the preflood soil surface. We used a 25-centimeter diameter ring to standardize the sampling area (Figure 2). The sediments are currently being separated from the plant litter, which will provide the mass of dry sediment per unit area at each sample site.

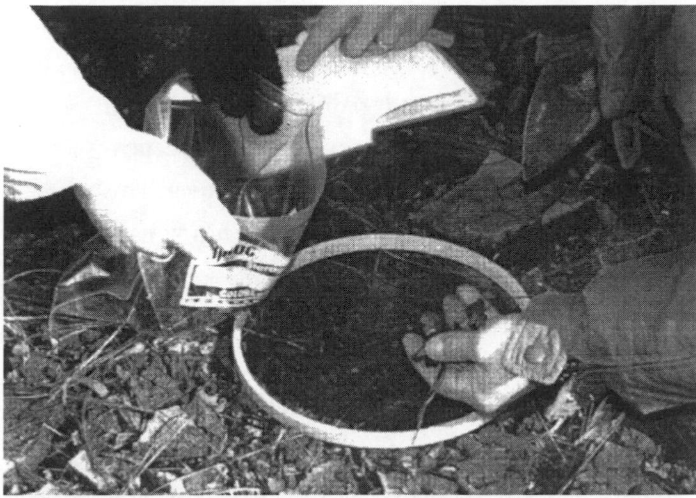

Figure 2. Collecting a sample of flood sediments intermixed with leaf litter within the 25 cm diameter ring. (Photo courtesy of Edge Magazine, East Carolina University)

Field Observations of Sedimentation

Although the lab work is not complete, and therefore we have no quantitative estimates of sedimentation rates associated with the 1999 flood, the field observations are relatively clear: little sediment was deposited on most of the Tar River floodplain. In many cases, only a "dusting" of sediment was observed within the plant litter or in abandoned homes (Figure 3). In many other instances we observed no measurable sedimentation in areas that clearly had been inundated by the floodwaters.

Larger accumulations of flood sediments were observed in three relatively isolated situations. First, overbank flow deposited coarser, sandier sediments along the top of channel banks immediately adjacent to the river (i.e., natural levees). These deposits were generally not very thick or spatially extensive (Figure 4).

Second, in locations where the bankfull channel of the Tar River angled across the floodplain, overbank flow during the flood transported sandy sediments from the channel bed onto the floodplain (Figure 5). The thickness of these deposits varied considerably, but was limited to a small section of floodplain immediately downstream of the source. Third, several tributaries draining the steeper southern part of the watershed provided a local source of sediment that was deposited on the floodplain immediately downstream from where the tributary flowed into the Tar River (Figure 5). In some cases, this sediment was derived from residential developments.

These observations indicate that during the 1999 flood few fine sediments (silt and clay) were deposited from suspension to Tar River floodplain, and that the thickest deposits were sandy sediments derived from the bed of the Tar River or small tributary channels. These sandy sediments, however, were localized and only transported a short distance on the floodplain before being deposited. There may be several as yet unresolved explanations for the lack of significant fine-grained floodplain sedimentation.

First, it is possible that the floodwaters in the Tar River were not transporting large amounts of suspended sediment, either because little sediment was mobilized within the watershed or because sediment was deposited in tributaries before reaching the Tar River. This may be related to the nature of the surface horizons of soils in the region, which tend to be quite sandy and lack the silt and clay that typically would be transported as suspended sediment. Second, it is possible that substantial quantities of sediment were transported by the Tar River but were not deposited. This may have transpired either because the sediments were too fine (i.e., clays) to settle from suspension, or because the sediment was transported through the Tar River to the Pamlico Sound in the early stages of the flood (i.e., during high flows from Hurricane Dennis) before floodwaters had spread onto the floodplain. Similar findings for the 1993 flood on the Mississippi River were reported (Gomez et al. 1995; Magilligan et al. 1998), where smaller winter flood flows transported more sediment than did the record flooding that occurred later that spring and summer. The earlier flows may have exhausted the supply of sediment available for erosion and transport. Thus, the sequencing of flood events may be more important than the magnitude of the events. Successfully explaining the relative paucity of sedimentation on the Tar River floodplain will require additional information on the timing and sediment concentrations of the flood flows associated with both hurricanes Dennis and Floyd. Estimates of sediment concentrations from remote sensing data may be useful in this regard.

Figure 3. Thin (1 mm thick) flakes of sediment deposited on the floor of an abandoned house in Princeville, N.C. Keys at top center are for scale.

a.

b.

Figure 4. a. Sand deposited on the floodplain along the south bank of the Tar River near Ironwood (northwest of Greenville). This sand is derived from two sources: a small, steep tributary draining a new residential development and the bed of the Tar River where the channel bends away from the south bank. b. Sandy flood sediments (2 cm thick) on the south bank of the Tar River at Ironwood.

Work Remaining

Assessing the quantity of sediment deposited on the floodplain of the Tar River is only the first stage in this ongoing research project. The second part of this project will focus on the factors influencing the particle-size characteristics of the deposits. Previous research has shown that the particle size and thickness of flood deposits decrease with increasing distance from the river channel, primarily due to the hydraulics of overbank flow (Allen 1985). However, these spatial patterns are also influenced by channel orientation, variations in valley width, floodplain geometry and topography, the nature of the vegetation cover on floodplains, and the particle size and availability of sediments within the watershed for transport and deposition.

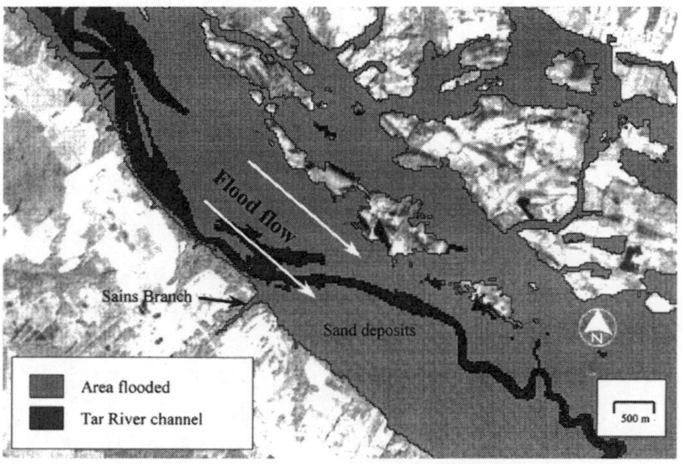

Figure 5. Localized deposition of thicker, sandy sediments from two sources. A small, relatively steep tributary (Sains Branch) transported sand from a residential development under construction along the west bank. Just upstream of this tributary confluence, the main channel of the Tar River turns to the east across the valley. This allowed the flood flow to cross over the channel and transport sandy bed sediments up onto the floodplain.

A third element of the project will examine the potential transport of trace metal contaminants associated with the sediments. Resolving the first two components of the research will play an important role in explaining trace metal concentrations in the flood deposits. Because many contaminants and nutrients are preferentially associated with fine-grained sediments (Horowitz 1991), floodplains are widely recognized as important sinks for the storage and potential remobilization of pollutants adsorbed (i.e., weakly attached) to suspended sediments (Bradley 1989; Marron 1992; Lecce and Pavlowsky 1997). Understanding spatial variations in the particle-size distribution of the floodplain deposits, therefore, is critical to understanding the distribution and environmental fate of contaminants transported by the flood. Likewise, trace metals are unlikely to pose significant contamination problems in floodplain environments if the sediments on which the metals were adsorbed were not deposited in significant quantities, which is likely to be the case on the Tar River. Nevertheless, if metal concentrations prove to be high on the floodplain, and large quantities of sediment were transported to the Pamlico Sound (with little deposited on floodplains), then assessments of contamination in the estuary may be quite different from the Tar River floodplain.

Summary

Although the 1999 flood on the Tar River was the largest event on record, little sediment was deposited on most of the floodplain. In isolated locations, sand derived locally from tributaries or the bed of the Tar River was deposited in greater thickness immediately downstream from the source. Future research will attempt to explain the lack of fine-grained sedimentation by examining the sediment concentration in the floodwaters and the timing and sequencing of the flows produced by hurricanes Dennis and Floyd. The sediments will also be analyzed for trace metals in order to assess the transport of contaminants by the flood. Event-based research of this nature is important to help improve our understanding of basic sediment transport/deposition dynamics during rare floods and to facilitate comparisons with the dynamics of rare floods on other river systems. It also provides additional evidence necessary to understand the significance of large events in the sedimentary record.

Acknowledgments

This research was supported by a grant from the National Science Foundation (#BCS-0000557). Mary Reid, Helen Burrell, and Rachel Keiffer assisted with the lab and field work.

References

Allen, J. R. L. 1985. Principles of physical sedimentology. London: George Allen and Unwin.

Bradley, S. B. 1989. Incorporation of metalliferous sediments from historic mining into floodplains. GeoJournal 19:5–14.

Gomez, B., L. A. K. Mertes, J. D. Phillips, F. J. Magilligan, and L. A. James. 1995. Sediment characteristics of an extreme flood: 1993 upper Mississippi River valley. Geology 23:963–966.

Horowitz, A. J. 1991. Sediment-trace element chemistry. Chelsea, Mich.: Lewis Publishers.

Lecce, S. A. 1997. Spatial patterns of historical overbank sedimentation and floodplain evolution, Blue River, Wisconsin. Geomorphology 18:265–277.

Lecce, S. A., and R. T. Pavlowsky. 1997. Storage of mining-related zinc in floodplain sediments, Blue River, Wisconsin. Physical Geography 18:424–439.

Magilligan, F. J., J. D. Phillips, L. A. James, and B. Gomez. 1998. Geomorphic and sedimentological controls on the effectiveness of an extreme flood. Journal of Geology 106:87–95.

Marron, D. C. 1992. Floodplain storage of mine tailings in the Belle Fourche River system: a sediment budget approach. Earth Surface Processes and Landforms 17:675–685.

Phillips, J. D. 1992. Delivery of upper-basin sediment to the lower Neuse River, North Carolina, USA. Earth Surface Processes and Landforms 17:699–709.

Phillips, J. D. 1995. Decoupling of sediment sources in large river basins. In: Effects of scale on interpretation and management of sediment and water quality. IAHS Publication No. 226, 11–16.

Phillips, J. D., M. Wyrick, G. Robbins, and M. Flynn. 1993. Accelerated erosion on the North Carolina coastal plain. Physical Geography 14:114–130.

Schumm, S. A., and R. A. Lichty. 1963. Channel widening and flood-plain construction along the Cimarron River in southwestern Kansas. U.S. Geological Survey Professional Paper 353-D:71–88.

Simmons, C. E. 1988. Sediment characteristics of streams in North Carolina. U.S. Geological Survey Open-File Report 87–701.

Slattery, M. C., P. A. Gares, and J. D. Phillips. 1998. Quantifying soil erosion and sediment delivery on North Carolina coastal plain croplands. Conservation Voices 1:20–25.

Trimble, S. W. 1977. The fallacy of stream equilibrium in contemporary denudation studies. American Journal of Science 277:876–887.

Wolman, M. G., and J. P. Miller. 1960. Magnitude and frequency of forces in geomorphic processes. Journal of Geology 68:54–74.

About the Authors: Dr. Scott A. Lecce is an assistant professor in the Department of Geography at East Carolina University. His research focuses on the processes associated with the movement of water in rivers, including the transport and storage of heavy metals in fluvial environments, human impacts on channel morphology, erosion and sedimentation, and the hydrologic and geomorphic responses to environmental change. Also an assistant professor in the Department of Geography at ECU, Dr. Patrick Pease is involved in studying the environmental and anthropogenic conditions associated with dust generation and the biogeochemical impacts of dust on people. Paul A. Gares is an assistant professor in the Department of Geography at ECU, with interests concentrated in the fields of coastal geomorphology and environmental management. Dr. Catherine A. Rigsby is an associate professor in ECU's Department of Geology. She is currently working on a diverse group of research topics, including the Quaternary environment and sedimentation and tectonics.

Obtaining Needed Water Quality Data Using North Carolina Ferries: The FerryMon Project

Joseph S. Ramus and Hans W. Paerl

Introduction

The Pamlico Sound has the distinction of being the largest estuary in the United States for which there is the least known. There has been no systematic program to measure water quality status and trends in the Pamlico Sound. Rather, measurements and surveys have been concentrated in its tributary rivers. But the need to predict ecosystem response to water quality change in the Pamlico Sound is critical to guiding future management action. Time is of the utmost importance, given the accelerated pace of land-use changes in tributary watersheds. A program is needed to "fast track" water quality status analysis in the Pamlico Sound, which will then form the basis of trends analysis and predictive modeling.

Recently, the consequences of "event-scale" physical forcing have become prominent. The event scale is hurricanes and nor'easters—deep, compact lows that deliver high surface wind velocities and precipitation rates. These episodic storms (e.g., Bertha and Fran in 1997, Bonnie in 1998, Dennis and Floyd in 1999) have been regarded largely as stochastic (random) rather than deterministic (cyclic). However, researchers have shown that the El Niño–Southern Oscillation (ENSO) cycle in the South Pacific Ocean affects global weather. Thus, the event scale may in fact be deterministic. For example, there is evidence of a persistent multi-decade enhancement of Atlantic hurricane activity associated with a major reconfiguration of Atlantic basin sea surface temperatures, and the reconfiguration is coupled to the ENSO through atmospheric drivers.

The Pamlico Sound is relatively shallow, with an average depth of 4.5 meters and a maximum depth of 7.3 meters. It has a surface area of 5,000 square kilometers. The sound is bounded on the seaward side by the Outer Banks, a barrier island system that greatly restricts water exchange with the Atlantic Ocean through four small inlets. The ratio of the volume of the sound (26 billion cubic meters) to the average annual inflow (780 cubic meters per second) leads to a water residence time of about 11 months (i.e., the time required for a volume equivalent to that of the entire sound to exit the system). Small tidal amplitudes (0.3–0.5 meters) and diverse, slow-flowing, nontidal tributaries make the sound a highly effective "trap" for particulate matter and nutrients. During normal conditions, these hydrologic and morphometric characteristics ensure high productivity and provide an ideal nursery habitat for an extremely diverse population of finfish and shellfish. However, these same features can prove stressful during years with extremely high nutrient loads because nutrients remain in the system for long periods, supporting excessive primary production, including algal blooms, that can overwhelm the capacity of grazers and higher levels (e.g., fish) of the food web. Moreover, the limited tidal flushing, low currents, and long residence time ensure that nutrients and detrital material are stored in the sediments, fueling future algal blooms and causing associated water quality problems such as depletion of oxygen levels (hypoxia).

The consequences of increased frequency and strength of event-scale storms to the physics and biology of the Pamlico Sound are predictably great. The feature of greatest vulnerability is the impounding barrier island chain. The number of inlets could be increased or decreased, or the inlets reconfigured, to allow more or less water and materials to exchange with the coastal ocean. Currently, inlets do not connect the Albemarle Sound to the coastal ocean, but they have in the geologic past.

Assessment of the impact of event-scale storms on water quality in the Pamlico Sound requires rigorous baseline data on current conditions. So, too, does distinguishing the effects of natural events (event-scale storms) from anthropogenic impacts (land-use changes). The North Carolina Department of Environment and Natural Resources is sponsoring a monitoring program that will begin to fulfill this need.

Goals and Objective of the Project

Goals

The goals of the water quality monitoring programs are as follows: 1) determine ecosystem responses to excess nutrient inputs; 2) quantify the relationships between land-use activities, hydrologic processes, and the ecological response of receiving waters of the Pamlico Sound system; 3) develop the capability to assess and predict the relationships between nutrient inputs, phytoplankton blooms, and associated water quality changes, which is important for determining ecosystem response; and 4) provide information critical to long-term water quality management in the sound and its tributaries.

Objectives

The objective is to employ the North Carolina Department of Transportation's system of ferries to fast track water quality status and trends analysis for the Pamlico Sound. This project will occur at a time when accelerated land-use change is occurring in the tributary watersheds and when legislatively mandated nutrient controls are being placed on tributary watersheds. At present, there is no rational basis for predicting water quality change on the Pamlico Sound in response to human activities in the watersheds, because no baseline data exist. The intent of this project is to begin the process of rapidly providing spatially and temporally intensive baseline data in a cost-effective manner using existing resources—namely, the ferries.

The Automated Monitoring System (AMS) will monitor surface waters continuously along ferry routes and include the following parameters: temperature, salinity, dissolved oxygen, turbidity, chlorophyll, and humic substances. The monitoring system will be continuous flow, PC-operated and data logged, and it will be navigated using the global position system (GPS). The components are "off the shelf" sensors, which have the reputation of being "field hardened." In addition, an automated and refrigerated discrete sampler component will take and store water samples for subsequent laboratory determinations of 1) phytoplankton bulk enumerations by pigments; 2) dissolved inorganic macronutrients (nitrate, ammonium, orthophosphate, silicate); 3) total Kjeldahl nitrogen; 4) colored dissolved organic material (or humics); and 5) on selected samples, dissolved organic carbon, dissolved organic nitrogen, and carbon-hydrogen-nitrogen.

The frequency of data and discrete sample collection will be determined empirically by the distribution of properties along the ferry routes, such that all important spatial and temporal scales are represented. Routes are crossed by multiple ferries; however, only one ferry per route will be equipped for unattended monitoring.

For data management and utilization, spreadsheets will be built from navigated cruise track data and analyzed with appropriate statistical (as Systat 8.0) and geographic information system (GIS; such as Surfer 7.0, ARC/INFO, and ArcView) software, which can establish daily, synoptic, seasonal, and interannual variability, cycles, and trends. In addition, horizontal analysis can establish frontal system dynamics and the effect on phytoplankton productivity. All data will be archived in digital form on CD-ROM(s) and made available for other analysis and modeling efforts. A web site will be established on the Internet to communicate data and interpretations to the public.

Expected Results and Benefits

If the pilot program proves to be as robust as expected, it could become a model for status and trends water quality analysis for the Albemarle-Pamlico Sound system, as well as the Cape Fear River estuary. These "ships of opportunity" can assume a monitoring duty cycle with little or no interference or cost to their operation, while providing water quality managers with unprecedented continuous data, in both time and space. This data stream would be difficult, if not impossible, to obtain through conventional monitoring programs. Given sufficient data collected in this manner, water quality monitoring could eventually be transferred to more efficient remote sensing technologies. However, there would always remain the need to "ground truth" and thus a continuing role for ferries.

Relevance to North Carolina

The Albemarle-Pamlico Estuarine Study (APES) produced a comprehensive conservation management plan (CCMP, November 1994) for the estuarine system, which will serve the system well. Because the Environmental Protection Agency (EPA) provides only maintenance funding for the APES, there are not sufficient resources to monitor the progress of the CCMP as it is implemented, particularly with regard to water quality. The proposed water quality monitoring program offers an opportunity to calibrate the implementation of the CCMP and river basin nutrient management plans.

Relevance to other work

The Neuse River Monitoring and Modeling Project (ModMon) is an intensive monitoring and modeling effort in the lower Neuse River, primarily quantifying and predicting the ecosystem response to excess watershed loading of nitrogen nutrients. ModMon is the most comprehensive effort in a river basin in the state. Coupling this Pamlico Sound project to ModMon presents the opportunity to investigate the fate of tributary nutrient loading in the Neuse and Pamlico river estuaries. Materials transformations and exchanges are particularly important to understanding the role of water quality in Pamlico Sound in relation to the coastal ocean, especially in the context of fisheries.

The National Oceanographic and Atmospheric Administration's (NOAA) Coastal Services Center and NOAA's Natural Environmental Satellite Data and Information Service (NESDIS), Office of Research and Applications (ORA) are working to bring remote sensing to the coastal management community. The NOAA scientists are working with streams of data produced by the AVHRR and SeaWiFS sensors flown on satellites and aircraft. Appropriately calibrated, the data provide a tool to monitor ecosystem change in coastal waters. The intensive data stream from ferry-based automated water quality monitoring provides an unprecedented opportunity to calibrate coastal remote sensing, which has proved more difficult than ocean remote sensing.

About the Authors: Joseph S. Ramus is professor of Biological Oceanography at Duke University Marine Laboratory in Beaufort, North Carolina. Dr. Ramus's research includes the study of physical forcing of phytoplankton biomass, productivity, and community structure in coastal plain estuaries. His research seeks to match physiological response and the temporal frequency of physical drivers and the phasing of phytoplankton dynamics with the environment. Hans W. Paerl is the William R. Kenan Professor at the Institute of Marine Sciences, University of North Carolina in Morehead City, North Carolina. Dr. Paerl studies the nutrient production dynamics of aquatic microbes at the base of the estuarine and coastal food webs, focusing on environmental controls of algal production, community structure, and assessment of the causes and consequences of human-induced eutrophication of rivers, lakes, estuaries, and coastal oceans.

Part IV / An "Extreme Event"—Hurricane Floyd, September 1999—Impacts on Groups and Individuals

Population and Economic Changes in Eastern North Carolina Before and After Hurricane Floyd

Albert A. Delia

Al Delia is the Associate Vice Chancellor for Economic and Community Development at East Carolina University. His responsibilities include directing and overseeing the five units at the university that are involved in public service and public outreach programs that relate to economic or community development. Prior to accepting his current position, Mr. Delia served with the North Carolina Small Business and Technology Development Center, first as director of the Eastern Regional Office at East Carolina University, then as associate state director at the University of North Carolina at Chapel Hill. In that capacity, Mr. Delia conceived and developed special statewide programs in technology development and transfer, international trade, and federal procurement. These programs still serve as national models. Before making North Carolina his home, Mr. Delia helped found a nonprofit company to finance small- to medium-sized businesses in New Jersey. He has helped to start and is currently a partner in and member of the board of directors of several small businesses. He gave a plenary presentation at the conference and was introduced by Dr. Stephen Culver, chair of the Department of Geology at East Carolina University.

" . . . if we fail to plan, we plan to fail.

—Jim Hunt, North Carolina Governor 1985–2000

Introduction

Eastern North Carolina is no stranger to the effects of major storms. Because this region of the state juts out into the Atlantic Ocean, it is at great risk to severe weather. Historically, the area has both benefited and suffered from its weather. Centuries of commerce and development have been dependent in some way on the region's weather. Production of many crops that are important to the state's economy, such as tobacco, depend on the high rainfalls typical of the area. But the forty-four counties that comprise this area, extending from the Outer Banks west past Interstate 95, have seen significant changes in its economic fortunes over the years, evolving through an era dependent on big tobacco and textiles until today as it looks to find its place in the new high-technology-based economy. However, there are historically significant obstacles to this region's pursuit of economic prosperity. Even before the flood of

1999, eastern North Carolina was disadvantaged due to a lack of political muscle, central location, and statewide impetus to ensure sustainable and focused development.

As the region strived for economic change, the population increased. Since 1950 people have moved into the low-lying coastal areas of the state in record numbers. But wetlands and broad floodplains dominate these lands, placing the growing population at a high risk of exposure to natural disasters, like hurricanes and floods.

Of the Atlantic states, only Florida is more vulnerable to hurricanes. But with its firm grip on economic prosperity, Florida is more resilient to calamitous storms, enabling it to recover more rapidly and effectively than other hurricane-prone states. Within North Carolina, residents of eastern North Carolina are the least able to recover from disasters.

The combined effects of the two hurricanes that came ashore in 1999 in eastern North Carolina will impact the economy and social structure of this region for many years. The greatest flood in the state's history left the coastal plain region with a tenuous economic future and great concern for recovery. How communities respond to this new challenge will determine whether the long-term effects will be for the betterment or detriment of the region. This paper describes the demographic conditions of eastern North Carolina before and after these two devastating hurricanes. Also described is a program initiated at East Carolina University (ECU) that was designed to help individuals and communities shape a better future for eastern North Carolina.

The Face of Eastern North Carolina—Before the "Flood of the Century"

Over 38% of North Carolina's population, or 2.9 million people, reside within the eastern forty-four counties. Even accounting for no growth or a decrease in population in eleven of these eastern counties, the 14.6% growth rate in eastern North Carolina led the state average (13.8%) since 1990. The population of many of the coastal counties has nearly doubled or quadrupled since 1970 (Table 1). Looking more deeply into the growth statistics, since 1970 this region has seen a growth rate of 52.7%, still surpassing that of the state (48.5%) (Maiolo et al. 1998).

The core of eastern North Carolina, the forty-four counties east of Interstate 95, was the area most affected by the floods resulting from hurricanes Dennis and Floyd. Although this area has been blessed by greater than average population growth, it has also been the most economically disadvantaged region of North Carolina. Through no fault of planning or design (and at times due to the lack of it), the legacies suffered as a result of this rural economy include the lowest levels of education in the state, the most outhouses in the nation, the poorest counties, and the highest illiteracy rates. In addition, eastern North Carolina has a large minority population, primarily serving the agriculture industry. Historically underserved, this minority population includes both African Americans and Hispanics, who

Table 1. Percent changes in population size in eastern North Carolina since 1970. (Counties in bold have had drastic population increases in the last thirty years.)

County	Percent Change (%)			
	1970-1980	1980-1990	1990-1998	1970-1998
Beaufort	12.2	4.8	2.7	20.8
Bertie	2.4	-3.0	-1.4	-2.1
Brunswick	**47.6**	**42.5**	**24.4**	**178.3**
Camden	6.9	1.3	6.6	15.9
Carteret	**30.0**	**27.9**	**12.2**	**89.5**
Chowan	16.5	7.5	5.7	32.8
Columbus	8.7	-2.8	5.1	11.3
Craven	13.6	14.9	8.9	43.1
Currituck	**59.0**	**23.9**	**18.9**	**142.9**
Dare	**91.2**	**70.0**	**19.4**	**303.4**
Duplin	7.7	-2.3	10.4	17.4
Edgecombe	6.6	1.3	-3.3	4.5
Gates	4.1	4.8	6.8	17.2
Greene	7.7	-4.5	14.9	20.7
Halifax	1.3	0.8	-0.6	1.5
Hertford	-4.4	-3.6	-3.9	-11.3
Hyde	5.4	-7.9	-2.1	-4.8
Jones	-0.8	-3.0	-7.1	-10.2
Lenoir	8.4	-4.3	3.0	6.9
Martin	4.9	-3.4	1.8	3.3
Nash	13.6	14.2	13.3	49.6
New Hanover	**24.7**	**16.2**	**19.8**	**80.7**
Northampton	-3.9	-6.3	0.2	-9.8
Onslow	**9.4**	**32.9**	**-1.0**	**43.8**
Pamlico	9.8	9.3	5.6	27.1
Pasquatank	6.1	10.0	10.9	31.0
Pender	**22.7**	**29.6**	**24.9**	**111.7**
Pitt	**22.0**	**20.3**	**11.9**	**66.7**
Tyrrell	4.4	-3.0	-6.4	-4.8
Washington	5.4	-5.4	-7.0	-6.8
Wayne	13.6	7.8	8.4	33.8
Wilson	9.8	4.6	4.4	20.3
State Total	**15.7**	**12.7**	**12.1**	**48.5**

Source: Maiolo et al. 1998

were ultimately most affected by the flooding.

Within the eastern region of North Carolina, unemployment has averaged approximately 6%. The state average has been under 4%, making the region's unemployment rate 50% higher than the state average. Rates of poverty in the thirty-two counties most affected by the flooding were among the highest in the nation, 15% to 20% higher than the overall state average. In some areas, one in three people live below the poverty line. And for those employed, the outlook was equally disheartening; per capita income is $3,700 below the rest of the state.

According to a 1999 study (Wilson et al. 1999), there are 96,502 businesses in the forty-four county region. Of these, 78,285 were considered small businesses with one to nine employees; 16,983 were medium-sized businesses with between ten and ninety-nine employees; and 1,234 were large businesses with more than 100 employees. In this region, wages were 86% of the North Carolina average, and the rate of business failure was above the state average.

After the Storms—The Scope of the Disaster

Social costs

Geographically, forty-four counties and seventy-three municipalities were affected by the 1999 floods. Compared to other regions of the United States, the flood area would cover a land mass larger than Rhode Island, Connecticut, and Massachusetts—*combined.* Had this event impacted these three states to the degree that it affected eastern North Carolina, the recovery response would have been far different. Those states have greater regional and national political muscle and many salient issues are focused in the more urban and affluent regions.

As the flood receded in eastern North Carolina, the devastation was marked with the misery of those in harm's way. Fifty-two people died, most from driving into floodwater and then trying unsuccessfully to extricate themselves. Over 60,000 sought temporary shelter, and power outages affected 1.2 million people. In total, more than 50,000 homes were damaged, of those 15,000 were left uninhabitable and 8,300 were totally destroyed. Over 11,000 homes will be bought out through the National Flood Insurance Program.

Economic losses

Economic losses to business were equally devastating. Losses to the agricultural and forestry industry, including producers and service providers, totaled over $955 million. It is anticipated that up to 5,000 families will sell their farms. In all, more than 60,000 businesses had some degree of loss, with over $1 billion in physical damage and $4 billion in lost revenues. On an individual level, average repair cost for physical damage to businesses following the flood was $39,091, with an average loss of revenue of approximately $78,600. As a result of the flooding, 30,000 jobs were lost. In the severely hit counties, 75% of businesses shut down and were closed for between 3.5 and 8.5 days.

Prior to the flood, eastern North Carolina was gradually diversifying its economy, expanding the economic base, and developing business plans that included business expansions. Sixteen percent of small businesses and 19% of medium-sized businesses included expansion as part of their future. Following the flood, only 5% of small- to medium-sized businesses expressed an ability or willingness to expand. An even greater impact involved proposed large business expansions. Nearly a quarter of the large businesses in this region planned to expand before Floyd, but after the flood, only 8% of businesses with over 100 employees kept expansion as an element of their development plans (Wilson et al. 1999).

Providing Solutions—The ECU Outreach Network

Like the community that surrounds it, the campus of ECU suffered flood damage. As the university began to meet the needs of its students and staff, it could not ignore its neighbors in surrounding counties who were struggling to recover from the disaster. A university community is an enclave of experts—experts that too often are not able to apply their knowledge to solve problems that are found outside the academic environment. Often they are constrained by the time-consuming demands of their positions or because the process of reaching out to the community is not always easy.

ECU developed a program to facilitate linking academic experts with the specific needs that arose after Hurricane Floyd. The Outreach Network offers expert advice in various areas, such as environmental plans, strategic planning, counseling, and hazard mitigation. (For more information, see the network's web page at <www.ecu.edu/on/>.) Its purpose is to help the impacted counties rebuild and move on. As of 2000, the ECU Outreach Network has 260 faculty and staff members available to provide assistance for those who need it most. Graduate students are providing additional services through graduate assistantships and classes. Over the last year, the ECU Outreach Network has provided assistance in more than thirty cases in the surrounding communities. These cases have dealt primarily with grant writing initiatives, strategic planning, small business assistance, environmental planning, mental-health counseling, and stress management.

The ECU Outreach Network does more than just offer expertise and advice. In addition to those services already mentioned, the network provides web site addresses for information about hurricanes, flooding, and other natural disasters. Photograph and statistical links allow viewers a firsthand look at the severity of the destruction that Hurricane Floyd caused. Finally, the ECU Outreach Network provides contact numbers for local, state, and federal agencies that might be useful for obtaining recovery assistance.

The network has assisted in many projects. In this volume, Carmen Rossoniello has summarized the results of one project involving counseling children at an elementary school in Tarboro, North Carolina. Here are just a few other examples of how this program has begun to address economic and social recovery needs:

Hazard mitigation and environmental concerns—Hyde County representatives contacted members of the ECU Outreach Network to ask for assistance in hazard mitigation planning and for information relating to home elevations and acquisition. After contacting the Hyde County Planning office to initiate a work schedule, members of the Outreach Network began designing implementation plans to deal with ongoing environmental needs. In addition to these plans, the faculty members also created a hazard mitigation plan for Hyde County. Although this project has met its initial goals, the faculty members are still consulting with Hyde County officials to ensure that the process continues to run smoothly.

Economic growth and recovery—Pollocksville was hit particularly hard by the flooding from Hurricane Floyd. Many of the homes and businesses located in this town were lost to the floodwaters. Representatives of Pollocksville contacted the Outreach Network to ask for assistance in capital facilities planning and economic recovery. Much of the work associated with these projects has been focused on deciding where the extra-territorial boundaries should be located, as well as determining the tax value for surrounding properties. These decisions will allow the town's representatives and members of the network to choose the best strategy for the future economic development of the town. Meetings are now being set up with town administrators to discuss the network's initial findings.

Wastewater drainage and treatment—The town of Lake Waccamaw has begun to address a problem with their wastewater system that resulted from the hurricane and floods. Town leaders recognized a need to study the design of the storm water drainage plan and the wastewater treatment facility. These same officials contacted representatives of the network seeking advice on wastewater management. After several meetings, the town's leaders and the network, representatives have developed a team approach to address questions regarding Lake Waccamaw's current wastewater system and facility. Information gathering is in progress, with results and recommendations to come in early fall 2000.

Summary

The floods following hurricanes Dennis and Floyd provide an opportunity for the communities of eastern North Carolina to expand their economic foundation and establish plans that will lead to a more sustainable and vital future. In addition to establishing plans, the thirty-eight affected counties have the opportunity to assess inefficiencies in their communities. Through their efforts of consensus building and evaluation, these communities have the potential to design improvements that will result in investments in their future rather than maintaining the status quo.

Those in the flood-impacted region must help decide whether needed improvements are made. To overcome a historically inferior position in the state and nation, a single voice of recovery must be heard from all impacted communities—a unified effort of tens of thousands. This is the voice that must be heard in order to attain sustainable growth and economic diversification, focusing resources for the betterment of the region and creating a region unified by its vision of the future.

References and Resources

Department of Regional Development Services, East Carolina University <http://www.ecu.edu/rds/rds.html>.

Maiolo, J. R., A. Delia, J. C. Whitehead, B. Edwards, K. Wilson, M. Van Willigen, C. Williams, and M. Meekins. 1998. A socioeconomic hurricane evacuation impact analysis and a hurricane evacuation impact assessment tool (methodology) for coastal North Carolina: A case study of Hurricane Bonnie. Greenville, N.C.: East Carolina University, Regional Development Services (RDS), Department of Sociology, Department of Economics.

Problem Solving Research, Inc. 1999. Outlook—North Carolina, Spring 1999. A socioeconomic hurricane impact analysis for coastal North Carolina: Hurricane Floyd, 1999, East Carolina University.

Wilson, K., P. Harrell, K. Arena, N. Johnson, R. Navarro, and H. Burguss. 1999. Public perceptions of the importance of science and technology to the North Carolina economy. Regional Development Services Survey Research Laboratory, Greenville, N.C.: East Carolina University, <http://www.governor.state.nc.us/govoffice/science/projects/nc2030/survey/index.html>.

Looking into the Face of the Storm: Small Businesses

Walter Fitts

Mr. Fitts is the director of the eastern regional office of the North Carolina Small Business and Technology Development Center (SBTDC), a business development service of the University of North Carolina system that helps support economic development by assisting companies throughout the state. Mr. Fitts assumed responsibility for shifting the center's work to serve as the Business Recovery and Assistance Center, providing disaster assistance to a twelve-county area in eastern North Carolina.

I want to talk briefly about the impact of hurricanes Dennis, Floyd, and the flood on small businesses. In reality, these storms impacted all businesses in eastern North Carolina, with two direct hits from Dennis, one from Floyd, and the flood. You can literally make a case for all businesses that are geographically located east of Interstate 95, including agribusiness, as being severely impacted, in one way or another, by these disasters. An estimate, and that's about what it is, an estimate, is that 60,000 businesses—small, mid-size, and large, including agribusiness—were impacted. At the Business Recovery and Assistance Center, we're beginning to see some agribusiness clients right now.

Most of my comments are going to be directed toward those twelve counties right in the middle of eastern North Carolina. On 27 September 1999, the Small Business and Technology Development Center office in Greenville, the one in Wilmington, and the one at Elizabeth State University in Elizabeth City were converted to business recovery assistance centers. Providing recovery assistance is essentially what we've been doing ever since. We primarily help businesses (small, mid-size, and large) cope with the Small Business Administration (SBA) disaster loan application process. People from these five centers go from county to county in our region of the state, setting up shop in cooperation with a sponsor and some host organizations, and trying to get individuals to at least come in and apply for SBA disaster loan rebates.

It's going to be a long recovery period. Real small businesses and business that have only been around for a short period of time are going to have a hard time recovering. If 50% of these types of business make it, I'll be satisfied. For small- to mid-sized enterprises that have a little bit longer track record, I think that four out of six are going to make it. The larger businesses, with a couple of exceptions, have pretty much recovered to pre-storm activity.

In general, I was surprised and pleased to see the coordination and cooperation among state, regional, and local agencies in providing assistance. The only thing you see in the media are the horror stories. You never hear the good news about how businesses and individuals received help from a variety of sources. That capability is all over the place, and, frankly, I saw an awful lot of it. I think that the lesson we have learned is that helping communities, helping individuals, helping businesses, and in general helping our region recover from this disaster is going to take a continuous and collaborative effort.

The Incidence of Injury, Illness, and Death During and After Hurricane Floyd

Karen M. Becker

Introduction

In the late summer and early fall of 1999, the rains from Hurricane Dennis, Hurricane Floyd, and Hurricane Irene caused extensive flooding along the Neuse, Tar, Roanoke, Lumbar, and Cape Fear rivers, affecting an estimated 2.1 million individuals in eastern North Carolina. This report presents data on injuries, illnesses, and deaths during and following Hurricane Floyd. The leading cause of death and sources for illness and injury are identified and recommendations for decreasing these human impacts during and after future storms are presented.

Gathering Data

The state medical examiner's office provided the Center for Disease Control (CDC) with epidemiologic information about deaths related to Hurricane Floyd. (For a complete list of the individuals and institutions that provided information, see CDC 2000a.) To monitor illness and injury related to the hurricane and subsequent flood, emergency department surveillance was established at twenty hospitals in eighteen of the flood-affected counties in eastern North Carolina. Standardized illness and injury classifications were developed and applied by a disaster response team and emergency department staff during the surveillance period for comparison with similar periods in 1998. To monitor trends from 16 September to 27 October 1999, diagnosis or chief symptoms for each patient visit were abstracted from daily emergency department logs. The 1999 illness and injury data were compared with data from four days in September 1998 (13 September [Sunday], 15 [Tuesday], 17 [Thursday], and 19 [Saturday]) and four days in October 1998 (11 October [Sunday], 13 [Tuesday], 15 [Thursday], and 17 [Saturday]). To compare a complete week of 1998 data with 1999 data, the September 1998 weekdays were weighted by multiplying by 2.5 and added to the weekend days; the same methods were applied to the October 1998 data. Analysis of variance was used to compare the number of emergency department visits for each weekday during the 1999 surveillance period.

The Incidence of Injury, Illness, and Death

Table 1. Number of deaths associated with Hurricane Floyd and the flood.

September 1999 Date	Number of Deaths
15	1
16	**35**
17	8
18	2
19	0
20	1
21	1
22	2
23	0
24	0
25	1

The medical examiner determined that fifty-two deaths were associated directly with the storm. The deceased ranged in age from 1 to 96 years (median age was 43 years). Thirty-eight (73%) were males. Twenty counties reported at least one death, and 40% of all deaths occurred in three counties. Of the fifty-two deaths, thirty-five (67%) occurred on 16 September, the day Hurricane Floyd made landfall in Wilmington, North Carolina (Table 1). The leading cause of death was drowning; twenty-four (67%) deaths involved occupants of motor vehicles trapped in floodwaters (Table 2). Seven deaths occurred during transport by boat, in which flotation devices were not worn by any of the victims. Five (10%) of the fifty-two deaths were rescue workers.

From 16 September to 27 October, 59,398 emergency department visits were reported; 67% related to illnesses and 33% to injuries. Four conditions accounted for 63% of all visits: orthopedic and soft tissue injury (28%), respiratory illness (15%), gastrointestinal illness (11%), and cardiovascular disease (9%). Nineteen cases of hypothermia occurred following the hurricane, including one death. Emergency departments reported no hypothermia cases during the 1998 reference period. During the 1999 surveillance period, ten cases of carbon monoxide poisoning were reported, compared with no reported incidences during the 1998 reference period.

No statistical differences were found when comparing the number of emergency department visits with different days of the week during the surveillance period in 1999. Comparing the first week following Hurricane Floyd with the first week of September 1998, significant increases were reported in suicide attempts, dog bites, febrile illnesses, basic medical needs (e.g., oxygen, medication refills, dialysis, and vaccines), and dermatitis. (For complete statistical results, see CDC 2000a.) Comparing a week that occurred one month after Hurricane Floyd with the same period in 1998 showed significant increases in 1999 reported incidences of arthropod bites (e.g., spiders), diarrhea, violence (i.e., assault, gunshot wounds, and rape), and asthma. Routine surveillance by local public health workers following Hurricane

Table 2. Deaths related to Hurricane Floyd listed by cause (there were 52 deaths).

Cause of Death	Number	Percent
Drowning	36	69%
in motor vehicle	24	
in boat	7	
as pedestrian	4	
in house	1	
Motor-vehicle Crash (excluding drowning)	7	13%
Myocardial Infarction	4	8%
Fire (burns and trauma from escape attempts)	2	4%
Hypothermia	1	2%
Electrocution	1	2%
Fall	1	2%

Floyd identified outbreaks in shelters of self-limiting gastrointestinal disease and respiratory disease.

The findings in this paper are subject to at least three limitations. First, the surveillance system was limited because the emergency departments did not represent the range of health-care services used by individuals in the flood-affected areas. Second, if emergency department logs contained misclassified diagnoses, some medical conditions might not have been identified and recorded properly. Third, on the basis of the assumption that diagnoses on weekdays do not vary, only eight days of data were collected for September and October 1998, potentially limiting the strength of the comparison with 1999.

Identifying Causes and Making Recommendations

In areas where flash flooding occurs, water rises quickly, forcing individuals to evacuate without preparation. During and after Hurricane Floyd, rural inland counties were the most severely affected (S. Yount, Federal Emergency Management Agency, personal communication, 2000). Individuals residing in affected areas may not have recognized or been informed about the risks associated with severe storms. Most mortality and incidences of illness caused by inland hurricanes have been attributed to the effects of high winds (Philen et al. 1992; Brewer et al. 1994; CDC 1996a); however, surveillance during and after Hurricane Floyd showed illness and mortality patterns similar to other flood-related disasters (CDC 1993b; CDC 1994; CDC 2000b). Drowning was a major cause of death, especially among individuals who attempted to drive through moving water.

Hurricane Floyd surveillance reports of nonfatal injuries and illnesses were similar to earlier storms, with reported increases in insect stings (CDC 1993a; Brewer et al. 1994; CDC 1996b), dermatitis, diarrhea (CDC 1993a), and psychiatric conditions (Longmire et al. 1988). Findings unique to Hurricane Floyd included increases in reports of hypothermia, dog bites, and asthma.

In the aftermath of Hurricane Floyd, some surveillance data suggest that public health intervention strategies could improve in future hurricane-related disasters. State agencies need to identify regional and local organizations that represent communities at risk. A coordinated disaster response could strengthen available resources and improve response scope and efficiency. Surveillance data also suggest that deaths from floods may be prevented by identifying flood-prone areas and advising individuals at risk to take appropriate actions. Public service announcements, educational materials, and training programs on hurricane preparedness should be made accessible to all communities before a hurricane season begins. For example, motorists should be warned not to drive through areas in imminent danger of flash floods or onto roads and bridges covered by rapidly moving water. If vehicles are necessary to evacuate a community, safe evacuation routes should be identified in advance. In addition, all individuals that use boats for transport should wear flotation devices. The deaths of five rescue workers suggest the need for occupational risk prevention training.

Individuals should take precautions with animals, especially if they are unfamiliar to the handler. Even though hurricanes typically occur during warmer periods of the year, care must be taken to avoid hypothermia, especially in situations where exposure to water occurs. People with asthma and other chronic respiratory conditions returning to homes and workplaces that have been flooded should guard against exposure to mold and mildew, which may exacerbate respiratory symptoms, especially during cleanup activities (National Institute for Occupational Safety and Health 1994).

Throughout all phases of disaster relief, including long-term recovery, appropriate mental-health services should be made available. The long-term psychological effects following a disaster such as this have not been well studied; it is likely that posttraumatic stress-like disorders have affected those suffering from the devastation caused by hurricanes Dennis, Floyd, and Irene. Community disaster planning for each hurricane season should begin by early spring. The current definition of areas vulnerable to flooding should be reevaluated and made clear to all communities. Optimally, steps should be taken to maximize the opportunity for timely and safe evacuation. For those that choose to stay behind, the adoption of behaviors that minimize risk should be facilitated.

References

Brewer R. D., P. D. Morris, and T. B. Cole. 1994. Hurricane-related emergency department visits in an inland area; an analysis of the public health impact of Hurricane Hugo in North Carolina. An nuals of Emergency Medicine 23:731–736.

Center for Disease Control (CDC). 1993a. Morbidity surveillance following the Midwest flood—Missouri, 1993. Morbidity and Mortality Weekly Report 42:797–798.

Center for Disease Control (CDC). 1993b. Public health consequences of a flood disaster—Iowa, 1993. Morbidity and Mortality Weekly Report 42:653–656.

Center for Disease Control (CDC). 1994. Flood-related mortality—Georgia, July 4-14, 1994. Morbidity and Mortality Weekly Report 43:526–530.

Center for Disease Control (CDC). 1996a. Deaths associated with hurricanes Marilyn and Opal—United States, September-October 1995. Morbidity and Mortality Weekly Report 45:32–38.

Center for Disease Control (CDC). 1996b. Surveillance for injuries and illnesses and rapid health-needs assessment following hurricanes Marilyn and Opal, September-October 1995. Morbidity and Mortality WeeklyReport 45:81–85.

Center for Disease Control (CDC). 2000a. Morbidity and mortality associated with Hurricane Floyd—NorthCarolina, September–October 1999. Morbidity and Mortality Weekly Report 49:369–372

Center for Disease Control (CDC). 2000b. Storm-related mortality—central Texas, October 17–31, 1998. Morbidity and Mortality Weekly Report 49:133–135.

Longmire A. W., J. Burch, and L. A. Broom. 1988. Morbidity of Hurricane Elena. Southern Medical

Journal 81:1343–1346.

National Institute for Occupational Safety and Health (NIOSH). 1994. Update: NIOSH warns of haz ards of flood cleanup work. Publication no. 94–123.Washington, D.C.:U.S. Department of Health and Human Services, CDC.

Philen R. M., D. L. Combs, L. Miller, L. M. Sanderson, R. G. Parrish, and R. Ing. 1992. Hurricane Hugo-related deaths: South Carolina and Puerto Rico, 1989. Disasters 16:53–59.

About the Author: Karen Becker completed this work while working as an Epidemic Intelligence Service Officer for the Center for Disease Control and Prevention (CDC). Currently, Dr. Becker is a Preventative Medicine Fellow in the Office of International and Refugee Health at the U.S. Department of Health and Human Services.

The Impact of Hurricane Floyd on the Elderly

Eleanor Krassen Covan, Marlene M. Rosenkoetter, Beth Richards, and Anita Lane

Introduction

This study specifically examines the impact of Floyd on the elderly residents in four counties in North Carolina that sustained considerable flooding due to Hurricane Floyd. For some elderly victims, the issues and events of the hurricane and floods of September 1999 are particularly serious due to impaired coping abilities, limited incomes, the limited availability of support systems, and concern for their own health, among others. At an age when the elderly need familiar people and possessions around them, the floods left many coping with existing sources of stress, uncertainty for the future, and an awareness that things will not return to the way they were before the storm. During and after a disaster, the needs and type of assistance required for older adults may be quite different from those required by other members of a community.

The overall purpose of this study was to investigate the impact of Hurricane Floyd on the elderly residing in southeastern North Carolina. But more importantly, we wanted to identify issues that should be addressed to prevent a reoccurrence of the problems that resulted after Hurricane Floyd. Emergency management officials can use this information to plan more effectively for future storms.

After Floyd—Listening to the Elderly

Prior to Hurricane Floyd, a sociology of aging course was designed in the Gerontology Program at the University of North Carolina at Wilmington (UNCW). In the course, students were to assist in a local collaboration of older adults and service agencies that were committed to improving the quality of life for older adults. Three weeks after Hurricane Floyd, the Cape Fear Area Agency on Aging approached the Gerontology Program to assist in the recovery process. Specifically, we were asked to develop methods for assessing the impact of the storm on older adults in our region. The service-learning activities of the original course were modified to meet this request.

In consultation with local service providers, three methods of gathering data were chosen. (The university institutional review board reviewed each method for compliance with regulations for the protection of human subjects.) The three methods used were: 1) video life-history interviews with twenty elderly volunteers whose lives and personal possessions were devastated by the storm; 2) a questionnaire administered to older adults in Brunswick, Columbus, New Hanover, and Pender counties; and 3) open-ended interviews with a small sample of service providers. Students gathered all the data under the supervision of gerontology faculty.

Video life-histories

The video project was described to the director of the Department of Aging in each of the four counties. The directors were asked to recommend five to ten clients for the project. Because storm survivors were bombarded with people offering them goods or services that did not meet their needs, researchers felt that it was best to have service workers assess which elderly clients might benefit from telling their stories to students.

The students were grouped into teams of two, and each team was assigned one interviewee. They contacted the older adult, described the project, and requested permission to meet with that person. Students received guidance from UNCW faculty and the staff of the Cape Fear Area Agency on Aging, and a documentarian in the Department of Communication Studies at UNCW helped sensitize students to the special needs of the elderly interviewees.

Each team had two or three conversations with their interviewee and visited that person at least once before obtaining written permission to videotape a life-history interview. During the interview, students asked about all aspects of the elder's life before asking about the recent storms. Interviewees were then specifically asked to discuss the impact of Hurricane Floyd. The interviewees decided what was recorded on their videos. Upon completion of the interview, each student wrote a short paper describing the older adult they interviewed and the impact of the storm on that person's life. The students and the course instructor then employed qualitative content analysis of all of the interviews to assess the collective impact of the storm on older adults. At the end of the project, the videos were presented to the interviewees as gifts.

Questionnaire

Researchers designed a questionnaire that thirty-two students in the sociology of aging course then administered to a group of older adults. Students were provided with guidance and instructions and were given the opportunity to meet and discuss their approach with the faculty researchers. In particular, students were told to remind interviewees that they could stop the interview at any time. Students could also discontinue an interview should an interviewee become upset. In addition, students were given information on how to ask open-ended questions, write up the responses, and code the data.

The questionnaire was divided into three sections and was designed to collect both quantitative and qualitative data. The first section elicited responses on demographic information. The second section concentrated on decisions concerning evacuation and the immediate impact of the storm, and the third section was devoted to hurricane-specific personal and situational issues. A thorough review of the questionnaire's reliability and value was not completed due to the urgency of testing soon after the storm and the nature of the questionnaire. However, content validity of the questionnaire was established through peer review and external consultants. Students pre-tested the questionnaire by interviewing older neighbors and family members. It was also tested with a small number of subjects to determine the length of time required for its completion, as well as its readability and completeness.

A sample of elderly residents in southeastern North Carolina, each of whom was at least sixty years old, was obtained using clients that were involved in nutrition programs in a four-county area. Each student in the course was asked to complete five surveys. Site managers and student interviewers explained the purpose of the survey to older adults. Each older adult was interviewed privately, in a face-to-face situation. Students recorded the elder's responses and each prepared a short qualitative analysis of the persons he or she interviewed.

Service agency interviews

Two students conducted eleven interviews with community service workers involved in disaster planning, evacuations, post-disaster work, and/or community safety. The students selected the interviewees. They used a qualitative questionnaire designed to determine how these providers and their agencies were personally affected during the disaster, how they could be better prepared for future disasters, and how they could better serve their clients. Both face-to-face interviews and telephone interviews were completed.

Areas of Concern for the Elderly After Hurricane Floyd

A total of 167 older adults participated in the study. A majority (93.4%) were between the ages of 60–89 years of age. Of these, almost half (41.9%) were between the ages of 70–79. Whites comprised 65.7% of the sample, African Americans 31.3%, with the remaining of other ethnic origins. Nearly 72% were females and 28.1% were males. Living arrangements varied, with 51.5% living alone, 31.1% living with a spouse, and 19.2% living with family. The majority (68.1%) lived in a single-family house, while 10.8% were living in an apartment, and the same percentage lived in a permanent mobile home. Most respondents (76%) had a neighbor living next door, and 69.9% had a family member within the same town or closer. Income levels included: 38.8% with $10,000 or less; 32% with $10,001–$20,000; and 12.9% with $20,001–$30,000. The group of interviewees is particularly involved with religious institutions. Of the twenty life-history respondents, five were either in the ministry themselves or were the sons or daughters of parents who were in the ministry. As one woman told us, "You always had to put the Lord first . . . going to church was a mandated thing."

Concern for pets

For the elderly, pets are a source of caring and closeness, and there is commitment to their welfare (Rosenkoetter 1993). Of the 167 participants in this study, 34.7%, or fifty-eight individuals, had a pet. This finding is particularly important when examining the impact of the pet on the decision to evacuate. Ten people indicated that they would stay with their pet and not leave, twenty-one indicated they would leave if there was a safe place to go with their pet, and twelve would not leave without their pet. These data suggest that many older people consider their pets to be family members. One woman who lives at the beach with two large dogs told the following tale:

> I had called [the animal hospital off the island] and reserved a place for Mutt and Jeff. The doctor there is so good to them and he knows them. But when the storm prediction was changed to category five, the receptionist called and said they couldn't chance taking any animals. Where was I going to go at the last minute? I called a friend in Wilmington who said I could go to her house, but she really didn't want me to bring Mutt and Jeff. She wouldn't let them in the bedroom so I slept on the floor in the hall with the dogs. They were so scared of all the noise and banging . . . I couldn't let them cry. . . .

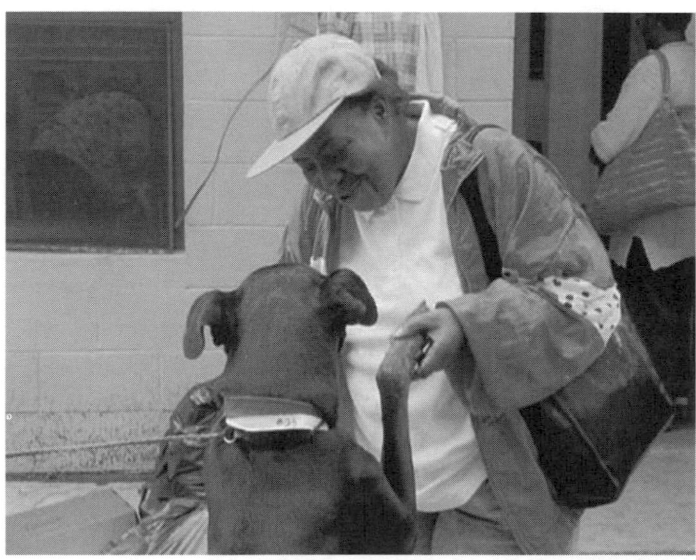

Joy in the midst of sorrow. A woman in Princeville, N.C, is reunited with her dog at the Animal Shelter in Tarboro. She and thousands of others in eastern North Carolina were forced to abandon their pets as floodwaters rushed into their homes. (Photo by Dave Saville, courtesty of FEMA News Photo)

The safest places considered for the pet were the homes of family or friends or a private kennel. When we consider the data on pets based on county of residence, the importance of pets is heightened. In our research area, Pender County elders were the least likely to have evacuated before the storm, they had the greatest likelihood of damage due to post-Floyd floods, and they were much more likely to have pets. In Pender County, 50% of the elders had pets and most factored their animals into the decision of whether, when, and where to evacuate.

Health concerns

Few of the respondents (5.5 %) noted that Hurricane Floyd affected their medication supply. The health status among respondents before Floyd did not change during or after Floyd, nor did their ability to get around change during or after Floyd. Service workers did recognize some health differences. They perceived more medical problems after the storm, especially in the counties experiencing the greatest amount of damage following Floyd (Pender and Columbus). In these counties, self-reported health ratings, both during and after the flooding, were significantly worse than in New Hanover and Brunswick counties, perhaps because they are more rural. Our data may not have detected storm-related differences due to a sampling bias. In our opportunistic sample of nutrition program participants, those who were sick were less likely to have been interviewed. Three of the twenty elders originally scheduled for home video life-history interviews later declined due to illness, and another person postponed her interview to allow time to recover from gallbladder surgery.

Concerns specific to elderly women

In a study of women and housing issues following Hurricane Andrew and the Red River Valley Flood, Enarson (1999) noted that women experienced conflict with men over priorities during household preparation and evacuation, their domestic work intensified when living conditions were disrupted, and gender was a factor in the decision to repair the home. Ollenburger and Tobin (1999) found that gender played a significant role in responses to natural disasters, and that women exhibited greater stress than men following the Des Moines flood in 1993. In another study of that flood, it was found that 71% of the respondents displayed symptoms of posttraumatic stress disorders (Tobin and Ollenburger 1996).

Data from life-history interviews with elders who lost their homes help explain the Ollenburger and Tobin (1999) findings. Among our interviewees, women were more likely to live alone (only one man lived alone) and to have lower household incomes (49.5% of women had incomes of $10,000 or less, compared to 13.6% of men). Living alone may mean that there is no conflict between spouses, but there is also no spouse to help with clean up or repairs. Two of our interviews were conducted with older residents who lived in the same community, within a mile of each other and in similar homes. Both homes suffered similar flooding damage. The Federal Emergency Management Agency (FEMA) offered the owners $19,000 to repair their homes. A couple in their seventies occupied one home, and the husband has been able to repair most of the damage with the FEMA funds as he had "worked in construction." The other home, occupied by an older widow, sits abandoned. Her funds were insufficient to hire anyone to do the work and she cannot do it herself. Of the older adults we studied, older women are more likely than men to have been employed in the service sector and less likely than men to have been employed in the construction industry.

Qualitative data reveal social/emotional issues that are related to age as well as gender. Men and women chose to talk about different things when students recorded their life-history interviews. Men spoke of their work history, their love of fishing, and then moved on to state that the only predictable thing about nature was how hard it was to control storms. Women, on the other hand, tended to speak of family or personal relationships. For the women we interviewed, life has been centered on home, family, and church activities. Several showed interviewers family Bibles and photos that they had managed to rescue. Three of the women were particularly distraught that the flood had destroyed the only photos of deceased family members. Men, on the other hand, were more likely to ask interviewers to "walk their property" with them, noting the things that needed to be repaired. These data suggest that men and women attach different meanings to "home."

Two of the elderly women said they evacuated against their better judgment because of nagging from their sons. One was later rescued with her son's family after his home flooded. Another woman explained that she went to her son's house because he was worried about her. The woman said that her son and his wife worried her to death and wouldn't let her sleep. They kept waking her up and checking on her every time they heard a noise in the house. She finally told them to go to bed and to let God take care of all of them. She also noted that she wished she had stayed at her own home where she would have "gotten some rest." These examples suggest that our interviewees are family-oriented and that older women will listen to the advice of male kinsmen even when it is inconsistent with their own needs and experience.

Coping with Stress

Of those who were interviewed, both men and women showed amazing resilience in terms of morale, and both genders relied on faith, family, and community in the months immediately following the floods. Only a few of our life-history interviewees complained about not receiving help, and these complaints were not from those who had completely lost their homes. Most did not dwell on what they no longer had; instead they were grateful for what they did have. They were thankful for the help of strangers. Most of all, they sang the praises of God. A comment from Elsie, age eighty-five, serves as an example:

> Well I declare, I sure have got some experience, because the Lord knows I never lived a life like this. I can't hardly explain it. I've never lived in a trailer. That's just one unit there. There's no room to put my clothes. But still, I declare, I appreciate it. I just thank the Lord. I lay in bed at night and I say, "Lord, I thank you for this house. It's yours and it's mine." You won't never hear me say nothing about it. What I want to say is praises, something good . . . Seems like I don't worry too much. Everything is doing fine. The Lord blessed us. Sending people in to help us be recovered. I just thank all of them for it. . . .

Several described themselves as having more faith in God following the storm. Almost all spent a lot of time at church in the months following the disaster, going there not to seek an explanation for what happened to them but to praise the Lord for how lucky they have been. Annie, for example, said that she had feared death and aging all her life, but that she does not fear it one bit anymore. She said, "It has brought me closer to the Lord, and the closer I am to the Lord, the less I fear death." Another said, "Without our good friends and faith we would have gone crazy. God has protected us."

Many coped with stress by volunteering to help others that they described as "worse off." One older couple in their seventies were involved in unloading trucks of donated supplies, aiding their neighbors, and were guests on a telethon. The couple is in counseling for psychological stress, but they said that helping others is the best therapy. Another respondent said, "The Lord serves those who serve God."

We asked residents to tell us about the help they needed before, during, and after Hurricane Floyd. The most common request concerned the need for help to prepare the home for evacuation and to help clean or repair the property following the storm. Many said that they could not install boards to cover the windows, or if they were installed it was hard to remove them. A few reported injuries related to this activity. One gentleman was knocked unconscious when a board hit him on the head. Another smashed his thumb with a hammer. While there are many individuals and agency personnel who volunteer to help those with special needs, services need to be coordinated and made available to all that need them. And these needs are especially acute for the elderly.

Recognizing Risk and Participation in Disaster Planning and Preparation

Perhaps the most critical element in the prevention of structural damage and the negative impact of hurricanes and floods on potential victims is planning and preparation. Lave and Lave (1991) interviewed residents of flood-vulnerable communities in Pennsylvania. In general, the respondents knew very little about how to protect themselves from floods. They frequently perceived that flood insurance was too costly, and they knew little about the causes of floods or how to protect themselves from floods. If people do not know to prepare, do not know how to prepare, or are themselves unable to prepare, they automatically become at risk.

As a hurricane approaches, including storms that may cause flooding, orders for evacuation are customarily given to those residents in high-risk areas; however, determining who will actually follow those orders and evacuate is another matter. Overall, people are more prone to evacuate if they feel they are at risk.

Nearly all of the respondents had experienced several hurricanes in the past, and the vast majority watched weather reports; however, neither their personal experience nor the advice of experts helped them prepare for the floods. An elderly woman who had lived in the same Pender County location all her life stated:

> We thought we made it safely through the storm. We were cleaning up. Then, two days after, my husband saw water under my car. I thought nothing of it and went to look for myself. Water was coming in the yard. I couldn't figure where the water was comin' from 'cause the river behind the house was at normal level . . . it was just flowin' in . . . In just a few hours the water was over my deck and I left. . . . There was no warning. . . . We were unprepared.

The story of a 77-year-old woman's experience in Columbus County is just as disturbing. She told us:

> My children didn't want me to stay at home during the storm so I went to Elizabethtown on Wednesday. By Thursday the storm had passed so I headed back home. It was difficult to get back because of all the water in the area. There was some water in my yard, but I decided all was well since I had had no problems in the past. By Friday morning, the water was rising. A neighbor pounded on my door. I got out and moved my car to higher ground, but there was already water all over my floor. I lifted what I could to high spots in the house. My son and grandson tried to come and get me, but they couldn't get here. . . . They were so worried. . . . I was rescued by boat. They got me at the shelter. I went home on Sunday and started to clean up.

Summary

Perry and Lindell (1991) noted that deference to evacuation warnings and orders are related to a person's perceived risk. The most consistent finding in our data is that older adults made decisions based on individual circumstances and personal experience. Because this was a convenience sample, we cannot generalize about the behavior of the overall elderly population; however, while 66% said they are confident in the reports from county officials, one out of four respondents say they may not heed county advice in the future. They seem to trust their own experience and the advice of their children when making hurricane-related decisions. Unfortunately, experiences before, during, and after Hurricane Floyd are likely to reinforce the notion that expert advice may be unreliable. Perhaps this is a consequence of how hurricane information has been presented to them. It is alarming that of the elders interviewed, 42.5%, or seventy-one individuals, reported that they saw no need to evacuate as a category five storm approached our coast. Only 21% said that they paid attention to evacuation warnings or orders and ultimately left. Outside of New Hanover County, an urban county with two beach towns, only 12.6% of respondents followed evacuation advice. This is not surprising given that emergency management personnel typically limit evacuation orders to coastal residents. Although residents in low-lying areas are told to be on alert and those in mobile homes, which are at high risk for damages, are told to go to a shelter, the media reports typically focus on dangers in beach communities. The media, before a storm, typically broadcasts from middle-class beach communities or from urban areas. In contrast, storm damage disproportionately impacts the poor, those in rural areas, and the elderly. Although computers make it possible for some to get updated information, these groups are the least likely to have access to such technology. Reporting practices have an impact on elders' perception of risk; thus, reporting practices should be reexamined. Perhaps the most important question remaining is: "What are we going to do with what we have learned to prevent such extensive damage and losses in the future?"

Acknowledgments

This research was supported in part by a grant awarded to E. K. Covan from the University of Pittsburgh Generations Together Service Learning Program and the Association for Gerontology in Higher Education.

References

Enarson, E. 1999. Women and housing issues in two U.S. disasters: Hurricane Andrew and the Red River Valley Flood. International Journal of Mass Emergencies and Disasters 17(1):39–63.

Lave, T., and L. Lave. 1991. Public perception of the risks of floods: Implications for communication. Risk Analysis 11(2):255–267.

Ollenburger, J., and G. Tobin. 1999. Women, aging, and post-disaster stress: Risk factors. International Journal of Mass Emergencies and Disasters 17(1):65–78.

Perry, R., and M. Lindell. 1991. The effects of ethnicity on evacuation decision-making. International Journal of Mass Emergencies and Disasters 9(1):47–68.

Rosenkoetter, M. (1993). Health promotion: The influence of pets on life patterns in the home. In: Readings in family nursing, edited by G. Wegner and R. Alexander. Philadelphia: J. B. Lippincottx.

Tobin, G., and J. Ollenburger. 1996. Predicting levels of postdisaster stress in adults following the 1993 floods in the upper Midwest. Environment and Behavior 28(3):340–357.

About the Authors: Dr. Eleanor Krassen Covan is the director of the Gerontology Programs in the Department of Sociology, Anthropology, and Criminal Justice at the University of North Carolina at Wilmington. Her research and teaching are focused on issues relating to medical sociology, gerontology, and social psychology. Dr. Rosenkoetter is also on the faculty of the Gerontology Programs and is a professor in the School of Nursing at UNCW. Beth Richards is presently a graduate student in the gerontology post-baccalaureate certificate program at UNCW, and Anita Lane is currently an undergraduate in UNCW's Department of Nursing.

Looking into the Face of the Storm: The Elderly

Stanley P. Oakley, Jr.

Dr. Oakley is an M.D. and an associate professor in Psychiatric Medicine at the Brody School of Medicine at East Carolina University. He has a special interest in general adult and geriatric psychiatry. He has worked closely with members of a Greenville retirement community, which flooded during the storms, causing damage to apartments and loss of important possessions.

I am a geriatric psychiatrist. I do a lot of work with older folks, both on an individual basis at the School of Medicine at East Carolina University and also at a retirement community. The one thing I've learned about older folks is that they have a lot of history. They've lived through an awful lot of things. When the elderly look back at Floyd, their lifetime of experience gives a new perspective. First, their experience emphasizes the uniqueness of this event for eastern North Carolina. A lot of times older people will say, well, I remember back in 1931 when this happened or I remember back in 1920 when that happened, but with the folks who grew up in eastern North Carolina I didn't hear that. I heard that this was truly a once in 100-year event. They had never seen anything like it. That really hammered home to a lot of the elderly patients that this was a unique experience in their lives. On the other hand, their experience helped them because older folks have a lot of benchmarks. They have a lot of milestones with which to measure things. When I'd ask the older patients, "Have you ever been through anything like this before?" I got a raft of stories, ranging from floods in Pennsylvania, dust storms in an Army tent hospital in Southern California during the war, to other hurricanes that hit in Florida or the Gulf Coast.

I had a unique experience working with the retirement home in Greenville. This retirement home is located near the Tar River. On Friday night and Saturday morning, September 17 and 18, it soon became apparent that the water was rising. On Saturday morning the residents were given about two hours notice to "get your stuff . . . we're going to move you out for a couple days." They responded to that fairly well, but it was not just a matter of moving the residents by putting them on buses. There were residents that required intermediate care, some were not very ambulatory, and some were bedridden. Moving the residents was a major project.

Unfortunately, the couple of days turned out to be about a month. The Tar River kept rising. The first level of the retirement center, about 50,000 square feet, wound up under four or five feet of water. This flooded some of the residents' apartments. But what impacted a lot of residents was the flooding of the storage lockers on the first floor, where many of their possessions were kept.

Because residents could not move back immediately, they were moved to a facility some 120 miles away, in Durham, North Carolina, for about one month. Although the new facility was ready to run, relocating these elderly folks was very difficult and at times disorienting. For this reason the staff from Greenville actually went up to Durham and continued to care for them. These staff people were under a tremendous amount of stress. Many of them had lost homes or had homes that were flooded, but they literally moved to the Durham area, sleeping on mattresses on the floor for three-day shifts and then returning to Greenville. The elderly patients really appreciated this; they realized the sacrifices that were being made.

Another thing that really impressed the elderly folks was how many people stepped forward to help. The residents of the retirement community went to Durham with three days' worth of stuff and very quickly they ran out of all sorts of things. So various groups in the Research Triangle area collected clothes and brought them in for the elderly residents. They were very appreciative of this.

When they came back, they were faced with numerous lost possessions: furniture, appliances, clothes, and memorabilia. The lost memorabilia—pictures from the war years that could not be replaced—hit them particularly hard. They also lost financial records. When it comes time for taxes this year, their receipts will be found somewhere down in Pamlico County, on the river.

There are a lot of differences between how school-aged children reacted and how the elderly reacted to the disaster. Unlike children, the elderly didn't have bad dreams. They didn't have the feeling that this wasn't really happening, a feeling of unreality. They were very, very grounded in reality. They had the most difficulty with recurring thoughts or images of the flood. Almost all of them had lost something, but that wasn't their primary worry. Their number one worry, throughout the whole disaster, was their families. They wondered if their families were okay. When they were moved up to Durham, they worried about whether their families knew where they were, and how their families would cope with the move.

I was very impressed by the resourcefulness of the geriatric patients I worked with. However, like a lot of people, the one area in which they did need help was in dealing with the vast bureaucracy of recovery assistance programs. It was hard for them to deal with the various levels of recovery—the county level, the state level, and the federal level. It was very confusing. I saw a lot of the families stepping in to help with this problem. All in all, the elderly dealt with the disaster fairly well. They were quite resilient as long, as they got a little extra help in the areas where they needed it.

An Assessment of the Impacts of Hurricane Floyd on East Carolina University Students

Marieke Van Willigen, Stephanie Lormand, Bob Edwards, Jayme Curry, John R. Maiolo, and Kenneth Wilson

Introduction

University students likely have different needs and responses to natural disasters than do other adult members of a community. On the one hand, students may have less immediate cash at their disposal, but on the other hand, they may have more financial support from family to help replace lost belongings. Students may also be less knowledgeable about community resources and may be less likely to heed warnings issued by emergency personnel. Traditional-age students may have less experience with adversity and may be unaccustomed to seeking assistance or resources on their own. Finally, while traditional-age students are less likely to have the family obligations that come with marriage and children, nontraditional students—those with families—may be more negatively affected by disasters than non-students in similar circumstances.

In order to know how to assist students, universities must first understand how students experience natural disasters. Research on how natural disasters affect students is probably lacking because not many universities have had to deal with this issue (but see Pickens et al. 1995). While Hurricane Floyd was a disaster of almost immeasurable proportion for the eastern North Carolina region, the flood did provide a tremendous opportunity to study the effects of natural disaster in a university setting. This research draws from a survey of a random sample of university students that addressed issues of evacuation, living situation changes, personal property losses, sources of assistance, as well as financial, psychological, and physical impacts.

Surveying Students after the Floods

This research (funded in part by the Natural Hazards Mitigation Center in Boulder, Colorado) focuses on the student population at East Carolina University (ECU). A paper and pencil survey was administered in classrooms to a random sample of students, using a random stratified clustered sample design. This method was chosen to ensure equal representation in the sample of graduate students and upper- and lower-division undergraduate students. Graduate students represented 20% of the sample; upper- and lower-division undergraduates each represented 40% of the sample. Approximately 900 students completed the survey during the month of October 1999, approximately one month after classes resumed. To illustrate some of issues identified in the survey date, we supplemented the data analyses with anecdotal accounts of student experiences.

The characteristics of the sample closely match those of the student body, except women and nonwhites are slightly overrepresented. East Carolina University has many commuter students, coming from the cities and towns that surround the city of Greenville. By relying on classroom contact, the researchers were able to include students that don't live on campus or even in the immediate community. The student sample consisted only of students who were enrolled after the storm. Unfortunately, students who were affected by the storm but did not return were not able to complete the survey. However, according to the university's Office of Institutional Research, only about 100 students, or less than one half of one percent of the student body, withdrew from the fall semester and attributed their action to the storm. Therefore, we feel confident that the sample is generally representative of the experiences of ECU students.

The focal points of the survey can be divided into several types of student impacts—evacuation, living situation changes, personal property losses, sources of assistance, as well as financial, psychological, and physical impacts. Questions were also included to assess whether students helped other individuals or volunteer organizations during either the evacuation or the cleanup. The data analysis presented in this chapter is primarily descriptive; however, we also include some preliminary analyses of group differences in impacts and helping behavior.

Impacts on Students

Evacuation

Our data indicate that Hurricane Floyd displaced approximately 10,620 of the approximately 18,000 ECU students for an average of ten days. Fifty-nine percent of the students reported that they evacuated. While part of this mass evacuation was due to the closing of the university, only 17% lived on campus. Twenty-nine percent of the students evacuated to friends' homes, and 78% evacuated to family homes, with notable but markedly smaller proportions staying with other relatives (8%), in shelters (1%), or in motels (2%). These numbers do not equal 100 percent simply because students often evacuated to multiple destinations, moving from one place to another over the course of the two weeks that the university was closed. Over one-third of the sample had someone else stay with them for at least eight days. For example, one male freshman from out of state did not have transportation to leave his residence hall. He also did not know that the university had opened one residence hall for people in a similar situation. Therefore, he evacuated first to a Red Cross shelter with a group of other students from his dorm. Then his parents arranged for a shuttle to pick him up and drive him to the airport in Raleigh, and he flew home. He returned a few days before classes began and stayed with friends until the residence halls reopened.

A majority of ECU students come from east of Interstate 95. This is the region of the state that was hit directly by Hurricane Floyd and was the site of some of the worst flooding. It stands to reason, therefore, that the majority of the student body would have families who were affected by the storm, which might have limited their ability to receive support from their family as well as increased their burden. More than half of the students who were forced to evacuate also had families that had to evacuate. The case of one sophomore illustrates the double impact felt by these students. She evacuated from her apartment to her parents' home in the middle of the night, carrying a trash bag full of belongings on her head. After two days at home, she and her parents were forced to evacuate to a relative's home, where they slept on the floor in the living room with several other relatives who were also forced to leave their homes because of the storm.

Anecdotal evidence also suggests that the evacuation was difficult for physically disabled students living on campus. There was a lack of accessible transportation and no handicap-accessible alternative dormitory. When the university closed, students who could not leave were consolidated into a single dormitory, but this residence hall was not handicap accessible. One student in a power wheelchair was unable to find a ride that would accommodate his large and heavy chair. He evacuated to the home of a faculty member. The next day his parents arrived with their van to take him home.

Property damage

Sixty-six percent of the students surveyed had no property damage. Twenty-five percent, or approximately 4,500 students, had property damage that could be repaired while they remained in the home. Five percent, or 720 students, had to move out of their home temporarily. Four percent of the students had their homes condemned. Many of these students lived in apartments along the Tar River, which crested at more than 14 feet above flood stage. Some woke up to find water up to the second floor of their apartment buildings, lapping against the feet of their beds. All of these apartments were unlivable after the storm.

Personal property loss also disrupted the lives of university students. Sixteen percent of the students said they lost personal property aside from their home. From the results of our sample, we estimate that approximately 1,400 students lost clothing items, 1,260 lost furniture and stereo equipment, and 1,000 students lost cars. One student shared photographs of her brand new car. She had moved it to higher ground away from her apartment because she knew the apartments were prone to flooding, but the water came up higher and faster than she had anticipated. Overnight, the car was flooded. The loss of textbooks and school materials was so common that the university bookstore established a loan program so students would not have to pay to replace their books. Faculty members were encouraged to help students network with other class members to replace lost notes.

We asked students to report the sum of their property damage and personal property losses. Twenty-six percent of those surveyed reported some financial loss. Among those who incurred some sort of loss, the average was $6,000, although half those surveyed had less than $1,000 in damages. Surprisingly, about 23% of students who did not live on campus reported that they owned their own homes. The mean cost for repair/replacement of damages for these students was $16,000. Renters had lower costs. One-third of the students had some form of insurance; however, only 10% had full coverage.

Relocation

Our data suggest that approximately 1,260 students, or 7% of the student body, had to move as a result of Floyd. Moving in the middle of the semester had a ripple effect on many students' lives and the university community as a whole. Of those students who had to move, 91% reported that they had difficulty finding a new place to live. Forty-three percent found housing that was more expensive by an average of $93 per month. About one-third of students who were forced to move saw their rents change, either increasing or decreasing by less than $20 per month. In contrast, 23% of the students who were forced to relocate found cheaper living arrangements; yet, in most of these cases the cost was cheaper because these students had more roommates sharing living costs after the flood than they had before the flood. Some of these cost-saving situations resulted in overcrowded rental houses or apartments, which might have subsequent effects on academic performance. This will need to be monitored. One student reported being relieved to have found a place to stay—on the couch in his friends' apartment. He remained there for the rest of the semester, reluctant to take advantage of the FEMA trailers offered to students because he was already settled and did not want to move away from his friends.

Transportation to and from campus was also an issue for many students. Mainly, students moved from traditional student living areas (near campus, which is in the floodplain) to areas that do not typically have a high student representation. The university bus routes were not accessible from these new locations. In general, those who walked to school before Floyd either had to ride a bike or drive after Floyd. Some students who previously rode the bus now drove to campus, which may have a subsequent effect on existing campus parking problems. Expanding bus route service to include the new areas where students are living may eliminate the increased car use that resulted after the flooding.

Roommates also changed as a result of the hurricane. Nine percent of the respondents were not living with the same people after Floyd as before. Fifty-six percent of these respondents expected this to be a long-term situation, beyond the end of the semester. One student returned to her flooded apartment to find that her roommate had found a new apartment—without her. She was forced to move in with strangers with whom she connected through the ECU Relief Center. Her new roommates were unreliable, and she moved out at the end of the fall semester, bearing the cost of paying off the bills because they were in her name. Also, 14% of the respondents who moved had a pet they could no longer keep after the hurricane.

Physical and psychological effects

Aside from material losses, there were also physical and psychological effects due to the impacts of the floods. Forty-six percent of the students surveyed reported having had some sort of headache, cold, or flu since Hurricane Floyd. While we cannot compare those numbers against pre-Floyd illnesses, students who reported having had direct contact with floodwaters were more likely to report having experienced an illness since the storm. During the flooding, some students decided it would be fun to swim in the floodwaters covering the main streets near campus. Other students were exposed to floodwaters while rescuing animals, personal belongings, and even people.

Psychologically, 63% of students said their experience with Floyd caused them to change their life priorities. When asked to describe these changes, some students reported positive changes, such as feeling that material goods were less important to them and that family and friends were more important. On the negative side, some stated that school was less important, and that they were less likely to listen to experts during the next disaster. One freshman talked about her "disgust" with the 911 system. When she called 911, she was told that she should not attempt to evacuate her apartment because it was dark and the waters "might be dangerous." She awoke several hours later to find her apartment flooded to the second floor and most of her personal belongings ruined. She declared that she would never again trust experts and would, instead, follow her own "gut instinct." About 49% of the students reported they were having a harder time keeping up with schoolwork after Floyd, and 45% felt their lives were still disrupted or very disrupted since the storm. One major complaint that students reported was that faculty were not responsive enough to students who were affected by the flood. Students also perceived that their workload had increased due to lost school days. How faculty responded to students after the storm seemed to vary. Some students reported that faculty checked with each student in the class to identify students who were in need and even offered to help replace personal items; other faculty picked up the class where they had left off as if nothing had happened and made few, if any, adjustments to the schedule. Faculty in fields where standardized exams are given, such as nursing, reported enormous pressure to cover all class material in order to prepare students for these exams.

Finally, students reported indirect effects on their stress level due to losses incurred by their families and friends. One woman's father lost his family business to the flooding. She reported that it was terribly difficult for her to focus on her schoolwork while her dad was under so much stress. In fact, she wanted to withdraw from school but her family talked her out of it. While previously she had been a consistent A student, during the fall semester she earned her first C and D.

Group differences in impacts

We undertook a preliminary analysis of group differences in property damages and other flood impacts. Overall, we found very few significant differences. Students who lived off campus were more affected than those who lived on campus. Students who were homeowners were more negatively affected than were renters. Compared to on-campus students, those who lived off campus were more likely to report that their lives were still "very disrupted" . Similarly, North Carolina residents and African American students were more likely to report that their lives were still "very disrupted" compared to the lives of out-of-state students or white students.

Students were also asked whether or not their hurricane and flooding experiences had caused them to reconsider their life priorities. We found that female students were more likely than males to indicate a change. Similarly, students living off campus and those who had suffered damages from the storm were more likely to indicate a change in priorities as a result of their experiences. Female students were also more likely to report having been ill since the storm.

Giving and Receiving Assistance

Sources of information

The main sources of pre-storm information that students reported can be split into three categories. The primary sources of pre-storm information were television (49%) and the Internet (33%). The secondary sources of information were radio (43%) and informal communication with friends (43%). The university was included in the questioning as a source of information; however, it did not show up with any significance. When asked about the type of information students received directly from the university, the most common response was the effect of the storm on class schedules (69%). Students also reported receiving some information about what to do in preparation for future hurricanes and about re-housing efforts. However, less than a quarter of students received either of these kinds of information from the university. Many students in apartments that flooded took the initiative to find a new place to live while the university was closed; therefore, by the time the university began providing re-housing information, they were already settled.

Sources of assistance

Among available sources of assistance, most students relied on family, friends, and landlords. Quite a few neighbors helped with cleaning and repairing. Friends were the largest source of assistance in finding new places to live. Only 3% of the students reported getting help from the ECU Relief Center. However, students did rely more on the relief center for financial assistance; about one-quarter of students needing financial assistance sought help from the center. In part, this may have resulted from the university's immediate offer of $100 to any member of the university community who indicated that they had incurred losses. This provided a significant incentive for students to seek out assistance from the center.

The primary source of financial assistance was, not surprisingly, family; one-third of those needing assistance received it from members of their family. Eighteen percent of students also got assistance from FEMA and the Red Cross. However, it is important to note that 45% of students who needed information and referrals to potential sources of financial or material assistance reported that they received no such help. The same is true for those who needed to obtain financial and material assistance, with 49% of affected students indicating they received no such assistance. One student said that he was reluctant to ask for help, although he had lost almost all of his personal belongings and was forced to move. He believed that there were other people who were worse off than he was who needed help more. Instead he chose to sleep on the floor of his new apartment until he could afford to replace the mattress he had lost in the flood.

Because families provided most of the monetary support for their children's relief efforts, it is understandable that students with families that also incurred damages were doubly affected. One-third of the respondents had family members who incurred damages due to the hurricane or subsequent flooding. About one-half of the students who had incurred losses themselves had family members who also had damages. We expect that these students had fewer resources available for the recovery process than did students whose families were not impacted. In fact, these students were more likely to report that their lives were still disrupted and that they felt their experiences had changed their life priorities. They were also more likely to report that they had no assistance in finding a new place to live. More than half of these impacted students reported receiving no financial assistance to recover their losses.

Student participation in relief efforts

Volunteerism, both organizational and informal, becomes an important factor in coping after natural disasters. East Carolina University students were an important resource in local relief efforts through both formal channels like the Red Cross, the Salvation Army, or the Emergency Animal Rescue Service (EARS) and informally by helping friends and neighbors. Thirty-nine percent of the students surveyed provided volunteer labor for local organizations. The Pitt County Red Cross was the organization with which students most frequently volunteered (15%), followed by local churches (12%). During the period when the university was closed, some of these students reported spending the majority of their time distributing clothes through the Red Cross, acting as Spanish translators in shelters, or working in emergency soup kitchens through their local churches. After the flooding, students also became involved in community cleanup programs, primarily through classes and organizations of which they were members. For example, many students in the sociology honors society organized a cleanup of an elderly woman's home. Students who had incurred damages—women, North Carolina residents, graduate students, and off-campus residents—were more likely to be involved in volunteer work than other groups. But, most of those who volunteered after Floyd had volunteered before Floyd (71%).

Significantly, 47% of the sample, representing about 8,460 students, reported providing some form of relief assistance through informal channels. The most common beneficiaries of informal assistance were friends (33%), and 18% helped family members clean and repair. While women became involved in formal relief efforts, men were more likely to get involved in informal assistance efforts. Many men reported helping neighbors repair damages to their homes. One student reported that he had spent most of his break in his neighborhood going from house to house with his chainsaw, cutting up trees and limbs that had fallen on people's homes, cars, and lawns. Students who had volunteered with service organizations before the flood were also more likely to provide informal assistance than those who had not previously volunteered.

Summary

This research indicates that Hurricane Floyd heavily affected ECU students. In part, because East Carolina University is largely a commuter campus, many students incurred property damages and the loss of personal property. Furthermore, relocations likely led to disruptions of support networks, which may have long-term impacts. At the time of this survey, many students still felt that the storm had directly or indirectly disrupted their lives. While previous research suggests that extended family networks have a positive impact on recovery (Quarantelli 1960; Bolin 1982), we found that those students whose families were also impacted by the storm reported the greatest level of life disruption and were less likely to have received assistance from any source.

If students' responses are consistent with those of other victims of natural disasters, long-term psychological impacts are not uncommon (Baisden 1979; Warheit 1985). Furthermore, most students are single, making them more vulnerable to long-term impacts (Peacock with Ragsdale 1997), and those who have children are likely to have young children, which decreases their ability to recover quickly after a disaster (Yelvington 1997). However, the lack of any systematic research on how students differ from other members of the community in their responses to a natural disaster means that we don't know how students are likely to recover. The long-term impacts of this disruption on students' well-being and academic performance should be monitored.

References

Baisden, B. 1979. Crisis intervention in smaller communities. In: The small city and regional community: Proceedings of the 1979 conference, edited by E. J. Miller, and R. P. Wolendsky, 325–332. Stevens Point, Wis.: University of Wisconsin.

Bolin, R. C. 1982. Long term family recovery from disaster. Boulder, Colo.: University of Colorado.

Peacock, W. G., with A. K. Ragsdale. 1997. Social systems, ecological networks, and disasters: Toward a socio-political ecology of disasters. In: Hurricane Andrew: ethnicity, gender, and the sociology of disasters, edited by W. G. Peacock, B. H. Morrow, and H. Gladwin. New York: Routledge.

Pickens, J., T. Field, M. Prodromidis, M. Pelaez-Nogueras, and Z. Hossain. 1995. Posttraumatic stress, depression, and social support among college students after Hurricane Andrew. Journal of College Student Development 36(2):152–161.

Quarantelli, E. L. 1960. A note on the protective function of the family in disasters. Marriage and Family Living 22:263–264.

Warheit, G. H. 1985. A propositional paradigm for estimating the impact of disasters on mental health. International Journal of Mass Emergencies and Disasters 3(2):29–48.

Yelvington, K. A. 1997. Coping in a temporary way: The tent cities. In: Hurricane Andrew: ethnicity, gender, and the sociology of disasters, edited by W. G. Peacock, B. H. Morrow, and H. Gladwin. New York: Routledge.

About the Authors: Marieke Van Willigen is an assistant professor in the Department of Sociology at East Carolina University. She is currently studying the impacts of Hurricane Floyd on rates of distress and mortality among residents in eastern North Carolina, with a particular emphasis on how these effects vary by gender. Stephanie Lormand and Jayme Curry are students in ECU's Department of Sociology. Bob Edwards is an assistant professor and graduate director in the Department of Sociology at ECU. Dr. John Maiolo was the committee chair of the In the Aftermath of Hurricane Floyd *conference and is an emeritus professor in the Department of Sociology at ECU. Dr. Kenneth Wilson is a researcher at the ECU's Survey Research Laboratory and a professor in the Department of Sociology.*

Part IV / An "Extreme Event"—Hurricane Floyd, September 1999—Impacts on the Natural Environment

The Effects of the Flood on the Water Quality and the Fishes of the Pamlico River Estuary

Joseph Luczkovich, Larry Ausley, Chris Pullinger, Garcy Ward, and Katy West

Introduction

Hurricanes Dennis and Floyd hit the East Coast in September 1999, dropping a combined total of twenty inches of rainfall in a three-week period. The heavy rainfall caused massive inland flooding in eastern North Carolina and the Pamlico River estuarine system (Figure 1). The combined effect of these two storms was greater than the amount of flooding from Hurricane Fran in 1996, as can be observed in the U.S. Geological Survey (USGS) hydrograph of the Tar River at Rocky Mount, North Carolina (Figure 2). The Tar and Pamlico River system was inundated with floodwater containing untreated sewage, algal nutrients, debris, and chemical contaminants. Changes in water quality that occur after hurricanes and large storms can cause stress for estuarine fishes, and hurricane-induced changes in water quality has been linked to the occurrence of fish kills (Creaser 1942; Beecher 1973; Van Dolah and Anderson 1991; Paerl et al. 1998) and changes in the fish community (Breeder 1962). We were interested in exploring the impact of this flood on the ecology of the Pamlico River Estuary, especially with reference to water quality and the occurrence of fish diseases.

The Pamlico River Estuary

The Pamlico River Estuary lies in the coastal plain of North Carolina. It receives input from and is a continuation of the Tar River, making it an oligohaline (salinity ranging from 0.5 to 5 part per thousand [ppt]) to a mesohaline (salinity ranging from 5 to 18 ppt) estuary (Copeland and Riggs 1984). The Tar River gradually widens east of the U.S. Route 17 bridge in Washington, N.C., to form a shallow (average 3.3 meter depth), drowned river valley estuary that empties into the Pamlico Sound about 65 kilometers downstream. The Pamlico River along with the Pamlico Sound and its tributaries forms the second-largest estuarine system in the United States.

In the Pamlico River Estuary, Tar River fresh water normally mixes with estuary water from Pamlico Sound, creating horizontal salinity gradients. Salinities range from 0 and 20 ppt, depending upon the exact position along the estuary's length, with lower salinity levels occurring toward the Route

17 bridge. Pamlico Sound salinities range between 10 and 29 ppt, and full ocean salinities (35 ppt) occur beyond the barrier islands. Water exchange with the ocean, due to tidal pumping, occurs at Oregon, Ocracoke, and Hatteras inlets. The fresh water in the estuary dilutes the salt water that enters through these narrow openings. Thus, the salinity level along this gradient is a balance between ocean input and river flow. Salinity gradients and river flow data can be used to estimate the *flushing time* of the estuary, which is the average amount of time it takes for a parcel of fresh water to reach the mouth of the estuary. Stanley (1992) estimated that the average flushing time for the Pamlico River Estuary is twenty-four days.

Vertical stratification of the water column in the estuary, due to salinity and density differences between sea water and fresh water, often leads to hypoxia, or low dissolved oxygen, in the bottom water of the estuary (Stanley and Nixon 1992). This occurs frequently during late summer when winds are light and thunderstorms produce runoff. When these conditions occur, the freshwater runoff floats above the denser salt water. Strong winds can vertically mix the more oxygenated surface water with the bottom water, but when the winds are light, vertical mixing does not occur. Without this mixing, low dissolved oxygen levels occur in the bottom water. In addition, algal growth, organic materials, and nutrients (nitrogen and phosphorous) in the surface water will eventually sink and provide energy for bottom-dwelling bacteria and other consumers (Paerl et al. 1998). As these bottom-dwelling consumers feed, they remove oxygen from the water, often causing hypoxia. Hypoxia is problematic because it is associated with fish kills.

Fish kills in North Carolina estuaries specifically involve juvenile Atlantic menhaden (*Brevoortia tyrannus*) (Paerl et al. 1998). In the summer, dissolved oxygen levels in the Pamlico River are normally greater than the North Carolina Department of Environment and Natural Resources (NCDENR) standard for hypoxia of 4.0 milligrams of oxygen per liter (mg/l). But during periodic hypoxic events it can drop to less than 4.0 mg/l. Winter-time dissolved oxygen levels are much higher due to the increased solubility of oxygen in cold water.

The Pamlico River estuary is one of the most important ecosystems supporting juvenile fishes in North Carolina (Ross and Eperly 1985). At least sixty-five species of fishes use the Pamlico River estuary (Copeland and Riggs 1984). Many of these juvenile species, such as the Atlantic menhaden, comprise the bulk of the adult commercial fish catch in North Carolina and elsewhere (Ahrenholz 1991). Rapid changes in water quality can produce physiological stress in fishes. For example, if salinity decreases, spot (*Leiostomus xanthurus*) and Atlantic croakers (*Micropogonias undulatus*) exhibit decreased respiratory rates (Moser and Gerry 1989). If dissolved oxygen levels decrease, physiological stress can result, which is exhibited by reduced swimming stamina, decreased blood oxygen saturation, and increased metabolic rates (Heath 1987). Some marine fishes, like Atlantic croaker, are very tolerant of low salinity (Moser and Gerry 1989), and other species such as sheephead minnows (Cyprinodon variegatus) are tolerant of hypoxic conditions (Peterson 1990), but all fishes are stressed to some degree. Atlantic menhaden appear to be particularly intolerant of hypoxia (Hall et al. 1991). In addition to the fish kills that may occur in low oxygen conditions (Paerl et al 1998), sublethal impacts may occur. Due to the physiological stress resulting from changes in salinity and dissolved oxygen, some fishes may show signs of disease, and changes in salinity may affect associated parasites (Plumb et al. 1976, Hearth and Padgett 1990, Shafer 1990).

Data Collection

Regular monitoring of water quality and the incidence of fish disease has been underway under NCDENR programs since 1998, so data were available from before and after the flood. We sampled the Pamlico River along a 50-kilometer transect using a water quality meter. The first sampling station was at the U.S. Route 17 bridge (Figure 1). Water was analyzed for salinity and dissolved oxygen levels and for the level of nutrient (nitrogen and phosphorus) inputs. Vertical salinity and dissolved oxygen profiles (at 1-meter depth intervals) were collected at seven stations (0, 5.4, 13.0, 24.2, 31.5, 39.8, and 49.9 kilometers) in the middle of the river on a bi-weekly schedule before and after the storm. We determined the flushing time by dividing the estuary into six regions and estimating the volume of fresh water in each region. The volume estimates were made using the salinity profiles and a calculated flushing rate, which was based on the river flow at Rocky Mount, N.C. (Figure 2). During the same period, an automated water pump sampler was used to collect daily water samples at the U.S. Route 17 bridge near Washington. Using U.S. Environmental Protection Agency methods, samples were analyzed for total phosphorus and total nitrogen (Kjeldahl) in order to measure the nutrient input into the estuary.

Each month fishes were sampled using cast, gill, and trammel nets at eight randomly selected stations in the upper, middle, and lower Pamlico River, for a total of twenty-four stations per month. Prevalence of fish diseases was re-

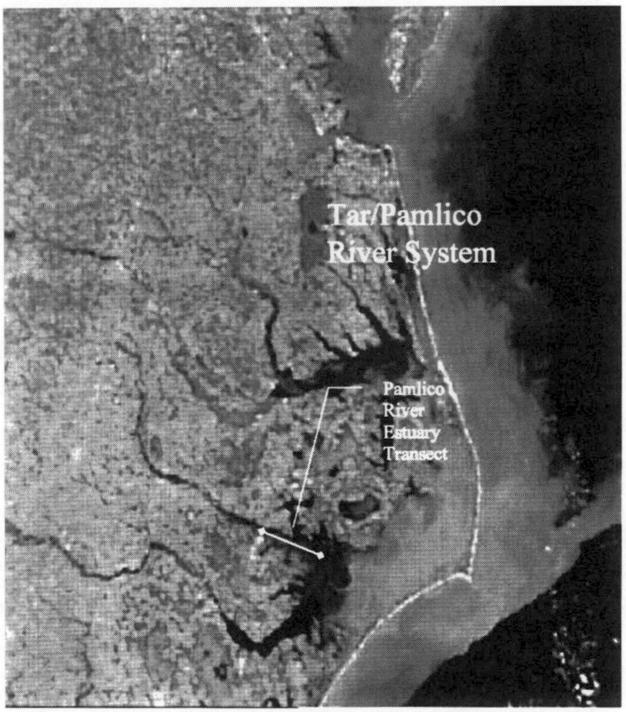

Figure 1. Landsat image of eastern North Carolina on 23 September 23 1999, showing the dark-colored floodwaters moving into Pamlico Sound.

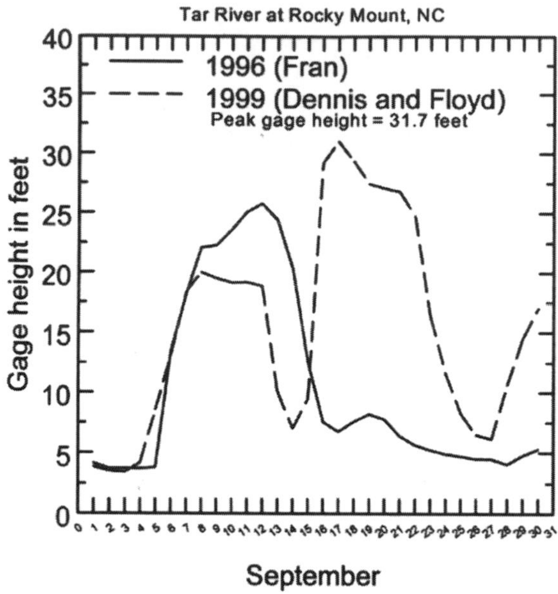

corded as the percent of fish in the total catch with visible skin lesions. No attempt was made to determine the cause of the lesions, but a sample of twenty Atlantic menhaden was sent each month to the North Carolina State University College of Veterinary Medicine for analysis (see "Pathogenesis of Ulcerative Dermatitis and Myositis in Coastal North Carolina Fish", J. Mac Law and Jay F. Levine, August 2000, unpublished report).

Figure 2. Hydrograph of the Tar River at Rocky Mount, N.C., at Highway 97 during September (USGS gauging station No. 02082585). River gage height in feet above the datum for that station (53.88 feet above sea level) is shown during 1996 (Hurricane Fran) and during 1999 (Hurricanes Dennis and Floyd). (USGS data, courtesy of Jeanne Robbins, Surface-Water Specialist, Data Chief, USGS, Raleigh, N.C.)

Water Quality Before and After the Floods

Salinity levels

Due to a drought that had been occurring in the summer of 1999, the salinity was relatively high at all stations before the storms (17 August 1999) (Figure 3). Salinity increased with distance from the Route 17 bridge in all months. Water quality measurements made after the storms (22 September 1999 and 13 October 1999) indicated that the floodwaters made the estuary largely fresh water (Figure 3). At all stations, surface water (less than 1.5 meters) and bottom water (greater than 2.5 meters) had lower salinity levels during the flood (September and October 1999) than they did in the pre-flood (17 August 1999) and post-flood (16 February 2000) periods. By 16 February 2000, salinity levels had not yet returned to the conditions that were present before the August flood, averaging only 5 ppt at the 49-kilometer station.

Dissolved oxygen

Dissolved oxygen was normal in the pre-flood samples in August 1999, averaging 6 mg/l. One station, the Route 17 bridge, had hypoxic conditions, with dissolved oxygen levels of less than 4 mg/l (Figure 4). This was not unusual, as low dissolved oxygen often occurs in the estuary during low-flow periods in the summer (Stanley and Nixon 1992). After Hurricane Floyd passed and the flood had begun (22 September 1999), dissolved oxygen concentrations averaged less than 5 mg/l in the bottom water. At four of the six stations sampled

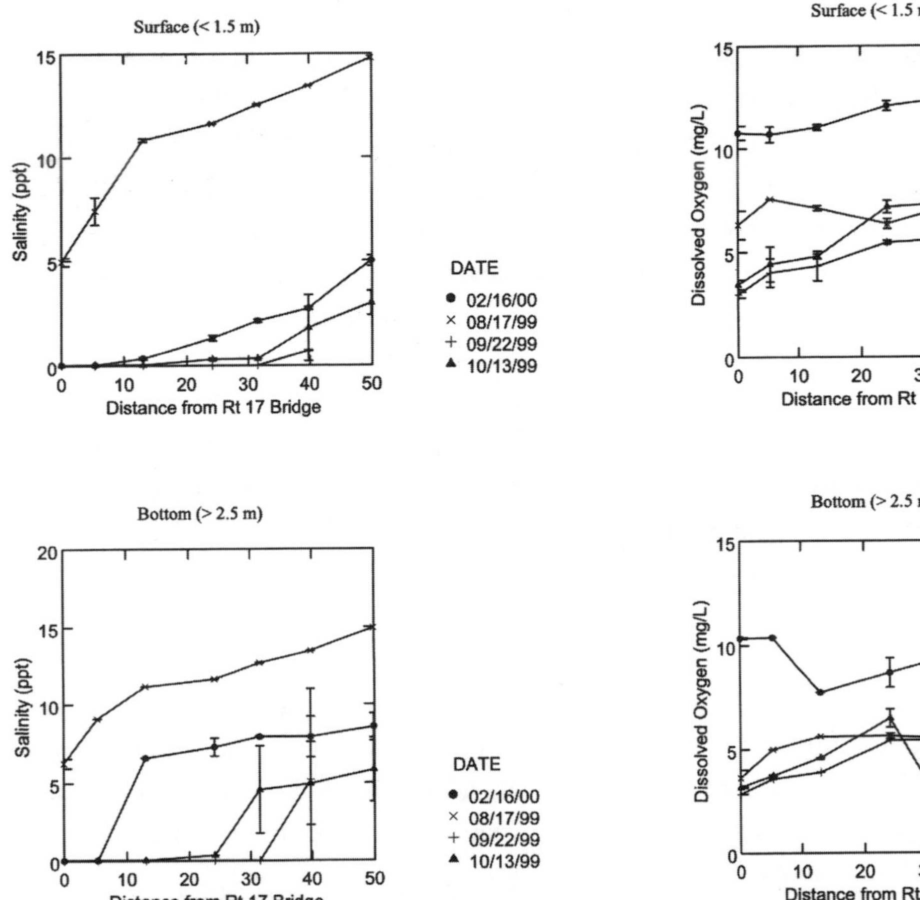

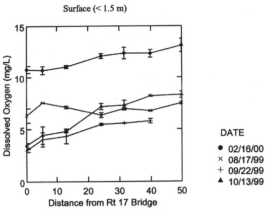

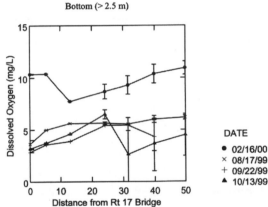

Figure 3. Salinity levels in the surface water (**top panel**) and bottom water (**bottom panel**) of the Pamlico River Estuary versus distance from the U.S. Route 17 bridge. Four dates are shown: one month before (17 August 1999), immediately after (22 September 1999), one month after (13 September1999), and five months after (16 February 2000) the flooding of the Tar/Pamlico River.

Figure 4. Dissolved oxygen levels in the surface water (**top panel**) and bottom water (**bottom panel**) in the Pamlico River Estuary versus distance from the U.S. Route 17 bridge. Four dates are displayed: one month before (17 August 1999), immediately after (22 September 1999), one month after (13 September1999), and five months after (16 February 2000) the flooding of the Tar/Pamlico River.

in September, dissolved oxygen levels fell below the NCDENR's hypoxia standard of 4 mg/l (rough weather prevented the 49.9-kilometer station from being sampled) (Figure 4). Oxygen levels were lowest at the Route 17 bridge and at the 39.9-kilometer station, with levels exceeding 5 mg/l in the middle section of the estuary. In October, dissolved oxygen in the bottom water remained very low, averaging 4.4 mg/l along the entire transect, with low levels near the Route 17 bridge (0-kilometer and 5.4-kilometer stations) and from the 39-kilometer station to the 49.9-kilometer station downstream. After the flood had subsided, dissolved oxygen levels in the bottom water rose to winter-time high levels (7.0 mg/l in November 1999, 9.4 mg/l in December 1999, 10.7 mg/l in January 2000, and 9.8 mg/l in February 2000).

Flushing time

The flooding greatly decreased the flushing time of the Pamlico River, from nineteen days before the storm (17 August 1999) to 4.5 days during the flood (22 September 1999). This short flushing time suggests that the high river flow associated with the hurricanes' passage over the Tar/Pamlico watershed caused a rapid exchange of fresh water with the Pamlico Sound. Flushing time after the flood on 16 February 2000 increased to forty-six days, due to the low river flow rate at that time and the large volume of fresh water still remaining in the estuary. This change in flushing rate indicates that the floodwaters may have rapidly flushed fresh water into Pamlico Sound immediately following the hurricanes, but the estuary became poorly flushed during the winter months. This lowered winter flushing time suggests that nutrients, organic materials, and pollutants associated with the flood may still be present in the estuary in February 2000. Depending on rainfall, Tar River flow rates should return to high levels in the spring of 2000 and lower the flushing time to the normal twenty-four days. But nutrients and contaminants may be trapped in the sediments and in the biota of the estuary; therefore, they may not flush from the system at the same rate as the fresh water.

Nutrient levels

Figure 5 (total phosphorus) and Figure 6 (total nitrogen) show the elevated nutrient inputs caused by the flood. Peak input of both phosphorus and nitrogen occurred in October 1999. These flood-associated nutrients will become part of the estuary's nutrient cycles, and because they represent a large proportion of the total 1999 nutrient load for the estuary, they could stimulate harmful algal blooms during the coming year.

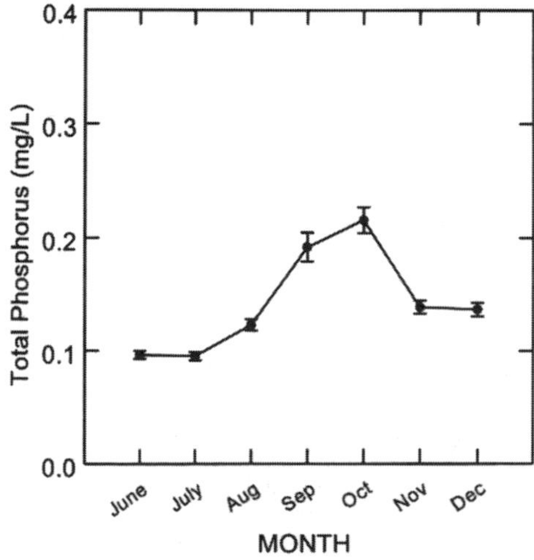

Figure 5. Monthly mean total phosphorus (mg/L) (plus or minus one standard error) in the daily water samples taken at the U.S. Route 17 bridge. EPA method 365.1.

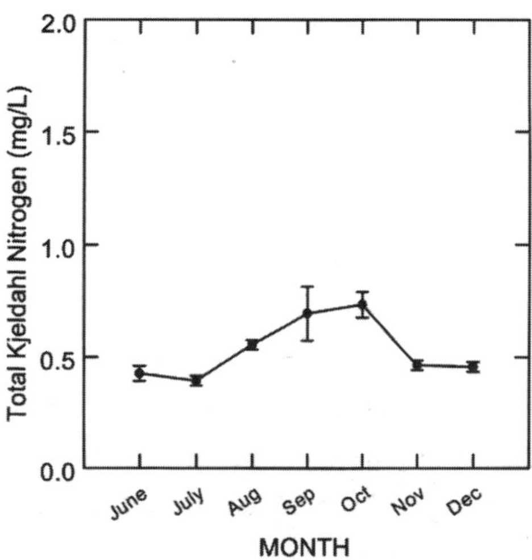

Figure 6. Monthly mean total Kjeldahl nitrogen (mg/l) (plus or minus one standard error) in daily water samples taken at the U.S. Route 17 bridge. EPA methods 350.1 and 351.1.

Incidence of Fish Disease Before and After the Floods

Fish kills and incidence of disease

Prior to the passage of Hurricane Floyd, there were two large kills that involved Atlantic menhaden (*Brevoortia tyrannus*). These fish kills (15,768 and 85,724 fish) occurred in July of 1999, when dissolved oxygen levels were low due to the seasonal hypoxia that occurs during the summer in the Pamlico River Estuary. The massive fish kills that many scientists had feared would occur after the storm did not materialize. In fact, just a single fish kill of 122 fish—bluegill (*Lepomis macrochirus*; also called bream), longnose gar (*Lepisosteus osseus*), and spot—was reported after the storm (Table 1). This kill was associated with low dissolved oxygen (dissolved oxygen at the two sites during the kill was measured at 0.6 mg/l and 3.6 mg/l) and is listed as a "probable" hypoxia kill. It appears that Hurricane Floyd and the flooding associated with the storms did not cause the direct deaths of many fish, at least those that could be observed in floating fish kills. The influx of fresh water in all probability caused many fish to move downstream in advance of the flood. Thus, they remained in the higher salinity waters. Many fishes can detect a change in the salinity, even a rapid change, and respond by increasing their swimming speed and moving away from areas where salinity is changing rapidly (Moser and Gerry 1989).

Table 1. Fish kills reported to the Rapid Response Team of the North Carolina Department of Environment and Natural Resources in Tar/Pamlico Basin during 1999.

Date	Location	Number	Species
26 May 1999	Rowland Creek	152	pumpkinseed sunfish, gar
13 June 1999	Pungo Creek canal	2,000	bream, menhaden, bass, spot
17 June 1999	Blounts Creek	411	perch, catfish, bass,gizzard shad
29 June 1999	Blounts Creek	757	bream, menhaden, bass, shad
29 June 1999	Blounts Bay	1,740	bream, bass, spot, flounder
30 June 1999	Blounts Bay	8,413	menhaden, anchoives, spot
20 July 1999	Pamlico River	**85,724**	menhaden
22 July 1999	Pungo River	**15,768**	menhaden
3 October 1999	Gar Gut Bayview	122	bream, bass, spot

However, our net collections showed that there were still many fish present after the flood. In the fall of 1998 (September through December), thirty-four species of fishes were captured, with spot (*Leiostomus xanthurus*) most common and Atlantic menhaden the next most common species. In contrast, during the fall of 1999, including the post-flood period, thirty-eight spe-

Table 2. The top ten most common fish and invertebrates caught in gill, trammel, and cast nets before the flood in September through December 1998 and after the flood in September through December 1999.

Pre-Floyd Abundance		
Rank	**Species**	**Mean Relative Abundance**
1	Spot	32.3
2	Atlantic menhaden	15.7
3	Bluefish	11.8
4	Flathead catfish	10.1
5	Blue crab	9.9
6	White perch	7.7
7	Longnose gar	6.7
8	Weakfish	6.6
9	Mullets	6.2
10	Percoid fish	5.5
Post-Floyd Abundance		
Rank	**Species**	**Mean Relative Abundance**
1	Lyre goby	60.0
2	Atlantic menhaden	25.9
3	Pinfish	18.8
4	Bluefish	17.8
5	Striped mullet	10.5
6	Red drum	8.1
7	Gizzard shad	5.8
8	Southern flounder	5.0
9	Spot	4.9
10	Blue crab	4.4

cies of fishes were captured in the nets after the storm, with lyre gobies (*Evorthodus lyricus*) most common, Atlantic menhaden as the next most common, and spot falling to the ninth most abundant species (Table 2). Thus, a shift in the fish community occurred in Pamlico River Estuary due to the flood's effects.

After the storms, there were some important indications of stress in the fish still present in the estuary. Various species of fish (such as the lyre goby, spot, silver perch [*Bairdiella chrysoura*] pumpkinseed [*Lepomis gibbosus*] and white catfish [*Ameiurus catus*]) showed skin lesions and disease, but none were found to be diseased as commonly as Atlantic menhaden (Figure 7). Juvenile Atlantic menhaden had a statistically significant increase in disease incidence in the fall of 1999 compared with the disease incidence in the same months in 1998 (October-December 1998 versus October-December 1999). Figure 7 shows that Atlantic menhaden actually exhibited elevated levels of disease earlier in the year, during July, before the storms hit. This increase was coincident with the large fish kills mentioned earlier. Nevertheless, the level of disease incidence observed after Hurricane Floyd was statistically higher than would have been expected based on a comparison of 1998 and 1999 data.

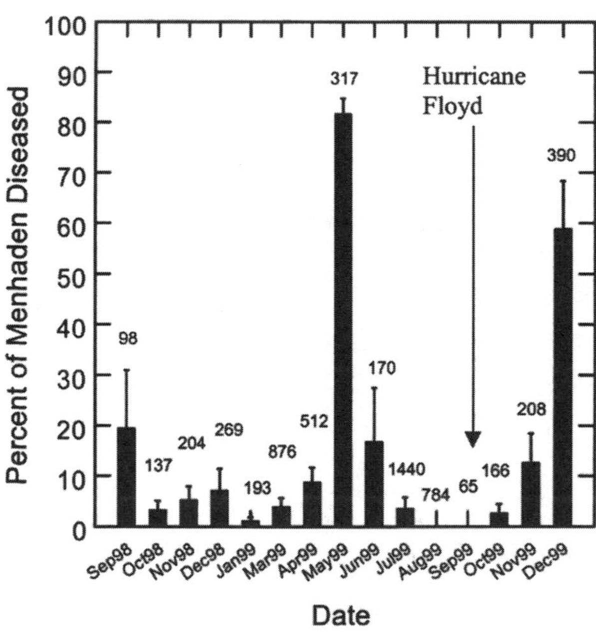

Figure 7. A comparison of the disease incidence for juvenile Atlantic menhaden (Brevoortia tyrannus) caught in cast nets, gill nets, and trammel nets during September 1998 through December 1999. Mean percentage of diseased fish in samples is shown along with the standard error. Numbers above each monthly sample represent the number of fish examined for disease.

Disease in juvenile Atlantic menhaden has been associated with a variety of microbial agents, but no definitive cause for this disease condition has been established. According to the "Fact Sheet on Estuarine Fish Kills in North Carolina," available at the state of North Carolina Division of Water Quality Environmental Sciences Branch web site (<http://www.esb.enr.state.nc.us/>), there are many possible causes of skin lesions in menhaden. Naturally occurring parasites, including bacteria, protozoans, viruses, worms, and crustaceans, can cause skin lesions. The fact sheet also discusses the hypothesized causes of the lesions in Atlantic menhaden: *Aphanomyces* fungal growth (Dykstra et al. 1986); *Pfiesteria* toxins (Noga et al. 1996, Burkholder and Glasgow 1997, Burkholder et al. 1999), *Kudoa*protozoan cysts (Harrell and Scott 1985), and hypoxia (Plumb et al 1976). Any of these pathogens may occur as opportunistic infections, which would not occur in unstressed fish but are possible results of a weakened immune response in the affected fish, possibly due to stress from salinity and dissolved oxygen changes. Contaminants in the sediments or water, which may have been higher than normal due to the flood, could also play a role in weakening the immune response of the fish. We cannot determine the cause of disease or death from field data alone. We must wait for the results of further, careful laboratory experimentation before we can establish the cause of these diseases in Atlantic menhaden. We must also wait to see if there is any detectable change in the catches of commercial fisheries, which depend on the Pamlico River Estuary as a nursery site. Only time will tell if hurricanes Floyd and Dennis have caused long-term changes to the fishes and estuarine ecosystems of the Tar and Pamlico rivers.

Summary

Before and after hurricanes Dennis and Floyd, routine environmental surveys were underway by NCDENR scientists. After the storm, we found a dramatic decline in salinity at all stations. Regions of the estuary became entirely fresh water. Dissolved oxygen declined in deeper parts of the estuary and fell below the NCDENR's standard for hypoxia at four of six stations immediately after the storm. Total phosphorus and nitrogen in the Tar/Pamlico River increased after the storm, reaching peak levels in October. Fish caught for the ongoing Disease Incidence Survey indicated an increase in the number of diseased Atlantic menhaden after the storm relative to samples taken during the autumn months in the previous year. These data indicate that the fishes in the Pamlico River Estuary were impacted by the huge volume of freshwater runoff from the rainfall, which caused the salinity and dissolved oxygen to decrease and brought an increase in nutrients. Such events represent stressful conditions for species such as the Atlantic menhaden. The cause of disease in Atlantic menhaden and the status of disease incidence of other fishes is uncertain, but these data warrant careful monitoring in the future to determine if there is a long-term change in the fish community and in the overall health of the Pamlico River Estuary.

References

Ahrenholz, D. W. 1991. Population biology and life history of the North American menhadens, *Brevoortia* sp. Marine Fisheries Review 53:3–20.

Beecher, H. A. 1973. Effects of a hurricane on a shallow-water population of damselfish, *Pomacentrus variabilis*. Copeia 1973:613–615.

Breeder, C. M. 1962. Effects of a hurricane on the small fishes of a shallow bay. Copeia 1962:459–462.

Burkholder, J. M., and H. B. Glasgow, Jr. 1997. *Pfiesteria piscicida* and other *Pfiesteria*-like dinoflagellates: Behavior, impacts, and environmental controls. Limnology and Oceanography 42:1052–1075.

Burkholder, J. M., M. A. Mallin, and H. B. Glasgow. 1999. Fish kills, bottom-water hypoxia, and the toxic *Pfiesteria* complex in the Neuse River and estuary. Marine Ecology Progress Series 179:301–310.

Copeland, B. J., and S. R. Riggs. 1984. The ecology of the Pamlico River, North Carolina: an estuarine profile. FWS/OBS-82/06 Washington, D.C.

Creaser, E. P. 1942. Fish mortality resulting from effects of a tropical hurricane. Copeia 1942:48–49.

Dykstra, M. J., E. J. Noga, J. F. Levine, D. W. Moye, and J. H. Hawkins. 1986. Characterization of the *Aphanomyces* species involved with ulcerative mycosis (UM) in menhaden. Mycologia 78:664–672.

Hall, L. W. Jr., S. A. Fisher, and J. A. Sullivan. 1991. A synthesis of water quality and contaminants data for the Atlantic menhaden, *Brevoortia tyrannus*: Implications for Chesapeake Bay. Journal of Environmental Science and Health. Part A. Environmental Science and Engineering 26:1513–1544.

Harrell, L. W., and T. M. Scott. 1985. *Kudoa thyrsitis* (Gilchrist) (Myxosporea: Multivalvulida) in Atlantic Salmon, *Salmo salar* L. Journal of Fish Diseases 8:329–332.

Hearth, J. H., and D. E. Padgett. 1990. Salinity tolerance of an Aphanomyces isolate (Oomycetes) and its possible relationship to ulcerative mycosis (UM) of Atlantic menhaden. Mycologia 82:364–369.

Heath, A. G. 1987. Water pollution and fish physiology. Boca Raton, Fla.: CRC Press.

Moser, M. L., and L. R. Gerry. 1989. Differential effects of salinity changes in two estuarine fishes, *Leiostomus xanthurus* and *Micropogonias undulatus*. Estuaries 12:35–41.

Noga, E. J., L. Khoo, J. B. Stevens, Z. Fan, and J. M. Burkholder. 1996. Novel toxic dinoflagellate causes epidemic disease in estuarine fish. Marine Pollution Bulletin 16:219–224.

Paerl, H. W., J. L. Pinckney, J. M. Fear, and B. L. Peierls. 1998. Ecosystem responses to internal and watershed organic matter loading: Consequences for hypoxia in the eutrophying Neuse River Estuary, USA. Marine Ecology Progress Series 166:17–25.

Peterson, M. S. 1990. Hypoxia-induced physiological changes in two mangrove swamp fishes: sheeps head minnow, *Cyprinodon variegatus* Lacepede and sailfin molly, *Poecilia latipinna* (Lesueur). Comparative Biochemistry and Physiology 97A:17–21.

Plumb, J. A., J. M. Grizzle, and J. Defigueiredo. 1976. Necrosis and bacterial infection in channel catfish (*Ictalurus punctatus*) following hypoxia. Journal of Wildlife Disease 12:247–253.

Ross, S. W., and S. P. Epperly. 1985. Utilization of shallow estuarine nursery areas by fishes in Pamlico Sound and adjacent tributaries, North Carolina. In: Fish community ecology in estuaries and coastal lagoons: towards an ecosystem integration, edited by A. Yanez-Arancibia. Mexico: DR (R) UNAM Press.

Shafer, T. H. 1990. Evidence for enhanced salinity tolerance of a suspected fungal pathogen of Atlantic menhaden, *Brevoortia tyrannus* Latrobe. Journal of Fish Diseases 13:335.

Stanley, D. W. 1992. Historical trends: water quality and fisheries, Albemarle-Pamlico Sounds, with emphasis on the Pamlico River Estuary. University of North Carolina Sea Grant College Program Publication UNC-SG-92-04. Greenville, N.C.: Institute for Coastal and Marine Resources, East Carolina University.

Stanley, D. W., and S. W. Nixon. 1992. Stratification and bottom-water hypoxia in the Pamlico River Estuary. Estuaries 15:270–281.

Van Dolah, P. R., and G. Anderson. 1991. Effects of Hurricane Hugo on salinity and dissolved oxygen conditions in the Charleston Harbor Estuary. Journal of Coastal Research (Special Issue) 8:83–94.

About the Authors: Joseph Luczkovich is an associate professor in the Department of Biology at East Carolina University, where he teaches and researches the ecology of estuaries, including seagrass, mangrove, and coral reef ecosystems, with special emphasis on the feeding ecology of marine fishes in those systems. Larry Ausley is a scientist at the North Carolina Department of Environment and Natural Resources (NCDENR). Chris Pullinger is an Environmental Technician and Garcy Ward is an Environmental Specialist on the Pamlico River Rapid Response Team of the NCDENR. Katy West is a biologist at the Division of Marine Fisheries at the NCDENR.

Monitoring the Coastal Ocean: Responses to Hurricane Floyd

Lawrence B. Cahoon, Michael A. Mallin, Frederick M. Bingham, Sharon A. Kissling, and Janice E. Nearhoof

Introduction

Data from a combination of monitoring programs were used to study the impacts of the September 1999 hurricanes and flood on the coastal ocean, particularly the discharges of contaminated floodwaters from the Cape Fear River to the coastal ocean. Among the monitoring programs used was a newly funded Coastal Ocean Monitoring program conducted by the University of North Carolina at Wilmington (UNCW). A series of sampling cruises yielded measurements of many important water quality parameters as the floodwater discharge proceeded. The very great volume of floodwater from the Cape Fear River produced a plume of highly discolored, relatively fresh water that extended well out to sea and into South Carolina coastal waters. The floodwater plume exhibited lower nutrient, fecal coliform, and chlorophyll concentrations and higher dissolved oxygen concentrations than were expected from the numerous waste spills upstream.

Public concerns about water quality and other impacts of the flooding were a major issue. The safety of water for drinking and recreational uses was a paramount concern, as was the safety of seafood products. Although data from the monitoring programs in place at the time of Hurricane Floyd helped address some of these issues, it is clear that major gaps in data collection, sampling efforts, and the distribution of information remain. Monitoring programs that plan data collection and dissemination efforts with disastrous events in mind can serve public needs much more effectively than routine data collection efforts.

Hurricane Floyd

Hurricane Floyd made landfall at Oak Island in Brunswick County, North Carolina, on 16 September 1999 as a category two hurricane with maximum sustained winds of approximately 100 miles per hour (167 kilometers per hour). The storm weakened considerably in the forty-eight hours prior to landfall. Its major impact was from torrential rains beginning in the early morning of 15 September. Rainfall totals for 14–16 September were as high as 50 to 60 centimeters (20-24 inches) in portions of eastern North Carolina, with the highest rainfalls in the lower Cape Fear River basin (data from the National Weather Service, Wilmington Office). These rains fell on an area that had already received substantial rains from Hurricane Dennis during the period of 30 August to 7 September, saturating soils throughout the coastal plain region. The resulting combination of heavy rains and saturated soils created record-setting flooding throughout eastern North Carolina, with especially severe flooding in the Northeast Cape Fear, Black, Neuse, and Tar river basins.

Flooding and storm-associated power outages caused extensive failures and discharges from waste treatment systems throughout the impacted region. Eastern North Carolina supports the densest concentration of concentrated animal feeding operations (CAFO) in North America, with especially large populations of swine and turkeys and somewhat smaller concentrations of broiler chickens and cattle. CAFOs produce waste manures that are generally land-applied, usually as dry litter by poultry CAFOs and as spray-applied liquid from waste lagoons by swine CAFOs. Animal wastes entered Hurricane Floyd's floodwaters from direct surface runoff of land-applied wastes, from lagoon breaches, and from the overtopping of waste lagoons at lower elevations. Human waste treatment systems also discharged large quantities of untreated or poorly treated wastes through bypasses of treatment facilities that were flooded or lost power, overtopping of treatment facilities at lower elevations, overflow of collection systems due to storm water infiltration, and flooding of septic tanks. Several industrial waste storage lagoons also breached, releasing various waste chemicals. Flooded vehicles, storage tanks, and other small but widespread sources released a variety of hydrocarbons and other chemicals into floodwaters. Finally, floodwaters flushed large volumes of swamp water, which is typically low in dissolved oxygen, from coastal plain wetlands and river-bottom swamps. Swamp water is also characterized as having a high biological oxygen demand (BOD). Water with high BOD has a high concentration of micro-organisms that use oxygen as a metabolic requirement and thus remove it from the aquatic environment. As a result of the influx of swamp water and the various pollutant releases, most of which were discovered quickly, the public was concerned about water quality downstream, particularly because flooding from previous hurricanes had created severe water quality impacts in this region.

Flooding caused by Hurricane Fran in September 1996 caused very large quantities of wastes and BOD from the same sources cited above to enter the Cape Fear River system, resulting in extremely low dissolved oxygen levels throughout much of the basin, especially the Northeast Cape Fear River. Flooding caused fish kills and malodorous conditions for up to one month after the storm (Mallin et al. 1999). Hurricane Bonnie in 1998 and the spring 1998 El Niño rains also produced flooding in the Cape Fear River system, but to a lesser degree and with relatively minor impacts. Consequently, many people were concerned that flooding from Hurricane Floyd might have severe water quality impacts, but there was had no firm basis for predicting actual impacts.

Monitoring Programs

UNCW, under the direction of Dr. Michael Mallin, has conducted monitoring in the lower Cape Fear River since 1995. This effort pools financial support from a group of NPDES (National Pollutant Discharge Elimination System) dischargers in the lower basin for the sampling work, satisfying their respective permit requirements and providing UNCW with a long-term water quality database. Sixteen sampling stations have been established throughout the lower Cape Fear basin, extending from stations on the lower Black, Northeast Cape Fear, and main stem of the Cape Fear River to the mouth of the estuary near Southport, North Carolina. Sampling is conducted monthly for a variety of parameters, including conventional physical, chemical, and biological variables such as salinity, temperature, dissolved oxygen, nutrients, chlorophyll *a* concentration, as well as metals.

UNCW also conducts a tidal creeks monitoring and research program with support from New Hanover County. This effort aims to monitor water quality in the small estuaries along the county's Atlantic side to identify possible remedies for problems and to evaluate their effectiveness. Water samples are collected monthly in five tidal creeks and in the adjacent Intracoastal Waterway. Dr. Mallin also directs this project.

A congressional appropriation through the National Oceanographic and Atmospheric Adminstration's (NOAA) Oceanic and Atmospheric Research office funds UNCW's new Coastal Ocean Monitoring program. Funding for this effort was received in late August 1999 and work began on 1 September, just before Hurricane Floyd struck the region. The overall monitoring program includes several elements that supported subsequent work in response to Hurricane Floyd's flooding, including studies of the Cape Fear River plume's chemical and biological effects on the coastal ocean and measurement of physical, chemical, and biological properties of coastal ocean waters. The principal investigator for this program is Dr. Lawrence B. Cahoon.

Response to Hurricane Floyd

Hurricane Floyd did relatively little damage along the coast, and it became quickly apparent that flooding was the major impact of the storm. News of the flooding effects also developed quickly, with numerous reports of waste spills and contamination. Consequently an effort to assess the effects of the flooding on coastal water quality was both physically possible and highly desirable.

The Cape Fear River program began water quality sampling efforts on 22 September, and the Coastal Ocean Monitoring program began on 23 September, using UNCW's research vessels. The extent of flooding impacts on the coastal ocean was quite impressive, so additional assets were sought to assist with the ocean monitoring work. NOAA's Natural Environmental Satellite Data and Information Service (NESDIS) program made satellite imagery available for use in assessing turbidity and chlorophyll levels in the coastal ocean. These images guided the research vessels' sampling efforts. Owing to the large extent of the plume of river water in the nearshore ocean, we used a larger oceanographic vessel, *R/V Cape Hatteras*, for two sampling cruises (1 October 1999 and 7–8 October 1999). Financial support was quickly provided by UNC Sea Grant, the National Sea Grant Office, the National Undersea Research Center at UNCW, and the Duke-UNC Oceanographic Consortium.

Coastal Ocean Water Quality

Experiences after previous hurricane floods suggested that several potential water quality problems were possible, including low dissolved oxygen, stimulation of algae blooms by nutrient loading, and microbiological contamination. Our sampling efforts were designed to determine if these problems occurred and, if so, quantify their magnitude and extent.

The floodwaters were characterized by high turbidity, high levels of coloring material, lowered salinity, and cooler temperatures than are typically observed at our sampling stations in September. Secchi depths (a measure of water transparency) in the mouth of the river were as low as 0.35 meters, compared to normal values, which are typically greater than 1 meter.

Dissolved oxygen

On the cruises conducted on 23 and 28 September and on 14 October, surface dissolved oxygen values were measured using a hand-held YSI 85 DO meter with automatic temperature and salinity compensation. Dissolved oxygen in surface water and in bottom waters was measured using the Winkler method for the more extensive cruises on 1 October and 7–8 October. Dissolved oxygen levels in the freshwater portions of the Cape Fear River were as low as 2.0 milligrams per liter (mg/l) in the first week after Floyd and rose subsequently. Some dissolved oxygen levels in the river's ocean plume were below the North Carolina standard of 5.0 mg/l in the first two weeks after the hurricane, but most sampled waters had reached levels above that standard by the 7–8 October cruise (Table 1). Stratification of the coastal ocean waters, with fresher water forming a layer above the denser ocean salt water, suggested the possibility of oxygen depletion in the lower

Table 1. Results of dissolved oxygen sampling in the Cape Fear River's lower estuary and ocean plume, 23 September 1999–14 October 1999, indicating surface or bottom samples (S/B), number of stations, and range of dissolved oxygen values in milligrams per liter (mg/l).

Sample Dates	S/B	Number of Stations	Dissolved Oxygen (mg/l)
23 September 1999	S	6	3.0–6.5
28 September 1999	S	6	3.45–6.35
1 October 1999	S	13	4.26–7.00
7–8 October 1999	S	25	4.53–7.73
7–8 October 1999	B	17	5.18–8.75
14 October 1999	S	8	4.46–6.06

layer. But dissolved oxygen levels in this layer were found to be as high as surface levels. As of 14 October dissolved oxygen values were generally above 5.0 mg/l in the Cape Fear River estuary and adjacent ocean waters. These dissolved oxygen data indicated that although there was a discernible impact from the flood, dissolved oxygen levels did not get low enough to cause major fish kills; no fish kills were observed in the estuary or coastal ocean.

Chlorophyll a concentrations

Chlorophyll *a* concentrations in the Cape Fear River estuary and the coastal ocean (measured by fluorometry using a Turner 10-AU fluorometer according to Welschmeyer [1994]) never exceeded 5.0 micrograms per liter (*μ*g/l) during the period 28 September to 14 October (Table 2). Concentrations in the surface waters of the flood plume averaged about 1 *μ*g/l, well below the North Carolina standard of 40 *μ*g/l, and were actually higher in ocean water unaffected by floodwaters.

Table 2. Results of chlorophyll *a* sampling in the Cape Fear River's lower estuary and ocean plume, 23 September 1999–14 October 1999, indicating number of stations and range of chlorophyll *a* values in micrograms per liter (μg/l).

Sample Dates	Number of Stations	Chlorophyll *a* (μg/l)
23 September 1999	6	0.7–2.6
28 September 1999	6	0.8–3.0
1 October 1999	13	0.6–1.1
7–8 October 1999	27	0.6–4.6
14 October 1999	8	1.22–2.52

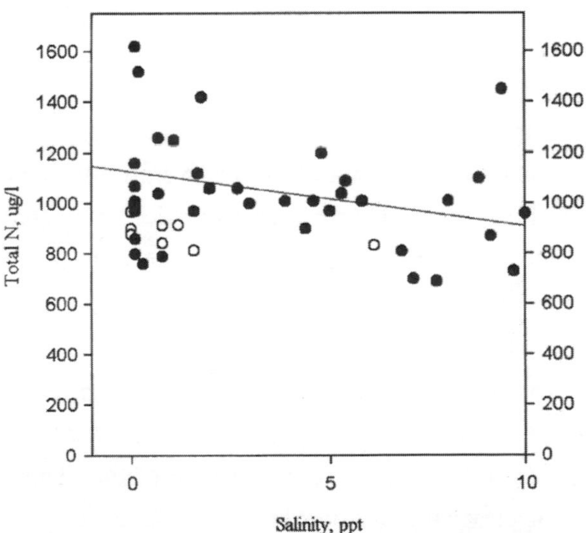

Figure 1. Total nitrogen (micrograms per liter [μg/l]) in the Cape Fear River versus salinity. Open circles are data from samples taken after Hurricane Floyd. Closed circles are data from samples collected twelve months prior to Hurricane Floyd.

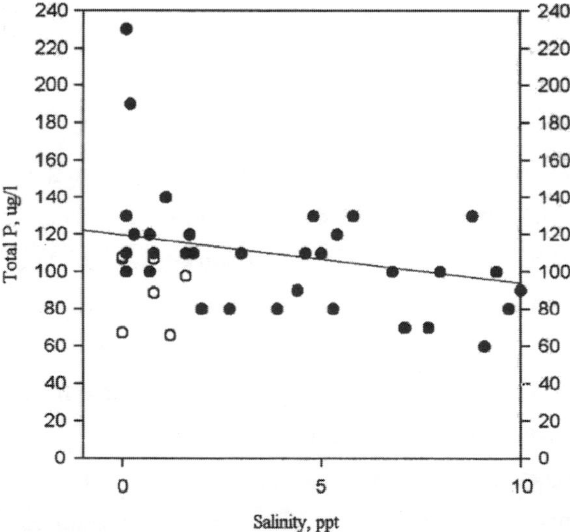

Figure. 2. Total phosphorus (micrograms per liter [μg/l]) in the Cape Fear River versus salinity. Open circles are data from samples taken after Hurricane Floyd. Closed circles are data from samples collected twelve months prior to Hurricane Floyd.

Nutrients

Water samples for total nitrogen and total phosphorus were digested using the wet persulfate method (Valderrama 1981) and analyzed for nitrate and orthophosphate using standard wet chemistry methods on an Alpkem Flow Solution 3000 autoanalyzer. Concentrations of total nitrogen and phosphorus were relatively low compared to values at comparable salinities typically observed by the Cape Fear River program during nonflood conditions (Figure 1 and Figure 2).

Microbiological contamination

Fecal coliform analysis was performed using the mFC method (APHA 1995). Subsequent analysis of anomalous colonies employed API 20 tests to identify bacteria species present on the coliform test filters. Fecal coliforms (usually *E. coli*) were present at low concentrations in all samples. The North Carolina standard for body contact is 200 colony forming units (CFU) per 100 milliliters (ml). All samples collected on 23 September were below this standard. All samples collected from ocean waters were at or below 3 CFU per 100 ml. These values would normally indicate that these waters were microbiologically safe for swimming. However, the pathogens *Salmonella, Shigella, Klebsiella*, and other potentially pathogenic species were identified in at least one sample, suggesting that coliform counts were not an adequate indicator of microbiological contamination in this situation. Much of the microbiological contamination observed was likely derived from local sewage and animal waste sources, not from sources much farther upstream.

Summary

The major water quality impacts feared in response to the flooding from Hurricane Floyd did not materialize in the Cape Fear River estuary or the coastal ocean downstream of the river mouth. Very high volumes of floodwater were discharged, but aside from the high turbidity and color associated with this water, nutrient and chlorophyll *a* levels remained low, and dissolved oxygen levels did not fall low enough to cause mortality among aquatic organisms. We attribute these results to the very high dilution of nutrient and organic loadings to the river by the extremely heavy rainfall associated with Floyd. Rain water is naturally low in nutrients and high in dissolved oxygen. Previous hurricanes, especially Fran, may have driven similarly heavy loadings of nutrients and organics but with substantially less dilution, thus causing major water quality impacts. Therefore, no two hurricanes are alike. There are a spectrum of possible effects. Also, a series of storms occurring in quick succession likely created different effects than if they had occurred with more time in between to allow return to pre-storm conditions.

Public concerns about water quality were a major issue for the Cape Fear region. Results of this monitoring effort were able to assuage many of these concerns. We have been able to reassure the local citizenry and visitors to the area that water quality in the coastal ocean recovered within about one month of Hurricane Floyd, and impacts were not as severe as first feared.

Although our response to Hurricane Floyd was reasonably effective, it was very much an effort that was tailored to this storm event. The lack of data on the normal conditions in the coastal ocean, lack of automated data collection systems that would have provided coverage throughout the storm and immediate aftermath, and the damage associated with such powerful storms all make effective, planned monitoring of these events difficult. Nevertheless, the importance of these events makes such efforts necessary. UNCW's monitoring programs are now well positioned to address this need in this region.

References

American Public Health Association (APHA). 1995. Standard methods for the examination of water and waste water, edited by A. E. Greenberg. Washington, D.C.: American Public Health Association.

Mallin, M. A., M. H. Posey, G. C. Shank, M. R. McIver, S. H. Ensign, and T. D. Alphin. 1999. Hurricane effects on water quality and benthos in the Cape Fear watershed: Natural and anthropogenic impacts. Ecological Applications 9:350–362.

Valderrama, J. C. 1981. The simultaneous analysis of total nitrogen and phosphorus in natural waters. Marine Chemistry 10:109–122.

Welschmeyer, N. A. 1994. Fluorometric analysis of chlorophyll *a* in the presence of chlorophyll *b* and phaeopigments. Limnology and Oceanography 39:1985–1993.

About the Authors: Lawrence B. Cahoon is a professor in the Department of Biological Sciences at the University of North Carolina at Wilmington (UNCW). One focus of his research has been the role of benthic microalgae in oceanic, estuarine, and freshwater ecosystems. He is also interested in evaluating water quality management practices in coastal areas and in the interactions of water quality with community function in estuarine habitats. Dr. Michael A. Mallin is the laboratory director of the Aquatic Ecology Lab at UNCW's Center for Marine Science. Among the current projects he is overseeing at the lab are the Lower Cape Fear River Program (since 1995) and the New Hanover County Tidal Creeks Project (since 1993). Dr. Frederick M. Bingham is a professor in the Department of Physics and Physical Oceanography at UNCW, with research interest in large-scale regional physical oceanography in the western equatorial Pacific, the Hawaiian Islands, and Onslow Bay, North Carolina, as well as other locations. Sharon A. Kissling is a research technician, and Janice E. Nearhoof is a research associate at UNCW's Center for Marine Science.

Water Quality and Fisheries Habitat Changes in the Pamlico Sound After Three Hurricanes: A Short-term and Long-term Perspective

Hans W. Paerl, Christopher P. Buzzelli, Malia Go, Benjamin L. Peierls, Richard A. Luettich, Tammi L. Richardson, Joseph S. Ramus, Lisa A. Eby, Larry B. Crowder, Larry W. Ausley, Jimmie Overton, and Jerad D. Bales

Introduction

Eastern North Carolina experienced four visits from three hurricanes (Dennis [twice], Floyd, and Irene) within a four-week period in September and October 1999. Hurricane Floyd alone led to an unprecedented 50- to 500-year flood event, depending on the exact location in the watershed (Bales et al. 2000). The flood inundated coastal rivers and the Pamlico Sound, the nation's second largest estuary and North Carolina's most valuable aquatic resource (Copeland and Gray 1991). The sound processes nearly half of North Carolina's freshwater runoff via its sub-estuaries (i.e., Neuse, Pamlico, and Roanoke-Chowan-Albemarle). It has a mean water residence time of nearly one year (Pietrafesa et al. 1996). The residence time, the amount of time necessary for a quantity of water equal to the volume of the entire estuary to pass out of the estuary, is an important characteristic. It indicates the type of interaction the estuary has with the open ocean and directly relates to water quality variables, including salinity and oxygen levels, and to the composition of the plant and animal community in the estuary. The long residence time of Pamlico Sound is in part due to the narrow inlets (e.g., Hatteras, Ocracoke, and Oregon inlets) that function to exchange water between the open ocean and the sound. From late September through early November 1999, the huge pulse of nutrient-laden runoff from Dennis, Floyd, and Irene reduced the sound's residence time to approximately two months.

Floodwaters also "freshened" the open sound, reducing surface water salinities from approximately 20 practical salinity units (psu; parts of sea salt per thousand parts water by weight, usually grams per kilogram) to less than 6 psu. This led to strong vertical salinity stratification, accompanied by excessive oxygen consumption (hypoxia) in bottom waters, which restricted the habitat for estuarine-dependent fish and shellfish species. Water and nutrient discharge from this single event approached the normal annual loads and turned the sub-estuaries into conduits for freshwater and nutrient discharge directly to the sound. Here, we report the immediate hydrologic, nutrient, and biological effects and discuss the long-term ecological and environmental ramifications for the sound.

Measuring the Impacts

On 23 September 1999 satellite imagery and ship-based observations indicated that the plume of sediment-laden floodwater following Hurricane Floyd's passage (15-16 September 1999) had entered Pamlico Sound. This large-scale intrusion triggered a rapid-response monitoring program, utilizing the research vessels *Susan Hudson* (Duke University Marine Laboratory) and *Capricorn* (University of North Carolina, Chapel Hill, Institute of Marine Sciences) to conduct monthly surveys of water quality and habitat conditions in the western Pamlico Sound. Water column data were collected along a grid of fifteen western Pamlico Sound sampling stations and at a site termed "C-3" (35° 7.22' N, 76° 28.66' W), which is near the mouth of the Neuse River Estuary and has been sampled since early 1998 as part of six instructional cruises conducted by Drs. Larry Crowder and Joesph Ramus. Parallel environmental data on the Neuse and Pamlico river estuaries were collected before and after the three 1999 hurricanes through ongoing cooperative monitoring programs including the Neuse River Monitoring and Modeling Project (ModMon) (see <www.marine.unc.edu/neuse/modmon>) and the U.S. Geological Survey (USGS) continuous monitoring on both the Neuse and Pamlico river estuaries (see <nc.water.usgs.gov>).

The following parameters and sampling protocols were employed: freshwater inflows, flood recurrence intervals, physical-chemical conditions, dissolved nutrients, dissolved organic carbon, particulate organic carbon, phytoplankton biomass (chlorophyll *a*), and fish assessments. For a detailed methodology description see Paerl et al. 2000.

Ecosystem Impacts and Ramifications

Hydrology

Hurricanes Dennis, Floyd, and Irene brought record rains to the Pamlico Sound watershed. The central Tar-Pamlico basin received 96 centimeters (cm) of rain during September and October. This was equivalent to about 85% of the average annual rainfall (Figure 1). Portions of the Neuse basin received about 75 cm of rain during the two months, which represented more than 50% the average annual rainfall (Figure 1). In most other regions of eastern North Carolina at least 50% of the annual rainfall fell during September and October, and regional flooding continued throughout October. Flood recurrence intervals ranged from 50 to over 500 years in the Tar-Pamlico basin, with 500-year or greater floods occurring in at least one location in all Pamlico Sound drainage basins. (For details, see Bales et al. 2000.)

Pamlico Sound received a higher than normal flow of fresh water due to the floods. The flow to Pamlico Sound during September and October 1999 was equivalent to about 83% of the sound's normal volume, indicating a water residence (or a complete flushing) time of approximately two months. This is in stark contrast to a more typical mean inflow volume during this period, which is approximately 13% of the sound's volume (Table 1). September inflow volume from the Pamlico River Estuary to Pamlico Sound was more than 90% of the average annual flow volume. Inflow from the Neuse River Estuary was slightly less than from the Pamlico River, with September inflow volume equivalent to 55%–60% of average annual inflow. During September, water residence time for the Pamlico River and Neuse estuaries was about seven days, compared to a typical value of about seventy days (Bales and Robbins 1995, Robbins and Bales, 1995).

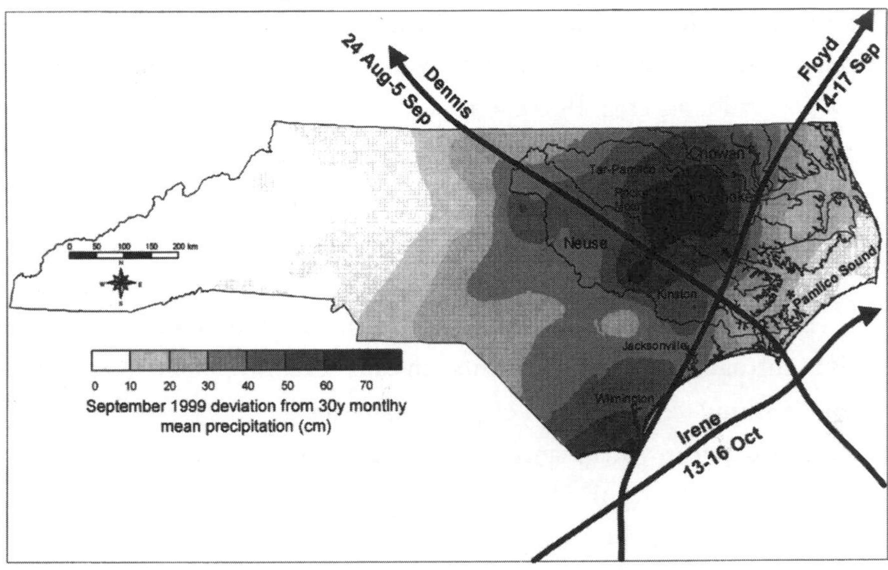

Figure 1. Map of North Carolina showing the tracks of hurricanes Dennis, Floyd, and Irene during September-October 1999. Also shown is the September 1999 deviation from the 30-year monthly mean precipitation in the various watersheds of the Albemarle-Pamlico Sound system.

Changes in salinity

Rapid change in salinity and low salinity levels can cause physiological stress to estuarine plants and animals. By late September to early October, the floodwaters rendered the Pamlico River and Neuse River estuaries fresh (0 psu), whereas typical late summer salinities are 10 to 16 psu near the mouths of these systems. Surface salinities in western Pamlico Sound typically range from 15 to 20 psu in September. Two weeks after the passage of Hurricane Floyd, which by far delivered the greatest rainfall of the three storms, the surface salinity in Pamlico Sound averaged 8.9 psu (plus or minus 1.4 psu), or about half of normal values, with the lowest

Table 1. Freshwater inflow to the Pamlico Sound during September and October 1999. "All others" refers to drainage from the Chowan basin, as well as direct rainfall to the surface of Albemarle and Pamlico sounds. (Table from Paerl et al. 2000)

		Freshwater Input to Pamlico Sound			
		In Volume (10^9 m^3)		As Percent (%) of sound volume	
Basin	**Drainage Area (km^2)**	**Normal**	**Sept–Oct 1999**	**Normal**	**Sept–Oct 1999**
Roanoke	25,320	0.93	2.49	3.57	9.55
Chowan	12,766	0.33	3.32	1.26	12.75
Neuse	14,499	0.54	5.58	2.07	21.41
Tar-Pamlico	11,142	0.31	4.61	1.21	17.68
All others	16,251	1.30	5.63	4.95	34.37
Total	79,978	3.41	21.63	13.08	83.01

salinities at the shallower locations. Rather than mix with the saltier waters of Pamlico Sound, the low-salinity floodwaters spread out over Pamlico Sound, "capping" the higher density salt water in an "oil on vinegar" manner. This resulted in a strong vertical stratification and the formation of a well-defined region where water density rapidly changed (i.e., a pycnocline) at a depth of 5 meters (m) in early October. The difference between surface and bottom salinity (stratification) for southwestern Pamlico Sound averaged 6 psu in October 1999, which is two to three times greater than was measured in previous years (Williams et al. 1967). A vertical salinity stratification of 3 psu is usually sufficient to induce strong enough vertical stratification to promote bottom-water hypoxia (Williams at al. 1967, Paerl et al. 1998).

Changes in nitrogen concentration

Although nitrogen is necessary for plant growth in terrestrial and aquatic environments, high levels of nitrogen and other nutrients can cause excessive plant growth. In aquatic systems, high nutrient levels stimulate the growth of phytoplankton (i.e., algal blooms), which depresses the amount of sunlight available to other plants and can deplete oxygen levels. Low dissolved oxygen levels can result in fish kills and in the death of other animals and plants. The process where high nutrient loads cause accelerated phytoplankton growth is called eutrophication, which is often caused by the input of pollution such as sewage or other fertilizers.

During early October 1999, dissolved inorganic nitrogen concentrations ranged from 0.71–11.06 micromolar (μM N) at the surface and the near-bottom locations of the Pamlico Sound. Sources of dissolved inorganic nitrogen came from within the estuary, due to the process of decomposition, and from input from outside sources, including floodwater runoff containing nitrogen from land-derived sewage, agriculture fertilizers, and other organic material. In the Neuse River Estuary, dissolved inorganic nitrogen concentrations were similar to the Pamlico Sound concentrations (6.64–15.56 μM N, measured at sixteen sites). In contrast, dissolved inorganic nitrogen in Chesapeake Bay, following a major flood that resulted from Hurricane Agnes (1972), increased only at the head of the bay and not throughout the bay (Ruzecki et al. 1976; Smith et al. 1976). Dissolved inorganic nitrogen concentrations are usually undetectable (less than 1 μM) at the mouth of the Neuse River Estuary in early fall (Hobbie and Smith 1975; Christian et al. 1991; Paerl et al. 1995, 1998), but in early October ammonium and nitrate concentrations at this location were greater than 10 μM and 2 μM, respectively.

During September and October 1999, dissolved inorganic nitrogen loading to the Neuse River Estuary was over 800 metric tons, which is 71% of the 1994–1997 average annual loading. Total nitrogen loading to the Pamlico River Estuary between mid-September and mid-October was about 1,600 metric tons. Total nitrogen loading to the Neuse River Estuary was about 3,500 metric tons, more than double the loading to the Pamlico River Estuary, despite the higher flows in the Tar-Pamlico River basin.

Biological responses

The enrichment of Pamlico Sound with nitrogen derived from outside the sound led to dramatic stimulation of planktonic microalgal biomass (i.e., phytoplankton) in this typically nitrogen-limited system (c.f., Kuenzler et al. 1979, 1982; Stanley 1983; Paerl et al. 1990, 1995). Phytoplankton are the dominant source of biologically available organic matter supporting the system's food web. At least 80% of primary production of the Neuse River Estuary is derived from phytoplankton (Paerl et al. 1998). Phytoplankton biomass, measured as chlorophyll *a* concentration, increased by three- to five-fold (from approximately 5 to 20 micrograms per liter [$\mu g/1$]) relative to pre-hurricane conditions (Figure 2). Elevated phytoplankton biomass was still evident seven months after the floodwaters entered the sound. This increase in phytoplankton production represents a sizable upward shift in trophic state (i.e., eutrophication) of this system and warrants close scrutiny to see if it will translate into increased production at higher trophic levels (i.e., finfish and shellfish) and/or greater hypoxia potential.

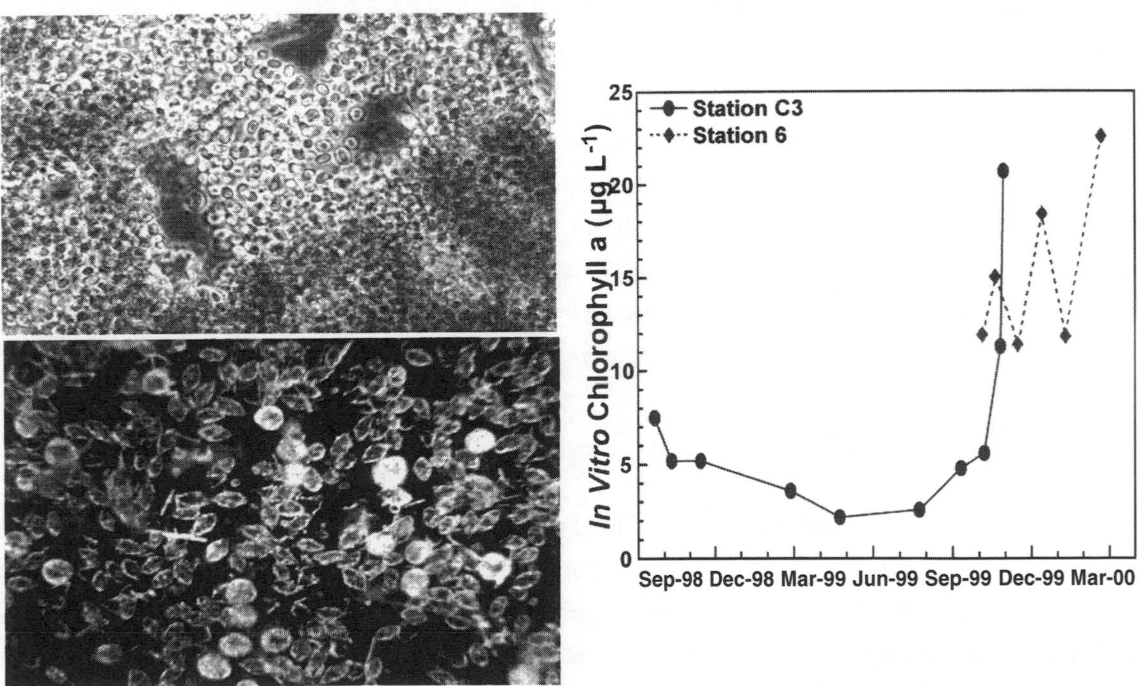

Figure 2. Surface water chlorophyll a concentrations at station C-3, the western Pamlico Sound index station that was sampled before and after the fall 1999 hurricanes. Chlorophyll a is an indicator of the amount (biomass) of planktonic algae in the water column. Representative members of the algal community are shown, including picoplanktonic blue green algae (cyanobacteria) (upper left frame) and dinoflagellates (lower left frame). Note the strong stimulation of algal growth following the entry of the flood hurricane waters in the sound in late September 1999. This stimulation was sustained into spring 2000.

Unusually strong vertical stratification, nutrient-enhanced production, and organic matter enrichment led to bottom-water hypoxia (less than 4 milligram of oxygen per liter [mg O_2/1]) in the estuary. These conditions cause stress to most motile finfish and shellfish species and are fatal to sessile biota (i.e., plants and animals that live attached to a substrate and therefore cannot necessarily move to less stressful regions) (Renaud 1986; Pihl et al. 1991; Lenihan and Peterson 1998; Eby et al. 2000). Hypoxia existed for approximately three weeks, beginning almost immediately after the floodwaters dispersed over Pamlico Sound in late September. The stratification and hypoxia persisted until 17 October when winds and rain from Hurricane Irene de-stratified, re-aerated, and further freshened the sound to approximately to 6 psu (compared to a more typical 18 psu). The sound subsequently restratified, in large part in response to the continued freshwater inflows from basin floodwaters.

On 8 October, following Floyd and before Irene, large numbers of dead and dying shrimp and blue crabs were collected in Pamlico Sound from below the pycnocline, where dissolved oxygen was less than 4 mg O_2 /1. Apparently, blue crabs were unaffected by floods following Hurricane Agnes in Chesapeake Bay. The number of live finfish and crabs caught during each of six Pamlico Sound trawls was about three-fold higher than before the flooding (11 September), although the number of different species (species richness) was lower. It appeared that the mobile species moved out of the estuaries ahead of the fresh water, but exposure to low-salinity, hypoxic water likely stressed or killed invertebrates that live attached to bottom substrates (i.e., sessile benthic animals). By 27 October, fish catches again increased by three-fold and the occurrence of disease increased substantially. Ten percent to 20% of three common species (pinfish, 17%; spot, 20%; and croaker, 14%) had lesions, sores or sloughing skin. Fifty percent to 70% showed signs of systemic bacterial infections (E. Noga, North Carolina State University, personal communication). During the same time frame in a non-hurricane year (October 1998), the incidences of external sores in the Neuse River Estuary were 0.18% in spot (of 566 spot collected) and 0.14% in croaker (of 718 collected). There is no data for pinfish.

The Long-term Perspective

It is likely that the shallow depths and long residence time in Pamlico Sound caused a substantial amount of the nutrient and organic inputs from the three 1999 hurricanes to be deposited in the sediments. The observed long-term enhancement of phytoplankton biomass, as of July 2000, appears to be linked to the ability of the sound to retain and recycle a relatively large fraction of the nutrients that were transported in the floodwater. Such a long-term ecosystem response was also observed in Chesapeake Bay after Hurricane Agnes (Ruzecki et al. 1976). The sequence of having increased nutrient loading via floodwaters, increased primary production, increased deposition of nutrient inputs, increased bottom-water oxygen consumption, and increased bottom-water inorganic nutrient release represents a mechanism that could extend the short-term enrichment effects of the flood of 1999 throughout 2000 and possibly beyond.

Nitrogen can leave the sound system by two mechanisms: water flow (outflow) out of the sound and from natural biological processes that remove nitrogen (i.e., denitrification). The sound's long residence time greatly retards outflow losses. Denitrification measurements in the Neuse River Estuary indicate that this process may remove only about 20% of the external nitrogen load (Thompson et al. submitted). Therefore, we expect nitrogen-enriched conditions to persist for several years. This extended response and recovery will likely translate to long-term higher trophic level response. In this regard, fisheries recruitment will depend on the time required for Pamlico Sound to return to typical salinity levels, biogeochemical characteristics, and food web structure.

The hurricanes of 1999 have provided a strong sense of awareness and respect for the large-scale, massive hydrologic and nutrient impacts storm runoff and flooding can have on a coastal ecosystem under the influence of human modification of its watershed. The observed and hypothesized estuarine responses also provide a perspective on the effects of climate change on the structure and function of coastal ecosystems. Increased tropical storm and hurricane activity is predicted over the next few decades (Gray et al. 1996; Landsea et al. 1999). The hurricanes of 1999 may be indicative of this phenomenon. Such a trend could seriously disrupt ecosystems critical for fishery resources, economic development, and habitability of the ecologically fragile coastal zone.

In conclusion, there is a need to assess both short-term and long-term hydrologic, nutrient, and sediment impacts on the sound, yet currently there is no long-term water monitoring and assessment program in place to evaluate these impacts and facilitate water quality and fisheries management strategies. A recent proposal to assess the effects of hurricanes and human-made watershed nutrient manipulations has received state funding (Hurricane Floyd Emergency Relief Bill). Three N.C. Department of Transportation ferries have been equipped for intensive "real-time" water quality monitoring of the sound. (See Ramus and Paerl's paper in this volume for a description of this project.) However, additional longer term state and federal funding will be needed.

References

Bales, J. D., and J. C. Robbins. 1995. Simulation of hydrodynamics and solute transport in the Pamlico River Estuary, North Carolina. Open-File Report 94–454, U.S. Geologic Survey, Raleigh, N.C.

Bales, J. D., C. J. Oblinger, and A. H. Sallenger. 2000. Two months of flooding in eastern North Carolina, September–October 1999: Hydrologic, water-quality, and geologic effects of Hurricanes Dennis, Floyd, and Irene. Report 00-4093, U.S. Geologic Survey Water-Resources Investigations, Raleigh, N.C.

Christian, R. R., J. N. Boyer, and D. W. Stanley. 1991. Multi-year distribution patterns of nutrients within the Neuse River Estuary. Marine Ecology Progress Series 71:259–274.

Copeland, B. J., and J. Gray. 1991. Status and trends of the Albemarle-Pamlico estuaries. Albemarle-Pamlico Estuarine Study Report 90-01, edited by J. Steel, North Carolina Department of the Environment, Health and Natural Resources, Raleigh, N.C.

Eby, L. A., L. B. Crowder, and C. McClellan. 2000. Neuse River Estuary modeling and monitoring project, stage 1: Effects of water quality on distribution and composition of the fish community. Report 325C, University of North Carolina Water Resources Research Institute, Raleigh, N.C.

Gray, W. M., J. D. Sheaffer, and C. W. Landsea. 1996. Climate trends associated with multi-decadal variability of intense Atlantic hurricane activity. In: Hurricanes, climatic change and socioeconomic impacts: A current perspective, edited by H. F. Diaz and R. S. Pulwarty. Denver, Colo.: Westview Press.

Hobbie, J. E., and N. W. Smith. 1975. Nutrients in the Neuse River Estuary, N.C. Report No. UNC-SG-75–21, University of North Carolina Sea Grant Program, Raleigh, N.C.

Kuenzler, E. J., D. W. Stanley, and J. P. Koenings. 1979. Nutrient kinetics of phytoplankton in the Pamlico River, N.C. Report No. 139, University of North Carolina Water Resources Research Institute, Raleigh, N.C.

Kuenzler, E. J., K. L. Stone, and D. B. Albert. 1982. Phytoplankton uptake and sediment release of nitrogen and phosphorus in the Chowan River. Report No. 186. N.C., University of North Carolina Water Resources Research Institute, Raleigh, N.C.

Landsea, C. W., R. A. Pielke, Jr., A. M. Mestaz-Nunez, and J. A. Knaff. 1999. Atlantic basin hurricanes: Indices of climatic changes. Climatic Changes 42:89–129.

Lenihan, H., and C. H. Peterson. 1998. How habitat degradation through fishery disturbance enhances impacts of hypoxia on oyster reefs. Ecological Applications 8:128–140.

Paerl, H. W., and D. R. Whitall. 1999. Anthropogenically-derived atmospheric nitrogen deposition, marine eutrophication and harmful algal bloom expansion: Is there a link? Ambio 28:307–311.

Paerl, H. W., J. Rudek, and M. A. Mallin. 1990. Stimulation of phytoplankton production in coastal waters by natural rainfall inputs: Nutritional and trophic implications. Marine Biology 107:247–254.

Paerl, H. W., J. L. Pinckney, J. M. Fear, and B. L. Peierls. 1998. Ecosystem response to internal and watershed organic matter loading: Consequences for hypoxia in the eutrophying Neuse River Estuary, N.C., U.S.A. Marine Ecology Progress Series 166:17–25.

Paerl, H. W., M. A. Mallin, C. A. Donahue, M. Go, and B. L. Peierls. 1995. Nitrogen loading sources and eutrophication of the Neuse River Estuary, N.C.: Direct and indirect roles of atmospheric deposition. Report 291, University of North Carolina Water Resources Research Institute, Raleigh, N.C.

Paerl, H. W., J. D. Bales, L. W. Ausley, C. P. Buzzelli, L. B. Crowder, L. A. Eby, M. Go, B. L. Peierls, T. L. Richardson, and J. S. Ramus. 2000. Recent hurricanes result in continuing ecosystem impacts on USA's largest lagoonal estuary: Pamlico Sound, N.C. EOS (in press).

Pietrafesa, L. J., G. S. Janowitz, T-Y. Chao, R. H. Weisberg, F. Askari, and E. Noble. 1996. The physical oceanography of Pamlico Sound. UNC-WP-86-5, University of North Carolina Sea Grant Publication, Raleigh, N.C.

Pihl, L., S. P. Baden, and R. J. Diaz. 1991. Effects of periodic hypoxia on distribution of demersal fish and crustaceans. Marine Biology 108:349–360.

Renaud, M. L. 1986. Hypoxia in Louisiana coastal waters during 1983: Implications for the fisheries. Fisheries Bulletin U.S. 84:19–26.

Robbins, J. C., and J. D. Bales. 1995. Simulation of hydrodynamics and solute transport in the Neuse River Estuary, North Carolina. Open-File Report 94–511, U.S. Geologic Survey, Raleigh, N.C.

Ruzecki, E. P., J. H. Schubel, R. J. Huggett, A. M. Anderson, M. L. Wass, R. J. Marasco, and M. P. Lynch, eds. 1976. The effects of tropical storm Agnes on the Chesapeake Bay Estuarine System. Publication No. 54, Chesapeake Bay Research Consortium. Baltimore, Md.: Johns Hopkins University Press.

Smith, C. L., W. G. MacIntyre, C. A. Lake, and J. G. Windsor. (1976). Effects of tropical storm Agnes on nutrient flux and distribution in lower Chesapeake Bay. In: The effects of tropical storm Agnes on the Chesapeake Bay Estuarine System, edited by E. P. Ruzecki, J. H. Schubel, R. J. Huggett, A. M. Anderson, M. L. Wass, R. J. Marasco, and M. P. Lynch. Publication No. 54, Chesapeake Bay Research Consortium. Baltimore, Md.: Johns Hopkins University Press.

Stanley, D. W. 1983. Nitrogen cycling and phytoplankton growth in the Neuse River, N.C. Report No. 20., University of North Carolina Water Resources Research Institute, Raleigh, N.C.

Williams, A. B., G. S. Posner, W. J. Woods, and E. E. Deubler. 1967. A Hydrographic atlas of larger North Carolina sounds. Data Report 20, U.S. Fish and Wildlife Service, Washington, D.C.

About the Authors: Hans W. Paerl is the William R. Kenan Professor at the Institute of Marine Sciences, University of North Carolina, Chapel Hill in Morehead City, North Carolina. Dr. Paerl studies the nutrient production dynamics of aquatic microbes at the base of the estuarine and coastal food webs, focusing on environmental controls of algal production, community structure, and assessment of the causes and consequences of human-induced eutrophication of rivers, lakes, estuaries, and coastal oceans. His colleagues in the research presented in this paper are Christopher P. Buzzelli, Malia Go, Benjamin L. Peierls, and Richard A. Luettich also from the Institute of Marine Sciences; Tammi L. Richardson from the Department of Oceanography at Texas A&M; Joseph S. Ramus, Lisa A. Eby and Larry B. Crowder are scientists at the Duke University Marine Laboratory in Beaufort, N.C.; Larry W. Ausley and Jimmie Overton are scientists with the Water Quality Division of the N.C. Department of Environment and Natural Resources in Raleigh, N.C.; and Jerad D. Bales is a researcher at the Raleigh, N.C., office of the U.S. Geological Survey.

Changes in Phytoplankton Biomass in the Pamlico Sound After Hurricane Floyd

Joseph S. Ramus

Introduction

The Pamlico Sound, with an area of 5,800 square kilometers, is the second largest estuary and the largest lagoonal estuary in North America. It processes freshwater runoff from 80,000 square kilometers of watershed, primarily in North Carolina, including the Chowan and Roanoke rivers to the Albemarle Sound and the Neuse and Tar-Pamlico rivers to the Pamlico Sound. Runoff waters are impounded by the narrow, sand barrier islands comprising the Outer Banks. The sound exchanges water with the coastal ocean through narrow, shallow inlets, primarily Oregon, Hatteras, and Ocracoke. The estuary is shallow, with an average depth of 4.5 meters and a maximum depth of 7.3 meters. The ratio of the volume of the Pamlico Sound (26 cubic kilometers) to the average annual freshwater inflow gives a theoretical residence time of eleven months. The large surface area to volume ratio and the long water residence time, allow up to 50% of the freshwater inflow to leave the Pamlico Sound by evaporation. Circulation is driven primarily by prevailing winds from northeast or southeast weather fronts (Weisberg and Pietrafesa 1983). Lunar tides are small and the sound is dominated by wind-driven tides.

The Pamlico Sound system is biologically productive and provides the principal nurseries for estuary-dependent finfish and shellfish species, which collectively account for about 80% of the commercial catch of the mid-Atlantic and south Atlantic bights (Miller et al. 1984). Given the biological importance of the Pamlico Sound, it is surprising how relatively little is known about it, especially in comparison to the neighboring Chesapeake Bay estuary. Its tributary rivers have been systematically studied, but the waters of the sound have not. Thus, a systematic study of the Pamlico Sound was begun in September 1998 to establish a database from which basic processes could be understood.

In September 1999, Pamlico Sound and its watersheds were visited by an unprecedented series of hurricanes, three in all (Dennis, Floyd, and Irene). During the storm events, record precipitation fell in the watersheds and soaked the soils (Dennis on 4–5 September; Floyd on14–17 September; and Irene on 17 October). In the preceding decades, the watershed floodplains were altered by stream channelization and land-use change, primarily conversion of forest lands to intensive agriculture and urban landscapes. Extensive flooding occurred following Hurricane Floyd. The tributary rivers of the Pamlico Sound were already known as sources for pollution, especially nitrogen nutrients that promote phytoplankton growth. Fertilized soil leaching, floodplain scouring, failed municipal wastewater treatment plants, and breached animal waste lagoons loaded enormous quantities of dissolved inorganic nitrogen and organic matter (dissolved and particulate) to the tributary rivers and estuaries.

Here the response of phytoplankton, measured as chlorophyll *a* and phaeophytin *a* biomass, to "event-scale" flooding is reported for the Pamlico Sound. In the Neuse River Estuary, it is estimated that at least 80% of primary production is derived from phytoplankton (Paerl et al. 1998), and it is a dominant source of organic matter supporting the sound's food web (i.e., small invertebrates and some fish graze phytoplankton, larger invertebrates and fish feed on the smaller animals). Thus, phytoplankton biomass and relative species abundances determine the size and structure of food chains in the sound. In some cases, excess phytoplankton production can drastically decrease the available oxygen (hypoxia) or completely deplete oxygen levels (anoxia) in bottom waters, leading to disrupted food chains and to salutary effects on the fishery. Thus chlorophyll *a* biomass is a bioindicator commonly used to gauge the ecological state of a body of water. Chlorophyll a is degraded rapidly to phaeophytin *a* in dying and dead cells no matter the cause, and here phaeophytin *a* to chlorophyll *a* ratios will be used as an indicator of grazing activity.

Measuring Biomass

Fourteen sampling stations on four transects were established in the western basin of the sound (Table 1). Transect A runs along the southeastern side of the basin, transect B and C run from the mouth of the Neuse River sub-estuary to near Ocracoke Inlet, and transect E runs from high in the Pamlico River sub-estuary to near Ocracoke Inlet. Stations were visited with the *Susan Hudson* oceanography vessel.

Table 1. Geospatial coordinates for the Pamlico Sound stations where water samples were collected.

Station	Coordinates
A1	35º 02.705' N, 076º 17.984' W
A2	35º 04.905' N, 076º 14.000' W
A3	35º 07.350' N, 076º 12.036' W
A4	35º 09.757' N, 076º 10.436' W
B1	35º 08.404' N, 076º 14.309' W
B2	35º 07.105' N, 076º 16.008' W
C1	35º 07.875' N, 076º 20.598' W
C2	35º 07.244' N, 076º 24.159' W
C3	35º 02.706' N, 076º 28.592' W
E1	35º 16.006' N, 076º 24.008' W
E2	35º 14.405' N, 076º 22.192' W
E3	35º 12.292' N, 076º 19.992' W
E4	35º 10.000' N, 076º 17.402' W
E5	35º 07.891' N, 076º 14.991' W

Fifty-milliliter raw water samples were gently filtered to measure concentrations of chlorophyll *a* and phaeophytin *a*. Six samples were collected per station, three surface and three bottom. (Note: Samples were filtered using 25 mm Whatman GF/F filters while adding a few drops of aqueous 1% magnesium carbonate. The filters were then placed in 20 milliliters of 90% acetone for extraction at -10°C. Fluorescence was used to determine concentrations of chlorophyll *a* and phaeophytin *a* [USEPA Method 445.0;

Arar and Collins 1996]).

For certain comparisons, the data are grouped into three time periods, the before Floyd period (program year 0.72–1.68, 20 September 1998–4 September 1999), the Floyd period (program year 1.68–1.96, 5 September 1999–17 December 1999), and the post-Floyd period (program year 1.96–2.52, 18 December 1999–6 July 2000). For other comparisons, the data are grouped into surface (S) and bottom (B) samples. (For a discussion of relevant hydrologic changes see Paerl et al. in this volume.)

Changes in Phytoplankton Biomass

Chlorophyll *a* concentration increased above seasonal levels only after Hurricane Floyd (Figure 1). This occurred most dramatically (up to a three-fold increase) in surface waters relative to bottom waters, especially in the high river estuary stations and persisted for two months before returning to seasonal levels. Phytoplankton enumerations (Tester, personal communication) indicate that the pelagic flora is dominated by flagellates, i.e., swimming cells, especially cryptomonads and dinoflagellates. The light-limited phytoplankton in the turbid waters that resulted following Floyd likely remained in surface waters to benefit from higher light levels. Bottom waters experienced a sharp increase in chlorophyll *a* in the post-Floyd period (Figure 1), which may be the consequence of increased water transparency and remineralization processes in the sediments. The highest chlorophyll *a* concentration was 21 micrograms per liter (µg/l), at station C3 in the Neuse River esturary, far short of the quantity defining the North Carolina statutory threshold for "nutrient sensitive waters" of 40 µg/l.

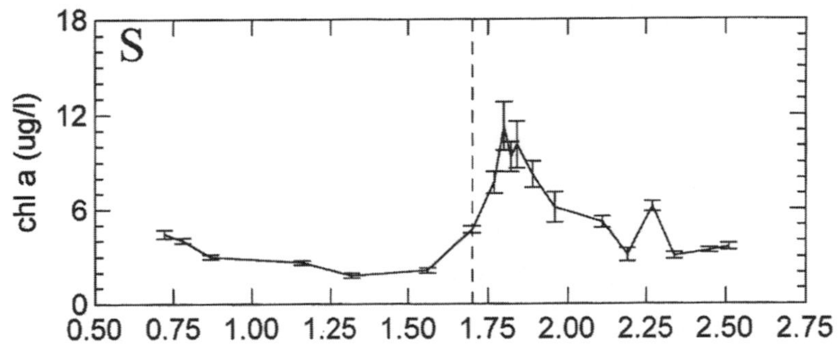

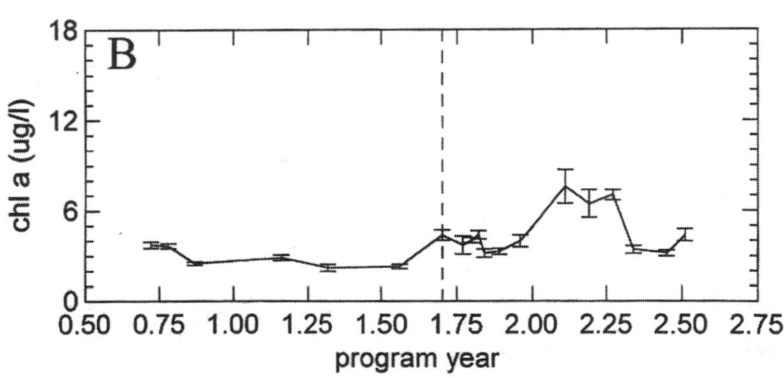

Figure 1. Time course of chlorophyll *a* concentration (plus or minus 1 standard deviation) pooled for all fourteen stations in the Pamlico Sound from 20 September 1999 to 6 July 2000 in surface (**S**) and bottom (**B**) waters. Dashed line represents date of Hurricane Dennis.

Phaeophytin *a* biomass increased more than three-fold in the Floyd period in both surface and bottom waters, but more in bottom waters than surface waters. The ratio of phaeophytin *a* to chlorophyll *a* remained statistically consistent in surface waters throughout the sampling program (Figure 2); however, the ratio increased sharply in the Floyd period in bottom waters. These observations are consistent with the notion that the highest chlorophyll *a* production rates are in nutrient-laden (fresh) surface waters. A variety of organisms subsequently grazed the chlorophyll, and it sank to bottom waters as fecal pellets containing high concentrations of phaeophytin *a*. The data also suggest that surface phytoplankton blooms are followed by grazer blooms. In general, data comparing whole transects were statistically equivalent, indicating a uniformity of response in the Pamlico Sound.

The phytoplankton biomass response to Hurricane Floyd flooding was not as large as might be predicted given the rate of dissolved inorganic nitrogen and particulate and dissolved organic that flowed into tributary rivers (see Paerl et al. this volume). Phytoplankton in the tributary rivers may have stripped phytoplankton growth nutrients from the surface waters upstream of the Pamlico Sound. Indeed, the upstream chlorophyll *a* concentrations, especially where the water was most turbid, were much higher than those that were observed in the sound. Also, humic substance concentrations (i.e., the organic component of soil that is derived from decomposition of animal and plant material) were very high in runoff surface waters and persisted in sound waters during the Floyd period; thus, the phytoplankton communities, which are normally nutrient-limited, were in fact light-limited.

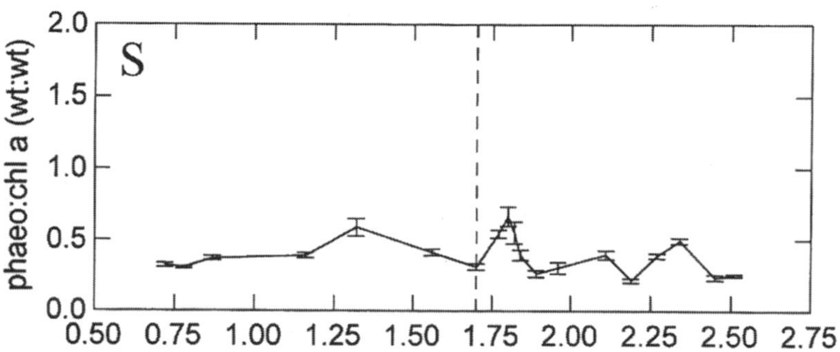

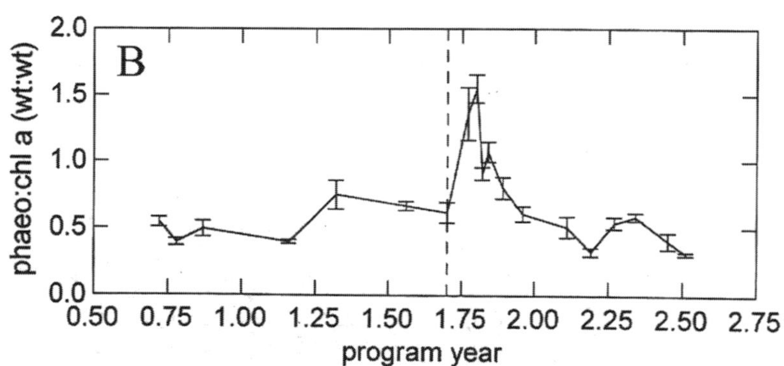

Figure 2. Time course of ratio of phaeophytin *a* to chlorophyll *a* (phaeo:chl *a*; plus or minus 1 standard deviation) pooled for all fourteen stations in the Pamlico Sound from 20 September 1999 to 6 July 2000 in surface (**S**) and bottom (**B**) waters. Dashed line represents date of Hurricane Dennis.

References

Arar, E. J., and G. B. Collins. 1996. In *vitro* determination of chlorophyll a and phaeophytin a in marine and freshwater algae by fluorescence. Revision 1.2. NERL, ORD, USEPA.

Miller, J. M., J. P. Reed, and L. J. Pietrafesa. 1984. Patterns, mechanisms and approaches to the study of migrations of estuarine-dependent fish larvae and juveniles. In: Mechanisms of migration in fishes, edited by J. D. McCleave, G. P. Arnold, J. J. Dodson, and W. H. Neill. NATO, Advanced Research Institute.

Paerl, H. W., C. Buzzelli, M. Go, R. A. Leuttich, B. L. Peierls, T. L. Richardson, J. Ramus, L. B. Crowder, L. W. Ausley, J. Overton, and J. D. Bales. 2000. Water quality and fisheries habitat changes in the Pamlico Sound after three hurricanes: A short-term and long-term perspective. *This volume.*

Weisberg, R. H., and L. J. Pietrafesa. 1983. Kinematics and correlation of the surface wind field in the South Atlantic Bight. Journal of Geophysical Research 88(C8):4593–4610.

About the Author: Joseph S. Ramus is Professor of Biological Oceanography at Duke University Marine Laboratory in Beaufort, North Carolina. Dr. Ramus's research includes the study of physical forcing of phytoplankton biomass, productivity, and community structure in coastal plain estuaries. His research seeks to match physiological response and the temporal frequency of physical drivers and the phasing of phytoplankton dynamics with the environment.

Part V / A Better Blueprint for the Future

Natural Hazards, Smart Growth, and Creating Resilient and Sustainable Communities in Eastern North Carolina

David R. Godschalk

Dr. Godschalk is an internationally recognized city and regional planner, scholar, and teacher. Currently, he holds the Stephen Baxter Chaired Professorship in the Department of City and Regional Planning at the University of North Carolina, Chapel Hill. His research interests include smart growth, hazard mitigation, coastal planning, consensus building, and distance learning. He is a registered architect as well as a planner, and has served as a consultant both in the U.S. and internationally. Dr. Godschalk has authored and edited a number of important books and reports that are crucial to regional planning. His most recent study is a national assessment of the effectiveness of intergovernmental policy and planning for hurricane, flood, and earthquake hazard mitigation under the Stafford Act. He has received numerous awards, most recently receiving the Distinguished Alumnus Award from the Department of City and Regional Planning. Dr. Godschalk gave a plenary presentation at the conference and was introduced by Dr. Ron Mitchelson, chair of the Department of Geography at East Carolina University.

Introduction

Future natural disasters are likely to become more frequent and more damaging everywhere in the nation, but particularly in eastern North Carolina. Because of its growth patterns, its low-lying land, its rivers, its wetlands, and its exposure to Atlantic Ocean storms, this region is especially hazard-prone. But what can the state and region do to enhance its ability to bend without breaking in the face of severe flooding and high winds? How can this state sustain itself into the future without losing quality of life, strong economies, and a healthy environment? North Carolina needs communities that are resilient and sustainable—communities that are able to rebound after a natural disaster while maintaining their economic growth and not compromising their present-day and future quality of life. One issue detailed in this paper is how North Carolina can create this type of community throughout the eastern region of the state.

I present both the bad news and the good news. If we believe the scientists, the bad news is that more severe storms are coming. But the idea of restricting property use to decrease the impact of flood hazards is a politically explosive proposition in a region where some older parts of communities lie almost entirely in the floodplain. However, the good news is that several places in eastern North Carolina have learned how to reduce the impacts of recurrent storms. They have shown that if we are smart about how we grow and are willing to change some old ideas and behaviors, then we can maintain our desired quality of life, economy, and environment. The key is to combine hazard mitigation with smart growth.

Integrating hazard mitigation with smart growth makes good sense. In order to demonstrate why this is important, this paper defines these terms then discusses the nature of the natural hazard problem and why this problem is increasing. Also described are effective ways that natural hazard impacts can be mitigated, particularly through smart growth. Finally, a vision of a resilient community that is able to sustain its vibrancy and resiliency in the face of future floods and hurricanes is proposed.

Defining Hazard Mitigation

In the context of planning, mitigation is the measures that are taken to avoid, reduce, or eliminate adverse impacts. The impacted environment includes the natural environment and human communities. Mitigation also can include restoring, rehabilitating, or repairing the effected environment. *Hazard mitigation* protects people and property from the destructive impacts of natural hazards (Godschalk et al. 1999; N.C. Emergency Management Division 1999) and includes:

- Planning—identifying hazards and vulnerability and making and carrying out smart growth and hazard mitigation plans before disasters occur.
- Avoiding hazard areas—directing new development away from hazardous locations and relocating existing structures and land uses to safer areas.
- Strengthening buildings and public facilities—flood-proofing and wind-proofing existing and new structures and public facilities through building codes and engineering design.
- Conserving natural areas—maintaining and enhancing the functions of wetlands, dunes, and forests, which naturally reduce hazard impacts, by acquiring property or development rights in hazard areas and then limiting development in these areas.
- Limiting public expenditures—withholding subsidies for roads, sewage treatment systems, and other public facilities that could induce development in hazard areas.
- Communicating the mitigation message—educating developers about mitigation techniques and notifying the public about the existence of hazard areas and the consequences of locating in these areas.

Defining Smart Growth

Smart growth connects development and quality of life, leverages new growth to improve community, restores city centers and older suburbs, and preserves open space and other environmental resources. It is town-centered, transit- and pedestrian-oriented, and mixes housing, commercial, and retail uses (ICMA 1998). Smart growth programs manage development location, amount, type, design, rate, and cost to achieve livable communities, efficient transportation systems, safe and orderly urbanization, and healthy natural resources (Godschalk in preparation).

Smart growth programs combine processes, goals, and features to achieve their objectives, including:

- Comprehensive planning—ensuring an adequate supply of land for development and integrating land-use and transportation decisions.
- Compact urban areas—protecting natural resources and open space, lessening automobile dependence, and reducing infrastructure costs.
- Mixed land uses and mixed densities—promoting walkable neighborhoods, a variety of housing choices, and a sense of community.
- Transportation options—encouraging the use of safe transit, walking, and cycling in addition to automobile use.
- Infrastructure within planned urban areas—making use of existing infrastructure services and providing schools, water and sewer services, and roads concurrently with development.
- Human-scale design—encouraging attractive and compatible buildings, streetscapes, and civic spaces.
- Review predictable and efficient development—reducing costly delays and promoting innovative project design.

Existing Natural Hazard Problems and Why They're Getting Worse

Eastern North Carolinians face a difficult problem. Already battered by catastrophic flooding from hurricanes Floyd and Fran, residents of this region may well have to look forward to an increasing number of future natural disasters.

Disasters result from the *intersection* of natural hazards (e.g., floods and hurricanes) with human settlements and activities on the land. If no human settlements or activities were located

Figure 1. September 1999–Flooded subdivision in Greenville, North Carolina.

in hazard areas, then the hazards would not cause damage to property or harm people. But towns and neighborhoods built in floodplains and on exposed shorelines bear the brunt of floods and hurricanes. Developments that drain wetlands and clear forests not only face flooding themselves, but also increase the likelihood of damage to their neighbors because they have compromised the natural ability of the environment to absorb hazard forces (Figure 1).

Table 1. Actual and projected percent increases in the population size of twelve eastern North Carolina counties.

County	1980-1990 (Actual)	1990-2000 (Projected)	2000-2010 (Projected)
Brunswick	42.5%	39%	23%
Carteret	28%	17%	23%
Currituck	24%	28%	23%
Dare	70%	30%	23%
Hoke	12%	36%	23%
Johnston	15%	37.5%	23%
Nash	14%	18%	13%
New Hanover	16%	29%	18%
Onslow	33%	0.4%	17%
Pasquotank	10%	40%	10%
Pender	30%	14.5%	24%
Pitt	20%	21%	11%

source: N.C. Office of State Planning <http://www.ospl.state.nc.us/demog/>.

Population growth and development

Unfortunately, the rising rates of urban development in a number of eastern counties combined with increasing natural hazard occurrences have compounded the disaster problem in North Carolina. Many people assume that eastern North Carolina is not growing, but at least a dozen counties belie that assumption (Table 1). Brunswick, Carteret, Currituck, Dare, Hoke, Johnston, Nash, New Hanover, Onslow, Pasquotank, Pender, and Pitt counties have had significant growth. The population in seven of these eastern counties grew by at least 20% between 1980 and 1990, and five counties grew by at least 30% between 1990 and 2000. Future steady growth is projected to continue in these counties between 2000 and 2010.

The location of new growth is a more serious issue than the amount of new growth. If future development could be steered away from the hazard areas, then its safety would not be in doubt. But even after the ravages of Hurricane Floyd in 1999, much of eastern North Carolina is rebuilding in the 100-year floodplains.

In March, reporters at the *News and Observer* (Raleigh, N.C.) found that against the advice of disaster experts, many towns and counties are allowing more new homes to be built in the floodplains. This is contrary to what state leaders had envisaged—replacing homes, businesses, junk yards, hog operations, and sewage treatment plants in floodplains with wetlands and forests that are able to soak up the water from overflowing rivers (Shiffer and Stradling 2000).

Most of the seventy towns and counties affected by Floyd are choosing not to curb floodplain development because they don't want to tell people what to do with their land, increase construction costs, or interfere with victims trying to "get back to normal," even if the government is footing the bill. The rebuilding in the floodplains is also occurring under the mistaken belief that there won't be another flood for 100 years.

While the state wants to spend $424 million to acquire and demolish 8,000 flood-prone houses—

the largest post-disaster buyout in U.S. history—the program is voluntary and many owners do not want to sell and move. Local governments that accept buyout money are required to prepare hazard mitigation plans, but there's no requirement that they implement them. Meanwhile, the disaster threat continues.

The occurrence of natural disasters is increasing

Presidentially declared disasters in the U.S. almost doubled during the past two decades, going from 237 in the 1980s to 460 in the 1990s. This number is larger than in any previous decade on record.

North Carolina has some of the most expensive disasters in the country. It ranks with Florida, Texas, and Alabama as having the highest number of billion-dollar weather disasters during the past twenty years.

Unfortunately, the future could be even worse. Scientists expect the number of extreme weather events, such as floods and hurricanes, to increase as global warming progresses. The last ten months in the U.S. were the warmest on record, leading D. James Baker, administrator of the National Oceanic and Atmospheric Administration, to say that "...changes in global temperatures can lead to more extreme weather events including droughts, floods, and hurricanes." And the last decade has seen seven of the warmest years in recorded human history, along with a 20% increase in the number of severe storms that dumped two or more inches of precipitation in a twenty-four-hour period (McKibben 2000).

Warmer air can contain more water vapor, leading to more intense rainfall. Sea level can rise. With this rise, the width of shorelines and beaches, which act as coastal barriers, will diminish. When this happens, historical records may no longer be an accurate harbinger of the future. Regions not previously considered as susceptible to flooding may experience floods in future storms. Overall, floods in the future are likely to be larger and shorelines are likely to be smaller. So what can be done to ensure that the cities and towns and the farms and forests of eastern North Carolina not only survive but also avoid some of the worst impacts of future floods and hurricanes?

A Strategy for Mitigating Natural Hazards

Hazard mitigation is a mix of forethought and common sense. It is not easy. There are lots of obstacles to overcome, including changing some bad development habits and getting rid of some past mistakes. But there are heartening success stories where communities, including some in North Carolina, have overcome obstacles and are prepared to weather future storms. Looking at these communities reveals some clear lessons on how to effectively mitigate the impact of natural hazards.

Refuse to collaborate with disaster

Since disasters only occur when people make the mistake of building in or disrupting natural hazard areas, those that allow or encourage such unsafe practices are collaborating with disaster (Godschalk 2000). Following World War II in Europe, those who collaborated with the enemy were shot. Without advocating such drastic measures in the case of natural hazards, better behavior would result if those who permitted such unsafe practices were penalized. Thus, local governments that allow unsafe land uses in their floodplains could lose their access to future state and federal disaster assistance. The goal would be to create a positive incentive and climate for smart growth, sustainable development, and effective hazard mitigation.

Identify natural hazards

Communities should not hide their heads in the sand. Community leaders must identify and map hazard areas and make sure the community is aware of them (Burby et al. 2000). The National Flood Insurance Program has identified flood hazard areas on Flood Insurance Rate Maps (FIRMs). Paper copies are available, and generalized versions can be downloaded from the Federal Emergency Management Agency's (FEMA) Project Impact web site (<http://www.esri.com/hazards>). These maps delineate:

- The 100-year floodplain—the area adjacent to a river or stream that has a 1% chance of flooding in any given year. The floodplain map shows A Zones and AE Zones with determined base-flood elevations.
- The 500-year floodplains—the area inundated by 100-year flooding with an average depth of less than one foot, drainage areas of less than one square mile, or areas protected from 100-year flooding by levees (designated as X500 Zones).

Coastal communities should also identify areas subject to wave action (V *Zones* on FIRMs) and hurricane storm surges, which are shown for category one to category five storms on Sea, Lake, and Overland Surge from Hurricanes (SLOSH) maps generated by the National Weather Service.

However, federal flood maps are not necessarily complete or current. Communities should prepare and maintain local

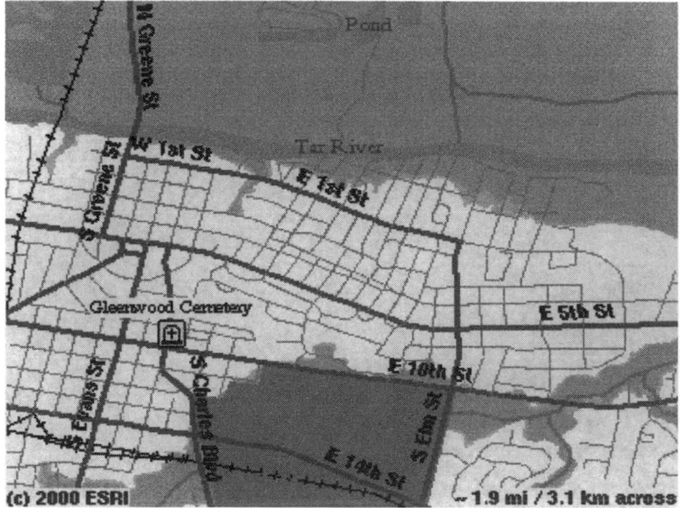

Figure 2. A flood hazard map for the city of Greenville, N.C. (Source: <http://www.esri.com/hazards>.)

maps that show the extent of flooding from the most recent flood events (Figure 2). For example, it is estimated that 1,914 parcels encompassing 1,129 acres in Selma, North Carolina, are in an unmapped FIRM zone (Geographic Technologies Group, Inc. 2000)

Assess community-level vulnerability

Communities need to identify the populations and properties within a hazard area and indicate the potential injury and damage that can result from an extreme natural event. Measuring vulnerability not only tells what losses to expect but also what benefits can be realized from strengthening or relocating buildings or implementing other mitigation actions. Overlaying hazard maps on census blocks can provide an estimate of the number of people at risk. In Johnston County, North Carolina, almost two-thirds of the total population of 81,306 are vulnerable to floods. About 33,077 people (41%) are located in the 100-year floodplain, and another 17,131 (21%) are located in a 500-year floodplain (Geographic Technologies Group, Inc. 2000).

Property vulnerability maps can be created by overlaying hazard areas maps on property assessor maps. These maps can be used to calculate the dollar amount of the properties and the number of households or businesses subject to a hazard. For example, Johnston County is extremely vulnerable to floods with almost $484 million of its tax value located within the 100-year floodplain and another almost $289 million of tax value in the 500-year floodplain (Table 2).

Table 2. Parcels within flood zones in Johnston County, N.C.

Status	Number of Parcels	Acres	Tax Value
		100-Year Floodplain	
Developed	1,510	4,233	$174,070,960
Undeveloped/developable	4,849	193,084	$309,598,650
		500-Year Floodplain	
Developed	1,001	1,919	$136,541,300
Undeveloped/developable	1.591	64,353	$152,026,580

source: Geographic Technologies Group, Inc. (2000)

Involve the community

Public participation is crucial in the decision-making processes that deal with hazards. A number of approaches are available to initiate public participation. They range from using an existing body, such as the planning board, to creating a new mitigation committee or creating a task force that can advise decision makers. An awareness campaign is an important first step to inform and motivate the community to address natural hazards. The exact form of participation is less important than ensuring that all affected groups have an opportunity to be involved and are satisfied with the fairness of the process.

Make a plan

The mitigation plan may be prepared as a stand-alone hazard plan or as a component of the community's comprehensive plan (Godschalk et al. 1998). Stand-alone plans often are created during the recovery period following a disaster. Most of the post-Floyd plans in eastern North Carolina are stand-alone mitigation plans. (For example, see the Johnston County plan by Geographic Technologies Group, Inc. 2000.) However, over time these mitigation plans should be incorporated into comprehensive plans, so that hazard mitigation and land-use planning can be integrated and carried out in tandem.

The land-use plan can map the hazard areas and related mitigation policies, as well as mapping areas that are less vulnerable and where development can be encouraged. It can also tie community facility site-selection policies, particularly for lifeline facilities such as transportation, water supply, and waste disposal.

Carry out mitigation

Implementing mitigation plans is an ongoing public and private effort. Governmental regulation and spending powers can be directed toward implementing mitigation strategies. Building codes set standards for a building's design, engineering, and structural features. Zoning codes address allowable land-use types, locations, and densities. Public funds can be budgeted to acquire at-risk property, to construct hazard control systems such as stormwater retention and drainage systems, and to hazard-proof existing public buildings and facilities such as sewage treatment plants and emergency operations centers. Private sector mitigation can be encouraged with informational and technical assistance so that businesses prepare and carry out their own strategies.

For example, in North Carolina, the Wilmington-New Hanover Project Impact Partnership has undertaken a number of initiatives to implement its mitigation strategy (N.C. Emergency Management Division 1999). These include:

- Installation of emergency generators in public facilities.
- Dune stabilization and beach nourishment to minimize flood damage.
- Elevation of new homes and electrical equipment.
- Preparation of business continuity and employee preparedness plans.
- Construction of disaster-resistant emergency operation centers at two schools.
- Conducting education and awareness programs to protect homes and businesses.

Monitor outcomes

To ensure that a mitigation strategy is working as anticipated, mitigation results must be tracked. Both pre-disaster and post-disaster mitigation efforts stretch over several years. As conditions change or more disasters occur, the plan may require revision to meet new situations. Ensuring that someone has responsibility for tracking progress and recommending revisions is important.

Kinston, North Carolina—A Community Adopts a Smart-Growth, Hazard Mitigation Strategy

Kinston is a mid-sized town located in Lenior County, North Carolina. It is situated at a mid-point between the state capital and the coast and adjacent to the Neuse River. The town was economically depressed when Hurricane Fran hit the region in 1996. The required evacuation of about 600 homes and total losses of tens of millions of dollars compounded the city's existing economic and social problems. Because of the flooding impact from hurricanes Fran and Floyd, Kinston is implementing a hazard mitigation plan based on smart growth principles and many of the hazard mitigation strategies outlined in the previous section. Kinston has taken the following practical steps to stop collaborating with disaster and to begin reducing natural hazard injury and damage:

- Mapped areas susceptible to hazards.
- Assessed hazard vulnerability for population and property at risk.
- Involved the community in mitigation policy-making through hazard planning committees and outreach programs.
- Prepared a comprehensive hazard mitigation plan.
- Initiated actions to carry out the mitigation plan.

As was stated previously, a willingness to reassess and change a plan is crucial to the success of any mitigation strategy. Kinston has made a commitment to track the outcomes of mitigation decisions and to revise their plan as necessary to meet new conditions.

The mitigation plan was initially formed following Hurricane Fran in 1996. The town's goals after the hurricane were to permanently reduce flood hazards and to revitalize existing neighborhoods and improve quality of life. The town is still in the process of acquiring 420 houses, three mobile home parks, and sixty-eight vacant lots, at a cost of approximately $31 million. To re-house the relocated people, they are stimulating investment in existing homes and new development on vacant in-fill lots around the downtown and using salvaged materials to help create affordable housing (N.C. Emergency Management Division 1999).

The more recent plan, the *Greater Kinston's 2000-2020 Smart Growth Plan*, includes maps of the Neuse River's 100-year floodplain and of the flood buyout areas where damaged housing will be targeted for relocation. The plan identifies primary, secondary, and long-term growth and development areas, where future growth will be encouraged and supported. The plan has clear goals. It seeks to relocate at-risk families from the floodplain and to build a menu of different types of new homes located on safe, high ground so that the families will have a choice of housing type and location. The plan seeks to make full use of the capacity of existing infrastructure—streets, schools, and water and sewer systems—rather than extending new services beyond the existing city. It seeks to ensure that affordable housing is high quality and to build new housing quickly to deal with demand. Finally the plan seeks to inspire in the community hope that the future can be bright once again.

Kinston's recovery strategy identifies timed-buyout phases in specific hazard area redevelopment locations—three following Hurricane Fran and two more following Hurricane Floyd. The buyout program is voluntary, so property owners may choose not to participate. When this occurs, it can leave a problematic, "snaggle-tooth" land-use pattern, with occupied private houses situated next to publicly owned vacant lots. These areas are difficult to redevelop and only partially reduce the areas' vulnerability to future floods. The town has made a number of efforts to encourage more complete buyout participation. After Fran, Kinston created the HELPS recovery program. This program links acquisition of flood-prone substandard housing with job training, skill development, homeownership, and ultimately, self-sufficiency. It seeks to create tenant-driven leadership through a housing institute that relocates families from the buyout area and promotes sustainable development. Also, the *Call Kinston Home* program brings together government, civic and professional groups, builders and realtors, businesses and industries to revitalize existing neighborhoods (N.C. Division of Emergency Management 1999). The *2000-2020 Smart Growth Plan* has a housing opportunity site map that identifies infill housing sites within the city, areas where new development is encouraged. The 700 families slated to leave the floodplains of the Neuse River and Adkin branch will be offered housing in one of these areas.

Kinston also adopted stricter flood elevation standards. They beefed up their building regulations, requiring a 2-foot elevation of living areas above the 100-year base flood level. They also require substantial improvements to existing homes in the floodplain.

Kinston expects to realize a number of benefits from its smart growth, hazard mitigation strategy. Some 1,750 residents will be moved out of high hazard flood areas. The town's sewer lines and other public facilities will be protected from repeated flooding and disruption. By keeping relocated households in the city, they will replace the tax base that is lost due to the buyouts and retain utility customers. They will also add to the tax base by reinvesting their recovery and redevelopment funds inside the city. At the same time, Kinston will use the recovery to improve their older, substandard housing stock and add business opportunities. They will address blight within their poorer floodplain neighborhoods. The town plans to create new green spaces from the recovered floodplains and improve water quality in the Neuse River. If done well, these steps should lead to a future community that is able to anticipate and withstand severe floods and hurricanes and recover from disasters in an orderly and effective manner.

Summary: A Vision of a Resilient Community

If communities like Kinston maintain a commitment to planning for recurrent natural disasters with forethought and common sense, they will be resilient, sustainable communities. Buildings, facilities, organizations, and activities will remain strong and supple in the face of natural hazards. In the year 2020, the resilient community will be able to look back and pride itself on successfully weathering any floods or hurricanes that occurred, while sustaining its economy, environment, and quality of life.

In twenty years, the resilient community will look back and see that it brought its citizens together after Hurricane Floyd and resolved to be prepared for any future severe weather event. The community's recovery plan after Floyd was not only to get back on its feet but also to begin a systematic and long-term mitigation strategy to move structures and people out of harm's way.

The community's plan started with the investment of state and FEMA funds in relocation and flood-proofing projects and continued with regular investments of local budget funds to acquire and preserve critical hazard areas. A new land-use plan and new development regulations were adopted. A public education program ensured that all citizens, from school children to adults, learned where the hazard areas were located and what future hazard risks could be expected. Developers of residential and business property were guided to safe locations.

Over time, the resilient community reduced the amount of its tax base in the floodplain from 60% to 30% or 15%. It replaced floodplain housing with parks, greenways, and recreation fields. It restored the functioning of its wetlands and carried out an urban forestry program along its riverfront, reclaiming the river corridor as a natural resource. It restored older neighborhoods outside the floodplain and built new compact neighborhoods within its urban service area.

While the community's population and economy continued to grow, its development did not intersect with its hazard areas, so its growth was sustainable. Unfortunately the neighbors of the resilient community did not take mitigation as seriously, and their growth was much less sustainable. Problems in their hazard areas reduced their development potential. But the resilient community found that it could maintain a high quality of life and safe living and working areas outside its hazard zones. When the next flood took place, the majority of its housing, schools, and critical facilities were out of reach of the floodwaters.

In short, through its responsible mitigation strategy and its smart growth plan, the resilient community was able to ensure that all of its population—its children, its elderly, and its adults—enjoyed future housing, employment, and recreation opportunities that were equal to or better than their current opportunities. Its long-term quality of life was not threatened by repetitive damage from natural hazards. Its good planning paid off in a safe and livable community.

References

Burby, R. J., R. E. Deyle, D. R. Godschalk, and R. B. Olshansky. 2000. Creating hazard resilient communities through land-use planning. Natural Hazards Review 1(2):99–106.

Burby, R. J., T. Beatley, P. R. Berke, R. E. Deyle, S. P. French, D. R. Godschalk, E. J. Kaiser, J. D. Kartez, P. J. May, R. Olshansky, R. G. Paterson, and R. H. Platt. 1999. Unleashing the power of planning to create disaster-resistant communities. Journal of the American Planning Association. 65(3):247–258.

Geographic Technologies Group, Inc. 2000. Johnston County, North Carolina hazard mitigation plan. Goldsboro, N.C.

Godschalk, D. R. 2000. Collaborating with disaster. N.C. APA Newsletter. 28(2):4–5.

Godschalk, D. R., E. J. Kaiser, and P. R. Berke. 1998. Integrating hazard mitigation and local land use planning. In: Modernizing state planning statutes: The growing smart working papers. Vol. 2, PAS Report 480-481. Chicago, Ill.: American Planning Association.

Godschalk, D. R., T. Beatley, P. Berke, D. J. Brower, and E. J. Kaiser. 1999. Natural hazard mitigation: Recasting disaster policy and planning. Washington, D.C.: Island Press.

International City/County Management Association (ICMA). 1998. Why smart growth: A primer. Washington, D.C.: ICMA.

McKibben, B. 25 May 2000. Acquaintance of the earth. The New York Review of Books, XLVII: 9, 48–50.

North Carolina Emergency Management Division. 1999. Hazard mitigation successes in the state of North Carolina. Raleigh, N.C.: Department of Crime Control and Public Safety.

Schiffer, J. E., and R. Stradling. 2000. Disaster down east: Six months and counting. News and Observer (Raleigh, N.C.), 12 March.

A Dialogue: Building Resilient Communities in a Disaster-Prone Region

Harold Stone and Joseph Luczkovich

Starting the Dialogue

The Questions: *What are the impediments to moving development out of harm's way? What are acceptable risks and how should they be assessed? What can be done in risk-prone communities to achieve the goals of smart growth and sustainability?*

The discussion was guided by **David Godschalk** and **David Brower**, professors in the Department of City and Regional Planning at the University of North Carolina, Chapel Hill. The discussion participants included agricultural producers, local planners and response personnel, academics, state emergency management officials, and private emergency management consultants.

Introduction

Intermingled in our discussion of the impediments for effectively mitigating disaster impacts were suggestions of the possible tools and activities that would aid in creating a more sustainable community in the aftermath of the 1999 floods. The group agreed that a primary problem impeding effective disaster mitigation is the inability of individuals and communities to effectively assess their risk to disasters. Did the individuals and communities most affected by the floodwaters lack knowledge of their potential risks or did they lack the determination and motivation to prevent the impending disaster? Based on the diverse experiences of the group, it was concluded that both elected officials and the public were responsible, and both are obligated to reduce future disasters. All responsible parties must address the problem of increased disaster losses, or the goal of creating a sustainable community will not be achieved. (See Godschalk, this volume, for a discussion and summary of disaster mitigation and sustainable communities.)

We began our discussion by identifying and describing the issues that prevented individuals and communities from rebounding after the flooding disaster. If, after future disasters, these issues are ignored, eastern North Carolina will experience impacts similar to those that occurred after Hurricane

Floyd. We also explored the concept of risk—how it is defined and who is responsible for its assessment—while also focusing on many specific mitigation issues such as federal housing buyout programs and responsible development. The need for community education programs and regional political determination were also identified as crucial to reducing the long-term impacts from future disasters. We then listed recommended tools and actions that could be implemented to initiate the needed changes we identified.

What Is Acceptable Risk?

Discussion participants agreed that people in eastern North Carolina had an awareness of the threat of natural disasters, but few, if any, had assessed their risk accurately. In general, people were prepared to respond to a disaster, either by protecting their business interests or their possessions. But the level of response was inadequate to meet the level of need. Both public and elected officials greatly underestimated their perceived risk of loss from the flood.

One functional designation of risk is the 100-year floodplain lines on hazard and planning maps. This designation gives decision makers—private homeowners, real estate agents, and politicians—the perception that there is a 1% chance of a flood every 100 years, or that they have 99 years until the next flood. It further infers that outside of this area, properties will be out of harm's way in the event of a flood. Participants noted the repetitive losses due to flooding that have occurred over the years in eastern North Carolina, and drew attention to the rebuilding and new construction in areas perceived to be relatively safe. These losses raise the concern that the method of conveying risk and/or the measurement and designation of risk is flawed.

Who Is Responsible For Assessing Risk?

No group is inherently more culpable than another for the decisions that resulted in the losses suffered after the disaster. But for those affected by the flooding after Floyd, three groups were identified as having inadequately assessed flood-related risks: home and property owners, the real estate industry, and governmental/quasi-governmental officials. Each group has a set of problems that contributed to total flood-related losses.

Property owners do not have adequate information about natural processes to accurately assess their risk. They are also placed at greater risk because they lack experience with flood hazards and because they mistrust government regulations (e.g., issues related to land acquisition).

Developers and realtors could serve as an initial step to educating prospective real estate buyers about a property's potential exposure to flooding. Historically, there are two reasons why developers and realtors have not adequately advised property owners. First, they have inadequate information regarding flood zones.

Second, property descriptions do not provide potential buyers with information on the risk of flooding.

At closing, a buyer is notified whether a property is located within the 100-year floodplain, which signals a need for federal flood insurance. However, the real estate agent often does not know this information. Although property boundaries are available to the agent, the primary source of information used to inform both the buyer and the agent is the Multiple Listing Service (MLS) data. Even when the agent knows that the property is within the floodplain, the value of that information is only as significant as the agent's understanding of the data. In some cases, a calculated 100-year flood may have previously struck the area. An uninformed real estate agent, land developer, or buyer may have a false sense of their safety, leading them to offer, buy, or build on a property that may be far more hazardous than is realized.

Developers and realtors should provide perspective property buyers with all the information that will allow them to evaluate their potential risks, including the larger geographic setting of the property, its detailed topographic characteristics, and instructions on how to interpret this information. This will allow perspective buyers to make an educated decision about the purchase of the property, balancing risk with the value of the property.

Our discussion also focused on the final group that affects disaster mitigation and recovery—government and quasi-governmental entities. This group includes municipal, state, and federal government elected and appointed officials as well as associated utilities and services that support these officials and the entities they oversee. Several issues were identified after the September floods that were directly linked to these decision makers: 1) problems with the federal flood insurance program and buyout requirements; 2) the process for making decisions that relate to construction requirements for building in floodplains; and 3) the lack of knowledge and political determination to resolve issues relating to flood hazards. Each of these issues is discussed in detail below.

Problems with the federal flood insurance program and buyout requirements

Historically, people have had difficulty with the Federal Flood Insurance Program because of unbalanced restrictions on recovery and mitigation choices. Property owners with homes or business in the floodplain who want to move, remain where they are because of federal-level delays in buyouts. In Kinston, North Carolina, many properties that were slated for federal buyout after Hurricane Fran in 1996 were still occupied when the floods of Hurricane Floyd hit. People who had wanted to move were unable to because of a housing shortage that resulted from delays in the buyout program after Fran. Families still recovering and anticipating a move out of harm's way found themselves once again struggling to replace belongings after Hurricane Floyd. Also, the goal of the buyout program, to decrease losses after future storms, will not be accomplished if those who choose the buyout option relocate to another flood-prone residence.

Homeowners can also mitigate loss by elevating their homes. But owners are faced with regulations that prevent them from implementing changes that would decrease their perceived risk. For example, the floods after Hurricane Floyd were considered a 500-year event. Many homeowners want to raise their properties high enough to ensure that another event of this magnitude would not affect them again. But the federal yardstick for home elevations is based on an agreed height above the 100-year flood level. Each incremental increase in elevation diminishes the calculated damage risk, but it also increases the cost. Elevations above FEMA standards are not approved because they are considered too costly, regardless of the perceptions of the homeowner.

Needed changes for building infrastructure in the floodplains

Roads built in the floodplains are engineered with little consideration for the volume of flow experienced in a 100-year flood event. Solid, raised roadbeds crossing the floodplain restrict high volume water flow, forcing water to funnel through culverts and road cuts that were designed to handle significantly less water. This lower water volume capacity allows water to back up behind the road cut, resulting in flooding, sometimes retaining water for days after the storm event.

Often these engineering problems arise from conflicts in regulation. The intrinsic value of wetlands to store runoff water is a natural means of flood control. Bridges could be constructed to span these wetlands, but bridges are expensive to construct and maintain. To reduce costs, wetlands are often filled, creating a road dam in the floodplain. Although federal regulations (section 404 of the Clean Water Act) prevent the construction of dikes, berms, and rip-rap in many low-lying areas as a means of protecting the intrinsic values of wetlands, permits to fill wet-lands are issued for commerce.

The St. James Street bridge in Tarboro, N.C., was washed out from the floods of Hurricane Floyd, leaving this main artery unusable. The waterway is a tributary of the Tar River. (Photo by Dave Gatley, courtesy of FEMA News Photo)

Initiating education programs and political determination

We discussed at length the need for educating all the groups that were affected by the floods. This includes educating property buyers, real estate agents, and developers; community-wide education programs that emphasize flood preparation and prevention; and getting information to important decision makers.

Decisions to mitigate future disasters require that adequate information is distributed and then integrated into the state, regional, and local development and disaster preparedness strategies and plans. The group agreed that simply "telling elected officials" doesn't bring about large-scale changes. Often decision makers do not have necessary information. Such information includes local understanding of buyouts, adequate mapping, and an understanding of the consequences of building in floodplains. Even when information is available, participants agreed that many other factors could limit the effectiveness of creating regulations to mitigate disaster losses. Special interest groups such as lawyers (e.g., local Bar Associations) and developers oppose laws that require complete risk disclosure to property owners and buyers.

Underpinning many government-level decisions, or the lack of decisions, is insufficient political determination for change. Identifying mitigation opportunities in a community requires political determination to understand and limit activities that place residents in harm's way. This element of decision making is often overlooked until after a disaster occurs or until an election year, when the issue is of highest salience. After a disaster, there is a narrow window of opportunity to force political change. It is during this time that required tools and resources are identified, created or improved, and are made available to the political officials who will need them to ensure a quick recovery after the next disaster.

Recommended Tools and Actions to Create a Resilient Community

To support the hazard mitigation strategy, the discussion group made general recommendations that spanned the breadth of the needs and specific tools required by the impacted groups we identified: property owners, realty industry, and government agencies.

Tools for smart growth and hazard mitigation plans

The first proposed mechanism for mitigating flood disaster addresses city and regional planning. Smart growth encourages the creation of a sustainable community by considering the natural environment as a functional element of social and economic development. Effective hazard mitigation plans are essential in smart growth plans. However, local governments often have more pressing priorities than mitigating unpredictable disasters. To encourage the development of hazard mitigation plans, the discussion group suggested linking municipal eligibility for federal and state grant funds to the development and implementation of an effective hazard plan.

In support of hazard mitigation plans, the group proposed several improvements to available tools that would function to reduce and eliminate losses resulting from floods. These improvements included:

- **Accurate and up-to-date hazard maps**—Floodplain maps are out of date and need to be recalculated to include existing and planned impermeable surfaces (e.g., parking lots, roads, sidewalks, etc.), which exacerbate flooding.

- **Define acceptable risk**—A consensus of a community's willingness to accept risk and what constitutes acceptable losses is essential in designing an effective mitigation plan.
- **Risk assessment**—Rather than waiting until a disaster strikes, communities should assess their vulnerability to risk and mitigate these risks to eliminate losses.
- **Regional planning**—Natural disasters do not occur in isolation. Communities are affected by the choices made by adjacent communities and landowners. By creating a regional plan, rather than a city or town plan, it is possible to develop policy that reduces the potential of disaster for an entire region.

Tools to increase political determination

A community cannot realize the mitigation opportunities listed above, unless there is a political determination for change. The participants considered the following to be essential additions and improvements for creating political determination:

- **Educate officials**—The first line of defense to reduce flood loss is the education of the officials that propose and vote on ordinances that could result in loss. Although it is not a guarantee to eliminate loss from flooding, education makes it more difficult to develop ordinances that unwittingly increase losses.
- **Place experts on local planning boards**—Local municipal boards are comprised of civic-minded individuals with personal interest in the health and growth of their community. Issues related to flood hazards are often complex, and expert assistance to uncover broader implications of policies could aid in reducing flood hazards.
- **Provide elected officials with "vulnerability maps"**—As a tool for education, create vulnerability maps that differentiate the potential vulnerability of an area. Areas of high vulnerability should be clearly demarcated, thus allowing easy reference for decision making. Also, multiple hazards (flooding, wind damage, hazardous materials, etc.) should be shown on one map; therefore confounding hazards can be easily identified (e.g., flooding in areas with hazardous material storage).

Translating smart growth issues into development policy

Three proposed policies were suggested to reduce the impact of development in the floodplain. These policies were developed as a part of the smart-growth strategy and focus on the location and type of construction that is allowed in areas of flood risk.

- **Disallow development in flood-prone areas**—Although it requires significant political determination and public saliency, the most effective way to mitigate disaster is to eliminate the object at risk.

- **Establish impermeable surface fees for builders**—Impermeable surfaces increase the volume of floodwater, causing additional losses. The developer who indirectly creates these losses does not pay for their cost. By charging a fee, the cost of the loss can be realized by the cause. The increased cost of impermeable structures may encourage the development and use of alternative surface materials.
- **Establish impact fees for developers**—Similar, but less defined than the above, impact fees would be assessed based on the impact of a development in a floodplain. This could encourage development that is more sensitive to the natural functioning of floodplains.

Education as a mitigation strategy

The most far-reaching recommendations made by participants dealt with using education as the primary tool for mitigating future losses from flooding. Many of these education opportunities are combined with several of the concerns listed above.

- **Public notification of high flood-risk areas**—Although flood insurance maps are available to the public, a significant percentage of the population who were impacted by the flooding following Hurricane Floyd were completely unaware that their property was at risk. Public notification could include signage near roadways that identify the height of water during floods and detailed flood maps in newspapers or distributed to communities at risk.
- **Up-front notification of flood risk to property buyers**—Individuals often invest significant time and energy looking for "the perfect" home. At closing, information related to the need for flood insurance may be considered a minor formality in relation to the overall stress of the actual home purchase. By addressing the issue well before closing, the buyer has a better opportunity to gain additional information and weigh the risk they are willing to take.
- **Put flood-risk information in realtor MLS books**—In conjunction with the above educational tool, realtors would be better able to represent a property if information related to the property's location in the floodplain was as prominent as the square footage and number of bedrooms.
- **Appropriate pricing of property in flood-prone areas**—Property in flood-prone areas is priced lower than nonflood-prone property. The price of these properties should reflect their cost to society—the federal, state, and local money that is required to compensate for property losses after a flood. Pricing properties relative to their societal cost would enable the public, as well as elected officials, to make cost-effective decisions and would raise public awareness of the true costs of these properties.

Create a Disaster Extension Service

The most innovative recommendation to emerge from our discussion was for the creation of a

Disaster Extension Service. This would be modeled after the current Agricultural Extension Service, which operates through the Land Grant and Sea Grant University systems. Every state has an agriculture outreach component that applies university research directly into the field. Most of these programs are run in conjunction with county governments.

A growing percentage of the population is moving into locations that are at risk of damage due to natural hazards. The creation of a disaster extension service would provide homeowners, businesses, and local governments with practical information about all phases of emergency management, based on the latest available research. This service could parallel the existing Agricultural Extension structure, coordinated by the university in each state that was currently taking the lead in hazard research and outreach. It is suggested that such a service would pay for itself by reducing losses from disasters in an amount that would be greater than the cost of the program.

About the Authors: Harold Stone is an associate professor in the Department of Planning at East Carolina University. His current research includes the evaluation of decision making as it relates to the social, economic, and political aspects of environmental planning and sustainable development. Joe Luczkovich is an associate professor in ECU's Department of Biology, where he teaches and researches the ecology of estuaries, including seagrass, mangrove, and coral reef ecosystems, with special emphasis on the feeding ecology of marine fishes in those systems.

Looking into the Face of the Storm: Hispanics

Javier Y. Castillo

Although he is busy in his role as vice president of LBA Group, Inc., a telecommunications company headquarted in Greenville, North Carolina, Mr. Castillo remains civic-minded. He served on the North Carolina Governor's Advisory Council on Hispanic/Latino Affairs and was co-chairman of the council's Economic Development Committee, as well as numerous other community and civic organizations. During Hurricane Floyd, he broadcasted news and information in Spanish on the local CBS affiliate station, WNCT-TV 9.

I know what it is like to be deprived of everything, no matter what you've had before. It's tough when you are in an area where you do not speak the language, or you know only some of the language. You have come looking for the "promised land," when suddenly you are confronted with a natural disaster. This is what happened to a vast majority of the Hispanic community living east of Interstate 95. There are probably about 150,000 Hispanics working the land in this region of the state. In a study conducted by East Carolina University's Regional Development Institute, Hispanics were said to have a $2.5 million impact on the economy of eastern North Carolina. Hispanic people are working the land; they are blue-collar workers; they are business owners. You see Hispanics working everywhere in this region.

Nine years ago I started a Saturday morning radio program that is a communication link for the Hispanic community. In a way, the Spanish-speaking community has entrusted me to serve as an information source. Also, during and after the last three hurricanes, I worked with the local TV station, Channel 9, providing storm information in Spanish. The Hispanic community learned that if they had electricity in their home, they could watch Channel 9. And whenever the community lost power, the station still had electricity and was able to rebroadcast the news on local radio stations. Unfortunately, during Hurricane Floyd, one station, I don't want to say which one, switched to music when Allen Hoffman, the Channel 9 anchorman, announced that I would now give important hurricane information in Spanish. The sad part is that it was a Christian station. This is one of the things we faced.

We also had to contend with government red tape. If you're an illegal, you cannot receive federal funds, although you can apply on behalf of your U.S.-born children. Thankfully, Governor Hunt's relief fund was for everybody. The governor recognized that everybody suffered losses from the storm—everybody, no matter if you had a green card or not. Hispanics contribute to the economy. They are not a drain on the economy. They are taxpayers. Therefore, there was no reason to deny these individuals at least state assistance.

One local commissioner wanted the Mexicans to go back to Mexico to seek help. Yet, Hispanics were picking his crops, working in his area, and are probably customers of his business. This is the type of attitude that the Hispanic community encountered. As a result, the community had the feeling that they are after us, so we had better lay low. Given this situation, how did the community react when the flood came? On Sunday, a few days after the hurricane, I went to one shelter where some Hispanics had arrived. They were not sitting; they were working. They were helping as people dropped off goods, clothing, and food. Hispanics were loading and unloading trucks and helping out the best they could. The shelter volunteers couldn't speak Spanish, so translators were provided. Some of these translators remained at the shelters for many days.

But many Hispanics did not seek help from the shelters. They stayed with friends, relatives, and acquaintances who opened their doors to them. In Greenville, we have the office of Catholic Social Ministry, which for years has been working with the Hispanic community to help with immigration issues. During the disaster, this was a place that was known and trusted. Churches also became the central points where people came and gathered information. Unfortunately, because they were not in the shelters, the Red Cross and FEMA did not count Hispanics as having been very impacted by the storm.

Although FEMA said that they had set up a Spanish help-line, nobody would answer the telephone. I am not saying that we are demanding Spanish-speaking workers at agencies, but it helps when someone knows the language, even a little bit. This was the situation that many encountered at the height of the emergency. The governor's office did open a 1-800 hotline that was available in Spanish. The 1-800 number was set up on the very first day of the storm. I remember announcing the number on Channel 9. Calls came from Wednesday to Thursday morning from the entire area that was affected by the hurricane. We are also fortunate in Greenville to have Channel 9, which provided good storm coverage for eastern North Carolina.

Overall, the Hispanic community bonded together; they were not in despair. They were not a drain on the system, and they did not go on welfare. After the floods, many Hispanics managed to find places to work or continued working where they did before the storm. I see at the Catholic Church, for example, 300 people every Sunday, and they seem to be very happy and content.

But we learned that when a situation like the flood disaster occurs, we need to be prepared. For example, there's nothing wrong with preparing information in another language. The Pitt County government did pretty well in providing information in Spanish, like how to clean your house after the floods. They provided this information in Spanish, despite some commissioners' complaint that is was a waste of money. It is positive when the government works with the Hispanic community, because we are citizens. We pay taxes. One suggestion I have, as we prepare for another hurricane season, is for the storm alerts and warning messages that are shown on TV be provided in Spanish. This will help people be aware about what's going on and allow them to prepare. Right now, this type of information is spread by word of mouth.

A Dialogue: Coordinating Recovery Efforts to Minimize the Impact of Future Disasters

William R. Mangun

Starting the Dialogue

The Question: *How should the specific responsibilities of different government agencies be coordinated to assure that future natural disasters are less catastrophic for the diverse people, communities, and businesses of eastern North Carolina?*

The discussion was guided by **Rutherford Platt**, Professor of Geography and Planning Law, Department of Geosciences, University of Massachusetts, Amherst. Approximately thirty individuals participated in the discussion, representing state and local agencies, the U.S. Department of Commerce, private relief organizations, universities, the medical community, Wachovia bank, and a few private citizens. The state agency participants came primarily from the mid-Atlantic coastal emergency and disaster management agencies in Georgia, Maryland, South Carolina, and North Carolina. Most local government representatives were from eastern North Carolina and had participated in the disaster relief effort through emergency support services and fire departments. Represented nonprofit organizations included the American Red Cross, the Salvation Army, the United Way, and religion-based groups. Most participants were directly involved in the Floyd disaster relief efforts or worked in agencies that provide disaster assistance.

Introduction

The responsibilities associated with providing aid after a disaster, developing long-term recovery strategies, and preparing for future disasters are distributed among many groups, both public and private. Most people know that the Federal Emergency Management Agency (FEMA) plays a role in disaster recovery, but the role of local governments and nonprofit groups is not well known. Over the course of our discussion, the participants in this dialogue recognized that disaster relief, recovery, and preparation is a linked system of responsibilities. Whether the domain of responsibility is the federal government, state or local governments, a community, a family, or an individual, each bears a level of responsibility.

As participants discussed the various roles of different government agencies, a primary interest was how relief is organized and dispensed at the state and local level. There was less interest in the details of federal government funding. Of greatest concern was coordination among units of government, collaboration between government and different segments of the community, and communication from government officials to the media and the public. We also discussed public education for disaster preparedness and personal and corporate responsibility.

Developing Statewide and Regional Disaster Plans to Coordinate Relief Efforts

Disaster relief efforts during the flood were plagued by a lack of structure and coordination in the distribution of resources to those in need. One of the more important coordination issues centered on the communication of information and decisions from state disaster relief agencies to governments below the county level. Although the state typically works closely with counties, the flow of official information to cities and towns, including local nongovernment organizations, was fragmented during the most pressing Floyd relief activities.

The state of North Carolina needs more effective coordination of disaster planning efforts. The state should develop regulations that require local governments to take specific actions that produce a specific and defined response. For example, immediately after the Hurricane Floyd disaster, the local resources of some counties often were depleted or overwhelmed by people fleeing from other counties. Local governments in eastern North Carolina lacked the authority to tell people to go to another county that could more quickly address their needs. In comparison, South Carolina has a disaster coordination process that funnels people out of congested areas.

Under the Emergency Planning and Community Right-to-Know Act of 1986 (U.S. Code 1986), which is an amended provision of the Comprehensive Environmental Response, Compensation and Liability Act (U.S. Code, Vol. 42, 1980), state governments must designate a state emergency response coordinator and create a state emergency response plan. The act also requires each county government to designate an emergency response coordinator and to establish an emergency response plan that fits with the plans of the state and other counties. Coordination of state and local response plans was not evident during the Floyd disaster. Strict adherence to the *right-to-know* provision would better utilize mutual assistance and transfer agreements among local governments within eastern North Carolina. It would also improve the coordination of statewide and local emergency response efforts.

Preparing for Future Disasters

Before Hurricane Floyd impacted eastern North Carolina, collaboration between public and nongovernment organizations in disaster preparation activities was inadequate. When the disaster struck, few people were aware of the types of resources that were available from nongovernment organizations. Community-based, nongovernment organizations (e.g., church groups, Salvation Army, Red Cross chapters) need to be more involved in disaster planning and decision making. Once plans are made, government and nongovernment organizations need to engage in regular, full-scale disaster simulations in order to identify problem areas and to develop familiarity with operating procedures. Specific positions should be established at the county, city, and town level to promote such collaboration and coordination. The discussion participants agreed that there is a need to create such positions and that the description of the position must be well defined. Informal assignment of disaster preparation responsibilities is ineffective. An individual informally assigned to perform certain disaster preparation tasks may leave an area, the tasks are not reassigned, and when a disaster occurs, the tasks are not performed.

Tied to the need for collaboration among public agencies and between public agencies and private groups is the need to integrate underrepresented groups into disaster planning. In eastern North Carolina, African Americans, migrant Latino farm workers, lower socioeconomic strata, and the elderly often are more negatively impacted by natural disasters than are other groups. Segments of the population that typically are not politically powerful must be drawn into the disaster planning and decision-making processes. In disaster planning activities, Geographic Information System (GIS) protocols could be used to demonstrate how potential natural disasters may differentially affect different populations. For example, U.S. Census Bureau data could be used to delineate areas where economic or ethnic patterns may indicate potential areas of need. Once these areas are identified, they could be targeted for disaster education or community-level involvement in the regional disaster planning process.

Getting Information Before and Immediately After a Disaster

Accurate and accessible communication is another important issue during catastrophes such as Floyd. People typically rely on local social networks for information such as family, friends, and church congregations. More formal mechanisms need to be designed and implemented in eastern North Carolina. One approach would be to design a system similar to that used in South Carolina. South Carolina has a disaster public-information telephone system that is a twenty-four-hour, 1-800 telephone number that citizens can use to find answers to practically any question.

When telephone systems collapsed during Hurricane Floyd, ham radio operators performed valuable communication functions during crisis situations, including conveying medical information. A satellite-based communication network could supplement or, possibly, supplant the service that was provided by ham operators during Floyd. Public authorities could be provided with the necessary equipment through a federal or state grant program.

Public communication systems are particularly vulnerable during natural disasters. Therefore, public information needs to be disseminated through multiple sources—television, radio, the Internet, telephone calling networks, and at designated public locations. However, a centralized coordination point for releasing public information about a disaster is crucial. Most radio and television stations have Internet connections and many have back-up power systems that allow them to continue operating when other power sources fail. Specific Internet communication links could be designated at radio and television stations. Through such links, a centrally based state coordination agency could provide up-to-date information to the radio and television stations that could be retransmitted to the public.

Disaster Education

Education is an essential step in preparing people for a disaster. Discussion participants deemed disaster preparation as essential to the improvement of eastern North Carolina's capacity for action after a natural disaster and for long-term disaster planning. At the start of the 2000 hurricane season, the government of South Carolina embarked on a public education campaign to prepare its citizens for disaster. A separate section in Sunday newspapers was prepared for bulk delivery. The section provided emergency checklists, typical precautions, descriptions of life in a shelter, etc. Businesses could help fund similar public information campaigns in North Carolina. Specifically, chambers of commerce could train small business owners on how to better prepare for floods, hurricanes, and other disasters. Such preparation could reduce damages and help small businesses to quickly recover and thus be able to provide needed services for the public.

Preparation for hurricanes and floods should also be integrated into public school curriculum. Like the axiom that students are taught about fire, "stop, drop, and roll," eastern North Carolina students should be taught what to do in the event of floods and hurricanes. The University of South Carolina produced a CD-ROM atlas on environmental risks and hazards for use in public schools. It is interactive and written at an eighth-grade reading comprehension level. North Carolina, as well as other states, should develop similar educational materials to assist their citizens to more effectively prepare for natural disasters and to cope with the aftermath. As global warming continues and climates continue to change, the occurrence of climate-induced natural disasters may increase, which will demand greater disaster awareness and preparation.

Who is Responsible? Everyone.

Self-sufficiency is a multi-layered issue. The first question that needs to be answered is "Who's responsible?" In the first seventy-two hours of a natural disaster, a local government is expected to respond to the immediate needs of the community. However, events can create situations in which the local government's resources are simply overwhelmed. In anticipation of such events, a system of cross-jurisdictional support must be in place. Established cooperative agreements among counties, cites, townships, and the state could be activated when the demands on certain local resources are high.

In order to lessen the impact of future disasters, lending institutions need to direct development away from disaster-prone areas. But to effectively direct development, businesses will need to refer to established government standards that support their decisions. After the Northridge Earthquake in 1994, California imposed new building standards and required old buildings to be retrofitted. Such standards allowed lending institutions to deny loans for buildings that did not meet the standards. Homeowners and homebuilders need to accept greater personal responsibility for their decisions. They can be made more responsible for building in hazard-prone areas by agreeing to sign waivers that would disallow them from receiving assistance after a flood, hurricane, or similar disaster.

Recommendations for Creating a Cooperative Response to Natural Disasters

Response to weather-based natural disasters requires an inordinate amount of cooperation among diverse segments of the population. In order to cope more effectively with a major disaster, the response effort must be carefully coordinated, inclusive, and collaborative. To achieve this goal the following recommendations should be considered:

- Efficiently distribute resources by coordinating public and private organizations.
- Following the provision of the Emergency Planning and Community Right-to-Know Act, establish mutual assistance and transfer agreements among local governments and coordinate disaster preparation plans.
- Involve community-based, nongovernment organizations in the disaster planning and decision-making process. Most importantly, this must involve populations that do not typically have much political power.
- Create a public-information telephone service which would provide citizens with a means to find answers to a wide variety of questions.
- Establish a public education campaign to prepare citizens for disaster.
- Train small business owners on how to better prepare for natural disasters.
- Integrate natural disaster education and preparation into public school curriculum.
- Local governments, businesses, and individuals should develop greater self-sufficiency.
- Establish government building standards that would direct development away from disaster-prone areas.

About the Author: Dr. Mangun is a professor in the Department of Political Science and the Coastal Resources Management Program at East Carolina University. He has been and remains involved in a wide range of environmental policy issues, including air and water pollution control, hazardous waste management, wetlands, wildlife management, natural resource management, and outdoor recreation.

Part VI / Recommendations

Lessons Learned, Alternative Paths to Recovery, and Specific Recommendations

John R. Maiolo and Harold Stone

As more people choose to live near the coast, land use becomes more diverse and more compressed, requiring planning that emphasizes sustainability. When the floodwaters from Hurricane Floyd receded, a wide range of needs was evident. Many were not met, which related directly to deficits in local and state disaster preparedness. Others were related to basic infrastructure challenges that, if changed, would serve as tools for better management of future disasters. But as we plan for the future, it is important to translate these disaster experiences into a learning opportunity to reduce future impacts.

This final chapter represents information gathered from two sources. The first is the North Carolina Division of Emergency Management (NCDEM), Department of Crime Control and Public Safety. The DEM was asked what they had learned from Floyd, both in terms of short-term and long-term response and recovery, and how those lessons could be translated into policies the DEM could use after future disasters. We would like to express our thanks to Steve Yount of the NCDEM for providing us with this information.

The second source was the discussion at the closing session of the conference. This discussion was driven by remarks and suggestions from the presenters, moderators, and note takers at the technical sessions, the roundtable discussion leaders and report writers, and the presenters and moderators at the plenary presentations. It also included comments from audience members. Although the conference focused on the effects of flooding in eastern North Carolina, recommendations outlined in this chapter have implications for the improvement of emergency management practices for all coastal regions that are susceptible to hurricanes and flooding.

A Central Recommendation: Create a Disaster Extension Service

Among the ideas resulting from the conference, one stands out. The creation of a disaster extension service, patterned in structure and design to the nationwide Agriculture Extension Service, was repeatedly offered as a needed resource for disaster preparation and recovery.

In 1862, the U.S. Department of Agriculture was created, and with it was passed the Morrill Land Grant College Act to create the Agricultural Extension Service. The purpose of this act was to ensure that quality education was provided to farmers and homemakers in the newly developed and rural areas of the U.S. We are currently facing comparable growth, as the U.S. population migrates to coastal areas. In fact, the threat of coastal-related losses resulted in the elevation of the Federal Emergency Management Agency (FEMA) to cabinet status.

A Disaster Extension Service would provide structure to an existing relationship between educators and the public. Pre-disaster education has proven to be an essential element for the reduction and elimination of loss. Currently, academic institutions provide a wide range of informational and training opportunities for governmental and nonprofit organizations and the public. Given the levels of loss and needs that were exhibited in the floods of September 1999, a more deliberate and focused approach must be undertaken to maximize available research and translate that research into practical information that is readily available to the public.

To prepare and educate the population effectively, however, a program as equally ambitious as the Agricultural Extension Service must be created. One of the constituent institutions in the University of North Carolina System could initially development the Disaster Extension Service. An "Emergency Management Agent" position could be assigned to each county, and educational materials and services for residents and businesses could be provided from them. Appropriate information materials could be customized to the needs of each county and could focus on the unique needs of the local community.

A Framework for Further Recommendations

The high probability of recurring flood events in North Carolina's coastal regions requires the integration of recommendations into a framework that reflects the needs of the impacted communities. Linkages between emergency management officials, public and private organizations, and the public are illuminated in the Emergency Management Cycle framework. This cycle provides a mechanism for evaluating effective improvements in disaster situations and is based on the following actions:

Response—actions that involve reacting to an *impending threat* of loss.
Recovery—actions that are an attempt to return the impacted community to pre-disaster *wholeness.*
Mitigation—actions that minimize risk by *removing the potential* of future losses.
Preparation—actions that minimize potential future losses that are *unavoidable.*

Although each phase of the cycle provides opportunities to reduce losses, the conference provided significantly more recommendations that involved mitigation and preparation than it did for the other stages of the cycle. On the other hand, many conference participants expressed a majority of their concerns in the areas of response and recovery. Therefore, the importance of recommendations in this chapter should not be measured by the number of recommendations in each category. However, each element in the cycle is related. Recommendations for effective mitigation and preparation can lead to more effective response and recovery. Also, some recommendations can apply to more than one category (e.g., education initiatives), and some recommendations are listed in more than one area.

Response

Hurricane Floyd's floodwaters uncovered a shortage of crucial emergency information that was needed by many vulnerable populations. Improving the access of information to the public cannot focus on just advanced technologies, but must include a broader distribution of basic information that will aid in a more efficient disaster response. This includes refining how the public accesses information about a forecasted disaster, meeting the specific information needs of different members of the community, and providing information about homeowner's and renter's insurance.

Meet the public's immediate emergency information needs

- Expand the toll-free telephone system for information exchange beyond the "Governors Hot Line" and 911. This system would convey and receive information related to flooded roadways, the areas that are flooded and the areas that are under a flood threat. This would involve the N.C. Department of Transportation and the N.C. Department of Environment and Natural Resources.
- Create a public-information telephone system, similar to the system developed in South Carolina, that would provide citizens with a means to find answers to a wide variety of questions.
- Mass communication on demand such as those offered on the Internet can replace or supplement many traditional informational outlets (e.g., the telephone system). This would reduce the usage pressure on traditional sources, which are needed to coordinate service delivery and triage.

Extensive flooding on the Highway 264 bypass between N.C. State Route 33 and 43. (Courtesy of the city of Greenville, N.C.)

Provide emergency information in a variety of forms

- We must recognize that mass media serve as a primary information source for the sight and hearing impaired. The needs of this vulnerable population should be considered when disaster-related decisions are made and information is distributed.
- We need to ensure the availability of foreign language interpreters, particularly Spanish translators. Translators can convey information about a pending disaster and relate safety information in all the venues within a community.

Make flood insurance information easy to attain and understand

- Provide a list of the companies that offer insurance for a particular region.
- Provide guidelines so individuals can determine whether they need flood insurance.
- Provide a list of what is and what is not covered by different levels of insurance.
- Provide the name of the organization that underwrites the insurance.

Recovery

Recovery extends past the disaster event. In the year following Hurricane Floyd, problems with the communication and organization between and within public-needed service agencies led to recommendations for the improvement of future relief efforts. But the recovery needs after future disasters can be minimized if mitigation and preparation activities remove the threat for loss. Recovery and mitigation are tied together in terms of the information provided to the public, government agencies' specific recovery actions, the community organizations that are utilized to assist with recovery, and ensuring that the promises for recovery are fulfilled.

Improve both short-term and long-term recovery programs

Responsibility for the initial phases of recovery requires both an effective and efficient use of resources. Too often the lack of coordination results in slow recovery and community frustration and animosity toward public official and agencies. The following could be implemented to improve current programs:

- Streamline the entire assistance application process, changing the names of programs and forms so they make sense to those seeking help.
- Increase the number of FEMA caseworkers so victims can receive more one-on-one assistance.
- Decrease job losses and small business failures by providing temporary debt relief to new business owners who have yet to establish the financial profile required to secure a low-interest loan.

- Include disaster preparation, response, and land-use in growth plans. Too often disaster-related plans are appendages to community planning. The process is best served if disaster planning is a natural and integral part of the total community planning process.
- Develop recovery programs to match the diversity of the region.

Improve agency distribution of information to the public

A lack of information often results in rumor and miscommunication. As a strategy for long-term assistance, information meetings could reduce the frustration of those most impacted by a disaster, and serve as a foundation for a more effective recovery strategy. Improving the availability of information to the public and how this information is received could be accomplished from the following recommendations:

- Hold public, town hall-type meetings to discuss issues related to floodplains, the status of flood plain management rules and regulations, as well as to identify appropriate reforms. The federal, state, and local government officials who are responsible for floodplain management should lead these meetings. The meetings should also be advertised widely in local newspapers and on radio and television stations.
- Provide information on the agencies responsible for enforcement of floodplain regulations at agency offices, in post offices, listed in phone directories, and made available on the Internet.

Recognize, value, and utilize community organizations and relationships

Often, individuals and families are the exclusive focus of emergency recovery efforts. By providing services focused at the community level, it is possible to reduce the trauma of a disaster, allow for empowerment of the community, and ensure the culture of the self-identified communities are recognized. A cohesive community approach can also be more cost effective. The following could be steps toward achieving these goals:

- Too many communities in the eastern North Carolina continue to reflect an unequal distribution of opportunities and resources based on race and ethnic differences. The tragedy of Hurricane Floyd could be an opportunity to restructure social relations and communities. Many of the programs needed to assist recovery can be altered to address this problem with little, if any, additional cost.
- Enhance recovery by developing and supporting social networks for victims who face finding a new home. These alternative pathways could be used to communicate the details of the recovery assistance process, thus ensuring that those who need aid receive it.

- Utilize interfaith and other volunteer groups at assistance application centers. These groups represent a valued community asset that can help direct victims to needed resources and could put a more sympathetic face on the recovery assistance process.
- Encourage joint relocation efforts for groups of households or entire blocks. This will allow victims to retain a sense of community and continuity. An effort such as this, if successful, could save time, money, and a great deal of grief in the future.

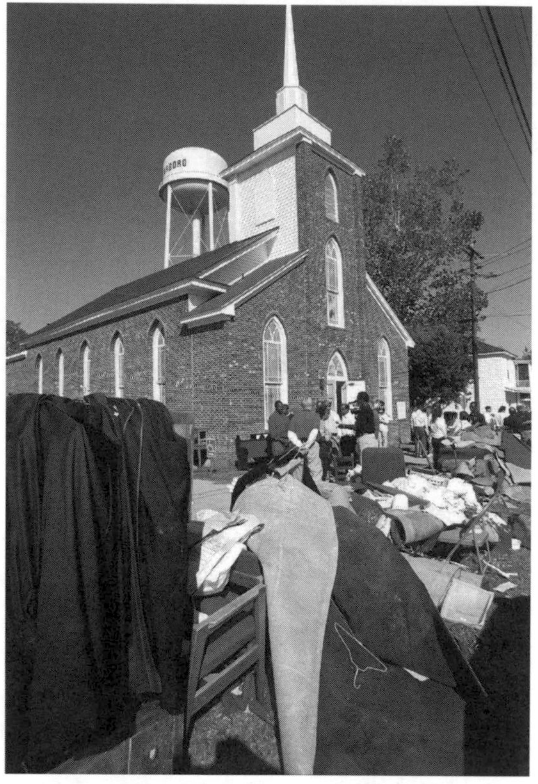
Church members come together to begin renovating the Eastern Star Baptist Church in Tarboro, N.C. (Photo by Dave Gatley, courtesy of FEMA News Photo)

Political accountability in the recovery process is essential

Often, plans for recovery are developed that reflect the political climate of urgency directly following a disaster. Over time, the pressures of political reality shift to the next "disaster," leaving some communities with unfulfilled promises. Thus, we need to find ways to:

- Recognize that economic, social, and environmental goals can co-exist if properly and realistically framed within the context of long-range community values and goals, especially if all community groups see that they have a stake in those goals.
- Hold public officials accountable for the decisions they make that effect floodplain management and mitigation, and find ways to substantially reward communities where sound decisions are made.
- Designate a statewide recovery office to oversee and focus recovery activities.

Mitigation

The majority of recommendations focused on eliminating future losses. Actions should be taken to remove communities and property out of harm's way and to decrease the impact of a potential disaster. To be effective, however, requires an investment of time and planning, and should include effective dissemination of information, education programs, local and regional disaster plans, floodplain management plans, and accurate floodplain maps.

Make disaster awareness information easily available to the public

In the aftermath of Hurricane Floyd, the need to improve the quality and quantity of certain types of information to meet the diverse needs of the public was evident. To decrease the public's risk, adequate information related to construction and living in flood zones is essential to reduce loss. Implementing the following could make information more accessible:

- Provide public notification of high flood-risk areas. A significant number of people that were impacted by the flooding following Hurricane Floyd were completely unaware that their properties were at risk. Public notification could include signage near roadways that identify the height of water during floods and detailed flood maps in newspapers, or distributed to the communities at risk.
- Develop programs to foster better disclosure of hazard information by real estate agencies and mortgage lenders. Provide a potential buyer with upfront notification of a property's flood risk by including flood-risk information in realtor Multiple Listing Service (MLS) books. This issue should be addressed well before closing, allowing the buyer to have the opportunity to gather additional information and weigh their risk.
- Provide information on what can and cannot be done to maintain streams. Information should include profiles of the agencies that oversee regulations of activities in streams and floodplains. This information could be available at post offices and libraries and distributed in the annual tax statements received by public and private property owners.
- Establish a public education campaign to prepare small business owners on how to better prepare for natural disasters.
- Create educational materials written at a level that is understandable across generations. Materials can be distributed at primary and secondary schools and to civic groups and public employees and made available to the public at post offices, libraries, and other public facilities.

Create better disaster mitigation plans

The work of local governments and businesses should result in greater community self-sufficiency. Often in the early stages of post-disaster emergency management, planning quickly becomes a secondary activity as the memory of the floodwaters fade. Only by retaining a focus on planning can sustainable development be achieved. Disaster or hazard mitigation plans should:

- Define acceptable risk; a consensus of a community's willingness to accept risk and what constitutes acceptable losses is essential in designing an effective mitigation plan. Communities should assess their vulnerability to risk and mitigate these risks to eliminate losses.

- Require local governments to disallow development in flood-prone areas or to direct development away from these areas. Although it requires significant political courage, determination, and public saliency, the most effective way to mitigate disaster is to eliminate the object at risk.
- Require impact fees for developers, including fees for the installation of impervious (impermeable) surfaces. Assessments should be based on how the development impacts a floodplain. This could encourage development that is more sensitive to the natural functioning of floodplains. By charging a fee, at least a portion of the cost of the loss can be returned. The increased cost of impervious structures may encourage the development and use of alternative surface materials.
- Emphasize regional planning. Natural disasters do not occur in isolation. Communities are affected by the choices made by adjacent communities and landowners. By creating a regional plan, rather than a city or town plan, it is possible to develop policies that reduce the potential of disaster for an entire region.
- Revisit building standards for areas with high winds and wind-driven water. Existing standards vary greatly across communities and regions, and many are simply insufficient to allow structures to stand up to hurricane conditions. Lending institutions can be an important source of support on this issue by providing loans only for structures that meet standards appropriate for a high-risk area.
- Establish monitoring systems (physical, health, socioeconomic, business) to quantify the impacts of policy changes on both human and physical systems.
- Blend hazard plans into local comprehensive plans.

Design more sensible floodplain management plans

- Move existing federal, state, and municipal infrastructure (e.g., sewage treatment facilities and electrical power stations) out of the floodplain. This would facilitate the ability of these government entities to quickly respond to community needs, such as marshaling areas for supplies and evacuation locations.
- Improve the management of watersheds and runoff districts. The need to restore natural systems was an important lesson learned from Hurricane Floyd.

Many public facilities are located in flood-prone areas, which can strain or completely eliminate many public-needed services during and after a natural disaster. During the floods that followed Hurricane Floyd, high water inundated this water treatment facility in Greenville, N.C. (Courtesy of the city of Greenville, N.C.)

- Index flood insurance premiums so they are more appropriate to the level of risk. Current programs do not sufficiently provide the necessary incentives to assess risks and take the necessary steps to reduce them. A careful restructuring of insurance premiums, making them more proportional to the level of risk, would go far toward resolving this problem.
- Implement appropriate pricing of property in flood-prone areas. Property in flood-prone areas is priced lower than nonflood-prone property. Pricing properties relative to their long-term costs to society would aid in making cost-effective decisions and raise public awareness of the true costs of these properties

Revise flood zone maps and create vulnerability maps

The continuing rapid growth in the coastal plain requires coordinated planning. As a regional phenomenon, losses from floods are often suffered as a result of a fragmented jurisdictional responsibility. The following actions could be an effective framework for preparing for and responding to coastal disasters:

- Develop an aggressive floodplain mapping program, including creating topographic maps that overlay geographic information system (GIS) data to enable the identification and correlation of changing demographics, development, and land use to floodplain locations.
- Create easily attainable maps that contain clear and easy-to-understand cartographic and topographic information, with GIS overlays that delineate the 10, 30, 50, 75, and 100-year flood line for a specific community.
- Provide elected officials with "vulnerability maps." Areas vulnerable to disaster impacts should be clearly demarcated, thus allowing easy reference for decision makers. Also, multiple hazards (flooding, wind damage, hazardous materials, etc.) should be shown on one map, so confounding hazards can be easily identified.
- Create accurate and up-to-date hazard maps. Floodplain maps are out-of-date and need to be recalculated to include existing and planned impermeable surfaces. Maps and other information should be available in hard copy as well as on each agency's Internet web site.

Preparation

Where mitigation actions are mostly focused toward minimizing losses due to a disaster, preparation actions focus on planning for disaster losses that cannot be avoided. For example, in eastern North Carolina, many homes and business remain in high-risk, flood-prone areas. Preparation activities should include actions that will minimize flood damage to these structures. Furthermore, many of the lessons learned after the flood emphasize the need for more structure and coordination of emergency management procedures. Unlike localized emergencies, disasters require the coordination of resources beyond local capacity.

Covering windows during a tropical storm can often prevent severe interior damage to a home. This Wrightsville Beach, N.C., home, with its protective storm shutters, was prepared for Hurricane Floyd. (Photo by Dave Gatley, courtesy of FEMA News Photo)

Clearly define agency responsibilities and coordinate disaster response

Preparation actions rely on a diversity of jurisdictions. In order to respond to a disaster effectively and efficiently, the following is recommended:

- Formulate a hierarchical chain of command that delineates the emergency management responsibilities of federal, state, and county governments.
- Clarify the responsibilities between the different levels of government.
- Restructure municipal and county Emergency Operations Centers' responsibilities to mirror that of the state Emergency Operations Center. This will maximize communication between levels of government and allow for the formation of a common language and focus.
- Establish mutual assistance and transfer agreements among local governments and coordinate disaster preparation plans, following the provisions of the Emergency Planning and Community Right-to-Know Act.

Improve communication among and between agencies

Interagency communication during disaster preparation phases provides a framework that determines the effectiveness of the response to a disaster. Failures in communication between agencies result in waste, the duplication of effort, or failures in the response "safety net." Thus, we need to:

- Create a system for effective communication among different government agencies and between government agencies and nongovernment organizations.
- Expand communication between the emergency agencies across different states, thus aiding in the required coordination of resources.

- Encourage closer, well-defined links between levels of response and recovery using cellular telephones, CB radios, and laptop computers, which were needed and often were not available during the flooding.

Alter the composition of planning and emergency response organizations

Taking advantage of the knowledge of planning and disaster experts would help improve regional planning for future growth and disaster protection. Disaster preparation should include the advice and recommendations of available experts. Individuals could be recruited to fill staff positions or to serve as advisors for existing organizations. For example:

- Install experts on local planning boards. Local municipal boards are comprised of civic-minded individuals, but issues related to flood hazards are often complex. Expert assistance to uncover broader implications of proposed policies could aid in reducing flood hazards, which often cannot be provided by nonexperts, no matter how well intended.
- Involve community-based, nongovernment organizations in disaster planning and in the decision-making process. Most importantly, this must involve populations that may not typically have much political power (e.g., church groups).
- Identify groups that are responsible for creating long-term plans and clearly define the specific responsibilities of each group.
- Establish a centralized management and planning office that could serve to integrate the responsibilities of each group.

Develop public disaster preparation programs

As with mitigation, the preparation phase of the emergency management cycle requires unique skills. When there is a high probability of disaster, education should be focused to meet the specific needs of a community, relative to the type, magnitude, and speed of onset of the disaster. Through education, a threatened population can quickly focus on the actions that need to be taken to limit loss. Education programs should include the following:

- Train the officials who propose and vote on ordinances that directly impact the type and magnitude of losses. This is the first line of defense to reduce disaster losses. Although it is not a guarantee for the elimination of loss due to flooding, education makes it more difficult to develop ordinances that unwittingly increase losses.
- Regularly show disaster preparation and response videos on television.

Summary

An effective emergency management structure is an integration of many policies that affect a variety of normal human activities. It is not an easy task to develop such a structure. But if Hurricane Floyd and its predecessors have taught us anything, it is that we have not done a sufficient job to protect our citizens and our communities from the ravages of extreme weather events. As those in charge assess the costs and benefits of the recommendations we have presented, we hope they will see that the more costly alternative is *not* to act on the recommendations.

Epilogue

John R. Maiolo

"Those who cannot remember the past are condemned to repeat it."

—George Santayana

The Life of Reason or the Phases of Human Progress: Reason in Common Sense, 1905

And there we have it. Some of the most informed and experienced minds in the world who study extreme weather events and related disasters have given us their best recommendations. It will be a testimony to our collective insight, wisdom, and courage to meet their challenges when we look back from a distant future and assess how we have reacted to the aftermath of Hurricane Floyd. Will we, after experiencing the continuation of extreme weather in our coastal margin for the next two decades, continue to lament at the destruction, or heed Santayana's warning so we can celebrate our willingness to be better prepared? Will we use this event as an opportunity to correct not only those social issues that specifically relate to recovery from Floyd's flooding but also those that have haunted us throughout our state's history?

Santayana also informs us that "The environing world can justify itself to the mind only by the free life which it fosters there" (from *Interpretations of Poetry and Religion,* 1900). It is essential for human society to confront the truths of the "environing world" to decrease the impacts from natural disasters for future generations and to develop a more harmonious co-existence with nature.

It appears that those who can begin to make a difference in this regard have learned some important lessons. Since Hurricane Floyd, state agencies in North Carolina have begun to take some steps in the right direction. For example, FEMA, in cooperation with the state, is in the process of buying out about 4,000 homes in the Tarheel state's floodplains, converting the land to permanent green space. To help guide reasonable and sensible development in watersheds and floodplains, North Carolina has become the first state in the nation to sign an agreement with FEMA to prepare and update its flood maps. After Floyd, many questions were raised about the adequacy of these maps. The new maps will be digitally designed so they can be updated as development occurs in sensitive watersheds, and should serve as excellent tools for local officials. The state also has improved evacuation preparation and planning, having made provisions to quickly reverse the east bound lanes of Interstate 40 so coastal residents can exit the coast more efficiently. On the federal level, FEMA is working with other federal transportation-related agencies to ensure that interstate evacuation coordination is in place.

Regarding needed actions once the disaster event is underway, FEMA and the state are examining funding options for new state swift-water rescue capacities. The availability of swift-water rescue teams and equipment for the eastern counties was questioned during Floyd, but the next time this type of rescue situation evolves, the state hopes to have improved its ability to respond in a timely manner.

Finally, in order to warn citizens of the potential for inland flooding, forecasters are working on a warning scale, equivalent to the Saffir-Simpson hurricane scale, that will project the amount of *water* contained within a given hurricane. This appears to be a new component in hurricane warning systems.

While these new and innovative initiatives are welcomed, and will, no doubt help us in the future, there is still much work to be done, as is evident from the many recommendations outlined in the previous chapter. This is especially true if we accept the predictions that numerous and severe weather events are likely for at least the next twenty years. The reality of future storms may be frightening, but their ability to destroy us is entirely in our hands—as citizens, scientists, agency personnel, and elected officials.